# Unreasonable Searches and Seizures

# UNREASONABLE SEARCHES AND SEIZURES

## *Rights and Liberties under the Law*

Otis H. Stephens

Richard A. Glenn

ABC◉CLIO

Santa Barbara, California • Denver, Colorado • Oxford, England

Cataloging-in-Publication data is available from the Library of Congress.
ISBN 1-85109-503-9—ISBN 1-85109-508-X (e-book)

09 08 07 06  10 9 8 7 6 5 4 3 2 1

This book is also available on the World Wide Web as an e-book. Visit abc-clio.com
for details.

ABC-CLIO, Inc.
130 Cremona Drive, P.O. Box 1911
Santa Barbara, California 93116-1911

This book is printed on acid-free paper.
Manufactured in the United States of America

*To my grandchildren: Caroline, Katherine, Elizabeth, Clark, Grace, Annie, and Charli*
O.H.S.

*To my sons: Ryan and Andrew*
R.A.G.

# Contents

# SERIES FOREWORD

*America's Freedoms* promises a series of books that address the origin, development, meaning, and future of the nation's fundamental liberties, as well as the individuals, circumstances, and events that have shaped them. These freedoms are chiefly enshrined explicitly or implicitly in the Bill of Rights and other amendments to the Constitution of the United States and have much to do with the quality of life Americans enjoy. Without them, America would be a far different place in which to live. Oddly enough, however, the Constitution was drafted and signed in Philadelphia in 1787 without a bill of rights. That was an afterthought, emerging only after a debate among the foremost political minds of the day.

At the time, Thomas Jefferson was in France on a diplomatic mission. Upon receiving a copy of the proposed Constitution from his friend James Madison, who had helped write the document, Jefferson let him know as fast as the slow sailing-ship mails of the day allowed that the new plan of government suffered one major defect—it lacked a bill of rights. This, Jefferson argued, "is what the people are entitled to against every government on earth." Madison should not have been surprised at Jefferson's reaction. The Declaration of Independence of 1776 had largely been Jefferson's handiwork, including its core statement of principle:

We hold these truths to be self-evident, that all men are created equal, that they are endowed by their Creator with certain unalienable Rights, that among these are Life, Liberty, and the pursuit of Happiness. That to secure these rights, Governments are instituted among Men, deriving their just powers from the consent of the governed.

Jefferson rejected the conclusion of many of the framers that the Constitution's design—a system of both separation of powers among the legislative, executive, and judicial branches, and a federal division of powers between national and state governments—would safeguard liberty. He believed strongly that even when combined with elections, such structural checks would fall short.

Jefferson and other critics of the proposed Constitution ultimately had their way. In one of the first items of business in the First Congress in 1789, Madison, as a member of the House of Representatives from Virginia, introduced amendments to protect liberty. Ten were ratified by 1791 and have become known as the Bill of Rights.

America's Bill of Rights reflects the founding generation's understanding of the necessary link between personal freedom and representative government, as well as their experience with threats to liberty. The First Amendment protects expression—in speech, press, assembly, petition, and religion—and guards against a union of church and state. The Second Amendment secures liberty against national tyranny by affirming the self-defense of the states. Members of state-authorized local militia—citizens primarily, soldiers occasionally—retained a right to bear arms. The ban in the Third Amendment on forcibly quartering troops in houses reflects the emphasis the framers placed on the integrity and sanctity of the home.

Other provisions in the Fourth, Fifth, Sixth, Seventh, and Eighth amendments safeguard freedom by setting forth standards that government must follow in administering the law, especially regarding persons accused of crimes. The framers knew firsthand the dangers that government-as-prosecutor could pose to liberty. Even today, authoritarian regimes in other lands routinely use the tools of law enforcement—arrests, searches, detentions, as well as trials—to squelch peaceful political opposition. Limits in the Bill of Rights on crime-fighting powers thus help maintain democracy by demanding a high level of legal scrutiny of the government's practices.

In addition, one clause in the Fifth Amendment forbids the taking of private property for public use without paying the owner just compensation and thereby limits the power of eminent domain, the authority to seize a person's property. Along with taxation and conscription, eminent domain is one of the most awesome powers any government can possess.

The Ninth Amendment makes sure that the listing of some rights does not imply that others necessarily have been abandoned. If the Ninth Amendment offered reassurances to the people, the Tenth Amendment was designed to reassure the states that they or the people retained those powers not delegated to the national government. Today, the Tenth Amendment is a reminder of the integral role states play in the federal plan of union that the Constitution ordained.

Despite this legacy of freedom, however, we Americans today sometimes wonder about the origin, development, meaning, and future of our liberties. This concern is entirely understandable, because liberty is central to the idea of what it means *to be American.* In this way, the United States stands apart from virtually every other nation on earth. Other countries typically define their national identities through a common ethnicity, origin, ancestral bond, religion, or history. But none of these accounts for the American identity. In terms of ethnicity, ancestry, and religion, the United States is the most diverse place on earth. From the beginning, America has been a land of immigrants. Neither is there a single historical experience to which all current citizens can directly relate: Someone who arrived a decade ago from, say, Southeast Asia and was naturalized as a citizen only last year is just as much an American as someone whose forebears served in General George Washington's army at Valley Forge during the American War of Independence (1776–1783). In religious as in political affairs, the United States has been a beacon to those suffering oppression abroad: "the last, best hope of earth," Abraham Lincoln said. So, the American identity is ideological. It consists of faith in the value and importance of liberty for each individual.

Nonetheless, a long-standing consensus among Americans on the *principle* that individual liberty is essential, highly prized, and widely shared hardly assures agreement about liberty *in practice.* This is because the concept of liberty, as it has developed in the United States, has several dimensions.

First, there is an unavoidable tension between liberty and restraint. Liberty means freedom: We say that a person has a "right" to do this or that. But that *right* is meaningless unless there is a corresponding *duty* on the part of others (such as police officers and elected officials) not to interfere. Thus, protection of the liberty of one person necessarily involves restraints imposed on someone else. This is why we speak of a *civil* right or a *civil* liberty: it is a claim on the behavior of another that is enforceable through the legal process. Moreover, some degree of order (restrictions on the behavior of all) is necessary if everyone's liberties are to be protected. Just as too much order crushes freedom, too little invites social chaos that also threatens freedom. Determining the proper balance between freedom and order, however, is more easily sought than found. "To make a government requires no great prudence," declared English statesman and political philosopher Edmund Burke in 1790. "Settle the seat of power; teach obedience; and the work is done. To give freedom is still more easy. It is not necessary to guide; it only requires to let go the rein. But to form a *free government;* that is, to temper together these opposite elements of liberty and restraint in one consistent work, requires much thought; deep reflection; a sagacious, powerful, and combining mind."

Second, the Constitution does not define the freedoms that it protects. Chief Justice John Marshall once acknowledged that the Constitution was a document "of enumeration, and not of definition." There are, for example, lists of the powers of Congress in Article I, or the rights of individuals in the Bill of Rights, but those powers and limitations are not explained. What is the "freedom of speech" that the First Amendment guarantees? What are "unreasonable searches and seizures" that are proscribed by the Fourth Amendment? What is the "due process of law" secured by both the Fifth and Fourteenth Amendments? Reasonable people, all of whom favor individual liberty, can arrive at very different answers to these questions.

A third dimension—breadth—is closely related to the second. How widely shared is a particular freedom? Consider voting, for example. One could write a political history of the United States by cataloging the efforts to extend the vote or franchise to groups such as women and nonwhites that had been previously excluded. Or consider the First Amendment's freedom of speech. Does it include the expression of *all* points of view or merely *some*? Does the same amendment's protection of the "free exercise of religion" include all faiths, even obscure ones that may seem weird or even irritating? At different times questions like these have yielded different answers.

Similarly, the historical record contains notorious lapses. Despite all the safeguards that are supposed to shore up freedom's foundations, constitutional protections have sometimes been worth the least when they have been desperately needed. In our history the most frequent and often the most serious threats to freedom have come not from people intent on throwing the Bill of Rights away outright but from well-meaning people who find the

Bill of Rights a temporary bother, standing in the way of some objective they want to reach.

There is also a question that dates to the very beginning of American government under the Constitution. Does the Constitution protect rights not spelled out in, or fairly implied by, the words of the document? The answer to that question largely depends on what a person concludes about the source of rights. One tradition, reflected in the Declaration of Independence, asserts that rights predate government and that government's chief duty is to protect the rights that everyone naturally possesses. Thus, if the Constitution is read as a document designed, among other things, to protect liberty, then protected liberties are not limited to those in the text of the Constitution but may also be derived from experience, for example, or from one's assessment of the requirements of a free society. This tradition places a lot of discretion in the hands of judges, because in the American political system, it is largely the judiciary that decides what the Constitution means. Partly due to this dynamic, a competing tradition looks to the text of the Constitution, as well as to statutes passed consistent with the Constitution, as a *complete* code of law containing *all* the liberties that Americans possess. Judges, therefore, are not free to go outside the text to "discover" rights that the people, through the process of lawmaking and constitutional amendment, have not declared. Doing so is undemocratic because it bypasses "rule by the people." The tension between these two ways of thinking explains the ongoing debate about a right to privacy, itself nowhere mentioned in the words of the Constitution. "I like my privacy as well as the next one," once admitted Justice Hugo Black, "but I am nevertheless compelled to admit that government has a right to invade it unless prohibited by some specific constitutional provision." Otherwise, he said, judges are forced "to determine what is or is not constitutional on the basis of their own appraisal of what laws are unwise or unnecessary." Black thought that was the job of elected legislators who would answer to the people.

Fifth, it is often forgotten that at the outset, and for many years afterward, the Bill of Rights applied only to the national government, not to the states. Except for a very few restrictions, such as those in section 10 of Article I in the main body of the Constitution, which expressly limited state power, states were restrained only by their individual constitutions and state laws, not by the U.S. Bill of Rights. So, Pennsylvania or any other state, for example, could shut down a newspaper or barricade the doors of a church without violating the First Amendment. For many in the founding generation, the new central government loomed as a colossus that might threaten liberty. Few at that time thought that individual freedom needed *national* protection against *state* invasions of the rights of the people.

The first step in removing this double standard came with ratification of the Fourteenth Amendment after the Civil War in 1868. Section 1 contained majestic, but undefined, checks on states: "*No State* shall make or enforce any law which shall abridge the privileges or immunities of citizens of the United States; nor shall any *State* deprive any person of life, liberty, or property, without due process of law; nor deny to any person with in its jurisdiction the equal protections of the laws" (emphasis added). Such vague language begged for interpretation. In a series of cases mainly between 1920 and 1968, the Supreme Court construed the Fourteenth Amendment to include within its meaning almost every provision of the Bill of Rights. This process of "incorporation" (applying the Bill of Rights to the states by way of the Fourteenth Amendment) was the second step in eliminating the double standard of 1791. State and local governments became bound by the same restrictions that had applied all along to the national government. The consequences of this development scarcely can be exaggerated because most governmental action in the United States is the work of state and local governments. For instance, ordinary citizens are far more likely to encounter a local police officer than an agent of the Federal Bureau of Investigation or the Secret Service.

A sixth dimension reflects an irony. A society premised on individual freedom assumes not only the worth of each person but citizens capable of rational thought, considered judgment, and measured actions. Otherwise democratic government would be futile. Yet, we lodge the most important freedoms in the Constitution precisely because we want to give those freedoms extra protection. "The very purpose of a Bill of Rights was to . . . place [certain subjects] beyond the reach of majorities and officials and to establish them as legal principles to be applied by the courts," explained Justice Robert H. Jackson. "One's right to life, liberty, and property, to free speech, a free press, freedom of worship and assembly, and other fundamental rights may not be submitted to vote; they depend on the outcome of no elections." Jackson referred to a hard lesson learned from experience: basic rights require extra protection because they are fragile. On occasion, people have been willing to violate the freedoms of others. That reality demanded a written constitution.

This irony reflects the changing nature of a bill of rights in history. Americans did not invent the idea of a bill of rights in 1791. Instead it drew from and was inspired by colonial documents such as the Pennsylvania colony's Charter of Liberties (1701) and the English Bill of Rights (1689), Petition of Right (1628), and Magna Carta (1215). However, these early and often unsuccessful attempts to limit government power were devices to protect the many (the people) from the few (the English Crown). With the emergence of democratic political systems in the eighteenth century, however, political power shifted from the few to the many. The right to rule belonged to the person who received the most votes in an election, not necessarily to the firstborn, the wealthiest, or the most physically powerful. So the focus of a bill of rights had to shift too. No longer was it designed to shelter the majority from the minority, but to shelter the minority from the majority. "Wherever the real power in a Government lies, there is the danger of oppression," commented Madison in his exchange of letters with Jefferson in 1788. "In our Government, the real power lies in the majority of the Community, and the invasion of private rights is *chiefly* to be apprehended, not from acts of government contrary to the sense of its constituents, but from acts in which the Government is the mere instrument of the major number of the Constituents."

Americans, however, do deserve credit for having discovered a way to enforce a bill of rights. Without an enforcement mechanism, a bill of rights is no more than a list of aspirations: standards to aim for, but with no redress other than violent protest or revolution. Indeed this had been the experience in England with which the framers were thoroughly familiar. Thanks to judicial review—the authority courts in the United States possess to invalidate actions taken by the other branches of government that, in the judges' view, conflict with the Constitution—the provisions in the Bill of Rights and other constitutionally protected liberties became judicially enforceable.

Judicial review was a tradition that was beginning to emerge in the states on a small scale in the 1780s and 1790s and that would blossom in the U.S. Supreme Court in the nineteenth and twentieth centuries. "In the arguments in favor of a declaration of rights," Jefferson presciently told Madison in the late winter of 1789 after the Constitution had been ratified, "you omit one which has great weight with me, the legal check which it puts into the hands of the judiciary." This is the reason why each of the volumes in this series focuses extensively on judicial decisions. Liberties have largely been defined by judges in the context of deciding cases in situations where individuals thought the power of government extended too far.

Designed to help democracy protect itself, the Constitution ultimately needs the support of those—the majority—who endure its restraints. Without sufficient support among the people, its freedoms rest on a weak foundation. The earnest hope of *America's Freedoms* is that this series will offer Americans a renewed appreciation and understanding of their heritage of liberty.

Yet there would be no series on America's freedoms without the interest and support of Alicia Merritt at ABC-CLIO. The series was her idea. She approached me originally about the series and was very adept at overcoming my initial hesitations as series editor. She not only helped me shape the particular topics that the series would include but also guided me toward prospective authors. As a result, the topic of each book has been matched with the most appropriate person as author. The goal in each instance has been to pair topics with authors who are recognized teachers and scholars in their field. The results have been gratifying. A series editor could hardly wish for authors who have been more cooperative, helpful, and accommodating.

*Donald Grier Stephenson, Jr.*

# PREFACE

The central philosophical premise of the Bill of Rights—the first ten amendments to the U.S. Constitution—is that citizens should be free from unwanted and unwarranted governmental interference. Hence, the Bill of Rights is an enumeration of specific freedoms from governmental interference, protected by judicial guardianship. Chief among those freedoms is "the right of the people to be secure in their persons, houses, papers, and effects, against unreasonable searches and seizures." To guard against such searches and seizures, the Fourth Amendment stipulates that "no Warrants shall issue, but upon probable cause, supported by Oath or affirmation, and particularly describing the place to be searched and the persons or things to be seized." The Fourth Amendment thus keeps the government out of constitutionally protected areas until it has sufficient reason to believe that a specific crime has been or is being committed.

The U.S. Supreme Court, of course, has the unenviable task of defining "unreasonable searches and seizures" and of articulating the prerequisites for "probable cause." On these questions, as with most questions involving the Bill of Rights, disagreement is a near certainty. What separates a "reasonable" search from an "unreasonable" search is open to interpretation. What constitutes probable cause is open to interpretation as well. Even so, the judiciary, in a long line of cases, has recognized that the basic purpose of the Fourth Amendment is to safeguard the privacy and security of individuals against arbitrary invasions by governmental officials. The Fourth Amendment thus gives concrete expression to a right of the people that is "basic to a free society."

It is no doubt true that law enforcement officials would solve crimes more efficiently without the Fourth Amendment. For, in the absence of the Fourth Amendment, police could forcibly enter your home and seize evidence; rummage through your locker, your backpack, or the pockets on a pair of pants (even those you happen to be wearing); tap your telephone line; and intercept and read your mail, both standard and electronic—all without a warrant, probable cause, or reasonable suspicion. While the drafters and ratifiers of the Fourth Amendment might not have foreseen many of these specific intrusions, they were unquestionably aware of the potential for law enforcement officials to invade the privacy and security of individuals. Their experience with Great Britain—with its general warrants and writs of assistance—afforded an illustrious comment on the wisdom and necessity of specific protections against arbitrary invasions by government officials.

This book examines the Fourth Amendment—from its historical origins to its early development to its current controversies. Its intent is neither to praise nor criticize, but rather to explain. Accordingly, the function of this book is descriptive, not prescriptive. Because the primary audience consists of upper-level high school and college students, this book assumes that readers are being introduced to the topic for the first time. This book evidences thorough and well-balanced research; avoids technical terms wherever possible, while clearly defining those terms that are necessary; and simplifies complicated constitutional issues without obscuring the central and important problems presented by them. The primary purpose of this book is to supply readers of all levels with a rich and comprehensive source of information about search and seizure law. It is our hope that this book will provide the general reader with sufficient information about the development of the Fourth Amendment to serve as a basis for evaluating the question of its continuing relevance in seeking a balance between the protection of individual liberty and demands for effective law enforcement.

To accomplish that purpose, this book (1) discusses the significance of search and seizure law, its role in a dynamic society, and its implications for the American political system; (2) reveals the origins and early development of search and seizure law by looking at the English, colonial, and revolutionary experiences; (3) examines the early history of the Fourth Amendment and the Supreme Court's development of its requirements; (4) explores the evolution and (some might say) devolution of Fourth Amendment protections from the late nineteenth century through the opening years of the twenty-first century by analyzing significant judicial decisions; and (5) speculates on recent trends in search and seizure jurisprudence by examining closely those issues and controversies that have been most visible in the last decade, with particular emphasis on the potential adverse effects of the USA PATRIOT Act, passed shortly after the disastrous attacks of September 11, 2001, on Fourth Amendment protections.

Chapter One introduces the subject matter. Because the field of search and seizure law is vast and complex, this chapter provides the reader with a general overview of the Fourth Amendment, selectively highlighting major areas of law enforcement activity that illustrate well the scope of the amendment. This chapter also makes clear the significance of the protection against unreasonable searches and seizures in the American political system.

Chapter Two explores the origins and early development of the Fourth Amendment. It surveys important developments in Great Britain and in the American colonies prior to the American Revolution, including discussions of general warrants, writs of assistance, and the remarkable "Malcom Affair" (characterized as the "most famous search in colonial America"), which had the effect of fueling the resentment and resistance to the search and seizure tactics of the British Crown. It touches upon search and seizure provisions in the early state constitutions adopted during the American Revolution. Major emphasis is given to the debates in the First Congress in 1789 that produced the final wording of the Fourth Amendment. The last part of the chapter briefly surveys nineteenth-century developments prior to the *Boyd* case of 1886 and discusses that case in some detail. This chapter seeks to explain the purposes that motivated the authors of the Fourth Amendment and the Supreme Court's early understanding of those purposes.

Chapter Three selectively analyzes the U.S. Supreme Court's complex development of search and seizure law during the twentieth century. It addresses such issues as the demands of the Fourth Amendment; the prerequisites for obtaining a warrant; the proliferation of exceptions to the warrant requirement (of which there are dozens); electronic surveillance; and the exclusionary rule (from its promulgation in the early twentieth century to its heyday in the 1960s to its decline during the last quarter of the twentieth century). Evident throughout this chapter is the enormous impact of the "war on drugs" in eroding Fourth Amendment protections during recent decades.

Chapter Four looks at emerging Fourth Amendment issues in the twenty-first century. It gives particular attention to the curtailment of Fourth Amendment guarantees in the purported interest of protecting the population of the United States against the threats of both international and domestic terrorism. Major attention is given to provisions of the USA PATRIOT Act authorizing warrantless telephone taps of American citizens. As is evident in this chapter, new Fourth Amendment claims continue to confront the justices, and search and seizure law remains a developing concept.

Chapters Five and Six support the preceding four. Chapter Five offers an alphabetically organized reference section on important cases, concepts, events, persons, and terms that are central to understanding the Fourth Amendment. Chapter Six is a source materials section, consisting of twenty primary documents. Because virtually the only law relating to search and seizure has been the law created by the courts, eleven of these documents are excerpts from cases decided by the U.S. Supreme Court. Preceding the cases is a 1749 general customs warrant from the British government; a 1761 writ of assistance from the British government; and an abridged reprint of James Otis's 1761 speech arguing against the colonial writs of assistance. Following the cases are copies of present-day warrants and warrant-related materials, both state and federal. Each item in this section is preceded by a brief headnote explaining the significance and background of the reproduced material. The entries included in these chapters are related to, and drawn from, the material presented in the first four chapters.

The book also includes a brief chronology of pertinent Fourth Amendment events, a table of cases providing the legal citation to all cases mentioned in the preceding chapters, and an annotated bibliography of useful works on the Fourth Amendment.

# ACKNOWLEDGMENTS

This book was made possible only through the assistance of a number of individuals. To each of them, we offer our sincere thanks.

D. Grier Stephenson, professor of government at Franklin and Marshall College and ABC-CLIO's America's Freedoms series editor, offered sound advice and timely encouragement at every stage of the project. Alicia Merritt, ABC-CLIO's senior acquisitions editor, and Peter Warwick, ABC-CLIO's submissions editor, provided insightful comments and prompt responses to our inquiries. Our production editor, Christine Marra, generously and readily gave of her technical expertise.

Nick Barca, Tracy Tipton Jenkins, and Linda C. Noe, recent graduates of the University of Tennessee College of Law; Aaron Belville, Fermin DeLaTorre, Adam Ruff, and Caitlin Shockey, current law students at the University of Tennessee; and Rachel Pearsall, a graduate student in political science at the University of Tennessee, supplied valuable research assistance.

Daniel Hull and Mary Kennon Walker, recent graduates of the University of Tennessee College of Law, gave extensively of their intellectual talents, thus greatly benefiting this book. In addition, Mary Kennon Walker lent (time and time again) her exceptional computer expertise to the completion of this project.

John M. Scheb, II, professor of political science at the University of Tennessee, and Howard C. Ellis, professor of business administration at Millersville University, enhanced our understanding of search and seizure law in numerous ways and offered helpful suggestions for making the topic more understandable to our target audience.

Thomas Y. Davies, National Alumni Association Distinguished Service Professor of Law at the University of Tennessee, reviewed and reacted to successive drafts on the historical origins of the Fourth Amendment, making detailed suggestions that undoubtedly improved the final manuscript. His contribution stretched beyond what we would have the right to expect.

James P. Jacobs, Jr., provided us with the opportunity to see the Fourth Amendment from the perspective of law enforcement. Our task—discussing search and seizure law—is most certainly easier than his—applying it on the street. Police officers must make instantaneous decisions on Fourth Amendment matters with incomplete information and in situations where indecision may result in danger to self or others. Authors write books (and courts render decisions) in pleasant and relaxed surroundings with the luxury of time, full disclosure, and the knowledge that our choices rarely result in harm. We remain mindful of the risks that Officer Jacobs and other law enforcement agents take to protect our communities.

Lianna Stewart, secretary in the Department of Government and Political Affairs at Millersville University, offered clerical support.

Of course, even with all this help, we alone are responsible for errors of fact and interpretation.

As always, our families merit the most thanks.

**O.H.S.:** My wife, Mary, supported this project throughout with her steadfast encouragement and remarkable patience.

**R.A.G.:** My parents, Kenneth and Beth, continue to support and encourage me, even if from a distance. My wife, Lorena, lifts my vision each morning and reminds me throughout each day of what is important in life. My older son, Ryan, tells me more often than I deserve that I am the best dad ever. I will never receive a more important accolade, nor do I aspire to one. And my younger son, Andrew, makes my departure each morning and my return each evening events of monumental significance, and ones that confirm my belief that I have been richly blessed as a father. Words are inadequate to express the joy each of you provides me.

*Otis H. Stephens*
*Knoxville, Tennessee*

*Richard A. Glenn*
*Lancaster, Pennsylvania*

# UNREASONABLE SEARCHES AND SEIZURES

# 1

# INTRODUCTION

No provision of the U.S. Constitution has been more difficult to interpret or more controversial in its application than the Fourth Amendment's guarantee of the right of personal security against unreasonable searches and seizures. The bare words of the amendment provide little guidance and raise at least as many questions as they answer. The Fourth Amendment declares:

> The right of the people to be secure in their persons, houses, papers, and effects, against unreasonable searches, and seizures, shall not be violated, and no warrants shall issue, but upon probable cause, supported by oath or affirmation, and particularly describing the place to be searched, and the persons or things to be seized.

As part of the Bill of Rights, this two-pronged restriction obviously applies to searches and seizures conducted by the government and not to searches and seizures by businesses or other private entities. But what is meant by "unreasonable," and what exactly is a "search"? What is the meaning of "probable cause"? How does the broad restriction against unreasonable searches and seizures contained in the first clause of the amendment relate to the more specific warrant requirement outlined in the second clause? And how will the provisions of the Fourth Amendment be enforced against officials who violate them?

In the American legal system the ultimate answers to such questions are provided by the U.S. Supreme Court. Of course state courts, construing their own constitutions—which contain similar search and seizure restrictions—play an important role in this, as in other areas of constitutional interpretation. On the basis of clearly stated "adequate and independent state grounds" (*Michigan v. Long,* 463 U.S. 1032, 1038; 1983), a number of these courts have in recent years extended search and seizure rights beyond the requirements of the Fourth Amendment as interpreted by the U.S. Supreme Court. In establishing standards for state courts to follow in this complex area of constitutional jurisdiction, the U.S. Supreme Court has noted that:

> If the state court decision indicates clearly and expressly that it is . . . based on bona fide separate, adequate and independent [state] grounds, we . . . will not undertake to review the decision." (*Michigan v. Long,* 463 U.S. at 1041)

Fourth Amendment requirements thus represent a uniform national *minimum* standard. The states may exceed this standard so long as they do not violate other provisions of the federal Constitution, but under our federal system, they cannot fall short of it. At the outset it is important to understand this basic feature of American federalism, since most criminal prosecutions raising search and seizure issues originate at the local level and are first addressed by state courts. While we will have occasion to comment on a few state decisions that go beyond nationwide Fourth Amendment restrictions, we will be concerned primarily with the historical origins of the Fourth Amendment and with the U.S. Supreme Court's development of standards applicable to contemporary issues of law enforcement throughout the United States.

The Supreme Court had little occasion to interpret the Fourth Amendment until almost a hundred years after its ratification. In the 1886 case of *Boyd v. United States* (116 U.S. 616), the Supreme Court suggested that evidence obtained in violation of the Fourth Amendment should be excluded at trial. Almost thirty years later, in *Weeks v. United States* (232 U.S. 383; 1914), the Court turned this suggestion into a formal requirement. The federal exclusionary rule, barring the admission of evidence obtained in violation of the Fourth Amendment, departed sharply from the old common law rule that determined the admissibility of evidence based on its reliability without regard to how it was obtained. From its inception the exclusionary rule was highly controversial and remains so to this day. For a number of years the exclusionary rule was limited to federal prosecutions. By the mid-twentieth century, however, the Supreme Court, employing a process known as "selective incorporation," had begun to apply various provisions of the Federal Bill of Rights to the states through the Fourteenth Amendment. This movement toward "nationalization" of the Bill of Rights had important and far-reaching implications, especially in the field of criminal law. The Fourth Amendment was one of the first procedural rights provisions to be applied to the states through the Fourteenth Amendment. This occurred in the 1949 case of *Wolf v. Colorado* (338 U.S. 25). The *Wolf* decision, though, did not apply the controversial federal exclusionary rule to the states. That important development did not take place until the Supreme Court's landmark decision in *Mapp v. Ohio* (367 U.S. 643; 1961). Thus the Supreme Court's application of Fourth Amendment standards to federal, state, and local levels of law enforcement and its accompanying extension of the exclusionary rule as a means of enforcing the requirements of the Fourteenth Amendment date only from the mid-twentieth century.

During the 1960s the Supreme Court, under the leadership of Chief Justice Earl Warren, significantly expanded the procedural rights of criminal defendants. This expansion, especially in the areas of search and seizure and police interrogation, added significantly to the increasing controversy surrounding the Warren Court as a result of its decisions on such "hot button" issues as school desegregation, school prayer, and legislative reapportionment. (Periods of Supreme Court history are often referred to by the name of the chief justice, in this case Earl Warren.) In 1968 two presidential candidates, Republican Richard Nixon and American Independent George Wallace, in effect "ran against the Court" and aimed pointed criticism at its criminal procedure decisions. Nixon, as the newly elected president, vowed to change the direction of the Court in this area through judicial appointments, and promptly proceeded to make good on this promise. His four Supreme Court appointees, Chief Justice Warren Earl Burger, and Associate Justices Harry A. Blackmun, Lewis F. Powell, and William H. Rehnquist, although differing on a number of other constitutional issues, generally agreed that the exclusionary rule should be limited. As a result, the 1970s and 1980s witnessed a substantial weakening of the protections afforded by the exclusionary rule as well as other safeguards recognized by earlier Fourth Amendment interpretation. (See, for example, *United States v. Leon;* 1984; and *Illinois v. Gates;* 1983. Discussed in Chapter Three.) The rise and decline of the Fourth Amendment exclusionary rule reflects the ongoing conflict between the values of liberty and the imperatives of law enforcement.

The field of search and seizure law is vast and complex. In this short book it will be examined selectively in a broad historical and social context. The principal objective is to provide the general reader with sufficient information about the development of the Fourth Amendment to serve as a basis for evaluating the question of its continuing relevance in seeking a balance between the protection of individual liberty and the demands for effective law enforcement. Fourth Amendment issues arise in a wide range of settings and pose a seemingly endless variety of difficult questions.

Accordingly, it is not surprising that Supreme Court decisions in this area often lack clarity and consistency, and that no unified theory of search and seizure law has emerged. Professor Anthony Amsterdam (1974, 353), a distinguished Fourth Amendment scholar, in commenting on the work of the Supreme Court some thirty years ago, observed that Fourth Amendment issues are "particularly fragile under the buffeting of rapid historical developments that incessantly place unprecedented strains upon the Court." Those "unprecedented strains" are no doubt greater in the post-9/11 era than ever before.

Over the years Congress and state legislatures have enacted numerous statutes designed to spell out the broad requirements of the Fourth Amendment and its counterparts in state constitutions. In the course of deciding cases courts are typically required to determine whether particular statutory provisions are consistent with constitutional requirements and whether they have been constitutionally applied. Sooner or later the most difficult questions work their way up to the U.S. Supreme Court, presenting the nine justices of that tribunal with the formidable task of transforming general abstract constitutional values into tangible, practical requirements for law enforcement agencies to follow.

## THE FOURTH AMENDMENT IN A DYNAMIC SOCIETY

Vast changes in transportation and modes of communication have revolutionized the techniques of law enforcement over the past two centuries. Yet the basic values implicit in the Fourth Amendment remain unchanged; safeguarding individual liberty, personal privacy, and the rights of property against arbitrary governmental intrusion—these are the core objectives of the Fourth Amendment. Imperatives of maintaining security in the face of violent crime and the looming threat of international terrorism nevertheless place constant pressure on law enforcement agencies to by-pass protections of individual rights in furtherance of the demands for public order and stability.

When the Fourth Amendment was ratified in 1791, police departments as we know them today did not exist. Law enforcement was a rather modest and informal enterprise, conducted largely by local constables with the assistance of private citizens. By the middle of the nineteenth century a distinct law enforcement profession began to emerge. The constable and his posse gradually gave way to a bureaucracy of professionally trained personnel organized along military lines in order to combat crime, seeking to maintain law and order in an increasingly urbanized society.

Like many other provisions of the Constitution, the Fourth Amendment has been interpreted in response to vast technological changes. This point is well illustrated by a classic sequence of Supreme Court decisions involving telephone wiretaps. In the 1928 case of *Olmstead v. United States* (277 U.S. 438) the Supreme Court took a strict view of the scope of the Fourth Amendment. Roy Olmstead, a suspected bootlegger, was charged with conspiracy to violate the national prohibition act, designed to implement the Eighteenth Amendment adopted almost a decade earlier. The government's evidence consisted of transcripts of Olmstead's telephone conversations obtained through a wiretap placed beyond the boundaries of his property. The law enforcement agents had not obtained a warrant authorizing the wiretap. Although there was no search or seizure of his person or physical property, Olmstead insisted that the Fourth Amendment had been violated. Obviously, the Fourth Amendment's reference to "effects" could have been interpreted to include telephone conversations. The Supreme Court, however, opted for a narrow, formalistic construction of the amendment. Writing for a five-member majority, Chief Justice William Howard Taft observed:

The reasonable view is that one who installs in his house a telephone instrument with connecting wires intends to project his voice to those quite outside, and that the wires beyond his house, and messages passing over them, are not within the protection of the Fourth Amendment. (277 U.S. at 465–466)

In one of his most famous dissenting opinions, Justice Louis D. Brandeis prophetically recognized the necessity of applying the Constitution to changing technological conditions:

The progress of science in furnishing the government with means of espionage is not likely to stop with wire-tapping. Ways may some day be developed by which the government, without removing papers from secret drawers, can reproduce them in court, and by which it will be enabled to expose to a jury the most intimate occurrences of the home. . . . Can it be that the Constitution affords no protection against such invasions of individual security? (277 U.S. at 473–474)

In 1928 the telephone was in fairly wide use. A few decades later it had become virtually omnipresent. Perhaps it was this reality that motivated the Court in 1967 to overrule the *Olmstead* case in *Katz v. United States* (389 U.S. 347). In *Katz* the Court reversed a conviction based in large part on evidence obtained by government agents who, without a warrant, had "bugged" a telephone booth from which Charles Katz, a suspected bookie, often placed bets. Writing for the Court, Justice Potter Stewart declared that "the Fourth Amendment protects people—not places." The new standard was spelled out by Justice John Marshall Harlan in an influential concurring opinion. The Fourth Amendment, Harlan explained, extends to any place or anything in which an individual has a "reasonable expectation of privacy." Consistent with this view, the Court has demonstrated a willingness to consider hotel rooms, garages, offices, automobiles, sealed letters, suitcases, and other closed containers as protected by the Fourth Amendment. (*Olmstead* and *Katz* will be discussed in greater detail in Chapter Three.)

The "reasonable expectation of privacy" standard has proved difficult to apply with consistency. This point is well illustrated by comparing two Supreme Court decisions, one involving aerial surveillance of private property and the other involving thermal imaging of a private residence. In *California v. Ciraolo* (476 U.S. 207; 1986), the Court addressed the question of whether the use of evidence based on visual observation of marijuana growing in the defendant's fenced backyard violated the Fourth Amendment. On the basis of an anonymous tip that Dante Carlo Ciraolo was cultivating marijuana plants, police officers hired a private plane and flew over his home at an altitude of 1,000 feet. They observed numerous marijuana plants growing in his backyard, shielded from ground observation by a ten-foot inner fence and a six-foot outer fence. Armed with this information, the police obtained a search warrant and seized seventy-three plants that were later used as evidence leading to his conviction. In rejecting Ciraolo's contention that his Fourth Amendment rights had been violated, the Supreme Court acknowledged that he had manifested a subjective expectation of privacy by building the fences around his yard. The Court concluded, however, that this expectation was not reasonable. Writing for a five-member majority, Chief Justice Burger said that police observation of an object within the "curtilage" of a dwelling (in this instance the enclosed backyard) is not always barred. The Fourth Amendment, for example, does not require that officers shield their eyes when passing by houses on public thoroughfares. Burger maintained that "the mere fact that an individual has taken measures to restrict some view of his activities does not preclude an officer's observations from a public vantage point where he has a right to be and which renders the activities clearly visible . . ." (476 U.S. at 213). Speaking for the four dissenters, Justice Powell pointed out that Ciraolo could not have done more, as a practical matter, to conceal his backyard from public view. He could have anticipated no real risk of a privacy violation from commercial or pleasure aircraft.

By contrast, the Court held in *Kyllo v. United States* (533 U.S. 27; 2001) that thermal imaging of a private residence is an illegal search in violation of the Fourth Amendment. Here, police received a tip that Danny Kyllo was growing marijuana in his house. Police followed up by checking Kyllo's utility bills for above normal energy consumption and by using a thermal imaging device to identify unusually high heat emissions normally associated with the growing of marijuana. Writing for the majority, Justice Antonin Scalia identified a reasonable expectation of privacy in the interior of a home. "To withdraw protection of this minimum expectation would be to permit police technology to erode the privacy guaranteed by the Fourth Amendment" (533 U.S. at 34). Accordingly, the government may not use a device not generally available to the public to explore details of a home that would otherwise be unknowable without physical intrusion. A search of this kind is presumptively unreasonable in the absence of a warrant. (*Kyllo* will be discussed in greater detail in Chapter Four.)

Advances in technology continue to occur at an accelerating rate. The *Ciraolo* and *Kyllo* cases illustrate the extent to which the Supreme Court has been able to apply Fourth Amendment values to problems posed by such advances. There appears to be nothing in the language of the Fourth Amendment to prevent its extension to unforeseeable technological change.

## Probable Cause and the Warrant Requirement

The Fourth Amendment imposes on government the requirement that searches and seizures be based on probable cause. With some notable exceptions to be discussed later, a police officer must have a good reason to believe that the search for which he seeks authorization will produce evidence of a crime. The Supreme Court has observed that police officers have probable cause when:

> the facts and circumstances within their knowledge and of which they had reasonable and trustworthy information [are] sufficient in themselves to warrant a man of reasonable caution in the belief that an offense has been or is being committed (*Brinegar v. United States*, 338 U.S. 160; 1949).

To ensure that probable cause does exist before police undertake to search a person's home, the Fourth Amendment also imposes a warrant requirement. The framers of the Fourth Amendment were careful to spell out with particularity the "place to be searched and the persons or things to be seized." Their concern grew out of the reckless use of "general warrants," under which British colonial officials often conducted wide-ranging searches of the homes and businesses of colonists. (For detailed background on the origins of the Fourth Amendment see Davies, "Recovering the Original Fourth Amendment." General warrants will be discussed more fully in Chapter Two). A search warrant is simply an order issued by a judge or magistrate authorizing law enforcement officers to conduct a search. Mindful of the principles of separation of powers, the Supreme Court in 1971 invalidated a warrant issued by a state Attorney General, a member of the executive branch, rather than by a judicial officer (*Coolidge v. New Hampshire*, 403 U.S. 443). The Court thus places great importance on the role of the "neutral and detached magistrate" in maintaining the integrity of the Fourth Amendment.

One of the most controversial questions concerning the issuance of search warrants involves the use of confidential informants. These persons, who refuse to cooperate with the police unless their anonymity is guaranteed, are vital to criminal investigations. As noted in the *Ciraolo* and *Kyllo* cases, previously discussed, police often rely on tips provided by confidential informants to obtain search warrants that lead to the discovery of incriminating evidence. In *Aguilar v. Texas* (378 U.S. 108; 1964), police obtained a warrant merely by swearing that they "had received reliable information from a credible person" that illegal drugs would be found at a certain location. The Supreme Court invalidated that warrant, ruling that an affidavit must inform the magistrate of

[1] the underlying circumstances from which the informant concluded that the narcotics were where he claimed they were, and [2] some of the underlying circumstances from which the officer concluded that the informant, whose identity need not be disclosed . . . was "credible" or his information "reliable" (378 U.S. at 114).

Five years later, in *Spinelli v. United States* (393 U.S. 410; 1969) the Court reaffirmed this two-pronged test. The *Aguilar-Spinelli* test made it more difficult for police to obtain warrants based on tips from confidential informants. On this issue, as on several others, the Warren Court was sharply criticized for "handcuffing the police." In 1983, a more conservative Supreme Court under Chief Justice Burger abandoned the *Aguilar-Spinelli* test in favor of a more flexible "totality of circumstances" approach, thus making it easier for police to obtain search warrants (*Illinois v. Gates*, 462 U.S. 213; 1983). Speaking for the Court, then Associate Justice Rehnquist asserted that the *Aguilar-Spinelli* test could not "avoid seriously impeding the task of law enforcement" because "anonymous tips seldom could survive a rigorous application of either of the Spinelli prongs" (462 U.S. at 237). In a strong dissenting opinion, Justice William J. Brennan argued:

[t]he court gives virtually no consideration to the value of insuring that findings of probable cause are based on information that a magistrate can reasonably say has been obtained in a reliable way by an honest or credible person. (462 U.S. at 289–290)

Justice Brennan agreed with Justice White, expressing fear that rejection of the *Aguilar-Spinelli* test might signal "an evisceration of the probable cause standard. . . ."

## WARRANTLESS SEARCHES

The Fourth Amendment places a high priority on search warrants. A number of scholars have argued, in fact, that the prohibition of unreasonable searches and seizures in the first clause of the amendment was, in effect, intended to bar warrantless searches. (See Cuddihy, *The Fourth Amendment: Origins and Original Meaning, 1602–1791*.) Nevertheless, the Supreme Court, beginning with the *Boyd* decision of 1886, has recognized a distinction between the general restriction against "unreasonable searches and seizures" and the more specific warrant requirement appearing in the second clause of the amendment. (For background see Landynski, *Search and Seizure and the Supreme Court*, Chapter Two.) This distinction has permitted the Court to hold that "exigent circumstances" may justify warrantless searches. With the increasing mobility of our society following the introduction and proliferation of the automobile and the broadening scale of law enforcement activity, warrantless searches have become more and more prevalent, and in fact are today more frequently conducted than those based on warrants. One familiar example is the legitimate warrantless search incidental to a lawful arrest. In *Chimel v. California* (395 U.S. 752; 1969), Justice Stewart stated for the majority:

> When an arrest is made, it is reasonable for the arresting officer to search the person arrested in order to remove any weapons that the latter might seek to use in order to resist arrest or effect his escape. . . . In addition, it is entirely reasonable for the arresting officer to search for and seize any evidence on the arrestee's person in order to prevent its concealment or destruction (395 U.S. at 762–763).

Legitimate warrantless searches may also be based on the consent of the individual whose privacy is being invaded. It is an elementary principle of law that individuals may waive their constitutional rights, so long as they do so knowingly, intelligently, and voluntarily. In *Schneckloth v. Bustamonte* (412 U.S. 218; 1973), the Supreme Court upheld a search based on consent even though the police had failed to advise the suspect that his consent was not required. The burden of proof rests, however, on the prosecution to show that no force or coercion was used to obtain consent. To determine whether consent was given voluntarily and knowingly, the Court looks to the totality of circumstances surrounding the search. Evidence within the "plain view" of an investigator or obtained in "hot pursuit" of a suspect may also be seized without a warrant. Blood tests for alcohol or illegal drugs may be conducted without search warrants under the "evanescent evidence" doctrine.

One of the most important and far-reaching exceptions to the warrant requirement is the automobile search. In the 1925 case of *Carroll v. United States* (267 U.S. 132), the Supreme Court upheld the warrantless search of an automobile believed to be carrying illegal liquor. The Court emphasized, however, that probable cause was essential to justify such a search. Indiscriminately stopping and searching passing motorists in an effort to discover evidence of crime could not be constitutionally justified. Over the years the Court has broadened and loosened the automobile exception to permit searches of luggage and closed containers, even those locked in the trunk. In *United States v. Ross* (456 U.S. 798; 1982), Justice John Paul Stevens clarified the legitimate scope of a warrantless automobile search as "no greater than a magistrate could have authorized by issuing a warrant based on the probable cause that justified the search" (456 U.S. at 818). Dissenting sharply, Justice Thurgood Marshall assailed the majority position as "flatly inconsistent . . . with established Fourth Amendment principles . . ." (456 U.S. at 831).

The Court has also held that when the police have made a lawful custodial arrest of an occupant of an automobile, the Fourth Amendment permits the police to search the passenger compartment of the vehicle as a contemporaneous incident of arrest (*New York v. Belton,* 453 U.S. 454; 1981). It should be noted that the Fourth Amendment reference to "seizures" extends to the arrest of a suspect as well as to items within his or her possession. In a recent decision, the Court further accommodated law enforcement officers by holding that even when the police do not make the arrest until after the suspect has exited the vehicle, they may nevertheless conduct a warrantless search of the passenger compartment (*Thornton v. United States,* 541 U.S. 615; 2004. This case is discussed more fully in Chapter Four.)

Other exceptions within the general category of automobile searches include border searches and highway checkpoints. For example, the Court recently held unanimously that the federal government's authority to conduct a warrantless inspection of an automobile entering the United States from Mexico need not be based on suspicion and could extend to removal, disassembly, and reassembly of the vehicle's gas tank (*United States v. Flores-Montano,* 541 U.S. 149; 2004. This case is discussed more fully in Chapter Four.)

In a number of situations, the Supreme Court has been willing to uphold warrantless searches at highway checkpoints. Common justifications of such searches are the "removal[] of drunk drivers from the road, . . . [and] verifying drivers' licenses and vehicle registration[s]." The Court has made it clear, however, that it does not approve of automobile checkpoints aimed primarily at the detection of "ordinary criminal wrongdoing" (*City of Indianapolis v. Edmond,* 531 U.S. 32; 2000). In the recent case of *Illinois v. Lidster* (540 U.S. 419; 2004), the Court again addressed this issue. Here the Supreme Court upheld the validity of a highway checkpoint set up to "ask vehicle occupants . . . for their help in providing information about" a hit-and-run accident in which a bicyclist had been killed (540 U.S. at 420). As Robert S. Lidster approached the checkpoint, the minivan he was driving swerved, almost hitting an officer. After smelling alcohol on his breath and administering a sobriety test, the police arrested Lidster, who was tried and convicted of driving under the influence of alcohol. The Supreme Court rejected Lidster's argument that the checkpoint violated the Fourth Amendment and that the evidence of his intoxication was thus inadmissible. The court reasoned that the checkpoint was only minimally intrusive and that the systematic stops were non-discriminatory. (This case is discussed more fully in Chapter Four.)

One other type of warrantless search falls entirely outside the field of criminal law. In recent years, the Court has recognized a "special needs" exception justifying searches and seizures within the public schools unrelated to criminal investigations. The Court has held that school officials may perform searches without individualized suspicion in the context of the "nationwide drug epidemic." In *Board of Education v. Earls* (537 U.S. 822; 2002), a divided Supreme Court, speaking through Justice Clarence Thomas, found no constitutional problem with a drug testing program extending to all students engaged in a wide range of extracurricular activities. (This case is discussed more fully in Chapter Four.)

## INVESTIGATORY DETENTION

One of the most controversial types of police searches is investigatory detention. This type of limited search usually takes the form of the "stop and frisk." In the typical situation, a police officer confronts a "suspicious" individual and conducts a limited "pat down" search in an effort to prevent a crime from taking place. The classic case in this area is *Terry v. Ohio* (392 U.S. 1; 1968). There, an experienced plainclothes officer observed three men who appeared to be preparing to rob a nearby jewelry store. Approaching the trio, he identified himself as a police officer and asked for their names. Unsatisfied with their mumbled responses, he subjected one of them to a "pat down" search that produced a gun for which the individual had no permit. In conducting this

search, the officer not only had no warrant but also lacked probable cause as traditionally defined. The Supreme Court nevertheless found the "stop and frisk" valid on the basis of "reasonable
suspicion." (This case is discussed more fully in Chapter Three.)

The *Terry* stop, widely used by police, permits law enforcement
officers to stop and question suspicious persons, pat them down
for weapons, and even subject them to nonintrusive search procedures, such as the use of metal detectors and drug-sniffing dogs.
While a suspect is being detained, a computer search can be performed to determine whether the suspect is wanted for crimes in
other jurisdictions. If so, then he or she may be arrested and a
search conducted incident to that arrest. In a recent decision, the
Supreme Court addressed the question of whether a state "stop
and identify" statute exceeded the constitutional boundaries of a
*Terry* stop (*Hiibel v. Sixth Judicial District Court of Nevada*, 542
U.S. 177; 2004. This case is discussed more fully in Chapter Four.)

## CONCLUSION

The preceding paragraphs have selectively highlighted major areas
of law enforcement activity illustrating the enormous expansion
of Fourth Amendment law in the United States. The Fourth
Amendment, as interpreted today, goes far beyond the concerns
of those who drafted and ratified it in the late eighteenth century.
Yet the Supreme Court has attempted time and time again to trace
its evolving application of search and seizure standards to the
Fourth Amendment's historical roots. Many scholars today maintain that the justices have largely misunderstood Fourth Amendment history and have moved far away from the concerns of the
founding generation. (See LaFave, *Search and Seizure: A Treatise
on the Fourth Amendment;* Davies, "The Fictional Character of
Law-and-Order Originalism"; and Levy, *Origins of the Bill of
Rights,* Chapter Seven.) In this book we will examine both the
early history of the Fourth Amendment and the Supreme Court's

development of its requirements from the late nineteenth century through the opening years of the twenty-first century.

## References and Further Reading

Amar, Akhil R. 1994. "Fourth Amendment First Principles." *Harvard Law Review* 107: 757–819.

Amsterdam, Anthony G. 1974. "Perspectives on the Fourth Amendment." *Minnesota Law Review* 58: 349–477.

Buffaloe, Jennifer Y. 1997. "'Special Needs' and the Fourth Amendment: An Exception Poised to Swallow the Warrant Preference Rule." *Harvard Civil Rights–Civil Liberties Law Review* 32: 529–564.

Cuddihy, William J. 1990. *The Fourth Amendment: Origins and Original Meaning, 1602–1791.* Unpublished dissertation, Claremont Graduate School. University of Michigan Dissertation Services, printed 1994.

Davies, Thomas Y. 1999. "Recovering the Original Fourth Amendment." *Michigan Law Review* 98: 547–750.

———. 2002. "The Fictional Character of Law-and-Order Originalism." *Wake Forest Law Review* 37: 239–437.

LaFave, Wayne R. 1996. *Search and Seizure: A Treatise on the Fourth Amendment.* Five volumes, 3rd Edition. West's Criminal Practice Series.

Landynski, Jacob W. 1966. *Search and Seizure and the Supreme Court: A Study in Constitutional Interpretation.* Baltimore, MD: Johns Hopkins Press.

Lasson, Nelson B. 1937. *The History and Development of the Fourth Amendment to the United States Constitution.* Baltimore, MD: Johns Hopkins Press.

Levy, Leonard W. 1999. *Origins of the Bill of Rights.* New Haven, CT: Yale University Press.

Maclin, Tracey. 1997. "The Complexity of the Fourth Amendment: A Historical Review." *Boston University Law Review* 77: 925–974.

Packer, Herbert L. 1968. *The Limits of the Criminal Sanction.* Stanford, CA: Stanford University Press.

Scheb, John M., and Scheb, John M., II. 2005. *Criminal Law and Procedure.* Belmont, CA: West Wadsworth. 5th ed.

Taylor, Telford. 1969. *Two Studies in Constitutional Interpretation.* Columbus: Ohio State University Press.

Wasserstrom, Silas J. 1989. "The Fourth Amendment's Two Clauses." *American Criminal Law Review* 26: 1389–1396.

# 2

## ORIGINS

### INTRODUCTION

One of the underlying objectives of the United States Constitution, as set forth in its preamble, is to "secure the blessings of liberty" to all generations of Americans. During the Constitutional Convention held in Philadelphia in the summer of 1787, however, the framers devoted most of their time and attention to the enumeration and allocation of powers among the three branches of the national government and between the national government and the states. On February 21, 1787, the unicameral Congress, in which each state had a single vote, had authorized the Philadelphia Convention for the purpose of strengthening the national government by revising the weak and ineffective Articles of Confederation. It quickly became clear to the Convention delegates that mere revision was an inadequate response to the problem, and they set about in secret session to fashion a new comprehensive blueprint of government. In reaching this momentous decision, these innovative leaders (some might call them revolutionaries) were transformed from delegates instructed to "revise" the Articles of Confederation into framers of a new constitution. The framers were chiefly concerned with distributing authority between the national and state governments (federalism); enumerating powers among three distinct branches of the national government (separation of powers); placing restrictions on those enumerated powers (checks and balances); and articulating certain limitations on both national and state governments (individual rights).

The incorporation of the first three of these defining principles minimized the threat of tyranny from any one government or any single branch of the national government. The incorporation of the fourth principle indicated the framers' highest ideals—protection of the liberty and property of the individual.

Federalism is a system of government in which a constitution divides power between a national government and subnational governments. Neither the state government nor the federal government receives its powers from the other. Instead, both governments derive their powers from the U.S. Constitution. The framers viewed the division of governmental authority as a means of checking power with power, and providing "double security" to the people. The national government would keep the state governments "in check," and the state governments would prevent excesses by the national government. In a federal system, both governments may act directly upon the people.

Separation of powers is a way of parceling out power among the three branches of the national government. James Madison was well aware of the writings of the eighteenth-century French philosopher Baron de Montesquieu regarding the dangers of concentrated governmental power. Reflecting Montesquieu's influence, Madison wrote in *Federalist, No. 47*, "the accumulation of all powers, legislative, executive, and judiciary, in the same hands . . . may justly be pronounced the very definition of tyranny." As such, the Constitution assigns the legislative, executive, and judicial powers of the national government to three separate, independent branches of government. This separation, Madison maintained, provided an "essential precaution in favor of liberty" (Hamilton 1961, 301).

In addition, power is checked and balanced. The legislative, executive, and judicial branches of the national government share certain powers so that no branch has exclusive domain over any activity. "The great security against the gradual concentration of several powers in the same department," Madison noted in *Federalist, No. 51,* "consists in giving to those who administer each department the necessary constitutional means and personal motives to resist encroachment by the others. . . . Ambition must be made to counteract ambition. . . . [E]xperience has taught mankind the necessity of auxiliary precautions" (Hamilton 1961, 321–322). The Constitution thus contains a number of "auxiliary precautions" so that each branch may "resist encroachment" by the others. For example, the legislature may check the executive by overriding a presidential veto, impeaching and removing the president, and rejecting presidential nominees, including federal judges. The legislature may check the judiciary by determining the jurisdiction of federal courts, and by rejecting, impeaching, and removing federal judges. The executive may check the legislature by vetoing bills passed by Congress, and check the judiciary by appointing all federal judges and by pardoning those accused or convicted of federal crimes. Much less was said about the powers of the judiciary. In fact, the Constitution is silent with respect to the means by which the judiciary may "resist encroachment" of the legislative and executive branches.

In attempting to create a more effective system of government, the framers provided for the expansion of congressional powers, established an executive branch that would, to some extent, share these powers, but would have a distinct and prominent identity of its own, and provided for an independent, life-tenured judiciary. The framers sought to provide for an effective national government but, at the same time, to preserve a degree of state autonomy and a sphere of individual rights by placing outer limits on that government. In Article I, Section 8, of the Constitution, for example, the framers specified a long list of powers, ranging from taxing and spending, to the regulation of commerce with foreign nations, and among the several states to declaring war, raising armies, and making "all laws which shall be necessary and proper for carrying into execution the foregoing powers, and all other powers vested by this Constitution in the government of the United States, or in any Department or Officer thereof."

Although these powers greatly enlarged the potential scope of national authority, their specific enumeration indicated that the national government was confined to the areas identified. The states, by contrast, continued to exercise inherent police power over a large unspecified array of activities and relationships for the purpose of protecting the health, safety, and general welfare of the public. In the 1780s this state police power included a limited role in enforcing criminal laws, the licensing and regulation of marriage and domestic relations as well as various occupations and professions, and the protection of property rights. Article I, Section 10, placed a few restrictions on the states, including provisions barring them from entering into treaties, alliances, or confederations or, without the consent of Congress, from entering into "any Agreement or Compact with another State, or with a foreign Power. . . ." As the language of Article VI clearly indicated, within its sphere of enumerated powers, the national government was to be supreme:

> This Constitution, and the Laws of the United States which shall be made in Pursuance thereof; and all Treaties made, or which shall be made, under the Authority of the United States, shall be the supreme Law of the Land; and the Judges in every State shall be bound thereby, any Thing in the Constitution or Laws of any State to the Contrary notwithstanding.

Although the framers were primarily concerned with the enumeration, allocation, and distribution of powers, they did recognize a few important safeguards of individual rights in the original Constitution. These included a definition of the crime of treason;

the prohibition of religious tests for holding federal office; the writ of habeas corpus; and prohibitions against ex post facto laws and bills of attainder.

The absence of a more comprehensive list of individual rights is not an indication that such rights were unimportant to the framers. They apparently thought that it was simply unnecessary to include a more detailed list of rights in the federal Constitution. Indeed, the Convention delegates were well aware that most of the state constitutions adopted during the American Revolution contained fairly detailed bills of rights placing limits on state and local governments. Because the framers anticipated a limited role for a national government exercising enumerated powers, they saw no critical need for a detailed federal bill of rights. Apparently, the framers did not even consider the possibility of adding a bill of rights until five days prior to the end of the Convention. After brief discussion, however, they hurried to adjournment without taking action on this matter.

The absence of a bill of rights immediately drew fire from such early critics as Thomas Jefferson and Patrick Henry, neither of whom attended the Philadelphia Convention. In fact, much of the opposition to the adoption of the Constitution by delegates popularly elected to state ratifying conventions centered on the absence of a bill of rights. The issue assumed critical importance during ratification debates in the pivotal states of New York and Virginia. Ultimately, delegates to the state Ratifying Conventions reached a compromise on this issue. The Federalists (those pushing for ratification of the Constitution in its original form) reached common ground with their anti-Federalist opponents. Both sides agreed that the states should be allowed to propose amendments to be added to the newly ratified Constitution as a bill of rights. The emerging consensus assured ratification of the Constitution in the summer of 1788.

Five states (Massachusetts, South Carolina, New Hampshire, Virginia, and New York) proposed amendments and promptly submitted them to the First Congress of the United States in 1789. In that year Congress proposed twelve amendments to the states. In December 1791 the requisite three-fourths of the states ratified ten of these amendments: the Bill of Rights. Amendments I through VIII provide for the protection of specific individual rights. These will be briefly summarized.

The First Amendment prohibits Congress from making laws "respecting an establishment of religion," prohibiting the "free exercise thereof," or "abridging" freedoms of speech, press, or "the right of the people peaceably to assemble, and to petition the government for a redress of grievances." The Second Amendment provides for "the right of the people to keep and bear arms. . . ." The Third Amendment prohibits the peacetime quartering of troops "in any house, without the consent of the owner," and during wartime except as "prescribed by law." The Fourth Amendment recognizes the "right of the people to be secure in their persons, houses, papers, and effects, against unreasonable searches and seizures" and imposes standards for the issuance of warrants. The Fifth Amendment contains provisions recognizing the extent of the right to indictment by a grand jury; provides that no person shall "be subject for the same offence to be twice put in jeopardy of life or limb," or compelled in a criminal case "to be a witness against himself," or "deprived of life, liberty, or property, without due process of law," or have his private property taken for "public use without just compensation." The Sixth Amendment lists a number of procedural protections to which criminal defendants are entitled, including "the right to a speedy and public trial," the right to trial by jury, the right "to be informed of the nature and cause of the accusation," and the rights of confrontation, "compulsory process," and defense counsel. The Seventh Amendment preserves a broad "right of trial by jury" in civil cases "where the value in controversy shall exceed twenty dollars. . . ." The Eighth Amendment bars the requirement of excessive bail, the imposition of excessive fines, and the infliction of "cruel and unusual punishments."

Beyond these safeguards of specific individual rights, the Ninth Amendment recognizes that the enumeration of rights in the Constitution "shall not be construed to deny or disparage others retained by the people." The Ninth Amendment reflects the widely held view of the Founding Generation that certain fundamental rights predated government itself. This "natural rights" perspective, grounded in the writings of such social contract theorists as John Locke and Jean Jacques Rousseau, had great influence in the late eighteenth century. It was invoked in a few early U.S. Supreme Court decisions (see for example *Calder v. Bull,* 3 U.S. 386; 1798 [opinion of Justice Samuel Chase] and *Fletcher v. Peck,* 10 U.S. 87; 1810 [especially the concurring opinion of Justice William Johnson]) but gradually gave way to a positivist interpretation that relied exclusively on the words of the Constitution as the only legitimate basis of interpretation. Nevertheless, the influence of natural rights theory has occasionally resurfaced, as in the debates over racial and gender equality in the middle and late twentieth century. Although the Supreme Court has given little attention to the Ninth Amendment, it was cited as one source of the unenumerated right of privacy in the seminal case of *Griswold v. Connecticut* (381 U.S. 479; 1965) (Stephens and Scheb 2003, 342, 662, and 685–690). In recent years the Ninth Amendment has figured more prominently in legal scholarship as a potential source of constitutional liberty (Barnett 2004). Finally, the Tenth Amendment declares that powers not delegated to the national government or prohibited to the states "are reserved to the States respectively, or to the people." It is interesting to note that the proposals originally recommended by the above-mentioned five states safeguarded "all the rights protected by the federal Bill of Rights (except the right to just compensation guaranteed by the Fifth Amendment)" (Schwartz 1977, 120).

The House of Representatives originally approved seventeen proposed amendments, twelve of which were ultimately accepted by the Senate and submitted to the states for ratification. Madison ranked one of the amendments, passed by the House but rejected by the Senate, as "the most valuable of the whole list" (1 Annals of Congress 755; 1789). It provided: "The equal rights of conscience, the freedom of speech or of the press, and the right of trial by jury in criminal cases, shall not be infringed by any state." If this amendment had been approved by the Senate and ratified, it would have fundamentally changed the relationship between the original Bill of Rights and the states. In 1789 the prevailing view was that the Bill of Rights applied only to the national government. Chief Justice John Marshall confirmed this interpretation authoritatively in his opinion for a unanimous Supreme Court more than forty years later in *Barron v. Baltimore* (32 U.S. 243; 1833), discussed below. As it turned out, freedoms of speech and press and the right to trial by jury were "incorporated" many years later into the Fourteenth Amendment and made applicable to the states. (See *Gitlow v. New York*, 268 U.S. 652; 1925; *Fiske v. Kansas*, 274 U.S. 380; 1927; *Near v. Minnesota*, 283 U.S. 697; 1931; and *Duncan v. Louisiana*, 391 U.S. 145; 1968.)

Section 1 of the Fourteenth Amendment, adopted in 1868, denied to each *state* the power to "make or enforce any law which shall abridge the privileges or immunities of citizens of the United States ... [or] deprive any person of life, liberty, or property, without due process of law ... [or] deny to any person within its jurisdiction the equal protection of the laws." Some members of Congress, including the two principal authors of the amendment—Representative John A. Bingham of Ohio and Senator Jacob M. Howard of Michigan—maintained that one objective of the Fourteenth Amendment was to make the Bill of Rights applicable to the states. The record of the Thirty-ninth Congress on this question, however, is far from conclusive. Nevertheless, plain-

tiffs in federal cases began to make this argument shortly after ratification of the Fourteenth Amendment.

The amendment's Privileges or Immunities Clause appeared to
be the most direct limitation on the activities of the states. Both
Bingham and Howard were on record in support of this view (see
*Congressional Globe* 1866, 2764–2765). Whatever potential for incorporation the Privileges or Immunities Clause had was soon
dashed by the Supreme Court's decision in *The Slaughterhouse
Cases* (83 U.S. 36; 1873). Upholding a Louisiana law that created a
monopoly on the operation of slaughterhouses, a five-four majority
of the Court, speaking through Justice Samuel F. Miller, concluded
that state citizenship was distinct and separate from national citizenship and that the Privileges or Immunities Clause protected
only those privileges or immunities that were granted by the federal
government and Constitution. Here, the plaintiffs had alleged a denial of a privilege—that of engaging in lawful trade. Yet that privilege was an aspect of state, not national, citizenship.

Justice Stephen J. Field, joined by three other justices, filed a
strong dissenting opinion, asserting that the Fourteenth Amendment protects "the citizens of the United States against the deprivation of their common rights by state legislation" (83 U.S. at 89).
These "common rights" included the fundamental right to secure
lawful employment in a lawful manner—a right denied the plaintiffs by the establishment of a state-created monopoly, preventing
them from engaging in their trade.

Given the Supreme Court's narrow interpretation of the Privileges or Immunities Clause, plaintiffs challenging the constitutionality of state restrictions on Bill of Rights guarantees began to
invoke the Due Process Clause of the Fourteenth Amendment as
a check on state power. In 1897 the Court "incorporated" into the
Fourteenth Amendment the Fifth Amendment provision that
"private property" cannot "be taken for public use, without just
compensation" (*Chicago, Burlington, and Quincy Railway Company v. Chicago,* 166 U.S. 226). This case reflected the Court's

strong support of laissez-faire capitalism at the height of the industrial revolution in America.

Not until well into the twentieth century did the Supreme Court begin to extend the Due Process Clause of the Fourteenth Amendment to other guarantees of the Bill of Rights. Eventually, through the case-by-case process of "selective incorporation," the Court, between the mid-1920s and the late 1960s, applied most of the provisions of the Bill of Rights to the states. (See, for example, *Gitlow v. New York,* 268 U.S. 652; 1925 [Freedom of Speech]; *Fiske v. Kansas* (274 U.S. 380; 1927) [freedom of speech]; *Near v. Minnesota* (283 U.S. 697; 1931) [freedom of the press]; *DeJonge v. Oregon* (299 U.S. 353; 1937) [freedom of assembly and petition]; *Cantwell v. Connecticut* (310 U.S. 296; 1940) [free exercise of religion]; *Everson v. Board of Education* (330 U.S. 1; 1947 [nonestablishment of religion]; *Wolf v. Colorado* (338 U.S. 25; 1949) [unreasonable searches and seizures]; *Mapp v. Ohio* (367 U.S. 643; 1961) [application of Fourth Amendment exclusionary rule]; *Duncan v. Louisiana* (391 U.S. 145; 1968) [jury trial in nonpetty criminal cases]; and *Benton v. Maryland* (395 U.S. 784; 1969) [prohibition of double jeopardy].) (The authors have adapted much of the foregoing discussion of "selective incorporation" from a companion volume in this series, Richard A. Glenn's *The Right to Privacy: Rights and Liberties under the Law* (2003, 35–38).)

Returning to the drafting of the original Bill of Rights, Madison, in a speech on June 8, 1789, proposed the provisions that became the first ten amendments. He mentioned two additional provisions merely as "other" amendments that would be worthwhile. These two provisions became the first and second proposed amendments only because Madison ordered them sequentially, based on where they would be inserted in the Constitution. Madison wanted to include the Bill of Rights in Article I, Section 9, the limitations on congressional power—instead of having it appended to the Constitution. Congress, however, did not accept Madison's placement recommendation.

Congress proposed a total of twelve amendments, including the two that Madison separated from the ten provisions later adopted as the Bill of Rights. No time limit on state ratification was imposed. As previously noted, the two "other" amendments were not ratified by the states in 1791. The first of these sought to fix the minimum membership of the House of Representatives at two hundred and to require that there be not "more than one Representative for every fifty thousand persons." (This proposed amendment is reproduced in full in Farber and Sherry, *A History of the American Constitution* 1990, 243.) The other amendment not adopted in 1791, interestingly, was resurrected from oblivion two centuries later and ratified as the Twenty-seventh Amendment. It limits the frequency with which members of Congress can alter their own compensation: "No law, varying the compensation for the services of the Senators and Representatives, shall take effect, until an election of Representatives shall have intervened."

Most of the individual safeguards contained in the federal Bill of Rights—the right to jury trial, protection against compulsory self-incrimination, and double jeopardy restrictions, for example—were well established in English common law long before American independence was declared. By contrast, the origins of Fourth Amendment limitations on search and seizure are rooted both in English and colonial experience prior to the American Revolution. In fact, the Fourth Amendment has been accurately characterized as "the one procedural safeguard in the Constitution that grew directly out of the events which immediately preceded the revolutionary struggle with England" (Landynski 1966, 19). In this chapter we will survey these prerevolutionary influences, selectively examine search and seizure provisions in the earliest state constitutions, analyze the factors that most directly influenced the drafting and adoption of the Fourth Amendment, and survey constitutional development between the adoption of the Bill of Rights and the emergence of the Fourth Amendment as a major source of Supreme Court interpretation early in the twentieth century.

## ENGLISH BACKGROUND OF
## SEARCH AND SEIZURE LAW

Although English political history prior to the eighteenth century seems far removed from the drafting of the Fourth Amendment, the unbridled power of the Crown to intrude upon the privacy of its subjects engendered growing discontent in England and the American colonies. Following the introduction of the printing press in 1476, the English Crown became increasingly concerned about published criticism of its policies and practices. Regarding such publications as "seditious and nonconformist," King Henry VIII introduced a licensing system in 1538 as a means of regulating publications (Landynski 1966, 21). The English Privy Council, the Court of the Star Chamber, and Ecclesiastical Courts, as well as Parliament, were empowered to authorize broad searches to identify and suppress objectionable books, pamphlets, and other publications.

While not directly related to the development of American search and seizure law, the licensing system illustrates the English government's lack of concern for individual liberty. Initially, the government entrusted the licensing authority to a private printers guild, the Stationers' Company. In return for the grant of monopoly privileges over printing, the Stationers' Company was charged with enforcing the system of censorship. In a detailed and informative study of the struggle for freedom of the press during this period, Professor Fredrick S. Siebert (1952, 64) concluded:

> The skillful use of the corporate organization of printers and publishers (The Stationers' Company) in the suppression and control of un-

desirable printing has long been considered a master stroke of Elizabethan politics.

Operation of the licensing system facilitated numerous prosecutions for seditious libel, especially from the mid-seventeenth century to the late eighteenth century. In 1637 Parliament enacted new libel and sedition laws. It was in response to these increased restrictions on freedom of expression that John Milton wrote *Areopagetica,* his famous defense of freedom of the press (Hall 2000, Section 1.2). The licensing system remained in effect until 1694 and "less direct methods of control" continued until the late 1700s (Landynski 1966, 21).

Throughout this period those conducting searches for seditious materials or as a means of gathering evidence for the prosecution of a wide array of offenses such as smuggling and tax evasion relied increasingly on general warrants (Hall 2000, Sections 4–6). The general warrant served as a basis not only for searches but for arrests as well. These warrants "lacked specificity as to whom to arrest or where to search . . . ." (Davies 1999, 558, n. 12). Accordingly, agents of the Crown, including designated private entities such as the Stationers' Company, could force their way into a private residence looking for allegedly libelous or seditious materials. Not surprisingly, this unbridled search power led to gross invasions of privacy. A vivid example is provided by the abusive treatment of the prominent English jurist and legal scholar Sir Edward Coke. In 1634, as Coke lay on his deathbed, agents of the Privy Council conducted a thorough search of his residence and law chambers for seditious and libelous papers "and seized not only the manuscripts of his voluminous legal writings but also his valuables, including money, keys, jewelry, his will, and a poem addressed to his children" (Levy 1999, 153).

English common law judges, adhering to the maxim that "a man's house is his castle," responded to the abuses posed by general warrants by gradually developing standards limiting the lawful scope of searches and seizures. Professor Thomas Y. Davies (1999, 579, n. 76) has noted that the most important English commentator on criminal procedure during the period under review, Serjeant William Hawkins, condemned general warrants in a legal treatise published in 1721. Hawkins observed that "it would be extremely hard to leave it to the discretion of a common Officer to arrest what Persons, and search what Houses he thinks fit" (Hawkins 1721, 82, quoted in Davies 1999, 579). Chief Justice Matthew Hale in his *History of the Pleas of the Crown*, completed prior to 1676 but not published until 1736, expressed the view that general warrants were void.

He went further by asserting that warrants must be based on standards of "probable cause" and "particularity" (Hall 2000, 6). In 1685, Parliament impeached Chief Justice William Scroggs, citing among other things his issuance of general warrants. This was Parliament's first recognition that general warrants amounted to an exercise of "arbitrary . . . governmental authority" (Landynski 1966, 25; Lasson 1937, 38–39).

Finally, in the 1760s, English judges began to rule against general warrants. The most significant of these rulings came in the cases of *Wilkes v. Wood* (19 Howell's State Trials 1153; 1763) and *Entick v. Carrington* (19 Howell's State Trials 1029; 1765). In 1762 John Wilkes, a member of Parliament, began the anonymous publication of the *North Briton,* a series of pamphlets highly critical of certain policies of the British government. The following year, in response to the publication of an especially offensive tract, Number 45 in this series, the government decided to prosecute for sedition the people responsible for disseminating this publication. Secretary of State George Grenville, Lord Halifax issued a general warrant to four messengers to search for and arrest "the authors, printers, and publishers of seditious and treasonable papers" (Hall 2000, 10). Under this open-ended warrant, the messengers proceeded to arrest some forty-nine persons on suspicion during a three-day period, "even taking them from their beds in the middle of the night" (Lasson 1937, 43–44). Among those arrested was the printer of the Number 45 who promptly informed on Wilkes. When the messengers came to arrest Wilkes, he refused to submit to the warrant and had to be forcibly removed from the premises. The messengers then conducted an extensive search of Wilkes's house. He later sued Robert Wood, the Undersecretary of State, who had supervised the execution of the warrant. In his trial court ruling, Chief Justice Charles Pratt held the warrant illegal "as totally subversive of the liberty [and] the person and property of every man in this kingdom" (Hall 2000, 10). Wilkes won a judgment of 1,000 pounds against Wood, and this judgment was affirmed on appeal. Some years later Wilkes obtained a 4,000£ judgment against Lord Halifax.

Shortly before the issuance of the warrant for Wilkes's papers, Lord Halifax had issued a warrant to seize all of the papers of John Entick, editor of the *Monitor,* another publication critical of the government. Entick's books and papers were seized on the authority of a general warrant. After learning of the success of Wilkes, Entick brought a trespass action against Nathan Carrington, one of the king's messengers. Entick won a judgment of 300 pounds. On appeal, Judge Pratt, recently elevated to the peerage as Lord Camden, affirmed the judgment and condemned the practice of issuing general warrants. To rule otherwise, he asserted, would be to throw open "the secret cabinets and bureaus of every subject in this kingdom ... whenever the secretary of state shall think to charge, or even to suspect, a person to be the author, printer, or publisher of a seditious libel" (19 Howell's State Trials at 1063). A year after this important decision, Parliament placed substantial limits on the issuance of general warrants, condemning them as illegal unless Parliament itself authorized them.

Shortly before the *Entick* decision, the prominent English statesman Sir William Pitt the Elder had given memorable expression to a growing spirit of opposition to the arbitrary power represented

by the general warrant. In a burst of impassioned rhetoric addressed
to the House of Commons in 1763, Pitt asserted that:

> The poorest man may, in his cottage, bid defiance to all the forces of
> the Crown. It may be frail; its roof may shake; the wind may blow
> through it; the storm may enter; but the King of England may not en-
> ter—all his force dares not cross the threshold of the ruined tenement"
> (Lieber 1853, 45).

*Wilkes v. Wood* and *Entick v. Carrington* were highly publicized in England. Short accounts of these and related cases appeared in colonial newspapers, although full legal reports of the
cases themselves did not cross the Atlantic until after the American controversies over general writs of assistance had largely run
their course. According to Professor Davies, "the widespread
colonial controversies over the general writ ran from the enactment of the Townshend Duties Act in 1767 to about 1774, at
which time they were displaced by more dire developments such
as the military occupation of Boston."

## COLONIAL BACKGROUND:
## THE WRITS OF ASSISTANCE CASE

The most important pre-Revolutionary development in the
American law of search and seizure occurred in Boston in 1761.
This fact supports the view that many colonial leaders regarded
general warrants as illegal even before the *Wilkes* and *Carrington*
cases were decided. A widely used 1742 treatise on *The Law of
Arrests* condemned "the Unreasonableness, and the Unwar-
rantableness of [general warrants]" (Davies 1999, 692, n. 416,
quoting 1 Legal Papers of John Adams 102 n. 74).

For some time the British government had imposed commercial
restrictions on the colonies in an attempt to prevent them from
trading with non-English industry. After the French and Indian

War, England, which had been somewhat lax in the enforcement of these restrictions, imposed new and stricter measures. Many merchants responded by resorting to smuggling illegal imports into the colonies. This in turn led to the issuance of writs of assistance, devices similar to general warrants. More specifically, writs of assistance authorized customs officers to search any houses or businesses at their whim and "commanded all officers and subjects of the Crown to assist in their execution . . . ." (Lasson 1937, 53–54; Bodenhamer and Ely 1993, 124). The writs were general in form and were limited in duration only by the lifetime of the monarch under whose authority they were issued. Because the writs contained no particularity requirement, customs officers could search for any import on which a duty had not been paid. Since they permitted virtually unlimited invasions of privacy, writs of assistance were just as arbitrary and subject to abuse as were general warrants. For this reason writs of assistance were particularly offensive to the colonists.

The question of the legality of writs of assistance was tested for the first time in 1761. Two critical events set the stage for *Paxton's Case,* more commonly known as the *Writs of Assistance Case.* First, the death of King George II on October 25, 1760, automatically limited the duration of writs of assistance issued in his lifetime. English law provided that these writs would expire no later than six months after the death of the monarch. The second critical event was the death of Chief Justice Jonathan Sewall of the Massachusetts Superior Court—a man John Adams regarded as a "friend of liberty," who was known to have doubts about the "legality and constitutionality of the writ, and the power of the court to grant it" (Adams 1961, III, 275). Sewall's successor was Thomas Hutchinson, who, at the time of his appointment, was serving as Lieutenant Governor of Massachusetts and who continued to hold this position even after his appointment as chief justice. Hutchinson, a supporter of the Crown, was thought not to share Sewall's misgivings about the writs.

Anticipating the expiration of the writs of assistance in 1761, Thomas Lechmere, Surveyer of the Customs in America, applied to the Superior Court of Massachusetts for renewal of his former writ and the writs of his officers, including that of Charles Paxton, Surveyer of the Port of Boston. Sixty-three Boston merchants who opposed reissuance of the writs to Paxton and other customs officers retained James Otis and Oxenbridge Thatcher to represent them at a hearing on this question in February 1761. Otis, a prominent Boston attorney, had recently resigned his Crown position as Advocate-General of Admiralty primarily because of his opposition to writs of assistance. John Adams, then a young member of the Boston Bar, attended the hearing. According to Adams's account written many years later, Otis, in a rousing speech that lasted over four hours, denounced the writs on the grounds that they were unenforceable and void because they were in conflict with the Magna Carta. Otis asserted that the writs were "putting the liberty of every man in the hands of every petty officer" (Landynski 1966, 34). Otis, however, did not stop there. He maintained that even if writs of assistance were within the purview of the statute (and this was debatable), the statute itself was not properly grounded in the fundamental precepts of English law. Indeed, Otis quoted Sir Edward Coke's famous dictum that even an Act of Parliament is void if it is "against common right and reason" (Dr. Bonham's case, 77 Eng. Rep. 646; 1610). He assailed the writs as instruments of "slavery" and "villainy" (Levy 1999, 158). The writs reminded him of the kind of power that had cost one king his head and another his throne. He denounced the writs of assistance as "the worst instrument[s] of arbitrary power, the most destructive of English liberty and the fundamental principles of law, that was ever found in an English lawbook" (Adams 1856, II, 523).

Arguing the case on behalf of the crown was the "father of the bar" in Boston, Attorney General Jeremiah Gridley. His argument in favor of the writs was based on English statutes. He argued—in a statement that sounds strange today—that the writs of

assistance provided a check on arbitrary power, because they required there to be a sheriff present to "have an eye" on the customs officers (Landynski 1966, 33).

Chief Justice Hutchinson later acknowledged that, immediately
following Otis's speech, "the court seemed inclined to refuse to
grant" the writs of assistance requested by Paxton and others
(Gray 1865, 415). Hutchinson, however, persuaded his fellow justices to postpone the decision until advice could be obtained from
England. He then wrote to William Bollan, the provincial agent
who had once served as Crown prosecutor in Massachusetts, in-
quiring as to how the customs writ was used in England. It so
happened that the attorney general in London at that time was
Charles Pratt, whose later opinion as Lord Camden in the *Entick*
case was strongly opposed to general warrants and who would
presumably have been just as critical of writs of assistance. After
receiving Bollan's opinion, which supported the legality of writs
of assistance, the court scheduled rearguments in November 1761,
followed Bollan's opinion, and issued the first of the new writs to
Paxton in December, some ten months after the initial hearing.

Even though James Otis lost the case, his impassioned speech
might have influenced events far more than the judicial decision
itself. Adams was so impressed that he later wrote:

> Mr. Otis' oration . . . breathed into this nation the breath of life. . . .
> He was a flame of fire! . . . Every man . . . appeared to me to go away,
> as I did, ready to take up arms against the writs of assistance. . . . Then
> and there the child Independence was born. In fifteen years, namely in
> 1776, he grew up to manhood, and declared himself free. (1961, I, 107)

A minority of scholars question the importance of the *Writs of
Assistance Case*. It has been argued that Adams was engaging in
historical revisionism in order to convince Americans that Boston,
not Virginia, had truly "been the cradle of the Revolution" and
that James Otis had preceded Patrick Henry as the first great ora-

tor of American liberty (Amar 2000, 66). It is more likely that the *Writs of Assistance Case* gained importance in retrospect. For the most part, knowledge of the case was initially confined to the Boston area. But with Otis's participation in the Stamp Act Congress as well as his interaction with such leaders as John Dickinson of Pennsylvania, the Case gained in visibility and influence (Davies 1999, 561–562, n. 20). Even apart from Adams's publication in 1772 of the abstract of Otis's speech, Davies and other commentators do agree that the case was an important moment in the political and philosophical lives of John Adams and other Founding Fathers (Davies 1999, 691). It is appropriate, then, that the *Writs of Assistance Case* is still widely recognized as one of the pivotal events leading to the American Revolution.

## REVOLUTIONARY BACKGROUND OF SEARCH AND SEIZURE LAW

Massachusetts reacted swiftly and decisively to the *Writs of Assistance Case.* In 1762 the legislature, then known as the General Court, passed a bill "outlawing general warrants and authorizing special writs only . . . " (Landynski 1966, 35). This bill, however, was vetoed by the colonial governor Francis Bernard, after which the writs were executed routinely until the confrontation with England occasioned by the Stamp Act of 1765. During this three-year period it appears that the Massachusetts Superior Court issued some fourteen writs of assistance in addition to the writ issued to Paxton in 1761. Popular agitation apparently persisted, however, and on July 24, 1765, "the Governor and his Council found it expedient to appoint a committee to inquire into the legality of the writs" (Landynski 1966, 36). Finding that the matter was "completely settled," the committee reported a week later that "the power to issue the writs did exist."

A month later, passage of the Stamp Act reawakened lingering "animosities" toward the writs of assistance (Landynski 1966, 36).

During the "Stamp Act riots" on the evening of August 26, 1765, a rampaging mob first threatened to destroy "the house occupied by [Charles] Paxton, which was saved by the present of a barrel of punch from the owner of the house." Governor Francis Bernard reported this event in a letter to Lord Halifax dated August 31, 1765 (quoted in Gray 1865, 422). Later that evening, the mob destroyed the houses of several leading colonial officials, including that of Chief Justice Hutchinson. Governor Bernard, in a letter to the Lords of Trade, stated that the destruction of Hutchinson's house was accomplished "with a savageness unknown in a civilized country." Referring to Hutchinson's role in the *Writs of Assistance* Case, Bernard concluded that the Chief Justice "took the lead in the Judgement for granting Writs, and now he has paid for it" (quoted in Gray 1865, 416).

The intensity of colonial opposition is well illustrated by the "Malcom Affair" of 1766. Characterized by Fourth Amendment historian William Cuddihy as "the most famous search in colonial America," this ransacking of the house of Daniel Malcom, a prominent Boston merchant, was based on a tip to customs officers that Malcom had recently smuggled brandy and other liquors into his cellar. Malcom at first cooperated with Benjamin Hallowell, the Boston Comptroller of Customs, who, accompanied by a deputy collector, came to Malcom's house armed with a writ of assistance. Malcom "opened every place in his house that his visitors wished to see, including his wood shed and two cellars." He refused, however, to open a third locked cellar, claiming that the keys were in the possession of a neighbor to whom he had rented the cellar. This person, when summoned, also denied possession of the keys. When Hallowell persisted in demanding the keys, "Malcom exploded in anger, and the threats escalated on both sides." Hallowell and his colleague threatened to break into the cellar and ordered their assistants to come inside the house to carry out the threat. This was precisely the kind of search that the authors of the Fourth Amendment found so offensive. Shortly after the assistants entered the house, Malcom, brandishing two large pistols, threatened to "blow the brains out of the first person who broke a lock or door" (Cuddihy 1990, 1019). This fiery response caused the officers to withdraw temporarily and to supplement their writ of assistance with a specific warrant. When they returned some five hours later, a large crowd had gathered outside Malcom's house, which had been converted into a "veritable fortress," with doors bolted and windows shuttered. Malcom ignored all entreaties to permit entry into his house, and when the specific warrant and writ of assistance expired at nightfall, the officers withdrew in frustration. "Malcom waited several more hours before congratulating the remnant of the crowd with buckets of wine" (Cuddihy 1990, 1002–1030; Lasson 1937, 68–69).

Legal doubts in London about whether Malcom could be prosecuted provided the impetus for Parliament to reaffirm the authority for writs of assistance in no uncertain terms in the highly controversial Townshend Revenue Act of 1767 (Smith 1978, 447–453). Meanwhile, the British government continued to expand its use of broad search and seizure power in Massachusetts as well as in other colonies, right up to the beginning of the American Revolution. This oppressive practice had the effect of fueling the resentment and resistance of the colonists. Even though Massachusetts judges continued to issue writs of assistance, they were, as a practical matter, almost impossible to enforce. The intensity of popular opposition to writs of assistance was expressed in a lengthy diatribe by a Massachusetts "Committee of Twenty-one" appointed by Boston residents in 1772 "to state the right of the Colonists—and . . . to communicate and publish the same . . . to the world." The Committee asserted, among other complaints, that "our houses and even our bed chambers are exposed to be ransacked . . . by wretches, whom no prudent Man would venture to employ even as Menial Servants" (Landynski 1966, 38, n. 90). As late as 1774 the First Continental Congress, in petitioning King George III for a "redress of grievances," specifically objected to the writ of assistance as an abuse of the search power: "The officers of the customs are empowered to break open and enter houses, without the authority of any civil magistrate, founded on legal information" (Lasson 1937, 75).

While Massachusetts judges readily issued writs of assistance during this pre-Revolutionary period, the judges in other colonies strongly resisted them, even after the Townshend Act made them clearly available to customs officers. In fact, the strong colonial reaction to the Townshend Act has been recognized as "the most direct catalyst for the Fourth Amendment" (Davies 2005, n. 21). In his important study of the Fourth Amendment, Professor Jacob W. Landynski (1966, 36) emphasized the influential role of other colonies and the leadership of their judges:

> Were it not for the fact that other colonies shared in the opposition, it is not likely that the events in Massachusetts, important as they were, would in themselves have been responsible for the Adoption of the Fourth Amendment. In Massachusetts resistance to the writs came from the people, elsewhere from the courts themselves.

For example, in Connecticut, Delaware, Georgia, Maryland, Pennsylvania, Rhode Island, and Virginia the courts either rejected or ignored applications for the writs. With the exception of New Hampshire, which typically followed the lead of Massachusetts, the other colonies either received no applications for writs or displayed reluctance to issue them. The judges, who served at the pleasure of colonial governors, displayed considerable courage in resisting the mounting pressure to issue writs of assistance. On the basis of a detailed study of writs of assistance in the colonies, O. M. Dickerson (1939, 75) concluded that the establishment of an American judiciary "free from executive control [grew] in no small degree out of this experience."

Beyond widespread public criticism, occasional legislation, and the resistance of many judges, the most tangible evidence of American opposition to abuse of the search and seizure power is found in the provisions of state constitutions adopted during the Revolution. Previous judicial and legislative restrictions were for the first time included in written constitutional provisions as part of the basic law of several of the newly independent states.

Even before the signing of the Declaration of Independence, Virginia had provided a constitutional guarantee against general warrants, grounded in the protections against arbitrary governmental invasion of individual privacy and liberty found in the Magna Carta. On June 12, 1776, Virginia adopted a constitution that included a Declaration of Rights. A drafting committee had originally delegated authorship of this declaration to George Mason, who produced a first draft that did not address the search and seizure issue. Memory of the *Wilkes* case influenced the committee to add a statement opposing general warrants. As modified and approved by the full Virginia Constitutional Convention, this statement provided that "general warrants whereby an officer may be commanded to search suspected places without evidence of a fact committed, or to seize any person or persons not named, or whose offense is not particularly described and supported by evidence, are grievous and oppressive and ought not to be granted" (Cuddihy 1990, 1237). While this language seems ambiguous to many modern legal scholars, this is largely because the modern meaning of words like "ought" have drifted from the meanings held at the time this declaration was written. The framers of the Virginia Declaration intended it as a strong condemnation of general warrants and a very strict standard of proof for officers seeking specific warrants (Davies 1999, 675, n. 349, 350).

The Maryland Declaration of Rights, while following its Virginia counterpart to some extent, explicitly used the term "illegal" to describe general warrants, as well as the terms "grievous and oppressive" (Cuddihy 1990, 1238). This does not imply that general warrants were legal in Virginia, merely that the Virginians took their illegality as a given and did not feel the need to restate that fact (Davies 1999, 675, n. 349). Maryland and Delaware were also more detailed in their requirements for obtaining a specific warrant. In those states "warrants could issue only on sworn complaint and had to specify places as well as persons" (Cuddihy 1990, 1251). Thus Maryland's search and seizure provision bears a closer resemblance to the Fourth Amendment than does Virginia's version, although both laws had the same intent and effect. The Pennsylvania Constitution of 1776 added the requirement that warrants "particularize objects as well as persons and places," thus moving a step closer to the language of the modern Fourth Amendment. The Pennsylvania Constitution also declared that "the people have a right to hold themselves, their houses, papers, and possessions free from search and seizure" (*Pennsylvania Declaration of Rights,* Chapter 1, Section 10, Paragraph 8).

The Massachusetts Constitution of 1780, in addition to its sweeping condemnation of general warrants, was the first to use the phrase "unreasonable searches and seizures." This constitution was written by John Adams, one of the strongest critics of unrestricted searches and seizures, and here we can clearly see the language evolving toward the modern form. Also, note that John Adams, who had been present during James Otis's argument in the *Writs of Assistance Case* in 1761, was likely influenced by Otis's denunciation of government intrusions "against common right and reason." This phrase, which Otis had borrowed from Sir Edward Coke, was later reused and reworded by Sir William Blackstone as an attack on "unreasonable" imprisonment under general warrants (Davies 1999, 692). The Massachusetts Constitution also provided that "every subject has a right to be secure from all unreasonable searches and seizures of his person, his houses, his papers, and all his possessions"(*Massachusetts Declaration of Rights,* Section 14). This language is similar to the opening words of the Fourth Amendment: "The right of the people to be secure in their persons, houses, papers, and effects against unreasonable searches and seizures shall not be violated. . . ." The Massachusetts and Pennsylvania Constitutions also provided that warrants be based on "oath or affirmation," a phrase that appears in the Fourth Amendment.

Massachusetts was the first state to submit its constitution to the voters. In town meetings held throughout the state, the citizens overwhelmingly approved the new constitution. Although the records of town hall votes are somewhat incomplete, it appears that sixty-one towns examined segments of the Massachusetts Constitution that contained the search and seizure restrictions. Over 97 percent of the 4,591 recorded voters in those towns approved these restrictions. Thus, when John Adams condemned general warrants, "he spoke the mind of nearly everyone in Massachusetts" (Cuddihy 1990, 1247–1248).

In all, seven of the original thirteen states—Virginia, North Carolina, Maryland, Pennsylvania, Delaware, Massachusetts, and New Hampshire—included search and seizure restrictions in their first constitutions. (Although not admitted as a state until 1791, Vermont also placed limits on search and seizure in its Constitution of 1777.)

While state constitutional provisions varied in some details, together they contained all the guarantees later embodied in the Fourth Amendment. The North Carolina Constitution of 1776 closely followed the Virginia Constitution, and the Constitution of New Hampshire, adopted in 1784, adhered fully to the Massachusetts Constitution. According to Cuddihy (1990, 1252–1253):

> [t]he pronounced similarity in state constitutional declarations on search and seizure reflected both similar historical experiences with general warrants and the extensive publicity those declarations received.

The most logical explanation for this similarity is that the Founding Fathers in each state were simply following and imitating the work of their counterparts in other jurisdictions (Davies 2005). It seems clear that by the time the Fourth Amendment was drafted in 1789, a national consensus had developed on the importance of placing federal as well as state constitutional limitations on searches and seizures.

The inclusion of formal restrictions against searches and seizures in a majority of the early state constitutions reflected a decided preference for specific as opposed to general warrants. Nevertheless, these formal provisions did not bring an end to the use of general warrants. In fact, during the Revolution general warrants were widely employed by many of the states, including several of those that disavowed them in their constitutions. General warrants were used most frequently in an effort to control military desertion and the activities of British loyalists. These warrants were also employed during the war to protect the interests of Southern slaveholders. It is not surprising that the states cast aside peacetime ideals of individual rights and reverted to "first principles," namely the right of self-defense against foreign and domestic threats during a time of war (Davies 1999, 746, n. 568).

The most extensive use of the search power during the Revolution was directed against Quakers in Philadelphia. In 1777, a number of prominent Quakers were suspected of collaborating with the British. Reacting to reports of an "imminent" invasion, the Second Continental Congress (the de facto national government sitting in Philadelphia) submitted two resolutions to the Supreme Executive Council of Pennsylvania. The first of these requested the Council "to search the house of every Philadelphian of dubious loyalty and disarm him." The second resolution rested on the presumption that a "pacifist manifesto" amounted to evidence that a number of prominent Quakers were disloyal. It called for the "seizure" of these persons as well as their "personal and official papers of political significance, and all other persons of questionable allegiance." Although these resolutions, both of which were carried out by the Executive Council, did not specifically authorize general warrants, the use of such warrants was clearly implied. Accordingly, the Council issued a general warrant authorizing the arrests of a number of Philadelphia Quakers and the seizure of their papers as well as records of Quaker meetings. Such sweeping search and seizure power could not have been enforced if specific warrants had been required for each house and suspect (Cuddihy 1990, 1267–1268).

During the Revolution the states were, to say the least, ambivalent about warrant restrictions. Specific warrants were widely used for searches to recover stolen goods. On the other hand, general warrants were readily available to assist the war effort and protect the security of the community. But according to Professor Davies (1999, 655, n. 299):

> the use of general warrants during the military emergency of the Revolutionary War—which amounted to a civil war—is not valid evidence of the Framers' view of the legality of such warrants in normal times.

This ambivalence reflected the tension between competing claims of order and liberty. The ongoing conflict between these claims has never been resolved. It continues to this day as a defining feature of Fourth Amendment jurisprudence. During periods of relative peace American constitutional liberties tend to flourish. This is true not only in the field of search and seizure but also with respect to freedoms of expression protected by the First Amendment. But these liberties are quickly curtailed in the face of a real or perceived threat to the safety and security of the country. The recent limitations on protections against unreasonable searches and seizures embodied in some provisions of the USA PATRIOT Act indicate the persistence of the intrinsic conflict between claims of liberty and order. Congress hurriedly passed the USA PATRIOT Act as the United States geared up for the "war on terror" initiated in the immediate aftermath of the horrendous attacks of September 11, 2001. This legislation might ultimately represent the most far-reaching challenge to Fourth Amendment values in American history (and will be discussed in Chapter Four).

The practical claims of law enforcement as exemplified by the "war on drugs" indicate that the war metaphor is not limited to military conflict. Fourth Amendment safeguards have given way since the 1970s in large part due to the demands of vigorous drug-law enforcement. The U.S. Supreme Court, which has assumed ultimate responsibility for interpreting the procedural and substantive requirements of the Fourth Amendment, has been sharply divided on many questions regarding the nature and scope of individual protections against searches and seizures. Long before the Supreme Court entered the field of Fourth Amendment interpretation, the competing claims of individual liberty and the safety and security of the country, as reflected in the values of the first state constitutions and the accompanying exigencies of war, were shaping the law of search and seizure in the United States.

## The Framing and Adoption of the Fourth Amendment

As previously noted, the ratification of the federal Constitution was jeopardized due to the absence of a bill of rights. Patrick Henry railed against the Constitution because, among other things, he thought it was incomplete without a ban on general warrants (Davies 2005). The anti-Federalists were concerned that the overarching unity provided by the federal government would be turned into overreaching intrusions into the lives and businesses of private citizens. They believed that pre-Revolutionary protections for the home would not adequately safeguard other private, nonresidential locations. One of the ways they sought to counteract this weakness in the common law was by arguing in the state ratifying conventions that a provision against unreasonable searches and seizures should be included in bill of rights, if not the Constitution itself (Davies 1999, 694).

Ultimately, James Madison put aside his initial objections and assumed leadership of the movement in the first Congress to add a bill of rights to the original Constitution. Among those opposing this effort were such luminaries as Alexander Hamilton and James Wilson. They contended that a bill of rights was both unnecessary and risky—unnecessary because all rights not already surrendered were retained, and risky because it would imply that rights not included in a bill of rights were surrendered. Critics were quick to point out that the Constitution did grant some rights, such as habeas corpus, "which, if the proposition were granted, should not have been necessary" (Landynski 1966, 40).

In any event, by the summer of 1789, Madison had persuaded his colleagues in the U.S. House of Representatives to consider a list of amendments that, after numerous alterations in wording and organization, would become the federal Bill of Rights. We are concerned here specifically with the search and seizure provisions that were shaped by a series of compromises into the final language of the Fourth Amendment. Madison wrote the original version of the amendment:

> The rights of the people to be secured in their persons, their houses, their papers, and their other property from all unreasonable searches and seizures, shall not be violated by warrants issued without probable cause, supported by oath or affirmation, or not particularly describing the places to be searched, or the persons or things to be seized. (quoted in Davies 1999, 697)

In contrast with the two-clause form of the Fourth Amendment as finally adopted, Madison's original version only banned general warrants. It did not extend to warrantless intrusions. According to the Congressional Register (an early, but incomplete, record of House proceedings), Representative Egbert Benson of

New York regarded this provision as too weak and formally moved to insert the phrase " . . . and no warrant shall issue, but upon probable cause . . ." in place of Madison's original language " . . . shall not be violated by warrants issued without probable cause . . ." (Bodenhamer and Ely 1993, 125). This motion failed by a wide margin. Traditional accounts have long maintained that Benson used his influence as chair of a drafting committee to send his defeated version to the Senate for its consideration. Recent scholarship, however, convincingly refutes the account in the Congressional Register and rejects the "conspiracy theory" associated with Benson. The evidence indicates that Elbridge Gerry, one of the strongest and most outspoken proponents of a bill of rights, thought that the language should be more imperative and proposed the addition of the words "and no warrants shall issue" to Madison's language, thus converting the amendment to its modern two-clause form. Furthermore, newspaper sources show that the motion passed when submitted to a vote (Davies 1999, 717–719).

Ultimately, Madison's single-clause version was rejected in favor of the two-clause form that Congress submitted with the other Bill of Rights amendments for ratification by the states:

> The right of the people to be secure in their persons, houses, papers, and effects, against unreasonable searches and seizures, shall not be violated, and no Warrants shall issue, but upon probable cause, supported by Oath or affirmation, and particularly describing the place to be searched, and the persons or things to be seized.

The importance of this small change has been magnified in subsequent attempts to interpret the framers' words. Where the first draft of this amendment was clearly aimed at forbidding only searches performed under general warrants, the final version is broader and was much later seen as more ambiguous, arguably invalidating all unreasonable searches, irrespective of whether accompanied by specific warrants. The contemporary Supreme Court has emphasized the reasonableness requirement in the first clause of the amendment and has greatly diminished the importance of the warrant clause. A growing minority of scholars, however, reject this interpretation, maintaining that the framers placed far greater emphasis on the warrant standards. According to this view, the phrase "unreasonable searches and seizures" is equivalent to "searches and seizures under general warrants" (Davies 1999, 723–724).

In September 1789, twelve amendments, including the search and seizure amendment discussed above, were submitted to the states. As previously noted, ten of these were approved and were added to the Constitution as the Bill of Rights. According to the original numbering of the amendments, the search and seizure provision appeared as Amendment Six. At least as late as 1806 Chief Justice John Marshall, in the first significant search and seizure case to reach the Supreme Court, still adhered to this original numbering (*Ex Parte Burford*, 7 U.S. 448; 1806). More than two years passed before Virginia, the requisite ninth state, ratified the amendments. The effective date of ratification of the Bill of Rights was December 15, 1791. Ironically, Virginia, the first state to include a search and seizure restriction in its own constitution, was the last of the required three-fourths majority to ratify the search and seizure amendment along with other provisions of the Bill of Rights.

## EARLY CONSTITUTIONAL DEVELOPMENT OF SEARCH AND SEIZURE LAW

As noted above, the first Supreme Court decision in which the Fourth Amendment received significant attention was *Ex Parte Burford* (1806). The principal issue in this case, however, was not the validity of a warrant, but the basis on which John A. Burford was committed to jail. Chief Justice John Marshall, writing for a unanimous Court in this habeas corpus proceeding, ordered that Burford be discharged from prison. Burford, an Alexandria, Virginia, shopkeeper, had been confined to jail, by order of eleven justices of the peace for the District of Columbia. He had failed to obtain sureties in what Marshall characterized as "the enormous sum of 4,000 dollars" securing his good behavior for life. Local authorities alleged, without supporting evidence, that Burford was "not of good name and fame, nor of honest conversation, but an evil doer and disturber of the peace of the United States, so that murder, homicide, strifes, discords, and other grievances and damages, . . . are likely to arise thereby" (7 U.S. at 450–451). Obviously unimpressed by this rush to judgment, Marshall, focusing only on the warrant of commitment, determined that the Fourth Amendment had been violated because the

> warrant state[d] no offence. It [did] not allege that he was convicted of any crime. It state[d] merely that he had been brought before a meeting of many justices, who had required him to find sureties for his good behaviour. It [did] not charge him of their own knowledge, or suspicion, or upon the oath of any person whomsoever. (7 U.S. at 452)

Marshall assumed without specific comment that the Fourth Amendment, which extended to "persons and things to be seized," was designed to protect against imprisonment without a criminal conviction as well as arbitrary searches. Although the amendment does not refer explicitly to arrests, Marshall took it for granted that this view of its scope was self-evident. He therefore concluded that in the absence of "some good cause certain, supported by oath . . ." the prisoner had been improperly committed (7 U.S. at 453).

In 1855 the Supreme Court ruled that the Fourth Amendment did not apply to civil proceedings. In this case a "warrant of distress" to recover a debt had been issued "without the support of an oath or affirmation." Writing for the Court, Justice Benjamin R. Curtis concluded that the Fourth Amendment had "no reference to civil proceedings for the recovery of debts," where no search warrant had been issued (*Murray v. Hoboken Land Company*, 59 U.S. 272, 285; 1855). This view of the scope of the Fourth Amendment did not prevent the Supreme Court some thirty years later from making an important search and seizure ruling in a forfeiture case. That 1886 case, *Boyd v. United States* (discussed in more detail later), was technically a civil matter, but had important parallels to the customs searches and seizures that had inspired the framers to write the Fourth Amendment. So we can see that while the language of the Fourth Amendment does not refer explicitly to either civil or criminal proceedings, the Supreme Court has long recognized that the amendment does apply in some situations to civil actions. For example, *Marshall v. Barlow's* (436 U.S. 307; 1978) held that the Fourth Amendment requires a search warrant or its equivalent for an OSHA inspection of business premises.

In 1878 the Supreme Court expressed the opinion that the post office could not open sealed mail without a warrant. Writing for a unanimous Court in *Ex Parte Jackson* (96 U.S. 727), Justice Field asserted that "No law of congress can place in the hands of officials connected with the postal service any authority to invade the secrecy of letters and . . . sealed packages in the mail: and all regulations adopted as to mail matter of this kind must be in subordination to the great principle embodied in the fourth amendment of the Constitution" (96 U.S. at 733). Although this view was offered as *dictum* (an observation made by a judge in announcing an opinion that is not necessary to its determination), it was influential in defining the scope of the Fourth Amendment.

Few criminal cases reached the Supreme Court until late in the nineteenth century. Prior to that period the vast majority of such cases were decided with finality by state courts. Furthermore, the

Supreme Court was not granted criminal appellate jurisdiction in federal cases until 1891. The Supreme Court's first extensive analysis of the meaning and scope of the Fourth Amendment did not come until 1886 with its landmark decision in *Boyd v. United States* (116 U.S. 616; 1886). According to Justice William J. Brennan, one of the Supreme Court's most ardent defenders of civil liberties, the *Boyd* case was "part of the process by which the Fourth Amendment . . . has become more than a dead letter in the federal courts" (*Abel v. United States,* 362 U.S. 217, 255; 1960 [dissenting opinion]).The *Boyd* case arose from the federal government's initiation of forfeiture proceedings against two New York merchants, George and Edward Boyd, to recover thirty-five cases of plate glass alleged to have been imported duty-free in violation of the federal revenue laws. The Boyds had previously contracted with the government to import a small quantity of glass without payment of customs duties, but had allegedly abused that privilege by importing more glass than the contract allowed. The trial judge invoked a customs statute under which he ordered the Boyds to produce as evidence an invoice specifying the value and quantity of an earlier shipment of twenty-nine cases of glass. After the Boyds complied with the judge's order under protest, the jury decided in favor of the government, with the result that the goods were forfeited. In subsequent proceedings, the Boyds raised important Fourth and Fifth Amendment questions about the constitutionality of the statute that enabled the judge to order them to produce invoices.

First, was the forced production of the invoice a search, even though it did not involve the kind of traditional invasion of privacy associated with the origins of the Fourth Amendment? In his opinion for a majority of the Court, Justice Joseph Bradley ruled that the forced production of the invoice allowed by the statute was a search because it "effect[ed] the sole object and purpose of search and seizure" (116 U.S. at 622). This interpretation, effectively equating a forfeiture procedure with a search, supports the view that Bradley's opinion amounted to "judicial activism at its worst" (Davies 2005).

Second, were unreasonable searches allowed under this law? Justice Bradley concluded that they were because, in the words of Professor Wayne LaFave (1996, 8) "[the search] was directed toward mere evidence of crime. . . ." In one of the most memorable passages from his opinion, Justice Bradley wrote:

> It is not the breaking of [a man's] doors, and the rummaging of his drawers, that constitutes the essence of the offense; but it is the invasion of his indefeasible right of personal security, personal liberty and private property, where that right has never been forfeited by his conviction of some public offense. . . . (116 U.S. at 630)

Without referring to the *Murray* decision, in which the Court had held that the Fourth Amendment did not apply to civil proceedings, Justice Bradley maintained that "proceedings instituted for the purpose of declaring the forfeiture of a man's property by reason of offenses committed by him, though they may be civil in form, are in their nature criminal" (116 U.S. at 633–634). Fourth Amendment protections therefore applied because the proceeding against the Boyds was "quasi-criminal" in nature.

The third and most important question presented in the *Boyd* case was whether competent evidence, seized illegally, could be used at trial. This is the difficult inquiry addressed later by the Fourth Amendment exclusionary rule. In *Boyd*, the Court indicated that such evidence was inadmissible, but it did not explicitly articulate the exclusionary rule adopted almost thirty years later in *Weeks v. United States* (232 U.S. 383; 1914). *Weeks* is a more direct progenitor of modern search and seizure law than *Boyd* (Davies 1999, 729–731). (Due to the organizational framework of this book, that discussion will be left to Chapter Three.) For the purposes of deciding the *Boyd* case, though, Justice Bradley linked the Fourth Amendment with the Fifth Amendment right against self-incrimination. He recognized that the self-incrimination and search and seizure provisions "throw great light on each other." After describing the close interrelations between the two amendments, Justice Bradley concluded that the Court had been "unable to perceive that the seizure of a man's private books and papers to be used in evidence against him is substantially different from compelling him to be a witness against himself" (116 U.S. at 633). He concluded that "the notice to produce the invoice . . . the order by virtue of which it was issued, and the law which authorized the order, were unconstitutional and void." Moreover, the inspection of the invoice and its introduction into evidence were "erroneous and unconstitutional proceedings" (116 U.S. at 638).

In what is labeled as a concurring opinion, but is actually a partial dissent, Justice Miller, supported by Chief Justice Morrison R. Waite, agreed that the Self-Incrimination Clause of the Fifth Amendment had been violated. He maintained, however, that the majority had inappropriately invoked the constitutional protections against search and seizure. Justice Miller's criticism of the Court's reliance on the Fourth Amendment is shared by a number of scholars, and the linkage of the Fourth and Fifth Amendments was rejected by the Supreme Court in later cases. Nevertheless, *Boyd v. United States* was for many years one of the most frequently cited of the Court's search and seizure decisions. Modern jurisprudence, however, has not followed *Boyd's* interpretation of either the Fourth or the Fifth Amendment.

*Boyd* is best remembered today for Justice Bradley's recognition of individual privacy as a constitutional value. In support of this interpretation, he provided a detailed review of the British and colonial antecedents to the Fourth Amendment, including the *Wilkes* and *Entick* cases and James Otis's eloquent argument in the *Writs of Assistance Case*. Justice Bradley's analysis brought the Fourth Amendment into a position of high visibility at a time when modern methods of law enforcement and their accompanying encroachments on civil liberties were beginning to pose difficult problems for trial and appellate courts. Therefore, *Boyd* is of great historical significance because it anticipated the development of modern search and seizure law, even though its precedential value has diminished (Landynski 1966, Chapter 2; Glenn 2003, 49–50).

The Bill of Rights, including the Fourth Amendment, originally applied only to the actions of federal officers or persons acting under the authority of the federal government. This was the generally accepted interpretation when the Bill of Rights was ratified in 1791. The First Amendment's opening provision—"Congress shall make no law respecting an establishment of religion or prohibiting the free exercise thereof . . ."—specifically applies to the national government. The only other Bill of Rights provision that refers to the national government is found in the Tenth Amendment: "The powers not delegated to the United States by the Constitution, nor prohibited by it to the States, are reserved to the States respectively, or to the people."

The question of whether any of the other amendments applied to the states was ultimately answered in the negative by Chief Justice Marshall in his 1833 decision in *Barron v. Baltimore* (32 U.S. 243). The basic constitutional question in this case was whether the Fifth Amendment's Just Compensation Clause applied to the states. In reaching the decision that it did not, Chief Justice Marshall, writing for a unanimous Court, commented generally on the relationship between the Constitution and the states: "The Constitution was ordained and established by the people of the United States for themselves, for their own government, and not for the government of the individual States" (32 U.S. at 247).

Chief Justice Marshall noted that a few guarantees such as habeas corpus and the restrictions against ex post facto laws and bills of attainder appeared twice in the Constitution—first, in Article I, Section 9, as restrictions on the national government, and second in Article I, Section 10, "by express words" as limitations on the states. He reasoned, however, that no other restrictions on state power could be inferred from the general language of the Constitution or any of the provisions of the Bill of Rights. Consistent with Chief Justice Marshall's reasoning, the Supreme Court in 1855 held that the Fourth Amendment offered no protection against searches conducted by state officers (*Smith v. Maryland,* 59 U.S. 71).

In the aftermath of the Civil War, the 1868 adoption of the Fourteenth Amendment fundamentally changed the constitutional relationship between the national government and the states. The Fourteenth Amendment placed broad restraint on the states by providing, among other limitations, that "no state shall deprive any person of life, liberty, or property without due process of law. . . ." Some of the framers of this amendment assumed that the Due Process Clause encompassed all of the individual guarantees contained in the first eight amendments, and that these amendments thus applied in full to the states. Others, however, rejected this "full incorporation" theory. The Supreme Court took a middle position on this issue, opting for a "selective incorporation" approach by which only those freedoms deemed essential to the preservation of a "scheme of ordered liberty" were extended to the states (*Palko v. Connecticut,* 302 U.S. 319; 1937). In fact, in the 1949 case of *Wolf v. Colorado* (338 U.S. 25), the Court absorbed only the "core of the Fourth Amendment"—that is, the right not to suffer "arbitrary intrusion[s] by the police." This was characterized by Justice Felix Frankfurter, in his majority opinion in *Wolf,* as "implicit in the 'concept of ordered liberty' and as such enforceable against the States through the Due Process Clause [of the Fourteenth Amendment]" (338 U.S. at 27–28). Thus, in spite of later references to the contrary (notably Justice Stewart's comment in *Elkins v. United States,* 364 U.S. 206; 1960), the Fourth Amendment was not applied in its entirety to the states in *Wolf.* This absorption of the core remained somewhat ineffective until the exclusionary rule, which prohibits the use of evidence obtained in violation of the Fourth Amendment, was extended to the states in *Mapp v. Ohio* (367 U.S.

643; 1961). Through the gradual process of "selective incorpora-tion," the Supreme Court had applied most of the Bill of Rights provisions to the states by the late 1960s. For example, the justices have incorporated the right to counsel (*Gideon v. Wainwright*, 372 U.S. 335; 1963); the right against self-incrimination (*Malloy v. Hogan*, 378 U.S. 1; 1964); the right of confrontation (*Pointer v. Texas*, 380 U.S. 400; 1965); the right to a jury trial (*Duncan v. Louisiana*, 391 U.S. 145; 1968); and the protection against double jeopardy (*Benton v. Maryland*, 395 U.S. 784; 1969).

Through interpretation of their state constitutions, state courts remain free to provide broader protections against unreasonable searches and seizures than the protection afforded by the U.S. Supreme Court's interpretation of the Fourth Amendment. Of course, such interpretation must be consistent with other require-ments of the federal Constitution. If, however, "the state court de-cision indicates clearly and expressly that it is . . . based on bona fide separate, adequate and independent [state] grounds," the Supreme Court "will not undertake to review the decision" (*Michigan v. Long*, 463 U.S. 1032, 1041; 1983). The importance of the "incorporation" of the Fourth Amendment into the Four-teenth Amendment is that it sets a basic standard of protection against unreasonable searches and seizures. The states may exceed, but cannot fall short of, this standard.

## Conclusion

In its final form the Fourth Amendment contains two clauses. The first of these provides, "[t]he people shall be secure in their per-sons, houses, papers, and effects against unreasonable searches and seizures. . . ." The second clause declares that "no warrant shall is-sue but upon probable cause, supported by oath or affirmation, and particularly describing the place to be searched, and the per-sons or things to be seized." As we have already seen, James Madison's original version of the amendment contained a single clause providing that the rights against unreasonable searches and seizures "shall not be violated by warrants issued without probable cause. . . ." Madison's language reflects his assumption, widely held by his contemporaries, that a specific warrant was a prerequisite to any reasonable search. In his view, warrantless searches were already forbidden as denials of the right to due process of law (Davies 2002, 391). His reference to warrants "issued without probable cause" and particularity was, in effect, a repudiation of general warrants.

Although the framers' intent probably did not change when they reworded the amendment, the final form of the amendment has been subject to multiple interpretations by judges and scholars down through the years. If the first clause is considered together with the second clause, then the warrant requirement automatically applies to all searches and seizures. If, however, the first clause is considered apart from the second clause, it can be interpreted as permitting *reasonable* searches and seizures without the requirement of any warrant at all. Everything then turns on the definition of the term "reasonable."

For many years the U.S. Supreme Court expressed a clear preference for adherence to the warrant requirement. Over time, however, the Court began to recognize "exceptions" to this requirement. These exceptions will be discussed in Chapter Three. Apart from the exceptions to the warrant requirement, for well over half a century the Court has been moving toward the position that the first clause of the Fourth Amendment confers an independent power to conduct "reasonable" searches not limited by the warrant standards of the second clause. (See, for example, the opinion of Justice Sherman Minton in *United States v. Ravinowitz,* 339 U.S. 56; 1950.) Despite the strong historical evidence that the Fourth Amendment did not authorize warrantless searches, this view has gained strong support. In recent years, the William Rehnquist Court, often led by Justice Antonin Scalia, has expressed preference for a "reasonableness" standard, independent of the warrant requirement altogether. Thus, irrespective of the likely "intent" of the framers of the Fourth Amendment, search and seizure requirements have become less stringent, reflecting the perceived needs of law enforcement and, more recently, the public demand for safety and security in an "age of terrorism." This development has had the effect of greatly reducing the significance of the second clause of the Fourth Amendment with its specific and more detailed warrant requirements.

Two other factors that have influenced a changing interpretation of the "reasonableness" clause may be briefly summarized. First, the nineteenth-century "invention . . . of armed, quasi-military, professional police forces" made it necessary for judges and scholars to "rethink both the relationship between 'reasonableness' and 'warrants' and the nature of Fourth Amendment remedies" (Steiker 1994, 824). Second, the persistence of racial conflict for more than a century following the Civil War and Reconstruction and "the myriad ways in which this conflict has intersected with law enforcement" require "new constructions of the Fourth Amendment" It is significant that, as a result of selective incorporation, the greatest extension of Fourth Amendment protections took place during the 1960s, the decade in which the civil rights movement transformed America (Steiker 1994, 824).

Many judges and scholars have attempted to sum up the basic values underlying the Fourth Amendment. In his famous dissent in *Olmstead v. United States* (277 U.S. 438; 1928), Justice Louis D. Brandeis offered the following appraisal:

The makers of our Constitution undertook to secure conditions favorable to the pursuit of happiness. They recognized the significance of man's spiritual nature, of his feelings and of his intellect. They knew that only a part of the pain, pleasure and satisfactions of life are to be found in material things. They sought to protect Americans in their beliefs, their thoughts, their emotions and their sensations. They conferred, as against the government, the right to be let alone—the most comprehensive of rights and the one most valued by civilized men. (277 U.S. at 478)

Regardless of whether one agrees with this idealistic view of the intent of those who wrote the Fourth Amendment and other provisions of the Bill of Rights, it seems clear that they had a realistic understanding of the strong tendency of those who hold political power to act arbitrarily and abusively unless checked by strong procedural safeguards.

The Fourth Amendment was designed as a constitutional limitation on the abuse of governmental power. The amendment, however, contains no enforcement provisions beyond an assumption that statutes passed in violation of the amendment would be overturned. Thus, it would be primarily up to the courts, and in particular the U.S. Supreme Court, to implement the values expressed in the amendment. Since the late nineteenth century the Supreme Court has produced a vast body of case law interpreting the Fourth Amendment—its meaning, scope, and limitations. In a general study of moderate length it is impossible to deal with all facets and nuances of Fourth Amendment law. In the following two chapters, however, a selective examination of major trends and highlights of this complex area of constitutional development will be undertaken. In analyzing and evaluating Fourth Amendment issues, emphasis will be placed on contemporary problems and the challenges they pose for the preservation of meaningful Fourth Amendment values.

## REFERENCES AND FURTHER READING

Adams, John, and Charles Francis Adams, eds. 1856. *Life and Works of John Adams.* Vol. II. Boston: Little, Brown.

Adams, John, and L. H. Butterfield, eds. [1755–1804] 1961. *Diary and Autobiography of John Adams.* Vol. III. Cambridge, MA: Belknap Press.

Adams, John, L. K. Wroth, and H. B. Zobel, eds. 1966. *The Legal Papers of John Adams.* Vol. I. Cambridge, MA: Belknap Press.

Amar, Akhil Reed. 2000. *The Bill of Rights: Creation and Reconstruction.* New Haven, CT: Yale University Press.

Banning, Lance. 1995. *The Sacred Fire of Liberty: James Madison and the Founding of the Federal Republic.* Ithaca, NY: Cornell University Press.

Barnett, Randy E. 2004. *Restoring the Lost Constitution: The Presumption of Liberty.* Princeton, NJ: Princeton University Press.

Bodenhamer, D. J., and J. W. Ely. 1993. *The Bill of Rights in Modern America.* Bloomington: Indiana University Press.

*Congressional Globe.* Thirty-ninth Congress, First Session. 1866.

Cuddihy, William J. 1990. *The Fourth Amendment: Origins and Original Meaning, 1602–1791.* Unpublished Ph.D. dissertation, Claremont Graduate School.

Davies, Thomas Y. 1999. "Recovering the Original Fourth Amendment." *Michigan Law Review* 98: 547–750.

———. 2002. "The Fictional Character of Law-and-Order Originalism: A Case Study of the Distortion and Evasions of Framing-Era Arrest Doctrine in *Atwater v. Lago Vista.*" *Wake Forest Law Review* 37: 239–437.

Dickerson, O. M. 1939. "Writs of Assistance as a Cause of the Revolution." In *The Era of the American Revolution,* Richard B. Morris, ed. New York: Columbia University Press.

Farber, Daniel A., and Suzanna Sherry. 1990. *A History of the American Constitution.* St. Paul, MN: West Publishing Co.

Glenn, Richard A. 2003. *The Right to Privacy: Rights and Liberties under the Law.* Santa Barbara, CA: ABC-CLIO.

Gray, Horace, Jr. In Quincy, Josiah, Jr. 1865. *Appendix to Reports of Cases Argued and Adjudged in the Superior Court of Judicature of the Province of Massachusetts Bay, between 1761 and 1772.* Boston: Little, Brown and Company. Reprinted 1948, Buffalo, New York: Dennis & Co.

Hall, John Wesley, Jr. 2000. *Search and Seizure.* 3rd ed. Two volumes. Charlottesville, VA: Lexis Law Publishing.

Hamilton, Alexander, James Madison, and John Jay. [1787–1788] 1961. *The Federalist Papers.* New York: Mentor.

Hawkins, Serjeant William. 1721. *Pleas of the Crown.* Vol. 2.

LaFave, Wayne R. 1996. *Search and Seizure: a Treatise on the Fourth Amendment.* 3rd ed. Vol. 1. New York: West Publishing Company.

Landynski, Jacob W. 1966. *Search and Seizure and the Supreme Court: A Study in Constitutional Interpretation.* Baltimore, MD: Johns Hopkins Press.

Lasson, Nelson B. 1937. *The History and Development of the Fourth Amendment to the United States Constitution.* Baltimore, MD: Johns Hopkins Press. Reprint edition. New York: Da Capo Press.

Levy, Leonard W. 1999. *Origins of the Bill of Rights.* New Haven, CT: Yale University Press.

*Massachusetts Declaration of Rights,* March 2, 1780.

McCullough, David. 2001. *John Adams.* New York: Simon and Schuster.

*Pennsylvania Declaration of Rights.* Chapter 1, Section 10, Par. 8.

Scheb, John M., and John M. Scheb, II. 2005. *Criminal Law and Procedure.* 5th ed. Belmont, CA: West Wadsworth.

Schwartz, Bernard. 1977. *The Great Rights of Mankind: a History of the American Bill of Rights.* New York: Oxford University Press.

Siebert, Fredrick S. 1952. *Freedom of the Press in England 1476–1776: The Rise and Decline of Government Controls.* Urbana: University of Illinois Press.

Slobogin, Christopher. 2002. *Criminal Procedure: Regulation of Police Investigation.* 3rd ed. New York: Matthew Bender.

Smith, M. H. 1978. *The Writs of Assistance Case.* London: University of California Press.

Steiker, Carol. 1994. "Second Thoughts about First Principles." *Harvard Law Review* 107: 820–857.

Stephens, Otis H., and John M. Scheb, II. 2003. *American Constitutional Law.* 3rd ed. St. Paul, MN: Wadsworth.

*Virginia Declaration of Rights.* June 12, 1776. Section 10.

# 3

## TWENTIETH-CENTURY ISSUES

### INTRODUCTION

As discussed in the previous chapter, the Bill of Rights may be properly viewed as a general expression of the drafters' prevalent fear of certain fundamental rights being deprived by government. In particular, the Fourth Amendment is a profoundly antigovernmental addendum to the Constitution. It denies "to government—worse yet, to democratic government—desired means, efficient means, and means that must inevitably appear from time to time throughout the course of centuries to be the absolutely necessary means, for government to obtain legitimate and laudable objectives" (Amsterdam 1974, 353).

Although the most detailed guarantee in the Bill of Rights, the key elements of the Fourth Amendment are not self-explanatory; its strictures have an open texture and an inescapable ambiguity (O'Brien 2005, 852). For example, is the Search and Seizure Clause an independent standard, prohibiting unreasonable searches and seizures in all circumstances, or does it stand in conjunction with the Warrant Clause, allowing such searches when certain preconditions—a warrant, based "upon probable cause, supported by Oath or affirmation, and particularly describing the place to the searched, and the persons or things to be seized"—are met? Who is prohibited from conducting these "unreasonable searches and seizures"? Are only the police restricted? Or are all government agents similarly bound? What differentiates a "reasonable" search and seizure from an "unreasonable" search and seizure? Does every arrest or search and seizure require prior judicial approval? Is every search and seizure based on a warrant "reasonable"? Are all warrantless searches and seizures automatically "unreasonable"? What constitutes "probable cause" for the issuance of a warrant? Equally important, how is the guarantee against "unreasonable searches and seizures" to be enforced? Does the Fourth Amendment require that all evidence obtained via unreasonable searches and seizures be excluded from use at trial? These and other important questions have confronted the Supreme Court over the past century, resulting in the development of a complex set of "sometimes cross-cutting and confusing rulings."

Without question, clarity and consistency were not hallmarks of the Supreme Court's Fourth Amendment jurisprudence during the twentieth century. Justice Felix Frankfurter noted that "[t]he course of true law pertaining to searches and seizures . . . has not . . . run smooth" (concurring in *Chapman v. United States*, 365 U.S. 610, 618; 1961). Justice Tom Clark referred to the law of the Fourth Amendment as a "Chinese Puzzle" (dissenting in *Wong Sun v. United States*, 371 U.S. 471, 498; 1963). One perceptive commentator concluded simply that the Fourth Amendment cases were a "mess" (Dworkin 1973, 329). This is, no doubt, in part because of the difficulty, not unique to the Fourth Amendment, of discerning concrete commandments from vague and unilluminating admonitions. Another contributing factor to this absence of clarity is federalism. Until the middle of the twentieth century, the typical Fourth Amendment case reaching the Court grew almost entirely out of federal law enforcement, which did not include much in the way of ordinary "street crime." Several mid-century decisions, most notably *Mapp v. Ohio* (367 U.S. 643; 1961), changed that reality. Today, there are few police encounters that do not pose some kind of Fourth Amendment question. The factual variables in those encounters are virtually limitless, and ultimately the Court must confront the need to clarify application of the Fourth Amendment in situations that, prior to 1961, the justices encountered only infrequently. And a third factor contributing to doctrinal inconsistency is, obviously, changes in the views of the members of the Court.

Any examination of the Fourth Amendment over the course of an entire century will, of necessity, be lengthy. This chapter, therefore, is divided into the following sections: The Search and Seizure Clause; The Warrant Clause; Exceptions to the Warrant Requirement; Electronic Surveillance; and The Exclusionary Rule. Although the exclusionary rule is discussed late in this chapter, it deserves a brief mention early. Because of the exclusionary rule, the admissibility of evidence at trial depends largely upon the legality of the search that uncovers the evidence. Generally speaking, evidence obtained in an unlawful search is inadmissible at trial. The various rules and doctrines discussed in this chapter are consequential, therefore, because of the exclusionary rule. Without it, the Supreme Court would be far less motivated to litigate many of these Fourth Amendment questions. Throughout this (and the next) chapter, the reader should be mindful of the principle that requires the exclusion of illegally seized evidence at trial. It is important to recognize, however, that most criminal prosecutions in the United States do not even reach the trial stage. Well over 90 percent of these cases are resolved through negotiated guilty pleas (plea bargaining). Undoubtedly, in some instances, prosecutors are willing to plea bargain with defendants because questionably obtained evidence might be subject to exclusion. Nevertheless, plea bargaining has the practical effect of making it unnecessary for the trial judge to rule formally on the exclusion of evidence.

## THE SEARCH AND SEIZURE CLAUSE

The right of the people to be secure in their persons, houses, papers, and effects against unreasonable searches and seizures, shall not be violated. . . ."

The Search and Seizure Clause grants to certain persons certain freedoms against certain types of searches and seizures. It does not guarantee to each individual freedom from all searches and seizures. Searches and seizures are not prohibited by the Fourth Amendment except insofar as they bear the requisite relationship to "persons, houses, papers, and effects." Even then, searches and seizures affecting those areas are prohibited only if they are "unreasonable"; reasonable searches and seizures, even if affecting those areas, are not proscribed. Similarly, law enforcement practices may be unreasonable—incredibly unreasonable—and still be constitutional, as long as those practices do not constitute searches and seizures within the meaning of the Fourth Amendment.

### Defining "of the People"

The phrase "of the people" does not refer to all of the people; rather it refers to "a class of persons who are part of a national community or who have otherwise developed sufficient connection with [the United States] to be considered part of the community" (*United States v. Verdugo-Urquidez*, 494 U.S. 259, 265; 1990). This protected community includes U.S. citizens (even those who are stationed or traveling abroad) and aliens who have voluntarily entered the United States (or its territory) and have developed substantial connections with this country. The Fourth Amendment thus does not constrain law enforcement officers in all places and against all persons.

## Defining Searches

Obviously, if a "search" has not occurred, the Fourth Amendment is not implicated. And if the Fourth Amendment is not implicated, the requirements of reasonableness, probable cause, and a warrant do not apply. So, what constitutes a search under the Fourth Amendment is a threshold question—one that has proved especially troublesome.

Searches of "persons" include, for example, any physical touching of an individual's body or clothing that causes hidden objects to be revealed; demanding that an individual disclose a concealed object; and extracting an individual's blood or urine for traces of alcohol or drugs. By contrast, discerning observable characteristics of an individual is not a search.

Searches of "houses" or other closed private premises—apartments, garages, business offices, stores, and curtilage (the grounds inside a fence or wall surrounding a building)—include not only any physical entry or physical intrusion of a surveillance device, but also observation from the outside when assisted by sophisticated technology, at least when such technology is not in general public use. (Until 1967, observation into such premises *from the outside* did not constitute a search, even when assisted by electronic amplifying devices.) Visual surveillance of a house, via naked-eye observation, is not a search; because "the eye cannot . . . be guilty of trespass," law enforcement officers are not required to shield their eyes or avert their other senses when surveilling a home. Additionally, it is not a search to examine an open field—an unoccupied or undeveloped area in close proximity to a dwelling, even if the area is privately owned—or an area otherwise readily exposed to the public.

Searches of "papers" and "effects" include any examination of an object—for example, letter, parcel, backpack, suitcase, trash can, and automobile—that attempts to disclose its contents, unless such object has been abandoned. Surface visual observation of an object is not a search. Also, while a law enforcement officer who has collected these items has engaged in a search, an officer who receives such items from a third party has not necessarily engaged in a search.

Prior to 1967, the Supreme Court employed the concept of a "constitutionally protected area" to define the scope of searches of "persons, houses, papers, and effects" in a Fourth Amendment context. This restrictive standard for determining a search came to an end in *Katz v. United States* (389 U.S. 347; 1967), replaced by the "reasonable expectation of privacy" standard. Under this standard, the touchstone of Fourth Amendment analysis is whether an individual has a constitutionally protected reasonable expectation of privacy. This requires, first, that a person manifest a subjective expectation of privacy in the object of the challenged search and, second, that the expectation be one that society is prepared to recognize. *Katz* and its implications will be discussed in much greater detail later in this chapter. (See "Electronic Surveillance" page 144.)

## Defining Seizures

Seizures include arrests, investigatory detentions, or other confinement against an individual's will. Historically, the definition of "arrest" was "the taking of a person into custody in order that he may be forthcoming to answer for the commission of an offense" (Foote 1960, 402). In 1968, however, the Supreme Court expanded the concept abruptly and unequivocally:

> There is some suggestion in the use of such terms as "stop" and "frisk" that such police conduct is outside the purview of the Fourth Amendment because neither action rises to the level of a "search" or "seizure" within the meaning of the Constitution. We emphatically reject this notion. It is quite plain that the Fourth Amendment governs "seizures" of the person which do not eventuate in a trip to the station house and prosecution for crime—"arrests" in the traditional termi-

nology. It must be recognized that whenever a police officer accosts an individual and restrains his freedom to walk away, he has "seized" that person. (*Terry v. Ohio*, 392 U.S. 1, 16; 1968)

As so defined, not all personal intercourse between a police officer and an individual involves a seizure of that individual. A seizure occurs only when the officer "by means of physical force or show of authority" restrains in some way the liberty of a citizen (392 U.S. at 19, n. 16). Years later, Justice Stewart noted that a seizure occurred "only if, in view of all of the circumstances surrounding the incident, a reasonable person would have believed that he was not free to leave" (*United States v. Mendenhall*, 446 U.S. 544, 554; 1980). A majority of justices (four in the plurality and dissenting Justice Harry Blackmun) endorsed this standard for determining if a seizure had occurred in *Florida v. Royer* (460 U.S. 491; 1983).

## Defining Unreasonable

To be consistent with the Fourth Amendment, searches and seizures cannot be unreasonable. The reasonableness requirement of the Fourth Amendment necessitates that, in most cases, law enforcement officers obtain a warrant from a judge prior to conducting either a search or a seizure. Additionally, before the judge may issue the warrant, such officers must convince the judge that the warrant is supported by probable cause. There are, to be clear, a number of exceptions to this warrant requirement. These exceptions will be discussed later in this chapter.

## THE WARRANT CLAUSE

... and no Warrants shall issue, but upon probable cause, supported by Oath or affirmation, and particularly describing the place to be searched, and the persons or things to be seized.

The Warrant Clause announces three prerequisites for obtaining a warrant. First, the warrant must be based upon probable cause (although that term is not defined in the Fourth Amendment or elsewhere in the Bill of Rights). Second, it must be signed by a neutral and detached judge or magistrate. Third, the warrant must state with specificity the place to be searched and the persons or items to be seized. Equally important, the Supreme Court has issued a number of rulings on various practices pertaining to the execution of warrants.

## Probable Cause

Rumor, simple suspicion, and even a strong reason to suspect do not constitute "probable cause." That said, the precise meaning of probable cause is illusive; multiple definitions survive. First, probable cause exists "where the facts and circumstances within [the government's] knowledge . . . [are] sufficient in themselves to warrant a man of reasonable caution in the belief that an offense has been or is being committed" (*Brineger v. United States,* 338 U.S. 160, 175–176; 1949). This is the "textbook definition." Second, probable cause is what would lead a person of reasonable caution to conclude that criminally related objects are in the place that the warrant authorizes to be searched and at the time when the search is authorized to be conducted. This is sometimes referred to as the "nexus definition." Nexus is the connection among the probable cause, the individual's participation, and the elements of criminal activity. Third, probable cause is also the sum total of information and synthesis of what police have heard, know, or observe as trained officers. The Supreme Court has referred to probable cause as the "accumulated wisdom of precedent and experience" (*Dunaway v. New York,* 442 U.S. 200, 208; 1979).

In requesting a warrant, police officers are not required to prove their assertions. The Fourth Amendment demands "probability," not "certainty." Officers regularly rely upon informants to convince a judge or magistrate that probable cause exists. As such, the affidavit (warrant request) need not reflect the direct personal observations of the affiant (person requesting the warrant). But, when information obtained from informants is used to establish probable cause, the officer has some convincing to do. The old standard for establishing probable cause based on information provided by an informant was established by the Warren Court (1954–1969) in *Aguilar v. Texas* (378 U.S. 108; 1964). In evaluating such information, the officer had to convince a judge or magistrate of the veracity of the informant (how it is that the informant knows what he or she claims to know); and the reliability of the informant's knowledge (why it is that the officer believes the information to be accurate). For each prong, the officer was required to articulate sufficient "underlying circumstances"—facts and information—from which the judge could independently gauge the informant's veracity and basis of knowledge. The two prongs had to be satisfied separately and independently. Thus, the test became commonly known as the "separate and independent" test. As such, an affidavit that simply stated that the affiant received reliable information from a credible person was insufficient to establish probable cause. Similarly, conclusions of an unidentified informant were not enough for the issuance of a search warrant.

The more conservative (Warren Earl) Burger Court (1969–1986) abandoned the two-pronged test of *Aguilar* in *Illinois v. Gates* (462 U.S. 213; 1983) because it had encouraged an excessively technical and unnecessary dissection of informants' tips and distracted from the central issues presented in each case, thus placing an undue burden on law enforcement and judges. In its place, the justices adopted a "totality of the circumstances" approach. After acknowledging that an informant's veracity, reliability, and basis of knowledge were "all highly relevant" in determining probable cause, the justices held that those elements should not be understood as

> entirely separate and independent requirements to be rigidly exacted in every case. . . . Rather, . . . they should be understood simply as

closely intertwined issues that may usefully illuminate the common-sense, practical question whether there is "probable cause" to believe that contraband or evidence is located in a particular place. This total-ity-of-the-circumstances approach is far more consistent with our prior treatment of probable cause than is any rigid demand that spe-cific "tests" be satisfied by every informant's tip. Perhaps the central teaching of our decisions bearing on the probable-cause standard is that it is a "practical, nontechnical conception." (462 U.S. at 230–231)

Veracity, reliability, and basis of knowledge were no longer in-dependent requirements. Strength in one element could compen-sate for a deficiency in another. Additionally, the justices left open the possibility that other factors might have a bearing on the de-termination of probable cause when based on information ob-tained from secondhand sources.

Probable cause is a subjective standard of expectation of re-sults—supported by facts and circumstances that would lead a reasonable person to that expectation—that must be met to justify a search and seizure. It is a "practical, nontechnical conception." By Fourth Amendment standards, search warrants are only issued upon finding of probable cause; and warrantless searches must ad-here to the standard of probable cause (or something akin to it) to be admissible in court.

### Neutral and Detached Judge or Magistrate

The scheme of the Fourth Amendment "becomes meaningful only when it is assured that at some point the conduct of [the po-lice] can be subjected to the more detached, neutral scrutiny of a judge who must evaluate the reasonableness of a particular search or seizure in light of the particular circumstances" (*Terry v. Ohio*, 392 U.S., 21; 1968). Determining probable cause is, therefore, the task of a judicial officer. Search warrants may be issued only by a "neutral and detached" judge or magistrate. If the issuing officer is not "neutral and detached"—that is, he or she has some personal interest in the matter to be prosecuted—then the resulting warrant cannot be objectively reasonable. For example, for years the state of New Hampshire permitted its attorney general to issue search warrants. When the attorney general issued such a warrant during a murder investigation in which he was the chief prosecutor, the defendant challenged the constitutionality of the warrant. In *Coolidge v. New Hampshire* (403 U.S. 443; 1971), the Supreme Court held that such a practice violated a fundamental premise of the Fourth Amendment because the state official who was the chief investigator and the prosecutor in this case was not the neutral and detached magistrate required by the Constitution. Similarly, in *Connally v. Georgia* (429 U.S. 245; 1977), the justices held that a warrant issued by a justice of the peace who was not salaried and, so far as warrants were concerned, was paid a fee of $5 if he issued a warrant but nothing if he denied the application, had not been issued by a neutral and detached magistrate. A warrant cannot be reasonable if issued by an individual with a vested interest in the matter. The Court summed up the justification for this requirement well more than half a century ago:

> The point of the Fourth Amendment, which often is not grasped by zealous officers, is not that it denies law enforcement the support of the usual inferences which reasonable men draw from evidence. Its protection consists in requiring that those inferences be drawn by a neutral and detached magistrate instead of being judged by the officer engaged in the often competitive enterprise of ferreting out crime. (*Johnson v. United States,* 333 U.S. 10, 13–14; 1948)

A comical example of a less than neutral and detached magistrate comes from *Lo-Ji Sales v. New York* (442 U.S. 319; 1979). In this case, a town justice accompanied a police investigator to an adult bookstore to execute a facially valid warrant authorizing the seizure of two films deemed to violate state obscenity laws. The investigator had requested the town justice's presence at the search so that the justice might determine independently if any other items in the store were in violation of state obscenity laws. At the time the justice signed the warrant, however, no items other than the two films were specifically listed in the warrant. The justice, investigator, and nine other law enforcement officials entered the bookstore, arrested the clerk, and conducted an exhaustive search that lasted nearly six hours. During the search, the justice viewed multiple adult films using coin-operated projectors that had been adjusted so that they did not require coins for their operation; examined numerous reading materials after the police had removed the clear wrappers in which they were displayed; and inspected pictures on boxes containing film that had been removed from a display case. After determining that many of the objects he had scrutinized were legally obscene, the justice ordered their seizure. Upon completion of the search and seizure, the police added the items seized to the warrant, and submitted the completed warrant to the justice. The Supreme Court declared the search inconsistent with the Fourth Amendment on two grounds. First, the warrant lacked particularity. (See "Particularity of Things to Be Seized," below.) The Fourth Amendment did not countenance an open-ended warrant to be completed either while the search was taking place or after the seizure had been carried out. Second, the Court held that, by conducting a generalized search, the town justice was not acting as a neutral and detached judicial officer. The justice had abdicated his detachment and neutrality by telescoping the process of the *application* for the warrant, the *issuance* of the warrant, and the *execution* of the warrant. To be clear, the Fourth Amendment requires judicial involvement, just not that much judicial involvement!

## Particularity of Place to Be Searched

A warrant must identify specifically the place to be searched to the exclusion of all others. Typically, this requirement is satisfied by the identification of the premises by street address or apartment number. In rural areas, a farm or tract of land may simply be described by the name of its owner, and general directions to the area and descriptions of the area are permissible. Most of the problems arising out of this requirement stem from inaccurate descriptions on the warrant. For example, a warrant may authorize law enforcement officers to search a "third floor" residence within a particular apartment building. Yet, when executing the warrant, the officer may discover that on the third floor of the apartment building multiple residences exist. These are precisely the facts that gave rise to *Maryland v. Garrison* (480 U.S. 79; 1987), which will be discussed in greater detail later in this chapter. (See "Exclusionary Rule.")

## Particularity of Things to Be Seized

The Fourth Amendment also requires particularity in the description of the items to be seized. This requirement is intended to prevent general searches, to prohibit the taking of objects that fall outside the warrant's scope, and to curtail the issuance of warrants on vague or doubtful bases of fact.

There are several general principles to be culled from the cases decided in this area (Moenssens 2003). First, a greater degree of ambiguity is acceptable when police officers have acquired all the descriptive facts that a reasonable investigation could be expected to uncover, and by ensuring that all of those facts were included in the warrant. Second, a more general type of description is sufficient when the nature of the objects to be seized is such that they could not be expected to have more specific characteristics. Third, contraband, because of its particular character, requires a less precise description. Drug paraphernalia, for example, might suffice for a search warrant for a place well known for trafficking in controlled substances. Fourth, failure to articulate all of the available descriptive facts is not grounds for questioning the adequacy of the description where the missing facts could not have been expected to be of any assistance to the executing officer. And fifth, an error in the statement of certain descriptive facts is not a basis for questioning the adequacy of the description if the executing officer was nonetheless able to determine from those facts provided that the object seized was that intended by the description.

## The Warrant

Police officers seeking a warrant must make application to a judge or magistrate. Most applications require the recitation of the same basic information. For example, the application for a search warrant in the Commonwealth of Pennsylvania requires a police officer to depose and say that there is probable cause "to believe that certain property is evidence of or the fruit of a crime or is contraband or is unlawfully possessed or is otherwise subject to seizure, and is located at particular premises or in the possession of the particular person. . . ." Additional instructions include the following:

1. If information was obtained from another person, e.g., an informant, a private citizen, or a fellow law officer, state specifically what information was received, and how and when such information was obtained. State also the factual basis for believing such other person to be reliable.
2. If surveillance was made, state what information was obtained by such surveillance, by whom it was obtained, and state date, time, and place of such surveillance.
3. State other pertinent facts within personal knowledge of affiant.
4. If "nighttime" search is requested (i.e., 10 P.M. to 6 A.M.) state additional reasonable cause for seeking permission to search in nighttime.

5. State reasons for believing that the items are located at the premises and/or on the person specified above.
6. State reasons for believing that the items are subject to seizure.
7. State any additional information considered pertinent to justify this application.

Copies of an "APPLICATION FOR SEARCH WARRANT AND AUTHORIZATION," an "AFFIDAVIT OF PROBABLE CAUSE," a "RECEIPT/INVENTORY OF SEIZED PROPERTY," and a "RETURN OF SERVICE AND INVENTORY" from the Commonwealth of Pennsylvania are included in Chapter Six.

A federal warrant, similar in many respects, requests the affiant to articulate "the facts to support a finding of probable cause" for issuance of a search or seizure warrant. Copies of an "APPLICATION AND AFFIDAVIT FOR SEIZURE WARRANT" and an "APPLICATION AND AFFIDAVIT FOR SEARCH WARRANT" from the federal government are also included in Chapter Six.

### Execution of the Warrant

The Fourth Amendment incorporates the common law requirement that law enforcement officers knock and announce their presence, identity, authority, and purpose before forcibly entering a residence to execute a warrant. The so-called "knock-and-announce" rule requires police officers to notify the occupants of their presence, identify themselves as police officers, express their specific legal purpose for requesting entry, and to wait a reasonable amount of time to allow the occupants to admit the officers voluntarily or to refuse to do so, at which time the officers may enter the residence forcibly. There is no "bright line" rule for distinguishing between a reasonable and unreasonable amount of time for officers to wait after announcing their presence but before entering a residence forcibly. Courts have traditionally evaluated each case on the basis of what time period was reasonable under the specific circumstances. Fifteen to twenty seconds has become the general standard employed by law enforcement officers and supported by numerous courts.

This knock-and-announce requirement is based in part upon the sanctity and privacy of the home, and was well established in England by the middle of the eighteenth century. Even in colonial America, some notice or request for admittance preceded the execution of general warrants and writs of assistance. At the time of the ratification of the Fourth Amendment, a majority of states had enacted constitutional provisions or statutes incorporating the common law knock-and-announce principle. Even today, most states and the federal government have statutes prohibiting most no-knock warrants.

The Supreme Court first addressed this issue in *Wilson v. Arkansas* (514 U.S. 927; 1995). While executing search and arrest warrants simultaneously, police officers found the main door to Sharlene Wilson's home open. After opening an unlocked screen door and entering the residence, the officers identified themselves and informed Wilson of the purpose of their visit. Once inside, the officers discovered drugs and drug paraphernalia and arrested the suspect. Wilson petitioned the trial court to suppress the evidence because the police had failed to knock and announce before entering. The trial judge refused the petition. The Arkansas Supreme Court affirmed, holding that the Fourth Amendment did not require officers to knock and announce their presence prior to entering the residence.

A unanimous Supreme Court reversed. Given the long-standing common law endorsement of the practice of announcement, the justices expressed little doubt "that the Framers of the Fourth Amendment thought that the method of an officer's entry into a dwelling was among the factors to be considered in assessing the reasonableness of a search or seizure" (514 U.S. at 934). Framers' intentions notwithstanding, the *Wilson* Court further ruled that not every entry had to be preceded by an announcement; in some circumstances, law enforcement officers could enter a home to execute a warrant unannounced. Declining to fashion a "bright line" remedy, the justices left it up to the lower courts to determine the circumstances in which an unannounced entry was reasonable under the Fourth Amendment.

Lower courts have recognized three exceptions to this general requirement. To justify a "no-knock" entry, police officers must have reasonable suspicion to believe that knocking and announcing their presence will (1) be perilously dangerous; (2) be useless; or (3) inhibit the effective investigation of the crime by, for example, allowing the destruction of evidence. The Supreme Court has subsequently held that these exceptions strike an appropriate balance between the legitimate needs of law enforcement at issue in the execution of warrants and the individual privacy concerns affected by "no-knock" entries.

First, where the totality of the circumstances suggests that there is a threat of physical violence either to the arresting officers or to others, officers need not announce their presence. This "apprehension of peril" exception comes into play when officers preparing to execute a warrant have a reasonable belief that persons inside a dwelling are armed and dangerous, and that, by announcing their presence, they will face an unusually acute risk of violence. The possibility of violence is not enough to trigger this exception. Knowledge of the presence of weapons in a residence, for example, is alone insufficient to justify a "no-knock" entry. For the most part, however, judges have been reluctant to handcuff police on this matter. Knowledge of the presence of weapons—along with knowledge of a violent crime and a propensity on behalf of the suspect to use weapons criminally—may justify an unannounced entry. Lower courts have also permitted "no-knock" entries when suspects have threatened to use weapons to avoid apprehension.

A second exception is the "useless gesture." This exception applies when the facts known to the officers justify them in being "virtually certain" that the occupants of the home are well aware of the officers' presence, identity, authority, and purpose. If the occupants of the home are sufficiently aware, the rule has already been satisfied; any announcement would be a useless gesture. Lower courts have held that it is not enough for police to show that the occupants were aware of their presence. To be "virtually certain," the occupants must be aware of the purpose of the visit also. For example, if officers knock and announce their authority repeatedly without eliciting a response, yet hear the occupants running down the back stairs, a reasonable interpretation of such events is that the occupants are well aware both of the presence *and* purpose of the police visit. To require the officers to repeat both their authority and purpose would thus be a mere formality and a futile act, perhaps resulting in the occupants evading arrest. Similarly, if the occupants refuse to answer the knock—or if the residence is unoccupied—any announcement would be a useless gesture.

Third, the destruction of evidence is an exigent circumstance that justifies dispensing with the knock-and-announce requirement. Under this exception, police officers must have an articulable basis upon which to justify a reasonable belief that evidence is about to be destroyed. In *Richards v. Wisconsin* (520 U.S. 385; 1997), the Supreme Court disallowed a blanket exception to the knock-and-announce requirement in drug felony investigations, but held that, in this case, the officers' decision not to knock and announce was reasonable under the circumstances at hand. The dispositive circumstances here were that the individual, after opening the door and confronting the police, quickly slammed the door; and that the drugs were of an easily disposable nature. The

Court in *Richards* reiterated that it was the duty of the court confronted with the question to determine whether the totality of the circumstances of the particular entry provided compelling reasons for disregarding the knock-and-announce requirement. In a more recent case, *United States v. Banks* (540 U.S. 31; 2003), discussed in Chapter Four, the Court held that police officers, in possession of a warrant to search for cocaine in a relatively small apartment, could enter the home forcibly after knocking on the apartment door, calling out "police search warrant," and waiting fifteen to twenty seconds without a response. The *Banks* majority concluded that the officers could fairly have suspected that the cocaine would be destroyed if the officers were reticent any longer. Lower courts have permitted even shorter wait times in cases involving easily disposable evidence.

## Is a Search Based on a Warrant a Constitutional Search?

Often, the presence of a warrant will be determinative of the constitutionality of the search, but not always. As *Boyd v. United States* (1886), discussed in the previous chapter, made clear, searches based on a warrant are sometimes unconstitutional. By the same token, though, warrantless searches are sometimes constitutional.

### EXCEPTIONS TO THE WARRANT REQUIREMENT

The Fourth Amendment protects citizens from unreasonable searches and seizures. Within the last half century, the Supreme Court has increasingly emphasized that "the definition of 'reasonableness' turns, at least in part, on the more specific commands of the [Fourth Amendment] warrant clause" (*United States v. United States District Court for the Eastern District of Michigan*, 407 U.S. 297, 315; 1972). As a general rule, searches and seizures conducted outside the judicial process, without prior approval by a judge or magistrate, are per se unreasonable under the Fourth Amendment, subject to only a few "jealously and carefully drawn" exceptions. (While the Court refers to the exceptions to the warrant requirement as limited in number and "jealously and carefully drawn," the list of exceptions now seems to include much of what is characterized as routine police activity.) At present, these exceptions include (1) consent searches; (2) international border searches; (3) investigatory detentions; (4) warrantless arrests; (5) searches incident to a lawful arrest; (6) plain view searches; (7) plain feel searches; (8) exigent circumstances; (9) automobile searches; (10) administrative/special needs searches; and (11) other various searches (container searches; inventory searches; airport searches; searches at sea; searches of abandoned property; and searches of property in foreign countries of individuals jailed in the United States). Each of these exceptions is discussed below.

## Consent Searches

Consent searches are justified on the grounds that individuals may waive their Fourth Amendment rights. Nevertheless, the Supreme Court's jurisprudence vis-à-vis consent has proven problematic. For example, what kind of consent is required? What circumstances require consent? And who may consent? Generally speaking, for a consent search to be valid, the consent must be voluntarily given by the individual affected or someone authorized by that person to control access to the place to be searched or the things to be seized.

It was not until *Schneckloth v. Bustamonte* (412 U.S. 218; 1973) that the Supreme Court addressed the issue of what constituted "voluntary" consent. The justices held (1) that the question whether consent to a search was voluntary was to be determined from the "totality of all the circumstances," including any coercive police tactics and the personal characteristics of the subject giving the consent; (2) that neither warning nor knowledge of the right to refuse consent was a necessary precondition of valid consent; and (3) that the requirement of a knowing and intelligent waiver of constitutional rights, while applicable to constitutional guarantees involving the preservation of a fair trial for a criminal defendant, was not applicable to the Fourth Amendment guarantee against unreasonable searches and seizures. The majority further noted that a prosecutor seeking to rely upon consent to justify a warrantless search had the burden of proving that the consent was, "in fact, freely and voluntarily given," and not the result of implicit or explicit coercion.

In determining the voluntariness of consent, courts regularly consider four factors (Holcomb 2002). First, courts carefully examine the characteristics of the individual asked to provide consent to a search. This may include the individual's age, education, background, experience with the legal system, physical condition, and the ability to understand and communicate in determining the voluntariness of the consent. Second, the environment in which the person is asked to consent is important. Factors potentially significant include the nature of the location where the consent is given, the number of persons present, the number of law enforcement officers present, and the time of day. Third, courts consider any actions taken, or statements made, by the individual who is asked to consent. Of particular importance may be whether the individual provided consent in writing, whether the individual requested or consulted with counsel, whether the individual indicated consent through a physical action (such as giving an item to an officer), and what the individual said in response to the officers' request to search. Finally, courts scrutinize the actions and statements made by police during the course of asking for consent to search. For example, courts may ask whether the officers identified themselves as law enforcement personnel; made their request for consent plain enough to be understood; gave *Miranda* warnings; made repeated requests for consent; informed the individual of his or her right to refuse to consent; were armed, displayed weapons, used force, made threats, or otherwise physically or verbally abused or intimidated the individual; claimed falsely to have a search warrant; or made promises or inducements to the individual. Because the government bears the burden of demonstrating the voluntariness of consent, any single action or statement made by law enforcement officers could result in the individual's consent being deemed involuntary.

The *Schneckloth* "totality of all the circumstances" approach may have been modified significantly in two ways (Love 2004, 1473–1474). First, where the test propounded in *Schneckloth* considered personal characteristics of the individual consenting—age, education, and intelligence, for example—a subsequent decision has called into question whether a court would find a consent search involuntary in the absence of police misconduct. When weighing a Fifth Amendment claim by a schizophrenic that his mental impairment precluded him from making a voluntary confession, the justices opined in *Colorado v. Connelly* (479 U.S. 157, 164; 1986):

> [a]bsent police conduct causally related to the confession, there is simply no basis for concluding that any state actor has deprived a criminal defendant of due process of law. . . . [Even the presence of subtle psychological persuasion] does not justify a conclusion that a defendant's mental condition, by itself, and apart from its relation to official coercion, should ever dispose of the inquiry into constitutional "voluntariness."

Second, the dispositive question in *Schneckloth*—whether the consent had, "in fact," been given—appears to have been replaced with an "objectively reasonable" standard. In *Florida v. Jimeno* (500 U.S. 248, 251; 1991), the justices held that it was "objectively reasonable" for the police to conclude that the general consent to search a vehicle included consent to search containers within the vehicle. This, in spite of the reality that the respondent had not, "in fact," consented to a search of a brown paper bag on the floor of his vehicle. While the *Connelly* holding has never been applied in the consent search context, and the *Jimeno* holding has yet to be applied broadly to all instances of consent, it is no great leap to conclude that police misconduct is a prerequisite to any finding of involuntariness in consent searches; and that police may rely on "objectively reasonable" conclusions as to consent, as opposed to *specific* consent.

**Who May Consent?** In *United States v. Matlock* (415 U.S. 164; 1974), the Supreme Court addressed the question of who may provide consent. In February 1971, William Earl Matlock was indicted in federal court for allegedly robbing a federally insured bank. Three months earlier, police officers had arrived at his place of residence. Living in the home at that time were the two owners, several of their children, one grandchild, and Matlock. Upon knocking on the door, the officers were greeted by one of the owners' daughters, who granted entry into the residence. The daughter then voluntarily consented to the search of the house, including the east bedroom, which was jointly occupied by herself and Matlock. During that search, officers found $4,995 in cash, and investigators later traced the money back to the bank heist. At trial, Matlock moved to suppress the evidence seized in the search. The district court granted Matlock's motion, finding that the daughter lacked the actual authority to consent to the search. After the appellate court affirmed, the Supreme Court reversed. The justices held that when the prosecution sought to justify a warrantless search by proof of voluntary consent, it did not have to prove that such consent was given by the defendant. Rather, police could search a bedroom inhabited by two persons so long as they had consent from one of the inhabitants "who possessed common authority over or other sufficient relationship to the premises or effects sought to be inspected" (415 U.S. at 171). In other words, the consent of one person who possessed common authority over the premises or effects was valid against the absent, nonconsenting person with whom that authority is shared.

The justices went one step further in *Illinois v. Rodriguez* (497 U.S. 177; 1990), permitting evidence to be admitted at trial even though law enforcement officers conducted a warrantless entry and search, based upon the consent of a third party who police mistakenly, but reasonably, believed possessed that authority to consent to the search. In July 1985, police went to the home of Dorothy Jackson. They were met at the house by Jackson's daughter, Gail Fischer, who showed signs of a "severe beating." She informed the officers that she had been beaten by Edward Rodriguez earlier that day in an apartment across town, and offered to take police there and unlock the door with her key so that the officers could enter the apartment and arrest Rodriguez. After arriving at the apartment, Fischer gained entry into the apartment with her key, as promised. Once inside, the officers, while attempting to locate Rodriguez, stumbled upon some cocaine. They seized the cocaine and arrested Rodriguez. At trial, Rodriguez moved to suppress the evidence seized, contending that Fischer had moved out of the apartment several weeks prior to the entry and arrest. A state trial court granted the motion, and the state appellate court affirmed. After the state's highest court denied review, the Supreme Court reversed. Because Fischer did not live at the apartment and because she had taken a key to the apartment without Rodriguez's knowledge, the justices found that Fischer did not possess "joint access or control" over the apartment. The issue then turned to whether the police were justified in acting solely on a reasonable belief that Fischer had authority to authorize the search, even though that belief later turned out to be false. Rodriguez argued that such a rule would amount to a vicarious waiver of his Fourth Amendment rights, which, like the Fifth Amendment right to remain silent and the Sixth Amendment right to a trial by jury, could only be waived "knowingly" and "intelligently." The Court disagreed, distinguishing between trial rights deriving from the violation of constitutional guarantees and the nature of those constitutional guarantees themselves:

> There is a vast difference between those rights that protect a fair criminal trial and the rights guaranteed under the Fourth Amendment. Nothing, either in the purposes behind requiring a "knowing" and "intelligent" waiver of trial rights, or in the practical application of such a requirement suggests that it ought to be extended to the constitutional guarantees against unreasonable searches and seizures. (497 U.S. at 183)

The majority opinion then explained why the officers' belief (that Fischer had the authority to consent to the search) only had to be reasonable and not, in the end, factually accurate. Drawing a parallel to search warrants, which must be supported by probable cause, and not ironclad facts, the justices offered a definition that is more circular in logic than beneficial: To satisfy the reasonableness requirement of the Fourth Amendment, "what is generally demanded of [agents of the government] . . . is not that they always be correct, but that they always be reasonable" (497 U.S. at 185). So, under *Rodriguez,* a reasonable belief by an officer that a person has authority to consent to a search—regardless of whether that person actually possesses such authority—is all that is necessary for such a search to be binding on the defendant.

**Voluntary Consent.** Police may request consent for a warrantless search; they may not demand it. Consent must be voluntarily given; it cannot be the product of official intimidation or harassment. In *Florida v. Bostick* (501 U.S. 429; 1991), the Supreme Court confronted the controversial practice of police boarding public buses, identifying persons who matched a drug-courier profile, and asking those persons for permission to search their luggage. In this case, two police officers, both of whom were wearing badges and one of whom had a recognizable pouch that was carrying a concealed weapon, boarded a bus traveling from Miami to Atlanta, during a stopover in Ft. Lauderdale, Florida. The officers approached Terrance Bostick, explained to him that they were looking for illegal drugs, and requested his permission to search his luggage, informing him that he was not obligated to comply. Nevertheless, Bostick consented to the search and cocaine was found; he was later convicted. The Florida Supreme Court reversed his conviction, reasoning that a reasonable passenger would not have felt free to leave the bus to avoid questioning by the police. Accordingly, that court adopted a *per se* rule against the practice of "working the buses."

On certiorari to the U.S. Supreme Court, the justices announced that the appropriate inquiry in determining whether an encounter between an individual and the police was consensual was whether a reasonable person would have felt free to decline the officers' request and terminate the encounter. Here, the officers had not shown any use of authority or displayed any weapons. Bostick *voluntarily* consented to the search after he had been specifically informed of his right to refuse consent. And Bostick could have left the bus to avoid the interrogation at any time. Because this encounter was entirely consensual, Bostick had not been seized under the Fourth Amendment. Obviously, examining the totality of the circumstances, if a reasonable person would not have felt free to refuse consent and terminate the encounter, then the individual would have been seized under the Fourth Amendment.

**Revocation of Consent.**   Numerous lower courts have held that a person having given consent may withdraw that consent at any time. When consent is effectively withdrawn, police must discontinue searching.

**Implied Consent.**   Not all circumstances require consent. In *Illinois v. Batchelder* (463 U.S 1112; 1983), the Supreme Court upheld an *implied* consent law, common in all fifty states, requiring automobile drivers to submit to breath-analysis tests or have their driver's licenses automatically suspended. Similar implied consent laws exist for individuals operating other forms of transportation, such as airplanes and boats.

### International Border Searches

Nonconsensual searches without either a warrant or any individual suspicion that the person or place to be searched is connected to criminal activity may be conducted at international borders. A variety of governmental officials may conduct such searches, including immigration officials, Coast Guard officers, and customs agents. In the interest of national security, courts have long authorized routine border stops and searches of persons, luggage, personal effects, and vehicles, based on the sovereign authority of the United States to protect itself by controlling what persons and property cross into the country. Because it is within the power of the federal government to exclude aliens from the country, and because the Fourth Amendment's "balance of reasonableness is qualitatively different at the international border than in the interior," routine border searches of incoming or outgoing persons and property do not require reasonable suspicion, probable cause, or a warrant (*United States v. Montoya De Hernandez*, 473 U.S. 531, 538; 1985).

While the Supreme Court has yet to specify the factors that make a border search "routine," federal circuit courts have considered the level of intrusiveness involved to distinguish between a "routine" and a "nonroutine" search. Because most border searches of persons and property are nonintrusive, they qualify as "routine." By contrast, circuit courts have consistently held that more intrusive searches—x-ray examinations and strip searches, for example—require reasonable suspicion (*United States v. Adekunle*, 2 F.3d 559, 562; [5th Cir. 1993]; *United States v.*

*Oyekan,* 786 F.3d 832, 837; [8th Cir. 1986]; *Brett v. Ashley,* 247 F.3d 1294, 1303; [11th Cir. 2001]). Courts typically require an even "higher level of suspicion" or "clear indication" of criminal activity for the most intrusive of searches, such as body cavity searches (*United States v. Handy,* 788 F.2d 1419, 1420–1421; [9th Cir. 1986]; *United States v. Pino,* 729 F.2d 1357, 1359; [11th Cir. 1984]).

The "border search" exception not only applies at the border, but also at its "functional equivalent." Such functional equivalents may include an established station near a border, a point marking the confluence of two or more roads that extend from the border, or an airport at which arriving passengers and cargo of an airplane are searched after a nonstop flight from a foreign country (*United States v. Almeida-Sanchez,* 413 U.S. 266, 272–273; 1973). As with the definition of "routine" searches, the Supreme Court has yet to enumerate explicitly what constitutes a "functional equivalent" of a border. Federal circuit courts, however, have generally agreed that the "functional equivalent" of a border is the first practical detention point after a border crossing or the final port of entry, so long as there is reasonable certainty that the travelers crossed the border and that there was no change in the object of the search between the time of the border crossing and the search (*United States v. Beras,* 183 F.3d 22; [1st Cir. 1999]; *United States v. Hill,* 939 F.2d 934; [11th Cir. 1991]; *United States v. Ogbuehi,* 18 F.3d 807; [9th Cir. 1994]). The "functional equivalent" thus may include an airport, a port, or a customs area, though each may be removed at some distance from the actual border.

Recognizing the importance in controlling the illegal entry of aliens into the United States, the Supreme Court has, in limited circumstances, permitted the use of roving border patrols to stop vehicles to question occupants as to their citizenship and immigration status (*United States v. Brignoni-Ponce,* 422 U.S. 873; 1975). Because stops of this sort are typically brief, result in no search of the vehicle or its occupants (other than that which can be seen by anyone standing alongside the vehicle), and require at most a response to a brief question or the production of certain documentation, probable cause is not required for the stop. The justices have been keen to point out, however, that such roving border patrols do not possess unlimited discretion and cannot, consistent with the Fourth Amendment, make border area stops on a random basis. Such stops may be made only if the border patrol agents are "aware of specific articulable facts, together with rational inferences from those facts, that reasonably warrant suspicion that the vehicles contained aliens who may be illegally in the country" (422 U.S. at 884). The justices have suggested that, while each case will turn on the totality of the circumstances, factors to be considered by the border patrol agents include (1) the proximity to the border; (2) information about recent illegal border crossings in that vicinity; (3) the driver's questionable behavior; (4) the type of vehicle; (5) the number of occupants in the vehicle; (6) the suspicious activity of the occupants; and (7) the ancestry of the occupants (although the ancestry alone is insufficient to furnish reasonable grounds to believe that the occupants are aliens). Searches involving more than inquiries regarding citizenship and immigration status required either consent or probable cause.

Additionally, automobile travelers may be stopped at fixed checkpoints near the border without individualized suspicion (*United States v. Martinez-Fuerte*, 428 U.S. 543; 1976), and boats on inland waters with ready access to the sea may be hailed and boarded with no suspicion whatever (*United States v. Villamonte-Marquez*, 462 U.S. 579; 1983). Searches that occur at greater distances from the border (or the sea) require either consent or probable cause.

## Investigatory Detentions

An investigatory detention is the intermediate stage in the stop-detention-arrest process, during which the law enforcement officer determines whether he or she has probable cause to make an arrest. This exception to the warrant requirement permits law enforcement officers to detain temporarily an individual to maintain the status quo while the officer obtains additional information. Unlike an arrest, an investigatory detention does not require probable cause. Instead, investigatory detention requires only that the officers have reasonable, articulable suspicion of criminal activity.

The Supreme Court first addressed the legality of warrantless investigatory detentions in *Terry v. Ohio* (392 U.S. 1; 1968). In the Court of Common Pleas of Cuyahoga County, Ohio, John W. Terry was convicted of carrying a concealed weapon. At his trial, the prosecution introduced into evidence a revolver and a number of bullets that had been seized from Terry and a codefendant, Richard Chilton. The evidence had been seized by Detective Martin McFadden, a thirty-nine-year veteran of the Cleveland Police Department. While patrolling his regular beat in plain clothes, McFadden witnessed the two strangers walking back and forth along an identical route, pausing to stare in the same store window. Taking up a post of observation at some distance, McFadden watched the two men repeat this behavior for a total of about twenty-four times. At the completion of each route, the men conferred with each other on a street corner, where they were joined from time to time by a third individual, also unknown to McFadden. Suspecting the men of "casing a job, a stick up," the detective approached the individuals, identified himself, and inquired as to their names. Upon hearing a mumble, McFadden stopped them, spun Terry around, patted down his outside clothing, and discovered, but was unable to remove immediately, a concealed weapon. The detective then removed Terry's overcoat, taking possession of the weapon. A similar pat-down search of Chilton's outer garments revealed the presence of another concealed weapon, shortly thereafter seized by McFadden. The pat-down search of the third individual revealed nothing. McFadden did not put his hands under the outer garments of Terry or Chilton until he had felt the guns; and never placed his hands under the outer garments of the third individual.

At trial the prosecution contended that the guns had been seized incident to a lawful arrest. Although the trial court rejected that contention, the judge denied the defendant's motion to suppress the weapons on the ground that McFadden had cause to believe that Terry and Chilton were acting suspiciously, that their brief seizure and interrogation were warranted, and that the officer, for his own protection, could pat down their outer clothing, having reasonable cause to believe that they might be armed. The trial court thus distinguished between an "investigatory detention" and an arrest. The former required only reasonable suspicion, the latter probable cause. The trial court also distinguished between a "frisk" of the outer clothing for weapons and a full-fledged search for evidence of a crime. Again, the former required only reasonable suspicion, the latter probable cause. With the evidence admissible, Terry and Chilton were convicted. The intermediate appellate court affirmed the convictions and the Ohio Supreme Court dismissed the appeal.

Before the high Court, the justices explicitly balanced the nature and quality of the intrusion on the individual's Fourth Amendment interests against the importance of the governmental interests alleged to justify the intrusion, recognizing that in some circumstances the government's need to conduct a search (or seizure) may outweigh the minimal intrusion of personal liberty and privacy that the search (or seizure) entails. The majority opinion, written by Chief Justice Warren, conceded that the Fourth Amendment applied to the "stop and frisk" procedure at issue here: Whenever a police officer accosts an individual and restrains his freedom to walk away, that individual has been "seized" within the meaning of the Fourth Amendment. Similarly, a police officer's careful exploration of the outer surfaces of a person's clothing in an attempt to find weapons is a "search" under the

Fourth Amendment. Nevertheless, too much emphasis on the actual terms "search" and "seizure" diverted attention from the central inquiry under the Fourth Amendment—"the reasonableness in all the circumstances of the particular governmental invasion of a citizen's personal security." Thus, the question became whether, given "all the circumstances," Officer McFadden's actions were reasonable. The Court concluded:

> We merely hold today that where a police officer observes unusual conduct which leads him reasonably to conclude in light of his experience that criminal activity may be afoot and that the persons with whom he is dealing may be armed and presently dangerous, where in the course of investigating this behavior he identifies himself as a policeman and makes reasonable inquiries, and where nothing in the initial stages of the encounter serves to dispel his reasonable fear for his own or other's safety, he is entitled for the protection of himself and others in the area to conduct a limited search of the outer clothing of such persons in an attempt to discover weapons which might be used to assault him. (392 U.S. at 30)

Notice from the above passage the Court's cautious tone—"We *merely* hold . . ." (emphasis added). Equally important is the limited application of this exception to the probable cause requirement. First, to initiate an investigatory detention, the officer must have reasonable, articulable suspicion of criminal activity. That is, the officer must articulate specific facts, together with rational inferences drawn from those facts, that lead a reasonable man to conclude that criminal activity has occurred or is about to occur. An unparticularized hunch or generalized suspicion will not suffice. Second, a search stemming from the initial detention is warranted only if the officer reasonably believes that the suspect is armed and dangerous and that the officer's safety or that of others in the vicinity is endangered. "We cannot blind ourselves to the need for law enforcement officers to protect themselves and other prospective victims of violence in situations where they may lack probable cause for an arrest." Or, as stated more memorably by Justice John Marshall Harlan in a concurring opinion: An officer confronting a person suspected of a serious crime should not "have to ask one question and take the risk that the answer might be a bullet" (392 U.S. at 33). And third, any resulting search must be limited to the suspect's outer clothing in an attempt to discover weapons that might be used to assault the officer or harm others. The search is confined to what is "minimally necessary" to determine whether the suspects are armed. A "pat down" search is permissible; a more thorough search for evidence of criminal activity is not.

However limited the *Terry* exception was intended to be, it quickly came to stand for the proposition that a citizen on the street could be legally stopped and frisked if a police officer had "reasonable suspicion," even though that precise phrase is nowhere found in Warren's opinion (Powe 2000, 406). One biographer of the former chief justice called *Terry* "a considerable bow in the direction of law enforcement" (White 1982, 277); another simply called it "practical" (Cray 1997, 468). A former law clerk of Chief Justice Warren observed:

> Individually, the Justices . . . may have felt differing degrees of sympathy with the arguments of the police, but collectively they were unwilling to be—or to be perceived as—the agents who tied the hands of the police in dealing with intensely dangerous and recurring situations on city streets. (Dudley 1998, 893)

The lone dissenter in *Terry,* Justice William O. Douglas, dismissed angrily the majority's reliance on "reasonableness" as the touchstone of constitutionality. He refused to budge from the Fourth Amendment's insistence on probable cause, noting that it was the only line that drew a meaningful distinction "between an officer's mere inkling in the presence of facts with the officer's personal knowledge which would convince a reasonable man that the person seized has committed, is committing, or is about to commit a particular crime." Any relaxation of Fourth Amendment standards was a "long step down a totalitarian path." Then Justice Douglas concluded bitterly:

> There have been powerful hydraulic pressures throughout our history that bear heavily on the Court to water down constitutional guarantees and give the police the upper hand. That hydraulic pressure has probably never been greater than it is today. Yet if the individual is no longer to be sovereign, if the police can pick him up whenever they do not like the cut of his jib, if they can "seize" and "search" him in their discretion, we enter a new regime. (392 U.S. at 38)

But perhaps the country had entered a new regime. Lucas Powe, Jr. (2000, 407), offers an apt observation: "[O]ne cannot help but wonder if *Terry* would have been similarly decided two years earlier." By June 1968, when *Terry* was decided, much had changed. Martin Luther King, Jr., and Robert F. Kennedy had been assassinated midway through a year "pocked with bombings, arson, demonstrations, and random shootings . . . preceded by three years of riot, crime and summer terror, in a climate of ever-rising hate and fear. . . ." These events prepared "the way for the great concern that now dominated the second half of the campaign of 1968"—law and order (White 1969, 188).

The Court recognized in *Terry* that certain governmental interests—in this case, public safety—may justify a brief investigatory detention on less than probable cause. That detention, however, was strictly circumscribed by the exigencies of the situation. Such circumscription was evident in *Sibron v. New York* (392 U.S. 40, 64; 1968), a companion case to *Terry* in which the justices disallowed the search of a drug suspect who police had no reason to believe was involved in criminal activity or armed. "[T]he police officer is not entitled to seize and search every person whom he sees on the street. Before he places a hand on the person of a citizen in search of anything, he must have constitutionally adequate, reasonable grounds for doing so."

The primary bases for reasonable suspicion in *Terry* were the personal observations, and rational conclusions drawn from those observations and other experience and special knowledge, of a trained police officer. Subsequent decisions, however, have enlarged the bases for reasonable suspicion. For example, the Supreme Court held in *Adams v. Williams* (407 U.S. 143, 148; 1972) that information obtained by the police from a reliable informant established reasonable suspicion. When an informant is used, police are required to demonstrate the reliability of the information received, either by corroborating the details independently or establishing the credibility of the informant.

*Adams* did not address directly the issue of anonymous tips, except to comment that tips received from reliable sources provided a stronger justification for warrantless searches than did tips received anonymously. In the ordinary course of police work, of course, law enforcement officers often rely upon anonymous tips to further their investigation. In *Alabama v. White* (496 U.S. 325; 1990), the Supreme Court determined that if officers were able to corroborate independently parts of an anonymous telephone tip, then the information in that tip pertaining to criminal activity could be presumed reliable and used to provide reasonable suspicion. Remarkably, the majority came to this conclusion in spite of the fact that *none* of the suspect's actions that were observed by the officers exhibited sufficient indications of reliability to provide reasonable cause that the suspect was involved in criminal activity.

*White* is subject to criticism on a number of points. First, it makes it possible for anyone with sufficient knowledge about another person to formulate an anonymous tip justifying an investigatory detention of that person. For example, most persons have fairly regular schedules, leaving their residences at about the same time every day, carrying the same briefcase or satchel every day, and heading off in the same direction every day. This information alone—told to the police by an anonymous neighbor or, for that matter, by another police officer, acting anonymously on a hunch—hardly rises to the level of a reasonable basis that criminal activity is afoot. This allows any person with knowledge of mundane, noncriminal behavior—be it a person who wants to play a prank on a friend or be it one who harbors serious ill will toward another—to trigger an investigatory detention. Second, declaring an investigatory detention constitutional based on this less than compelling information subjects every citizen to being stopped and questioned by any officer who is willing to testify that the warrantless stop was precipitated by an anonymous tip predicting whatever conduct the officer had just witnessed for him or herself.

More recently, in a nod to the critics of *White,* the justices disallowed a "stop and frisk" (as the *Terry* exception has come to be called) based solely upon an anonymous tip that a person was carrying a gun. In *Florida v. J. L.* (529 U.S. 266; 2000), a unanimous Court held that because the anonymous call left the police officers without means to corroborate the details or establish the trustworthiness of the informant, the tip alone did not exhibit sufficient indications of reliability to provide "reasonable suspicion" to make an investigatory detention. Though asked to do so, the justices declined to adopt a "firearms exception," under which an anonymous tip alleging the possession of an illegal gun would, by itself, justify a "stop and frisk." To be constitutional, the unknown and unaccountable informant would have to explain either how the informant knew about the gun or provide some other basis for establishing the informant's credibility. Lower courts have repeatedly held that corroboration of several details of an anonymous tip amounts to reasonable suspicion. Coming from a high Court decidedly unsympathetic to criminal rights, this case may serve as a warning to states and lower courts that, in spite of recent trends, the Fourth Amendment remains a check on overly aggressive law enforcement.

Of far more lasting significance is *United States v. Sokolow* (490 U.S. 1; 1990), which not only enlarged the bases for reasonable suspicion but also extended the rationale for investigatory detentions. To recall, the Court in *Terry* stated that neither inarticulable hunches nor generalized suspicion rose to the level of probable cause. Yet, in *Sokolow,* the justices held that agents of the Drug Enforcement Administration had reasonable suspicion to detain an airline passenger matching six characteristics common to drug couriers. At the time of the detention, the agents knew that Sokolow (1) paid $2,100 for two round-trip airplane tickets from a roll of $20 bills; (2) traveled under an alias; (3) had an original destination of Miami, a major source city for illicit drugs; (4) stayed in Miami for only forty-eight hours, even though his round-trip flight from Honolulu to Miami took approximately twenty hours; (5) appeared nervous during his trip; and (6) checked none of his luggage. After further examination, drug enforcement agents secured a search warrant and discovered 1,063 grams of cocaine in his carry-on luggage. Sokolow was subsequently indicted and convicted for possession with intent to distribute cocaine, a federal drug offense. The court of appeals reversed the conviction, holding that the agents did not have reasonable and articulable suspicion of ongoing criminal behavior at the time of the stop.

The Supreme Court disagreed. "Reasonable suspicion" to stop and detain briefly a person for investigatory purpose must be more than an "inchoate and unparticularized suspicion or hunch." The officer must have "some minimal level of objective justification" taken from the totality of the circumstances, the whole picture (490 U.S. at 8). Here the agents had "more than a . . . hunch." They had a reasonable basis to suspect that Sokolow was engaged in transporting illegal drugs. Even though any one of the factors considered alone was insufficient evidence of illegal conduct and was consistent with innocent travel, all of the factors considered collectively amounted to reasonable suspicion. *Sokolow* underscores the holding in *Terry:* Despite the textual commands of the Fourth Amendment, law enforcement officers do not need probable cause to stop and frisk suspicious individuals. While this is but one expansion of the *Terry* standard, the Burger and Rehnquist (1986–2005) Courts have consistently permitted greater leeway for police to conduct investigatory detentions.

Additionally, lower courts, taking their cue from *Sokolow,* have held that law enforcement officers acted reasonably when detaining persons on the basis of several apparently innocent activities. For example, the Court of Appeals for the First Circuit allowed an investigatory detention of a man emerging from a swamp near the location of a drug bust (*United States v. Velez-Saldana,* 252 F.3d 49; [1st Cir. 2002]). The Second Circuit held that police had reasonable suspicion to "stop and frisk" a suspect who communicated secretly with an unidentified man, showed alarm, and acted evasively upon seeing police (*United States v. Welbeck,* 145 F.3d 493; [2nd Cir. 1998]). The Tenth Circuit deemed it reasonable to detain an individual because he made "hand to hand" contact with numerous individuals outside of an apartment in a high drug-trade area (*United States v. Hinshaw,* 235 F.3d 565; [10th Cir. 1998]). And the Eleventh Circuit permitted an investigatory detention because a suspect, backpack in tow, made several brief trips to a known drug dealer's garage (*United States v. Powell,* 222 F.3d 913; [11th Cir. 2000]).

Equally important, *Sokolow* extended the rationale for investigatory detentions. *Terry* said that a "stop and frisk" was warranted only if the officer reasonably concluded that the suspect was armed and dangerous and that the officer's safety or that of others in the vicinity was endangered. Law enforcement officers must be able "to protect themselves," said the *Terry* majority. Yet in *Sokolow,* the immediate threat to public safety was, at best, tenuous and, more likely, nonexistent.

More akin to *Terry, Illinois v. Wardlow* (528 U.S. 119; 2000) held that a police officer had reasonable suspicion to stop an individual who, upon seeing a police caravan patrolling an area known for heavy narcotics trafficking, fled. When William Wardlow was cornered, the police found both a handgun and live ammunition in his possession. After conviction, two state appellate courts found the "stop and frisk" unconstitutional, holding that sudden flight from a high crime area did not create reasonable suspicion under the *Terry* standard. On writ of certiorari to the Supreme Court, however, the justices opted not to rely solely upon the *Terry* standard, instead invoking the aforementioned "totality of the circumstances" yardstick. The determination of reasonable suspicion must be based on "commonsense judgments and inferences about human behavior" (528 U.S. at 125). Law enforcement officers are not required to ignore relevant characteristics of a particular location (a high drug-trade area) or sufficiently suspicious activity ("headlong flight" being the consummate act of evasion and clearly suggestive of wrongdoing). In short, unprovoked flight in a high-crime area amounts to reasonable suspicion justifying an investigatory detention. Ironically, if Wardlow had simply stood his ground, he probably would have escaped conviction. Even though he was in a high drug-trade area, the justices had previously held that such a factor alone was insufficient to justify a "stop and frisk." It was only because Wardlow "beat feet" that the police were able to prove reasonable suspicion.

A related issue is the range of activities that may take place during an investigatory detention. In *Terry*, the Court insisted that the officer's action be "reasonably related in scope" to the circumstances that justified the detention in the first place. Action that is not "reasonably related in scope" becomes an arrest (as opposed to an investigatory detention), and must be supported by probable cause, an obviously higher standard than reasonable suspicion. The justices, however, have been reluctant to establish "hard and fast" rules as to when an investigatory detention becomes an arrest: "Much as a 'bright line' rule would be desirable, . . . common sense and ordinary human experience must govern over rigid criteria"

(*United States v. Sharpe,* 400 U.S. 675, 682; 1985). The absence of a mechanical checklist for distinguishing between investigatory detention and formal arrests has not prevented lower courts from considering certain factors, including the degree of intrusiveness (whether the officer's conduct was more intrusive than was necessary to investigate the suspicion) and the duration of the stop. While the justices have not articulated specific time limits on investigatory detentions, they have considered the due diligence (or lack thereof) of the investigating authorities. Due diligence, not speed, is the standard. A lengthy detention is permissible when it results from factors beyond the control of the authorities, such as an uncooperative suspect or a computer malfunction. By contrast, courts have disallowed even brief detentions when officials have wasted time, intentionally misinformed the suspects as to the course of the investigation, or otherwise failed to act with appropriate diligence.

Investigatory detentions of property are governed by the same standards as investigatory detentions of persons in possession of such property. Courts insist upon reasonable suspicion for the initial seizure of the property and require police diligence in conducting the subsequent investigation. In *United States v. Place* (462 U.S. 696; 1983), for example, the Supreme Court held that police were authorized to detain *briefly* a traveler's luggage upon a reasonable belief that the luggage contained contraband or criminal evidence. The rationale was simple: The detention of personal effects was only "minimally intrusive" of Fourth Amendment interests, and the countervailing governmental interest—detecting those who would traffic in deadly drugs for personal profit—was exceedingly strong. That said, the justices disallowed the search in this case for two reasons. First, it was unreasonable to detain a traveler's luggage for ninety minutes pending the arrival of a drug-sniffing dog. And second, the prolonged seizure was unreasonable since the police conduct exceeded the bounds of a permissible investigatory detention, by removing the luggage to another airport, and misinforming the suspect about the course of the investigation. Here, again, the dispositive factor appeared to be the absence of diligence on behalf of the police, who failed both to investigate quickly and to use minimally intrusive procedures.

## Warrantless Arrests

While police occasionally obtain arrest warrants, particularly if they must enter a building to make an arrest, most arrests today are conducted in the absence of such warrants. If a police officer has firsthand knowledge—say, for example, the offense occurs in the presence of an officer—the officer may make a warrantless arrest. Likewise, if a police officer has probable cause to believe that a felony has been committed, the officer may arrest the subject without a warrant. (A felony is a general name for a class of crimes regarded by the law as very serious; a misdemeanor is a less serious crime. Aggravated assault, arson, burglary, kidnapping, murder, and rape are commonly considered to be felonies. Historically, felonies were crimes for which punishment included forfeiture of property, imprisonment, or death.)

The Fourth Amendment, as interpreted by the Supreme Court, does not require that a judge or magistrate review the factual justification for an arrest *prior* to the arrest. While such a requirement for all arrests would assure "maximum protection of individual rights," it would undoubtedly constitute an "intolerable handicap for legitimate law enforcement" (*Gerstein v. Pugh,* 420 U.S. 103, 113; 1975). An officer's on-the-scene determination of probable cause provides the legal justification both for the arrest and the subsequent brief detention necessary to take the administrative steps incident to the arrest. The officer's on-the-scene determination, however, is subject to later judicial review. As soon as is practicable after the arrest, the officer must secure a judicial determination of whether probable cause in fact existed at the time of the arrest. Any extended restraint on liberty following the arrest is predicated on a judicial finding that probable cause existed.

In certain circumstances, a warrantless arrest, even if based on probable cause, is unconstitutional. *Payton v. New York* (445 U.S. 573; 1980) held that the Fourth Amendment prohibits law enforcement authorities from making a warrantless and nonconsensual entry into a suspect's home to make a routine felony arrest. The *Payton* holding is clearly based on the sanctity of the home, which has a long history in the common law. In his famous oration against the writs of assistance in 1761 (see Chapter Two), James Otis spoke of the sanctity of the home and the sovereignty of its inhabitants as being one of the fundamental principles of the law: "A man who is quiet, is as secure in his house, as a prince in a castle" (Commager 1958, 45). Shortly thereafter, Sir William Blackstone (1765, I, 223) noted that the law has "so particular and tender a regard to the immunity of a man's house that it stiles it his castle, and will never suffer it to be violated with impunity." And, to recall from Chapter Two, William Pitt in a speech before the English House of Commons in 1763, opined that the "poorest man may in his cottage bid defiance to all the forces of the Crown" (Lieber 1853, 45).

*Payton* confirmed these sentiments, distinguishing earlier pronouncements upholding warrantless arrests in public places on the grounds that the physical entry of the home was the "chief evil" against which the wording of the Fourth Amendment was directed. Such physical entry was too substantial to allow without a warrant, in the absence of exigent circumstances, even when supported by probable cause.

For purposes of a warrantless home arrest, an important factor to be considered when determining whether any exigency exists is the gravity of the underlying offense for which the arrest is being made. In *Welsh v. Wisconsin* (466 U.S. 740; 1984), the justices disallowed a warrantless home arrest because the arrest was for a minor, noncriminal, nonjailable, traffic offense, declaring that the state's interest in the prosecution of such a minor offense was insufficient to overcome the special protection afforded the individual in his home. Although it is a close question, it seems fair to conclude from these and other decisions that a presumption of unreasonableness attaches to all warrantless entries into the home.

Outside of the home, police ordinarily have broad latitude to make warrantless arrests when the criminal behavior occurs in their presence. As *Atwater v. City of Lago Vista* (532 U.S. 318; 2001) illustrates, this general grant of authority extends even to misdemeanors. (A misdemeanor, as contrasted with a felony, is a less serious offense.) *Atwater* will be discussed in Chapter Four.

## Searches Incident to a Lawful Arrest

Because there is no way for an arresting officer to reliably predict whether a suspect being arrested poses a serious threat to the arresting officer, courts have historically permitted police some leeway in conducting searches that are incident to lawful arrests. Under this "search incident to lawful arrest" principle, whenever an arrest is made, the arresting officer may search the person being arrested to remove any weapons that may be used against the officer to effect an escape, and to seize evidence on the arrestee's person to prevent its concealment or destruction. Additionally, the officer may search the area "within [the arrestee's] immediate control" to prevent the individual being arrested from grabbing a weapon or other evidence. After all, a gun in a drawer near the person being arrested may be as dangerous to the arresting officer as one concealed in the arrestee's clothing. Courts have construed the phrase "within the immediate control" as the area from within which the arrestee might reach to gain possession of a weapon or destructible evidence. Lower courts have referred to the area within the suspect's immediate control as the "grabbing area."

The leading case on searches incident to lawful arrests is *Chimel v. California* (395 U.S. 752; 1969), in which the Supreme Court drew a distinction between, on the one hand, a search of the person arrested and the area within his or her reach and, on the other hand, more extensive searches. In this case, local police officers possessed a warrant authorizing the arrest of Ted Chimel for burglary. When attempting to serve the warrant at Chimel's home, the officers were informed by Chimel's wife that the suspect was not present, but that they could wait in the house until his return. This they did. After serving Chimel with the warrant, the officers requested permission to conduct a comprehensive search of his residence. Chimel objected, but was informed by the officers that on the basis of a lawful arrest they could conduct a search without his permission. The officers then searched the entire three-bedroom house, including the attic, the garage, a small workshop, and various drawers. The search uncovered a number of items that were later used to convict Chimel at trial.

In a seven-to-two decision, the Court declared that in the absence of a search warrant, there was no constitutional justification for searching rooms other than the room in which the arrest occurred or, for that matter, for searching through closed or concealed areas even in the room where the arrest occurred. Emphasizing the importance of warrants and probable cause as necessary bulwarks against government abuse, the justices limited the scope of the search to that which was in "plain view" or in "the immediate area" surrounding the arrestee. Here, the search went far beyond the arrestee's person and the area from within which he might have obtained either a weapon or something that could have been used as evidence against him.

*Chimel* has been criticized for constraining police action. If the arrest was lawful, critics note, then police should be justified in conducting a comprehensive search without the delay of obtaining a search warrant due to the risk that the evidence could be removed in the meantime. Additionally, *Chimel* forces police officers to make a case-by-case determination of what locations are within the "grabbing area" of the arrestee. *Chimel,* decided in Warren's last term as chief justice, has never been overturned. The subsequent Burger and Rehnquist Courts, however, have extended the rationale for warrantless searches incident to a lawful arrest and, in the interest of protecting law enforcement officers, generally given wide construction to the term "grabbing area."

For example, the question of just what type of "search" is permissible incident to a lawful arrest was addressed several years later in *United States v. Robinson* (414 U.S. 218; 1973). *Terry,* to recall, had allowed a limited "pat down" search of a suspect's clothing if the officer had reasonable suspicion to conclude that criminal activity was afoot. In *Robinson,* however, the Supreme Court, citing an arresting officer's need to protect himself by disarming a suspect, held that once a police officer had lawfully placed a suspect under arrest, the officer could conduct a "full" search of the arrestee. It did not matter that the officer had no reason to suspect that the arrestee was armed. (After all, Robinson had been arrested only for operating a motor vehicle after revocation of his operator's permit.) Nor did it matter that the officer had no reason to suspect that the arrestee possessed further evidence of a crime. (By chance, the officer discovered heroin capsules, which were found in a crumpled cigarette package in Robinson's coat pocket.) Contrasting this situation with the "stop and frisk" procedure upheld in *Terry,* the Court stated that it was "scarcely open to doubt that the danger to an officer is far greater in the case of the extended exposure which follows the taking of a suspect into custody and transporting him to the police station than in the case of the relatively fleeting contact resulting from the typical *Terry*-type stop" (414 U.S. at 234–235). This distinction was an adequate basis for treating all custodial arrests alike for purposes of justifying a full search. Instead of litigating in each case the issue of whether there was an adequate reason establishing the authority for a "full" search, the Court held that the lawful arrest alone established the authority to search. Accordingly, in the case of a lawful custodial arrest, a "full" search is not only an exception to the warrant requirement, but is also "reasonable" under the Fourth Amendment.

In *New York v. Belton* (453 U.S. 454; 1981), the Supreme Court went one step further, upholding a warrantless search of the passenger compartment of an automobile and a "container" found within the passenger compartment as a contemporaneous search incident to a lawful arrest, the term "container" denoting any object, whether open or closed, capable of holding another object and included, among others, glove compartments, consoles, luggage, boxes, bags, and clothing. Because the item—in this case, a jacket—was located inside the passenger compartment of the vehicle, it was "within the arrestee's immediate control." As in *Robinson,* it mattered not that the police had no probable cause or reasonable suspicion to search the luggage and other containers in the interior of the automobile. The lawful arrest alone created a situation justifying the contemporaneous search of the arrestee and the immediately surrounding area.

*Chimel, Robinson,* and *Belton,* read together, stand for the proposition that, incident to a lawful arrest, police officers have unlimited authority to conduct searches of the persons being arrested. A search incident to a lawful arrest is not limited to a "pat down" of the suspect's outer clothing. Additionally, officers have wide latitude to conduct searches of any place within the "grabbing area" of the arrestee, and to search and seize personal effects (a crumpled cigarette package in a jacket, for example) that are not necessary to protect the officer from harm and cannot be used to aid in an escape from custody. Moreover, the officers need not have probable cause, reasonable suspicion, or fear that weapons or evidence would be found upon the suspect or in the immediate area.

Obviously, the justices have been reluctant to constrain police activity to any discernible degree in this exception to the warrant requirement. And the more recent Rehnquist Court has demonstrated a willingness to extend even further the permissible scope of searches incident to lawful arrests. For example, when police making an arrest have reason to believe that someone else may be present in another part of the house and that such person may pose a danger to them, police may make a "protective sweep" for safety purposes (*Maryland v. Buie,* 494 U.S. 325; 1990). Probable cause is not required.

## Plain View

The Supreme Court has also recognized a "plain view" exception to the warrant requirement. Announced in *Coolidge v. New Hampshire* (1971), mentioned earlier in a different context, this exception allows a police officer, in certain circumstances and in the absence of a warrant, to seize items that are within his or her sight. Reliance on this exception requires the coalescence of four conditions: (1) a justified intrusion by police; (2) the items must be found in plain view; (3) it must be "immediately apparent" that the items are incriminating; and (4) the discovery must be inadvertent (Wallin 2002, 307–345).

First, the officer must be in a lawful position to observe the evidence; in other words, he or she must have prior justification for the initial intrusion. This prior justification condition may be satisfied in several ways. It may be pursuant to consent, a search incident to a lawful arrest, a search warrant for another object, exigent circumstances, or based on any of the other recognized exceptions to the warrant requirement. A typical example here is a situation in which police have a warrant to search for a specific object in a specific location and, during the course of that search, observe some other object of an incriminating nature. Here, the police had a prior justification for being in the place where such an object was spied.

Second, the evidence must be in plain view. A police officer may not search for objects of an incriminating nature. The officer may, however, seize such objects when in plain view. The plain view exception is thus a justification for a warrantless seizure, not a warrantless search. In explaining this important distinction between searches and seizures, the Supreme Court has observed that the Fourth Amendment prohibition against general searches and general warrants was intended primarily to protect against unjustified intrusions on privacy. But, if an article were already in plain view, neither its observation not its seizure would involve any invasions on privacy (*Horton v. California*, 496 U.S. 128, 133–134; 1990).

Third, it must be "immediately apparent" to the officer that the objects observed may be evidence of a crime, contraband, or otherwise subject to seizure. After attempts by numerous state courts to define the "immediately apparent" condition more precisely, the Supreme Court weighed in on this matter in *Arizona v. Hicks* (480 U.S. 321; 1987). Here, police officers had justification for being in a residence: They were searching for an individual who had fired bullets through the floor of his apartment, striking and injuring a man in the apartment below. One of the officers noticed—in plain view—expensive stereo equipment that seemed "out of place" in the otherwise seedy apartment. Guessing that the stereo equipment was stolen, the officer recorded the equipment's serial numbers. To access the serial numbers, however, the officer had to move the equipment away from the wall. After reporting the serial numbers, the officer's initial suspicions were confirmed: The stereo equipment had been taken in an armed robbery. Accordingly, the officer seized the stolen equipment. Other equipment was seized later, pursuant to a valid warrant. The trial court suppressed the stereo equipment, concluding that the recording of the serial numbers constituted a separate search unrelated to the exigency that validated the entry into the apartment and, therefore, violated the Fourth Amendment. The state court of appeals affirmed the lower court's judgment and the highest court in Arizona denied review.

The Supreme Court unanimously held that the mere recording of the serial numbers did not constitute a search or a seizure; accordingly the Fourth Amendment was not implicated. Six of the justices, however, found that the officer's actions in moving the stereo equipment constituted a search independent of the search that was justified by the circumstances permitting the entry into the apartment; thus, the Fourth Amendment was implicated. Because the movement of the equipment constituted a warrantless search, the movement could only be lawful if it fell within one of the recognized exceptions to the warrant requirement. As to the plain view exception, the first two conditions—prior justification and plain view—were satisfied. But the third condition—that it must be "immediately apparent" that the objects observed may be evidence of a crime, contraband, or otherwise subject to seizure—was unsatisfied. "Immediately apparent," the majority said, meant probable cause. In other words, to be lawfully searched and seized, not only must the item be in plain view, its incriminating character must rise to the level of probable cause. It would be illogical, the opinion announced, "to hold that an object is seizable on lesser grounds, during an unrelated search and seizure, than would have been needed to obtain a warrant for it if it had been known to be on the premises" (480 U.S. at 327). Since the state conceded that the officer had only a reasonable suspicion—a lower standard than probable cause—that the equipment was stolen, the majority concluded that the plain view exception was inapplicable. To summarize *Hicks*: A warrantless search of an item within plain view during a lawful search requires that police have probable cause to believe that the object in question is evidence of a crime or contraband. Without probable cause (with only reasonable suspicion), the movement of the object—even if only a few inches—to obtain serial numbers constitutes an unreasonable search. (Three justices dissented, expressing the view that reasonable suspicion, not probable cause, was sufficient to justify a cursory examination of suspicious items. Furthermore, even if the latter were the standard, the dissenters argued that probable cause was satisfied.)

The fourth condition for the plain view exception is that the discovery must be "inadvertent," which is to say that the officer may not know in advance the location of certain evidence or contraband or go looking for the evidence with the intent to seize it (and use the plain view exception only as a pretext). This condition has been the most controversial of the *Coolidge* four, in part because it was supported by only a plurality and not a majority of the justices in *Coolidge*. Some lower courts thus held that inadvertency was not a requirement of plain view; others interpreted it as binding precedent. *Horton v. California* clarified the matter, stating definitively that inadvertency was not a prerequisite for the plain view exception. In this case, a police officer investigating an armed robbery obtained a warrant to search a suspect's home for property stolen in the robbery. During the course of the search, the officer failed to discover the stolen property specified in the warrant. Nevertheless, he did discover, in plain view, the weapons used in the robbery and other items that had been stolen in a previous robbery. The officer later testified that while conducting the search for the specified items, he was interested in finding other evidence connecting the suspect to the crime. The evidence, therefore, was not discovered inadvertently.

After two state courts denied the accused's request for suppression of the evidence, the U.S. Supreme Court followed suit, holding that there was no requirement that the officer discover evidence in plain view inadvertently, so long as the search and seizure were confined in area and duration by the terms of the warrant. In short, the plain view exception was applicable even if an officer expected in advance to find the objects in plain view. The majority rejected the inadvertency requirement on two grounds. First, the requirement was impermissibly subjective—far too dependent on the state of mind of the officer. Under the Fourth Amendment, the appropriate standard was whether the search and seizure were "objectively reasonable"; the officer's state of mind was irrelevant. Second, rejecting the inadvertency requirement would not grant to the officer the power to conduct searches and seizures beyond what the warrant authorized.

As is clear from *Hicks* and *Horton,* the Court's rulings vis-à-vis the plain view exception to the warrant requirement usually turn on the particular circumstances of each case. Nevertheless, the plain view exception is typically justified when the intrusion is lawful, the object is in plain view, and the police have probable cause to believe—it is "immediately apparent" to them—that the objects in plain view are evidence of a crime or contraband. More-over, so long as the officers stay within the terms of the warrant, they may seize items not mentioned in that warrant if they have an objectively reasonable basis to conclude that such items are evidence of criminal activity or contraband.

## Plain Feel

*Coolidge* and its progeny clarified "plain view" principles. *Minnesota v. Dickerson* (508 U.S. 366; 1993) introduced a corollary principle. The "plain feel" exception authorizes a police officer who is lawfully patting down a suspect's outer clothing (within the boundaries established by *Terry*) to seize any object—to include nonthreatening ones—whose shape or mass makes it immediately apparent as contraband. In *Dickerson,* police officers in a marked squad car observed Timothy Dickerson leaving what they described as a known "crack house." After spotting the police vehicle, Dickerson immediately turned around and began walking in the opposite direction. Based on these supposedly evasive actions, the officers approached Dickerson and executed a "pat down" search for weapons. Although the search did not reveal any weapons, it did reveal a small lump in the pocket of Dickerson's jacket. After examining the object carefully with his fingers, the officer concluded that it was a "brick" of crack cocaine. Upon reaching into Dickerson's pocket, the officer retrieved a small plastic bag of crack cocaine. The suspect was then immediately arrested.

Prior to trial, Dickerson requested the suppression of the crack cocaine. Relying heavily upon *Terry,* a court concluded that because the officers were justified in stopping Dickerson to investigate whether he might be engaged in criminal activity, the subsequent "pat down" search was also justified to ensure that the suspect did not possess a weapon. Then, by analogy of the "plain view" doctrine, the court held that the warrantless seizure of the crack cocaine did not violate the Fourth Amendment. Dickerson was tried and found guilty. The Minnesota Court of Appeals reversed, declining to adopt a "plain feel" exception to the warrant requirement. The Supreme Court of Minnesota affirmed, noting that suspicion developed by way of touch was markedly different than suspicion developed by way of sight. In short, the "plain feel" exception was not analogous to the "plain view" exception. Additionally, even if it were, the search was still unconstitutional because the officer, in making his determination, squeezed, slid, and otherwise manipulated the contents of the pocket, even after the officer knew that Dickerson did not possess any weapon.

Because the officer did not immediately identify the small lump as crack cocaine—but rather came to that conclusion only after squeezing, sliding, and otherwise manipulating the contents of Dickerson's pocket—the U.S. Supreme Court held that the officer had overstepped the "strictly circumscribed" limits of *Terry.* Nevertheless, the *Dickerson* Court embraced a limited "plain feel" exception: Police do not need a warrant to seize nonthreatening contraband if the officer's lawful search is confined to that which is necessary to discover weapons and the object discovered is immediately apparent as contraband. So, had the officer in this case determined that the small lump was contraband during the course of his initial pat down of Dickerson (without having to squeeze, slide, and otherwise manipulate the lump), the seizure would have been justified. *Dickerson* makes clear that once a limited warrantless search for weapons is complete, a second, more intensive, search for evidence of contraband is unconstitutional.

Support for this decision may be found in *Arizona v. Hicks,* discussed earlier in this chapter:

> Just as the *Hicks* Court found that moving an object for closer scrutiny without either the authority of a warrant or some recognized warrantless exception was unconstitutional, the *Dickerson* Court also analogized that a more intense warrantless search and exploratory frisk was equally offensive. In either event, the incremental search was simply unjustified. (Wallin 2002, 317–318)

*Dickerson* is subject to criticism on a number of fronts (Lehmann 1994, 268–273). First, it blurs the bright-line rule of *Terry.* The "stop and frisk" power upheld in *Terry* was based entirely upon safety considerations. A limited protective search was permissible *only* when the officer reasonably suspected that criminal activity was afoot and considered the suspect armed and dangerous. Because of this bright-line rule, officers knew that any incremental search was unlawful. *Dickerson* changed this, justifying an incremental search based on an officer's quick, affirmative judgment as to what he or she feels hidden under a person's outer garments. An officer's reasonable fear of danger—not any notions of criminal culpability of the person being frisked—should be the governing principle in determining the scope of the frisk power. Second, the requisite "immediately apparent" element lacks precision. Courts must somehow determine when the nature of a small object becomes "immediately apparent" to the officer as contraband.

While a police officer can generally determine immediately whether an item in plain view is contraband, an officer conducting a "pat down" in most cases cannot be so sure, particularly when the item is an especially small one that is never seen and only felt through an outer garment. Moreover, the essential conditions that justify a "plain view" exception to the warrant requirement cannot justify an exception for "plain feel" searches. The touching of an object, the identity of which is concealed by a covering, cannot conclusively establish an object's identity or criminal nature. Knowledge concerning an object by merely feeling it through an exterior covering is necessarily based on the police officer's expert opinion (Lehmann 1994, 270–271).

To summarize, the "plain feel" exception is applicable under the following conditions: First, there must be a valid *Terry* stop. The police officer must be reasonably justified in believing that criminal activity is afoot. Second, the officer is justified in conducting a limited, protective search of the outer clothing. The officer must reasonably believe that the individual whose suspicious behavior the officer is investigating at close range is armed and presently dangerous to the officer and others. And third, the object discovered by feel must be immediately apparent to the officer as contraband.

## Exigent Circumstances

There are, to be sure, all types of police emergencies. One type, however, justifies a warrantless, nonconsensual, and forcible entry into a home. Such searches may be conducted in cases "in which an individuating judgment of criminal activity is required but a fast-developing situation precludes resort to a magistrate" (Amsterdam 1974, 359). These "exigent circumstances" may exist if a person's life or safety is threatened; a suspect's escape is imminent; evidence is about to be destroyed or removed; or some other consequence improperly frustrates legitimate law enforcement efforts. As such, some of the exceptions discussed earlier—those to the knock-and-announce rule, for example—and some of the exceptions discussed later may also be categorized as exigent circumstances, for they also require immediate action. Under this doctrine, also known as the "emergency doctrine" and the "necessity doctrine," police must have probable cause at the time of the arrest, search, or seizure, and the circumstances must be so exigent that obtaining a warrant is impracticable. If both conditions are satisfied, law enforcement is excused from the procedural requirements of the Fourth Amendment.

The quintessential exigent circumstance is immediate danger to the life or safety of a person. Because one of the most basic functions of any government is to provide for the security of the individual, when human life or limb is threatened, circumstances may justify a departure from the warrant requirements. The most common types of exigencies in this category include a sick or injured person in need of immediate aid; a fire, burglary, or robbery in progress; and a homicide or crime scene. In *Mincey v. Arizona* (437 U.S. 385, 392; 1978), for example, the Supreme Court held that when police come upon a homicide scene, they may make a prompt warrantless search of the area to see if there are other victims or if the killer is still on the premises. The need to protect life or avoid serious injury to self or others provides justification for what would otherwise be an illegal search.

A more frequent type of exigent circumstance is the destruction or removal of contraband. If a law enforcement officer has probable cause to believe that destructible evidence is present *and* an objectively reasonable belief that such evidence might be destroyed should the officer delay in the interest of obtaining a warrant, exigent circumstances exist. A stock example in this category is illegal drugs, which can be easily destroyed. Furthermore, law enforcement officers may prohibit an individual from entering his or her residence alone while a warrant is being procured if they have probable cause to believe that contraband is present and that it could be destroyed (*Illinois v. McArthur*, 531 U.S. 236; 2001).

A third danger satisfying the exigent circumstances doctrine is the imminent escape of a suspect. Courts have long held that exigent circumstances exist if police officers are in "hot pursuit" of a fugitive. The Supreme Court first recognized this exception to the warrant requirement in *Warden v. Hayden* (387 U.S. 204; 1967). Hot pursuit is commonly defined as the immediate pursuit of a suspect from the location of a crime involving some sort of chase. Typically, a warrantless entry based on "hot pursuit" requires four elements: probable cause (to make the arrest), an attempted arrest (in some public location), flight (from that location to a home or other private place), and chase (pursuit by a police officer). The location or length of the chase is not relevant: "It need not be an extended hue and cry in and about the public streets; the fact that [the] pursuit end[s] almost as soon as it beg[ins] does not render it any less a hot pursuit" (*United States v. Santana*, 427 U.S. 38, 43; 1976).

Consider the following scenario. After an undercover agent has sold cocaine to a suspect, police officers approach the suspect, who is standing in the doorway of her residence. Upon seeing the officers, the suspect retreats quickly into the vestibule of her house, where she is apprehended. While trying to escape, the suspect drops envelopes containing heroin. Those envelopes are later recovered by the arresting officers, who do not have a warrant— either for the arrest or the search. In this case, however, the failure to obtain the warrant did not necessitate the exclusion of the evidence because the suspect's rapid retreat from the approaching police officers satisfied the exigent circumstances exception to the warrant requirement. Since there was a need to act quickly to prevent the escape (and the possible destruction of evidence), there was "hot pursuit" (even though the attempted arrest, flight, and chase all took place within a small area and over a brief period). As such, the circumstances of haste rendered the obtaining of a search warrant impracticable.

A second example—involving a warrantless search based on "hot pursuit" that was disallowed—demonstrates the elasticity of the Supreme Court's pronouncements in this area. In *Welsh v. Wisconsin* (1984), referenced earlier, a witness observed an "inebriated or very sick" driver abandon his vehicle on the side of the road after swerving out of control. After checking the car's registration, the police proceeded to the home of the owner of the vehicle (who happened also to be the driver). When a family member opened the door to the home, the police, without a warrant, entered and found the driver lying naked in bed. The suspect was then arrested for driving a motor vehicle under the influence of alcohol and taken to the police station, where he refused to submit to a breath analysis test. Under Wisconsin law, a refusal to take a breath analysis test was reasonable only if the arrest was not lawful. The trial court concluded that the arrest was lawful; therefore, the breath analysis test was reasonable. The Wisconsin Court of Appeals reversed, finding that while the officers had probable cause to arrest the suspect, they had not established the existence of exigent circumstances to justify the warrantless arrest of an individual in his home. The Wisconsin Supreme Court then reversed the appellate court, whereupon the suspect requested review from the U.S. Supreme Court.

For purposes of a warrantless home arrest, as was the case in *Welsh,* the justices recognized that an important factor to be considered when determining whether any exigency existed was the gravity of the underlying offense for which the arrest was made. "[A]pplication of the exigent-circumstances exception in the context of a home entry should rarely be sanctioned when there is probable cause to believe that only a minor offense, such as the kind at issue in this case, has been committed" (466 U.S. at 753). In other words, exigent circumstances may differ from case to case based on the severity of the alleged crime. Here, because the state had classified the crime as a civil, nonjailable traffic offense, thus indicating a low interest in an arrest, the standard justifications for exigent circumstances were either not present or not applicable. No person's life or safety was threatened. The offender had already abandoned his car at the scene of the accident and arrived at his home. The suspect's escape was not imminent. Though the state argued "hot pursuit," the justices noted that a warrantless home arrest for a civil, nonjailable traffic offense was not justified by the "hot pursuit" doctrine where there was no "immediate or continuous pursuit" of the offender from the scene of the crime. Finally, while it was true that evidence of the offender's blood-alcohol level might have dissipated while the police obtained a warrant, that fact alone could not justify a warrantless home arrest, especially for a noncriminal traffic offense for which no imprisonment was possible.

*Welsh* clearly indicates that "an important factor to be considered when determining whether any exigency exists is the gravity of the underlying offense for which the arrest is being made" (466 U.S. at 753). In other words, the courts are more likely to find exigent circumstances when the crime in question is more serious.

### Automobile Searches

Within a generation of the first mass production of combustible engine automobiles, the Supreme Court created an exception to the warrant requirement for automobile searches. The initial reason for the exception was the inherent mobility of automobiles, which made obtaining a warrant to search one often impracticable. In *Carroll v. United States* (267 U.S. 132; 1925), a prohibition-era case, the justices distinguished an automobile search—in this instance, the search of an automobile engaged in the illegal transportation of liquor—from searches of "persons, houses, papers, and effects" specifically protected by the Fourth Amendment. The justices recognized a necessary difference between a search of a store, dwelling house, or other structure in respect of which a proper official warrant readily may be obtained, and a search of a ship, motor boat, wagon, or automobile, for contraband goods, "where it is not practicable to secure a warrant because the vehicle can be quickly moved out of the locality or jurisdiction in which the warrant must be sought" (267 U.S. at 154). Presumably, if obtaining a warrant is practicable, the exception does not apply. The exigency that gives rise to the warrantless search is the likely disappearance of the vehicle. (Half a century after *Carroll,* the justices declared impermissible a warrantless search of a parked automobile. Because the vehicle was not in motion at the time, immediate action was not required. Thus, police may not conduct a warrantless search of an automobile just because the automobile is capable of moving. To justify a warrantless search, the vehicle must be in motion.)

*Carroll* then turned its attention to the circumstances under which such a warrantless search could be made, stipulating that the "automobile exception" did not grant unfettered authority to law enforcement to search vehicles for any reason. "It would be intolerable and unreasonable if [police] were authorized to stop every automobile on the chance of finding [contraband] and thus subject all persons lawfully using the highways to the inconvenience and indignity of such a search" (267 U.S. at 153–154). Rather, vehicles may be searched without warrants only if the officer conducting the search has probable cause to believe that the vehicle is carrying illegal goods. The search of the automobile need not take place immediately. A number of decisions have upheld warrantless searches that were not conducted contemporaneously with the stop. The justification to conduct a search "does not vanish once the car has been immobilized" (*Michigan v. Thomas,* 458 U.S. 259, 261; 1982). As a general rule, police may conduct vehicle searches even after the vehicle has been immobilized, as long as they could have lawfully done so (had probable cause to do so) at some point in the process. It is not uncommon for authorities to remove a vehicle to a police station before conducting the search, perhaps because darkness or a hostile crowd prohibits a thorough search at the scene, stop, or arrest.

By the end of the 1970's, the Supreme Court had enunciated a second reason for distinguishing between automobiles and other private property—a diminished expectation of privacy that surrounds the automobile based on its "configuration, use, and regulation" (*Chambers v. Maroney*, 399 U.S. 42; 1970; *United States v. Chadwick*, 433 U.S. 1; 1977; *Arkansas v. Sanders*, 442 U.S. 753, 761; 1979). "One has a lesser expectation of privacy in a motor vehicle," the *Chadwick* Court announced, "because its function is transportation and it seldom serves as one's residence or as the repository of personal effects. . . . It travels public thoroughfares where both its occupants and its contents are in plain view" (433 U.S. at 12).

While this reduced expectation of privacy rationale has obviously broadened the power of police to conduct warrantless searches of automobiles, courts have remained firm in insisting that most automobile stops be based on some probable cause or reasonable suspicion of a traffic or safety violation. Random stops of motorists to check drivers' licenses and vehicle registrations are unconstitutional if they are not supported by probable cause or reasonable suspicion (*Delaware v. Prouse*, 440 U.S. 648; 1978). By contrast, in *Michigan Department of State Police v. Sitz* (496 U.S. 444; 1990), the justices upheld fixed highway sobriety checkpoints, even in the absence of any individualized suspicion, because of the magnitude of the drunken driving problem; the minimal intrusion resulting from the checkpoint (merely visual observation for signs of intoxication); the direct relation of the checkpoints to roadway safety; and the randomness of the stops. Such checkpoints are indistinguishable for constitutional purposes from border checkpoints, the majority said. Fixed road checkpoints staffed by law enforcement officers with drug-sniffing dogs, however, violate the Fourth Amendment. The Rehnquist Court (although not Chief Justice Rehnquist) drew the line on checkpoints designed primarily to interdict unlawful drugs in *City of Indianapolis v. Edmond* (531 U.S. 32; 2000). Because the checkpoints were set up to detect ordinary criminal activity (as opposed to promote roadway safety), individual suspicion was required.

A related issue, no less controversial, is what police may do after they have lawfully stopped a vehicle. Generally speaking, the Supreme Court has favored the interests of law enforcement in these situations. As discussed earlier, police may, with probable cause, conduct a "full" search of a driver arrested for a traffic offense (*United States v. Robinson*). This ruling was extended in *Maryland v. Wilson* (519 U.S. 409; 1997), which allowed police to order both driver and passengers out of the vehicle and to frisk them all. In both cases, the justices focused on the need for law enforcement officers to protect themselves. Police may also search the areas within the vehicle that are in plain view.

In *some* circumstances, automobiles may be searched without a warrant. In *some* circumstances, persons in automobiles may be searched without a warrant. And in *some* circumstances, closed containers in automobiles may be searched without a warrant. *United States v. Chadwick* (1977) and *Arkansas v. Sanders* (1979) involved warrantless searches of pieces of luggage that just happened to be in the trunks of automobiles. In both cases, police had probable cause to believe that the "double-locked footlocker" (in *Chadwick*) and the suitcase (in *Sanders*) contained marijuana. In both cases, police waited until the items were placed in an automobile to conduct the search. And in both cases, the search was disallowed, the justices stressing the heightened privacy expectations in personal luggage, as opposed to the decreased privacy expectations in the automobile itself. In other words, the fact that the luggage just happened to be in an automobile did not diminish the owners' expectations of privacy. This rule would presumably keep police from waiting until a piece of luggage or other closed container or property for which police would ordinarily need a warrant was placed in an automobile at which time police could invoke the automobile exception and bypass the warrant to conduct the search.

Just a few years later, however, *United States v. Ross* (456 U.S. 798; 1982) held that if police have probable cause to search a vehicle lawfully stopped, they may search any portion of the vehicle in which such items might be located. This included any closed containers and packages found inside the car. This decision created what some have called the "*Ross* anomaly": With probable cause to search a closed container that just happened to be in an automobile (as in *Chadwick* and *Sanders*), a warrant was required. Yet if police had probable cause to search an entire automobile, no warrant would be needed to search a closed container that just happened to be in the automobile (as in *Ross*). "Police who have reason to search a car may coincidentally come across a container, just as police who have reason to search a container may coincidentally find it in a car" (Mason and Stephenson 2005, 403). The first can be done without a warrant; the second demands one.

The "*Ross* anomaly" was resolved in *California v. Acevedo* (500 U.S. 565; 1991), which demonstrates well the extent of the automobile exception. Law enforcement officers witnessed Charles Acevedo leave an apartment where officers knew drugs had been delivered earlier in the day. He was carrying with him a brown paper bag, about the size of a package of marijuana. Acevedo placed the paper bag in the trunk of his vehicle. After he drove off, officers stopped him, opened his trunk, searched the paper bag, and found marijuana. Acevedo was convicted, but his conviction was reversed on appeal, the state appellate court concluding that while the police had probable cause to suspect the paper bag contained marijuana, the police lacked probable cause to suspect that the vehicle itself contained contraband. Because the probable cause was directed specifically at the paper bag, the case was controlled by *Chadwick* and *Sanders*, not *Ross*. What the officers should have done, the state appellate court said, was seize the bag, but not open it until they had procured a warrant for that purpose. The U.S. Supreme Court reversed; *Ross* trumped *Chadwick* and *Sanders*:

[A] container found after a general search of the automobile and a container found in a car after a limited search for the container are equally easy for the police to store and for the suspect to hide or destroy. . . . [I]t is better to adopt one clear-cut rule to govern automobile searches and eliminate the warrant requirement for closed containers. . . . In other words, the police may search without a warrant if their search is supported by probable cause.

(To clarify, *Belton*, discussed earlier, permitted a warrantless search of a passenger compartment of an automobile and containers within it. That search, however, was allowed as a contemporaneous search incident to a lawful arrest.)

*Wyoming v. Houghton* (526 U.S. 295; 1999) extended *Ross*, holding that if police had probable cause for a warrantless search of a vehicle, they could search *all* personal belongings of *all* passengers in the car that were capable of concealing contraband. The relevant factor was whether the personal belongings could conceal the object of the search, without qualification as to the ownership of the belongings.

**Motor Homes.** Generally speaking, courts treat mobile homes more like automobiles than residences. Because such homes are often "readily mobile," the automobile exception applies to them also. The justices have yet to address the question of whether the exception applies to a mobile home that is not "readily mobile."

## Administrative Searches/"Special Needs" Exception

Arguably the most controversial exception to the warrant requirement of the Fourth Amendment, at least in recent years, has been in the area of "administrative searches." Housing, health, safety, or other inspections or searches conducted as part of a general regulatory scheme, often but not exclusively to ensure compliance with laws and regulations, are called administrative searches. One of the fundamental principles of administrative searches is that they may not be used as a pretext to search for evidence of criminal activity. Because these searches are justified by "special needs" beyond the normal need for law enforcement, they do not merit the same constitutional protections. In the last twenty years, courts have broadened the "special needs" doctrine to permit a variety of warrantless, suspicionless searches, to include mandatory drug testing of certain segments of the population. A brief history of the development of the administrative search exception reveals its justification.

In *Frank v. Maryland* (359 U.S. 360, 365; 1959), a narrowly divided Supreme Court upheld a warrantless home inspection conducted by a city health inspector and aimed at enforcing health regulations. In that case, the justices, after evaluating the history of the constitutional protection against the official invasion of the home, concluded that its primary purpose was to confer upon the citizen "a right to resist unauthorized entry which had as its design the securing of information to fortify the coercive power of the state against the individual, information which may be used to effect a further deprivation of life or liberty or property." In other words, only those searches aimed at obtaining evidence of criminal activity required a judicially issued search warrant; administrative searches, because they were not aimed at uncovering such evidence, did not require a warrant. The four dissenting justices rejected the majority's narrow interpretation of the Fourth Amendment, asserting instead that it was designed to protect the citizen against uncontrolled invasions of privacy; and dismissed its arbitrary dichotomy between criminal and civil searches:

> History shows that all officers tend to be officious. . . . One invasion of privacy by an official of government can be as oppressive as another. . . . It would seem that the public interest in protecting privacy is equally as great in one case as another (359 U.S. at 382)

The *Frank* doctrine—administrative searches fall outside the scope of the Fourth Amendment—was soon overruled in *Camara v. Municipal Court* (387 U.S. 523, 536–537; 1967). Here, the justices held that a citizen possessed a constitutional right to insist that home inspectors procure a warrant prior to conducting a health or safety inspection. The *Camara* Court was careful to point out, however, that administrative searches, because they were conducted as part of a general regulatory scheme and not to uncover evidence of criminal activity, benefited from a more relaxed Fourth Amendment standard. Unlike searches pursuant to a criminal investigation, which had to be based on probable cause, administrative searches required only "reasonableness," to be determined by balancing the intrusion on the individual's Fourth Amendment interests against the promotion of a legitimate governmental interest. So long as the intrusion was limited and the state's objective was a "special need" outside normal law enforcement (to prevent the unintentional development of conditions that were hazardous to public health and safety, for example), the reasonableness standard was satisfied.

From *Camara* emerged a long line of cases dealing with administrative searches. Under this category, the Supreme Court upheld warrantless searches of heavily regulated businesses by health, safety, and fire inspectors; warrantless searches of prison cells (not even limited by the reasonableness standard); a warrantless search of a high school student's personal belongings and locker by a public school official (*New Jersey v. T. L. O.*, 469 U.S. 325; 1985); a warrantless search of a public employee's office by his supervisor (*O'Connor v. Ortega*, 480 U.S. 709; 1987); a warrantless search of an automobile junkyard (*New York v. Burger*, 482 U.S. 691; 1987); a warrantless search of a probationer's home (*Griffin v. Wisconsin*, 483 U.S. 868; 1987); blanket suspicionless searches where the risk to public safety was great (such as in airports); and drug testing among certain classes of public employees and certain groups of public school students. In each of these instances (save the warrantless search of prison cells), the probable cause requirement was replaced with the less stringent reasonableness standard that weighed the government's regulatory interest against the individual's privacy interest. Lest one conclude that all warrantless administrative searches are reasonable, in at least two instances the justices came down in favor of the individual. The first involved random, suspicionless drug testing of candidates for political office. The second involved a state hospital program that tested pregnant women for drug use and reported the results of the tests to police for criminal prosecution.

**Mandatory Drug Testing of Public Employees.**   The Supreme Court's decisions with respect to mandatory drug testing—and the disagreements among the justices therein—demonstrate well the inherent difficulties in administrative searches based on "special needs."

In the mid-1980's, numerous federal agencies, encouraged by the (President Ronald) Reagan administration (1981–1989), developed and implemented plans for assuring that government employees were drug-free. The Federal Railroad Administration (FRA) adopted regulations requiring that drug and alcohol tests be administered to railroad workers involved in serious train accidents. When those regulations were challenged as violative of the Fourth Amendment, the district court sustained them. The Court of Appeals for the Ninth Circuit, however, found that the regulations were unconstitutional because they were not based on any individualized suspicion, a standard prerequisite for a legitimate search:

> Accidents, incidents or rule violations, by themselves, do not create reasonable grounds for suspecting that tests will demonstrate alcohol or drug impairment in any one railroad employee, much less an entire train crew. (*Railway Labor Executives' Association v. Burnley,* 839 F.2d 575, 587; [9th Cir. 1988])

Though conceding that the drug and alcohol testing amounted to a search under the Fourth Amendment and that privacy interests were implicated by them, the Supreme Court reversed in *Skinner v. Railway Labor Executives' Association* (489 U.S. 602; 1989). Applying *Camara*'s balancing test, the seven-person majority, in an opinion by Justice Anthony Kennedy, reasoned that the regulation of railroad employees to ensure safety constituted a "special need" beyond normal law enforcement, justifying the departure from the usual warrant and probable cause requirements. In doing so, the majority affirmed that individualized suspicion was not a prerequisite for all drug testing. Whatever individual privacy interests were implicated were outweighed by the compelling governmental interest in ensuring the safety of the traveling public and of the railway employees themselves.

In a caustic dissent, Justice Thurgood Marshall, joined by Justice William Brennan, criticized the majority for taking a giant step toward "reading the probable cause requirement out of the Fourth Amendment" (489 U.S. at 636). He observed that, by allowing a warrantless, suspicionless search of a "person," the Court had completed the cycle, displacing the probable cause standard in each of the four categories specifically enumerated in the Fourth Amendment: searches or persons (*Skinner*), houses (*Griffin*); papers (*Ortega*); and effects (*T. L. O.*). Obviously, the dissenters would have preferred that the Court reaffirm the indispensability of the probable cause requirement and disallow the search.

Though not a companion case, *National Treasury Employees Union v. Von Raab* (489 U.S. 656; 1989) was decided on the same day as *Skinner*. *National Treasury* was a challenge to a drug-screening program for employees of the United States Customs Service, which has as its primary enforcement mission the interdiction and seizure of illegal drugs smuggled into the country. The program mandated, among other things, that those applying for positions as custom's inspectors, whether directly involved in drug interdiction or who are required to carry a firearm, must submit to drug screening. The testing was limited to personnel seeking positions as custom's inspectors. Those who failed the test were denied positions, but not subjected to criminal investigation. When the program was challenged under the Fourth Amendment, the district court enjoined it. The Court of Appeals for the Fifth Circuit reversed, noting that the program was reasonable in light of its limited scope and the agency's strong interest in detecting and preventing drug use among certain employees.

As in *Skinner,* and for the same reasons, the Supreme Court sustained the drug-screening program. The urine tests were most assuredly searches within the meaning of the Fourth Amendment. Individual privacy interests were implicated. And the Fourth Amendment generally required that searches be supported by a warrant based on probable cause. Nevertheless, not all searches had to be supported by a warrant, probable cause, or individualized suspicion; those principles, though often required, were not *always* required. Because the search was not part of a criminal investigation, probable cause was optional. Instead, reasonableness, determined by a balancing of interests, was the touchstone. Standard affirmed, the five-person majority weighed the government's interest against the individual's privacy interest. Agents of the Customs Service were the nation's "first line of defense" against drugs entering the country; as such, the government had a compelling interest in ensuring that they were physically fit and had unimpeachable integrity and judgment. Both body and mind were adversely affected by illegal drugs, and "[t]he national interest in self protection could be irreparably damaged if those charged with safeguarding [the border] were, because of their own drug use, unsympathetic to their mission of interdicting narcotics" (489 U.S. at 670).

When weighed against the interference with individual privacy, the majority reasoned that the screening program was not overly intrusive; even if it were, some public employees, like Customs Service agents, had diminished expectations of privacy. Whatever individual privacy interests were implicated came up short when measured against the compelling governmental interest in ensuring the drug-free Customs Service work force.

Also as in *Skinner,* and for the same reasons, Justices Marshall and Brennan dissented. This time, however, there were two other dissenters. Justice Antonin Scalia, in an opinion joined by Justice John Paul Stevens, accepted the use of the reasonableness test, but concluded that, due to the absence of any evidence of a drug abuse problem among Customs Service agents, there was no justification for the program. He contrasted this program with the one upheld in *Skinner.* In *Skinner,* the search was justified because it was well known and documented that railway workers had drinking problems; but in *National Treasury,* no such evidence existed. Even the Commissioner of the Customs Service had testified that the agents were largely drug-free. Justice Scalia dismissed the drug screening program as nothing more than a symbolic gesture aimed at demonstrating to the attentive citizenry that its government was serious about the "war on drugs."

The vote in *Skinner* was seven to two. The vote in *National Treasury* was five to four. In both, seven of the nine justices agreed that the reasonableness test was the appropriate standard for administrative searches based on special needs. The presence of four dissenters in the Customs Service case, however, indicated that widespread mandatory drug testing might be constitutionally suspect, and especially so if the only justification were symbolic.

When the state of Georgia demanded that candidates for designated state public offices (including judgeships) certify that they were drug-free, the justices drew the line. There was no evidence of a drug problem among the state's elected officials. Moreover, most elected officials did not perform high-risk, safety-sensitive tasks (as in *Skinner*), nor were they directly involved in drug interdiction efforts (as in *National Treasury*). Where such risks were present, Justice Ruth Bader Ginsburg said for an eight-member majority, blanket suspicionless searches appropriately calibrated were reasonable; just not here. (Chief Justice Rehnquist was the lone dissenter.) "However well-meant, [the drug test] diminishes personal privacy for a symbol's sake" (*Chandler v. Miller,* 520 U.S. 305, 322; 1997).

It was not enough, the Court said, to compel a search of this sort and of these people solely for "public image" considerations (to be able to say that the state's candidates for public office were "drug-free"). Whatever obvious differences existed between elected officials on the one hand and railway workers and customs agents on the other, this search may have hit "close to home" for the justices. After all, if a state could require candidates for judgeships to submit to a drug test, arguably Congress could require federal judges, even justices, to do so.

**Mandatory Drug Testing of Public School Students.** For decades, the Supreme Court has attempted to reconcile the constitutional rights of public school students with the government's interest in promoting a safe learning environment. One of the more commonly repeated pronouncements on this topic came in *Tinker v. Des Moines Independent School District* (393 U.S. 503, 521; 1969): Students do not "shed their constitutional rights . . . at the schoolhouse gate." The *Tinker* majority was quick to point out, however, that public school authorities might have more latitude to infringe upon individual liberties where it could be demonstrated that the exercise of those liberties substantially interfered with the operations of the school or disrupted the learning environment. It would thus be inaccurate to deduce from *Tinker* that public school students retained the same degree of liberties within the schoolhouse gate as they possessed on the other side of that gate. The justices confirmed as much in a Fourth Amendment context in *New Jersey v. T. L. O.* (1985), holding that the legality of searches executed by public school officials should be assessed under a standard less exacting than probable cause because of the "special needs" of maintaining an environment conducive to learning. In lieu of probable cause, the justices concluded that the reasonableness standard was appropriate for determining the legality of searches conducted by public school officials.

The *T. L. O.* Court left the question of whether individualized suspicion was a prerequisite of the reasonableness standard unanswered. (It did so, no doubt, because the search in *T. L. O.* was based on individualized suspicion.)

*Skinner* and *National Treasury,* however, answered that question in the negative, at least for certain public employees: Individualized suspicion was not an indispensable element of the reasonableness standard. Taking a cue from *Skinner* and *National Treasury,* numerous public schools soon initiated random, suspicionless drug testing for certain school students. The first challenge to these policies to reach the high Court dealt with a mandatory drug testing for student athletes in *Vernonia School District v. Acton* (515 U.S. 646; 1995).

When teachers and school officials in Vernonia, Oregon, noticed a spike in drug use and disciplinary problems in the late 1980s, they assumed that student athletes were, at least in part, responsible for it. As a result, the school board adopted a compulsory drug-testing policy for all student athletes. At the beginning of each playing season, every student athlete was tested; additionally, throughout the season, 10 percent of student athletes were randomly tested each week. James Acton, a seventh grader, wanted to play football, but his parents refused to consent to the drug testing. The Actons then sued the school district. After the district court dismissed the suit, the Court of Appeals for the Ninth Circuit struck down the policy as violative of the Fourth Amendment.

After acknowledging that the drug testing constituted a search subject to the demands of the Fourth Amendment, the Supreme Court, in almost perfunctory fashion, found that the scheme fit squarely within the "special needs" analysis. Accordingly, neither warrant nor individualized suspicion was required as long as the search was a reasonable one. To determine reasonableness, the six-member majority first considered the individual privacy interests of the students, concluding that unemancipated minors and public

school students, because they were in the temporary custody of
the state as "schoolmaster," had a lesser expectation of privacy
than did adults. Moreover, those expectations were even less for
student athletes:

> School sports are not for the bashful. They require "suiting up" before
> each practice or event, and showering and changing afterwards. Public
> school locker rooms ... are not notable for the privacy they af-
> ford.... No individual dressing rooms are provided; shower heads are
> lined up along a wall, unseparated by any sort of partition or curtain;
> not even all the toilet stalls have doors.... By choosing to "go out for
> the team," they [school athletes] voluntarily subject themselves to a
> degree of regulation even higher than that imposed on students gener-
> ally. (515 U.S. at 657)

The justices then considered the government's interest in the
drug testing, concluding that the nature of the concern was "important—indeed perhaps compelling." Having balanced the intrusion
on the individual's Fourth Amendment privacy interests against the
promotion of a legitimate governmental interest, the Court held the
policy to be reasonable and, therefore, constitutional. This marked
the third time the justices had sustained a random, suspicionless
drug-testing program; it was, however, the first outside of the public employment context. While the holdings of *Skinner* and *National Treasury* were extended to public school student athletes, the
Court demonstrated some apprehension in doing so: "We caution
against the assumption that suspicionless drug testing will readily
pass constitutional muster" (515 U.S. 665).

Justices Stevens (who supported the program in *Skinner*, but opposed the program in *National Treasury*), Sandra O'Connor (who
supported the suspicionless drug-testing programs in both cases),
and David Souter (who had joined the Court since *Skinner* and *National Treasury*) dissented. They found the policy unreasonable for
three reasons: First, there was no basis for concluding that a vigor-

ous *suspicion-based* testing would be ineffectual. Second, there was no evidence at all of a drug problem at the actual school attended by James Acton. And third, the choice of student athletes as the class to subject to suspicionless testing was unreasonable. If the school district were really concerned about the rise in drug-related disorders and disruptions of the learning process, a far more reasonable choice would have been to test those students with some demonstrated drug-related disorder or those who had been involved in disciplinary matters. In sum, no justifiable reason existed to test every student athlete in the entire school district for drugs.

It is worth noting that Justice Scalia, who had voted to disallow the drug-testing program in *National Treasury* six years earlier, announced the opinion in *Vernonia*. Central to his position here (and perhaps to others in the majority) was the fact that this policy dealt with children temporarily entrusted to the care of the state. It is, therefore, highly questionable if such a policy would be upheld outside of the public school context. For example, the government would probably not be allowed to test all persons entering or leaving known drug-ridden neighborhoods, even though the need to fight the scourge of drugs provides a fairly compelling government interest.

The Supreme Court extended the *Vernonia* holding seven years later in *Board of Education of Independent School District No. 92 of Pottawatomie County v. Earls* (536 U.S. 822; 2002), where it upheld a public school policy that required suspicionless drug testing of all students who participated in any extracurricular activity. This case will be discussed in Chapter Four.

**"Voluntary" Drug Testing in Hospitals.** In 2001, the Supreme Court held that a state hospital could not test pregnant women to obtain evidence of cocaine use for law enforcement purposes if the pregnant women did not consent to the procedure with full knowledge of the purpose for the test. *Ferguson v. City of Charleston* (532 U.S. 67; 2001) will be discussed in Chapter Four.

**Warrantless Drug Testing and "Special Needs."**   As is obvious from the above discussion, warrantless searches based on the "special needs" exception are heavily context specific. The justices have, with great intention, refrained from making bold pronouncements in this area. Each of the cases decided by the high Court is justified on independent grounds. Sometimes a warrantless, suspicionless search is reasonable; sometimes it is not. The Court's decisions rely to a large extent on the facts and circumstances of each particular case. The Court has disallowed suspicionless drug testing when designed to accomplish symbolic purposes or achieve law enforcement ends; yet the same Court has been quite accommodating of suspicionless drug testing in public schools (even if widespread) and when supported by legitimate, occupationally specific concerns. The Court has struck down suspicionless drug testing when the nature of the privacy intrusion was great; and upheld it when the nature of the privacy intrusion was limited. There is much disagreement among the justices on this topic. Their disagreements, however, elucidate well the difficulties inherent in balancing competing constitutional claims. The "special needs" exception is more complicated than most.

## Other Exceptions to the Warrant Requirement

There are a number of other exceptions to the warrant requirement. Because these exceptions are less controversial and much less complicated, they are addressed rather perfunctorily.

**Container Searches.**   When police have reasonable suspicion to believe that evidence of criminal activity is located within a movable container—a suitcase, a package, or a safe, for example—they may seize the container to prevent its use (in the case of weapons) or its disappearance or destruction (in the case of contraband). *United States v. Place* (1983), discussed earlier, held that the Fourth Amendment did not prohibit police from temporarily detaining personal luggage for exposure to a trained narcotics detection dog as long as police had reason to believe that the traveler was carrying luggage that contained narcotics. The mobility of the luggage justified its temporary detention.

As a general rule, though, while police may seize the container without a warrant, they may not search the container without a warrant. (In *Place,* the justices ruled that subjecting the luggage to a "sniff test" by a well-trained narcotics detection dog did not constitute a search within the meaning of the Fourth Amendment. So, while a seizure had occurred, a search had not occurred. And because the seizure was reasonable, the Fourth Amendment was not violated.) The Supreme Court has created a number of exceptions to this general rule. A warrant is not required for searches (1) of containers "within the immediate control" or "grabbing area" of an arrestee (*Belton*); (2) of containers whose illicit contents are in plain view (*Sanders*); (3) of containers whose illicit contents are immediately apparent by plain feel (*Dickerson*); (4) of containers found in automobiles lawfully stopped (*Acevedo*); and (5) of abandoned containers (*Abel v. United States,* 362 U.S. 217; 1960).

**Inventory Searches.**    To substantiate a warrantless inventory search of personal property, two conditions must be satisfied. First, the property must be lawfully in police custody. Second, the search must be conducted according to standardized criteria or established routine. Permitting these inventory searches accomplishes three purposes: protecting an owner's property while it is in police custody; insuring the police against possible false claims of lost, stolen, or vandalized property; and protecting the police from danger. The legitimate governmental interests served by these searches outweigh the individual's countervailing privacy interests in the contents of the personal property. Courts have repeatedly noted that standardized criteria or an established routine is required in order to prevent police from using the inventory search as a ploy "for a general rummaging . . . to discover incriminating evidence" (*Florida v. Wells*, 495 U.S. 1, 4; 1990). Accordingly, the criteria governing inventory searches should be designed to produce the desired result—an inventory of the contents of the personal property in lawful possession of police. Within these general criteria, police may exercise discretion.

A police officer may be allowed sufficient latitude to determine whether a particular container should or should not be opened in light of the nature of the search and characteristics of the container itself. Thus, while policies of opening all containers or of opening no containers are unquestionably permissible, it would be equally permissible, for example, to allow the opening of closed containers where the officers are unable to determine the content by examining the exterior of the container. The allowance of the exercise of judgment based on concerns related to the purposes of an inventory search does not violate the Fourth Amendment. Police may not conduct warrantless inventory searches for investigatory purposes. If, however, during the course of a valid inventory search (one done for inventory purposes), police discover evidence of a crime exposed to plain view, the evidence may be seized.

**Airport Searches.**   Warrantless security searches conducted by Transportation Safety Administration (TSA) or other officials at airports are permissible because the purpose of such searches is not to uncover evidence of criminal activity, but to deter would-be hijackers. One of the many lessons of September 11, 2001, was that a hijacked plane can become a weapon of mass destruction. Once a plane is hijacked, the opportunities to prevent the potentially grave danger have dissipated. As such, deterrence must begin prior to boarding the plane. Lower courts are divided on where and when a warrantless search may occur within the airport. For example, the U.S. Court of Appeals for the Fifth Circuit upheld a warrantless search that took place in an airport lounge area (*United States v. Moreno*, 475 F.2d 44, 50, [5th Cir. 1973]).

Relying on the rationale of *Terry,* the judges held that the police officer reasonably concluded that, based upon the suspect's "nervousness, coupled with the bulge in his coat pocket and the fact that he had just purchased an airline ticket and headed in the direction of the airline gate," the suspect might pose an air piracy threat. To wait until he stepped onto the plane invited potential tragedy. (It is worth noting that this case was decided back when individuals other than actual airline travelers were permitted to pass through the security checkpoint and roam the concourses.) The same court, however, in the same year, drew a distinction between searches of persons "in the general airport area" and those "who actually present themselves for boarding on an air carrier" (*United States v. Skipwith,* 482 F.2d 1272, 1276; [5th Cir. 1973]). While searches of the former were to be evaluated under a case-by-case application of the reasonableness standard, searches of the latter could be based on mere or unsupported suspicion.

Airport security searches have also been sustained on the basis of implied consent. (See "Consent Searches," page 8.) A passenger is not obligated to travel by air; he or she does so voluntarily. Accordingly, numerous courts have held that a prospective airline passenger implicitly consents to a search of his or her person and immediate possessions as a precondition of boarding the aircraft. If, during the search, evidence of criminal activity—even if unrelated to airline terrorism—is discovered, authorities may seize such evidence and detain the traveler. To allow the traveler to leave without punishment in those situations would only serve to encourage individuals planning airplane mischief. Additionally, it is no stretch to conclude that these principles may apply equally in similar contexts—say, for example, the subway system in New York City.

**Searches at Sea.** Whatever limited safeguards are available to stops and searches of automobiles, fewer are available to boats. A warrant is not required. Probable cause is not required. Reasonable, articulable suspicion is not required. Authorized by a statute promulgated by the First Congress (1789–1791), and sustained in *United States v. Villamonte-Marquez* (462 U.S. 579; 1983), customs agents may, without *any* suspicion of wrongdoing, hail and board any vessel on the high seas or in U.S. territorial waters for purposes of examining documentation and conducting safety inspections. Once on board, authorities may visit the vessel's public areas and draw reasonable conclusions from observations of those areas. Those observations may then in turn justify a more intrusive search.

"Important factual differences between vessels located in waters offering ready access to the open sea and automobiles on principal thoroughfares in the border area" give reasons for a less restrictive rule governing searches of vessels at sea (462 U.S. at 588). For example, permanent checkpoints (such as those upheld for vehicles in *Prouse*) would be impractical on the high seas, because vessels can move in any direction at any time; they need not follow established avenues as automobiles must. Additionally, government has a "substantial" interest in enforcing documentation laws "in waters where the need to deter or apprehend drug smugglers is great" (462 U.S. at 593). As such, the "limited" (although not "minimal") intrusion occasioned by boarding the vessel for documentation examination and safety inspection was reasonable. Obviously, vessels occupy a curious place under the Fourth Amendment. Dissenting in *Villamonte-Marquez*, Justice Brennan noted as much when he remarked that, in spite of the commands of the Fourth Amendment, the Court had, for the first time, approved "a completely random seizure and detention of persons and an entry onto private, noncommercial premises by police officers, without any limitation whatever on the officers' discretion or any safeguards against abuse" (462 U.S. at 598). Indeed, that is precisely what *Villamonte-Marquez* said.

**Abandoned Property.** The Fourth Amendment is not violated when government appropriates abandoned property (*Abel v.*

*United States*, 1960). A person who voluntarily abandons his or her property forfeits any reasonable expectation of privacy in that property. *California v. Greenwood* (486 U.S. 35; 1988), discussed later in this chapter, is demonstrative of the abandoned property doctrine. (See "Electronic Surveillance," p. 144.)

**Property in Foreign Countries Belonging to Individuals Jailed in the United States.** The Fourth Amendment is not applicable to searches and seizures conducted by U.S. agents of property that is owned by a nonresident alien and located in a foreign country (*United States v. Verdugo-Urquidez*, 494 U.S. 259; 1990). The drafting history of the amendment demonstrates that its purpose was to protect the people of the United States against the arbitrary actions of their government, and not to limit their government's actions against aliens outside of the United States.

## *Summary*

The Fourth Amendment clearly indicates a preference for warrants. Consistent with that preference, the Supreme Court has noted repeatedly that warrantless searches and seizures are presumptively unconstitutional. But the absence of a warrant will not necessarily be determinative of the unconstitutionality of a search and seizure. The justices have time and time again permitted searches and seizures conducted without prior approval by a judge or magistrate. Not too many years ago, the Court referred to these well delineated exceptions as "few" in number and "jealously and carefully drawn." As is evidenced in the preceding pages, however, modern realities have made it difficult for these exceptions to remain both "few" in number and "jealously and carefully drawn." Today, under a vast array of circumstances, warrantless searches and seizures are nevertheless reasonable, at least in the opinion of the nation's highest court.

## ELECTRONIC SURVEILLANCE

Technological developments over the last century have heightened threats to individual privacy and Fourth Amendment values. Closed-circuit televisions scrutinize activities in supermarkets, shopping malls, workplaces, and along city streets. Traffic monitoring systems record the whereabouts of vehicles, and automobile "black boxes" record certain activities of their drivers. Wireless communication technologies identify cellular phone locations. Electronic communications systems generate information about credit card purchases and online browsing habits. Computer technology provides the means for central storage and easy accessibility of massive amounts of data, making information collection much easier. Millimeter-wave cameras, back-scattered x-rays, and magnetic gradient sensors identify at some distance weapons "concealed" in a coat pocket or tucked in a waistband. Thermal-imaging devices pointed at a residence or place of business from a public street detect relative amounts of heat within the residence or place of business. Powerful satellite technology reveals the locations and activities of individuals. And the Internet— the ultimate marketplace of ideas, a worldwide library and meeting room where individuals from around the globe can come together to communicate, organize, debate, and learn, unrestricted by geographic distances or national borders—facilitates the unprecedented and rapid dissemination of stored information. This explosive growth in network acquisition, storage, and dissemination of information, much of which links various facts with identifying characteristics of particular individuals and much of which is maintained by federal, state, and local authorities, poses a considerable threat to Fourth Amendment values by vastly increasing the potential for security breaches and the subsequent misuse of such information. These and related issues have presented the Supreme Court with new questions concerning possible encroachments on the Fourth Amendment protection against unreasonable searches and seizures. And the justices have been asked to pour new technological wine into old bottles.

As discussed in the previous chapter, the traditional understanding of what constituted a "search" under the Fourth Amendment was announced in *Boyd v. United States* (1886). To recall, here the Supreme Court declared unconstitutional a part of the Federal Customs Act requiring a person to produce his business papers in court when his goods had been seized as contraband or else have the charges of fraudulent importing taken as "confessed" and forfeit the goods. Noting that a close and literal construction of the Fourth Amendment would deprive it of "half [its] efficacy, and lead to gradual depreciation," the justices held that the amendment applied "to all invasions on the part of government and its employees of the sanctity of a man's home and the privacies of his life." Justice Joseph Bradley wrote, "[i]t is not the breaking of his doors, and the rummaging of his drawers, that constitutes the essence of the offence, but it is the invasion of his indefeasible right of personal security, personal liberty and private property . . ." (116 U.S. at 630). Four inventions in the latter part of the nineteenth century—the telephone, the microphone, the wiretap, and instantaneous photography—provided new means by which law enforcement could conduct surveillance. These developments set the stage for the Court to consider whether the Fourth Amendment protected individuals from electronic surveillance by government officials. *Olmstead v. United States* (277 U.S. 438; [1928]) provided the first opportunity.

Roy Olmstead was convicted in federal district court of transporting and selling liquor in violation of the National Prohibition Act. The evidence used to convict him was secured by a warrantless wiretap placed by federal agents on telephone lines between Olmstead's home and office. Olmstead challenged the admission of the evidence on the grounds that it was obtained in violation of the Fourth Amendment's guarantee against unreasonable searches and seizures. The Supreme Court held that because the interception of telephone conversations occurred without "trespass" on private property, there was no "search" of a constitutionally protected area: "persons, houses, papers, and effects." According to Chief Justice William H. Taft, who authored the Court's opinion, the Fourth Amendment was not meant to include within its protection telephone wires that reached to the whole world; those wires were

> not part of his house or office, any more than [were] the highways along which they [were] stretched. . . . The reasonable view is that one who installs in his house a telephone instrument with connecting wires intends to project his voice to those quite outside, and that the wires beyond his house, and messages while passing over them, are not within the protection of the Fourth Amendment. (277 U.S. at 465–466)

*Olmstead* thus established the trespass doctrine: For a search to occur, government officials must trespass on private property. No trespass, no search. Also important, the majority held that conversations were not tangible items that could be seized. No taking of a tangible item, no seizure.

In dissent, Justice Louis D. Brandeis, joined by three of his colleagues, "seized" the opportunity to argue for a broader construction of the Fourth Amendment. He contended, in one of the most forward-looking opinions ever written, that the amendment conferred upon each individual a general right to privacy, one not confined to traditional categories of searches involving actual trespass on private property or seizures of tangible items. In other words, it was possible for government to violate Olmstead's right to privacy without trespassing upon his property or seizing his belongings. The danger in concluding otherwise was far too great:

> Discovery and invention have made it possible for the Government, by means far more effective than stretching upon the rack, to obtain

disclosure in court of what is whispered in the closet. Moreover, "in the application of a constitution, our contemplation cannot be only of what has been but of what may be." The progress of science in furnishing the government with means of espionage is not likely to stop with wiretapping. Ways may some day be developed by which the Government, without removing papers from secret drawers, can reproduce them in court, and by which it will be enabled to expose to a jury the most intimate occurrences of the home. . . . Can it be that the Constitution affords no protection against such invasions of individual security? (277 U.S. at 473–474)

Then, in words reminiscent of James Otis's speech in 1761 thundering against writs of assistance, Justice Brandeis concluded:

The makers of our Constitution undertook to secure conditions favorable to the pursuit of happiness. They recognized the significance of man's spiritual nature, of his feelings and of his intellect. They knew that only a part of the pain, pleasure and satisfactions of life are to be found in material things. They sought to protect Americans in their beliefs, their thoughts, their emotions and their sensations. They conferred, as against the Government, the right to be let alone—the most comprehensive of rights and the right most valued by civilized men. To protect that right, every unjustifiable intrusion by the Government upon the privacy of the individual, whatever the means employed, must be deemed a violation of the Fourth Amendment. (277 U.S. at 478)

Justice Brandeis's arguments notwithstanding, *Olmstead*'s trespass doctrine defined the scope of the Fourth Amendment for close to forty years, from 1928 until 1967. During that period, most electronic surveillance for law enforcement purposes fell outside the protections of the amendment. As such, police conducting nontrespassory electronic surveillance were virtually unencumbered by judicial oversight. In *Goldman v. United States*

(316 U.S. 129; 1942), for example, the Supreme Court extended *Olmstead*'s trespass doctrine to surveillance utilizing an electronic "bugging" device known as a detectaphone. Unlike the tapping of a telephone line, a detectaphone was placed against a wall to overhear conversations on the other side. After being convicted based in part upon his statements obtained via a detectaphone, Theodore Goldman attempted to distinguish his case from Olmstead's. Olmstead had been talking on the telephone; from that, the justices inferred that he intended to project his voice to the outside world. Goldman, however, had not been on the telephone, his conversation being with others in the room; therefore, he did not intend for his communication to be projected to the outside world. The justices found this asserted distinction "too nice for practical application of the Constitutional guarantee" (316 U.S. at 135). They were, in brief, unconvinced of any logical difference between what federal officers did in *Goldman* and state officers did in *Olmstead*.

By contrast, consider *Silverman v. United States* (365 U.S. 505; 1961). Here, federal agents, attempting to overhear conversations in an adjacent apartment, drove a "spike mike"—a listening device consisting of a foot-long spike attached to a microphone, together with an amplifier—so far through a crevice in a party wall that it made contact with a heating duct serving a suspect's apartment. The Court held that the trespass constituted "an actual intrusion of a constitutionally protected area," thus bringing the case within the ambit of the Fourth Amendment. In so holding, the *Silverman* Court implicitly overruled the second rationale of *Olmstead*— that conversations, because they were not tangible, could not be seized. Though prodded to do so by concurring Justice William O. Douglas, who pointed out the trivialness of a Fourth Amendment jurisprudence based on the type or depth of the penetration of a particular electronic device, the majority was unwilling to overturn *Olmstead*.

By the 1960s, *Olmstead*'s trespass theory was under attack. Alan F. Westin (1966, 1006–1009), for example, argued that government listening to private speech was the most important type of physical surveillance because it bared the individual's real self to a world in which everyone else was hiding behind a mask. It was also among the easiest types of electronic surveillance. When government had access to the room in which the speech was to occur, microphones—as small as a sugar cube, as inexpensive as $10, and easy to activate—could be secreted in objects within the room and were capable of recording or transmitting verbal communication. Of course this type of eavesdropping might have necessitated a warrant, as trespass had occurred. When entry into the room was not possible, however, speech could still be monitored by contact microphones on walls, "spike" microphones inserted into the air space between walls, or through vibrations carried along pipes, vents, or ducts coming from the room. Additionally, garden-variety directional microphones made it possible to listen to conversations held on porches or balconies, or in rooms with open windows, and to do so from a distance of several hundred feet. This was, of course, the extent of the technology in 1966. Westin and others, like Justice Brandeis before them, talked about the prospects for physical surveillance technology in the decades to come. Increased miniaturization of recording devices, voiceprint identification systems, computer tapping, and electronic mail all posed serious threats to Fourth Amendment privacy concerns. By 1967 a sufficient number of justices agreed. In that year, the Supreme Court decided two cases that gave birth to the Court's modern day electronic surveillance jurisprudence.

*Berger v. New York* (388 U.S. 41; 1967) confirmed *Silverman*'s implicit rejection of the alternative rationale in *Olmstead:* The Fourth Amendment protected "conversation." Accordingly, electronic surveillance to capture conversation constituted a search within the meaning of that amendment and required a warrant or probable cause for legitimacy. In this case, the justices declared unconstitutional a state statute that authorized a judge to issue an eavesdrop order if there were "reasonable ground to believe" that evidence of a crime might be obtained. But the Court did not address whether the "reasonable ground" standard satisfied the Fourth Amendment because the statute had other constitutional deficiencies. Most notably, these included the lack of a particularity requirement regarding a description of the conversations to be seized and the absence of a termination date for the eavesdrop order. (See "Particularity of Place to Be Searched," page 76 in this chapter.) Shortly after *Berger* was decided, Congress enacted federal legislation (Title III of the Omnibus Crime Control and Safe Streets Act of 1968) regulating electronic surveillance.

Of much greater significance is *Katz v. United States* (389 U.S. 347; 1967), arguably the most important Fourth Amendment case of the last half of the twentieth century, in which the Court said nevermore to *Olmstead*'s trespass doctrine. Charles Katz was convicted in federal district court of placing bets and wagers in violation of federal law. The evidence used to convict Katz was obtained by an electronic listening device placed outside a public telephone booth in Los Angeles, California. The device was placed outside the booth by agents of the Federal Bureau of Investigation (FBI), who did not have a warrant. At trial, Katz unsuccessfully challenged the admission of this evidence on the grounds that it was obtained in violation of the Fourth Amendment's guarantee against unreasonable searches and seizures. After a federal appellate court rejected an appeal of his conviction, Katz petitioned the Supreme Court for review.

In *Katz*, the justices decided that a search could occur without a physical intrusion into a "constitutionally protected area": "[T]he Fourth Amendment protects people not places. What a person knowingly exposes to the public, even in his own home or office, is not a subject of Fourth Amendment protection. But what he seeks to preserve as private, even if in an area accessible to the public, may be constitutionally protected" (389 U.S. at 351). The relevant question was thus whether the government had "violated the privacy upon which [an individual] . . . justifiably relied." To make that determination, the Court had to look to the nature of the privacy interest and the nature of the intrusion.

Under the *Katz* standard, the touchstone of Fourth Amendment analysis is whether an individual has a constitutionally protected reasonable expectation of privacy. In a concurring opinion, Justice Harlan endeavored to clarify the majority's holding by proposing a two-part inquiry. First, that a person manifest a subjective expectation of privacy in the object of the challenged search. And second, that the expectation be one that society is prepared to recognize as reasonable. In pursuing the second inquiry, the test of legitimacy is not whether the individual chooses to conceal assertedly "private activity," but whether the government's intrusion infringes upon the personal and societal values protected by the Fourth Amendment. Justice Harlan's concurrence has become the governing standard for determining whether a search has occurred in the absence of physical intrusion.

It is worth noting that, in *Katz,* the Court specifically declined to extend its holding to cases "involving national security" or "with respect to the activities of foreign powers or their agents." Federal courts have been reluctant to apply Fourth Amendment protections to foreign intelligence surveillance, preferring instead to defer to the Congress and the president on matters of national security. Numerous federal courts even adopted foreign intelligence exceptions to the Fourth Amendment. In *United States v. United States District Court for the Eastern District of Michigan* (1972), for example, the justices were careful to note that, while judicial approval was necessary for foreign intelligence surveillance by executive branch officials, domestic security surveillance involved different policy and practical considerations from ordinary criminal surveillance. The majority even suggested that Congress consider different protective standards for surveillance concerning national security and criminal investigation. In the wake of the events of September 11, 2001—and with the passage of the USA PATRIOT Act—this invitation to distinguish between foreign intelligence surveillance and criminal investigation has received much greater attention. This topic will be explored more fully in Chapter Four.

For the last four decades, the Court has relied upon the *Katz* analysis to determine what constitutes a search within the meaning of the Fourth Amendment. Generally speaking, the Fourth Amendment extends to any place or any thing in which an individual has a reasonable expectation of privacy. On the one hand, courts have demonstrated a willingness to consider hotel rooms, garages, offices, automobiles, sealed letters, suitcases, other closed containers, telephone conversations, fax transmissions, electronic mail, and certain information about the home as protected by the Fourth Amendment. On the other hand, courts have refused to extend Fourth Amendment protection to the curtilage of the home, especially where such curtilage is observable from a public vantage point; to abandoned or discarded property; or to open fields. *Oliver v. United States* (466 U.S. 170; 1984) is illustrative of the "open fields" doctrine: Because an individual growing marijuana in an open field has no reasonable expectation of privacy in that field, a warrantless search of the field by police officers is permissible.

The justices have, from time to time, been criticized for taking a rather limited view of what privacy expectations are justified. For example, in *California v. Ciraolo* (476 U.S. 207; 1986), the justices held that a warrantless, naked-eye aerial observation of an individual's fenced-in backyard was not a search within the meaning of the Fourth Amendment, even if the observation was directed at identifying marijuana plants growing in that yard. Here the justices concluded that the respondent's expectation of privacy from all observations of his backyard was not an expectation that was reasonable. The fact that Ciraolo had taken measures to restrict some views of his activities does not "preclude an officer's observation from a public vantage point where he has a right to be and which renders the activities clearly visible" (476 U.S. at 213). By the same logic, *Florida v. Riley* (488 U.S. 445; 1989) held that surveillance from a helicopter, at an altitude of four hundred feet, of the interior of a residential backyard greenhouse did not constitute a search requiring a warrant under the Fourth Amendment.

Three cases—*O'Connor v. Ortega* (1987), referenced earlier in this chapter, *California v. Greenwood* (486 U.S. 35; 1988), and *Bond v. United States* (529 U.S. 334; 2000)—illustrate well what the justices will and will not allow under the reasonable expectation of privacy standard. In the first, the Court held that public employees possessed a reasonable expectation of privacy in their offices. In the second, the justices decided that a homeowner did not have a reasonable expectation of privacy in the garbage bags left for collection on the curb outside his home. In the third, the justices acknowledged a reasonable expectation of privacy in luggage carried aboard a Greyhound bus on a cross-country trip. It is true that none of these cases involved electronic surveillance, as was the issue in *Katz*. Nevertheless, these cases demonstrate how the Court has interpreted and applied *Katz*'s "reasonable expectation of privacy" standard.

Dr. Magno Ortega was a seventeen-year physician and psychiatrist at a public hospital. In his position, he had primary training responsibility over young residents. In July 1981 several hospital officials, including Dr. Dennis O'Connor, became concerned about possible improprieties with regard to Ortega's management of the residency program. On request from O'Connor, Ortega agreed to a paid administrative leave of absence. During that leave and unbeknownst to Ortega, hospital officials entered his office, rummaged through his files and cabinets, and seized personal effects. Some of the items seized were later used in an administrative proceeding against Ortega, which resulted in his termination. Ortega commenced an action in federal district court alleging that the search violated his Fourth Amendment rights. The district court found the search constitutional because there was a need to secure state property in the office. The Court of Appeals for the Ninth Circuit reversed, ruling that Ortega had a reasonable expectation of privacy in his office.

The Supreme Court readily acknowledged that it had no talisman for determining reasonable expectations of privacy in the public workplace. Instead, questions about reasonable expectations of privacy in the workplace had to be addressed on a case-by-case basis. Obviously, the workplace included some areas—such as hallways, cafeterias, and offices—that were within the employer's control. That did not mean, however, that all persons occupying or passing through those areas forfeited their expectations of privacy. For example, a public employee who brought a suitcase to the office had no reasonable expectation of privacy in the outward appearance of the luggage. But that same employee retained a reasonable expectation of privacy in the contents of the luggage. The justices thus rejected the hospital's contention that government employees abandoned all expectations of privacy in the workplace. The majority then concluded that regardless of whether the hospital administrators had a legitimate right to be in the office, Ortega had a reasonable expectation of privacy in his desk and file cabinets since the office belonged to him only and the hospital had no regulations prohibiting or discouraging employees from keeping personal effects in their desks or file cabinets.

A second issue in *Ortega* was whether the probable cause standard was applicable for a search conducted by a public employer. The Court said no, relying upon the "special needs" doctrine of the Fourth Amendment. Accordingly, public employer intrusions on constitutionally protected privacy interests of government employees for noninvestigatory, work-related purposes, as well as for investigations of work-related misconduct, are not subject to the probable cause standard, but are judged by the standard of reasonableness under all the circumstances. In this case, the search was justified at its inception because there was evidence that the administrators might have had a reasonable belief that state property within the office needed to be secured, and was reasonably related in scope to the circumstances that justified the initial interference.

*California v. Greenwood* involved privacy expectations in trash that had been set on the curb for pickup. In early 1984, police received information indicating that Billy Greenwood might be involved in illegal narcotics activity. A police officer staked out the house and observed regular late night and early morning visitors, none of whom stayed more than a few minutes. After weeks of surveillance, the officer began to monitor and search the trash set out for collection on the curb in front of Greenwood's house. One of those searches yielded evidence of drug trafficking. On that basis, the officer obtained a warrant and searched Greenwood's house, finding large quantities of illegal narcotics. Greenwood was arrested, but the state trial court dismissed the charges, finding the warrantless search violative of, among other things, the Fourth Amendment. The appellate court affirmed.

Appyling *Katz*'s two-pronged reasonable expectation of privacy test, the Supreme Court reversed. The justices conceded that Greenwood might not have foreseen his trash being collected and inspected by police or other members of the public. That absence of foresight, however, was insufficient to confer Fourth Amendment protection to his garbage. A warrantless search was impermissible only if Greenwood had manifested a subjective expectation of privacy. This the Court could not confirm. It was common knowledge, the majority said, that "plastic garbage bags left on or at the side of a public street are readily accessible to animals, children, scavengers, snoops, and other members of the public" (486 U.S. at 40). Moreover, Greenwood had placed his trash on the corner for the express purpose of having someone else pick it up. In other words, he put his trash on the curb presumably to abandon it. Interestingly, *Katz* had announced, "What a person knowingly exposes to the public, even in his own home or office, is not a subject of Fourth Amendment protection. But what he seeks to preserve as private, even if in an area accessible to the public, may be constitutionally protected" (389 U.S. at 351). The rule in *Greenwood*, however, can be boiled down thus: "BEWARE: What a person knowingly exposes to the public, even in his own home or office, is not necessarily subject to Fourth Amendment protection. Some things he seeks to preserve as private may not be constitutionally protected."

By contrast, the Supreme Court held in *Bond v. United States* (2000) that a law enforcement officer's physical manipulation of a bus passenger's carry-on luggage was a search under the Fourth Amendment, and thus necessitated a warrant or probable cause. Steven Dewayne Bond was a passenger on a Greyhound bus traveling from California to Arkansas. During a stop at a border patrol checkpoint in Texas, a border patrol agent boarded the bus to confirm the immigration status of the passengers. Having done so, the agent, while walking to the front of the bus, squeezed the soft luggage that passengers had placed in the storage bins above the seats. In conducting this examination, the agent noticed that Bond's luggage contained a "brick-like" object. After obtaining consent to search the luggage, the agent found a "brick" of methamphetamine. Bond contended that the officer's manipulation of his luggage constituted a search of a constitutionally protected "effect" under the Fourth Amendment. Because the search was warrantless and because it did not fall within any of the specifically established exceptions to the warrant requirement, he asserted that it was violative of the Fourth Amendment.

The Supreme Court agreed. Bond had, by his conduct, exhibited an actual expectation of privacy in his carry-on luggage: He had used an opaque bag and he had kept it near him as opposed to placing it in the cargo hold under the passenger compartment accessible only from the outside. Additionally, this expectation was reasonable. "[T]ravelers are particularly concerned about their carry-on luggage; they generally use it to transport personal items that, for whatever reason, they prefer to keep close at hand" (529 U.S. at 337–338). The only remaining issue was whether Bond reasonably expected that his luggage would not be manipulated by the border patrol agent. On this point, the government claimed that by exposing his luggage to the public, Bond forfeited any reasonable expectation that his luggage would be free from physical manipulation. It was, after all, not uncommon for other passengers and bus employees to move luggage that had been placed in the overhead storage bins. The majority conceded this point, but held that a bus passenger did not expect that others, to include law enforcement agents, would squeeze or otherwise manipulate personal luggage in an exploratory manner for the purpose of determining its contents. The justices distinguished this case from *Ciraolo* and *Riley* by noting that those cases involved only visual, as opposed to tactile, observation, the latter being a more physically invasive and intrusive inspection than the purely visual inspection.

In 1928 Justice Brandeis stated in *Olmstead*: "Ways may some day be developed by which the Government, without [ever coming in the home], will be enabled to expose to a jury the most intimate occurrences of the home" (277 U.S. at 474). The recent Supreme Court's reexamination of electronic surveillance and the Fourth Amendment demonstrates the prophetic nature of this comment. In *Kyllo v. United States* (533 U.S. 27; 2001), the Court held that law enforcement's warrantless use of a thermal imaging device aimed at a private residence from a public street—the purpose of which was to detect relative amounts of heat within the residence—violated the Fourth Amendment. Here the justices confronted squarely the limits upon the power of technology to shrink the realm of guaranteed privacy. *Kyllo* is indicative of the heightened protection made available to the home and the Court's seeming reluctance to permit law enforcement to use highly sophisticated technology to disclose information that could not be obtained without physical intrusion into the home. *Kyllo* and its implications will be discussed in Chapter Four.

## Summary

It is most difficult to apply the Fourth Amendment, written in the eighteenth century, by men brilliant but limited by their times, to modern conditions replete with the ever-advancing technology of surveillance. The Fourth Amendment's journey from *Olmstead* to *Katz* and beyond is a function of the Supreme Court's recognition that, to be effective, the Fourth Amendment must be adaptable. *Olmstead's* narrow construction was eventually replaced with *Katz's* broad construction only after the justices realized that a Fourth Amendment jurisprudence that failed to consider developing technology would leave the amendment either obsolete or irrelevant. The reasonable expectation of privacy test provides that means for the test turns, at least in part, on the current society's expectations as to what is reasonable. A positive response cloaks the expectation of privacy with constitutional protection. A negative response denies constitutional protection to the expectation of privacy. Though the *Katz* standard is commonly accepted and rarely criticized, its application is often a point of contention. The division among the justices in many of the cases discussed above is demonstrative of the inherent difficulties in applying Fourth Amendment principles to modern conditions.

## THE EXCLUSIONARY RULE

The Fourth Amendment is quintessentially a restriction on the police. By its very language it prohibits unreasonable searches and seizures. Yet it does not provide instructions as to how this right is to be enforced. It is true that the Fourth Amendment is enforceable by civil (tort) and criminal actions or internal disciplinary proceedings against law enforcement officers who conduct such searches (Wilkey 1982). Those actions, however, are seldom maintained; nor are they easily maintainable because they encounter assorted legal difficulties and practical impediments. Numerous commentators have noted the absence of any of these or other alternative means of enforcing Fourth Amendment standards. As such, the primary instrument for enforcing the Fourth Amendment has been the exclusionary rule—a judicially fashioned doctrine that requires the exclusion at trial evidence obtained from an unreasonable search and seizure. The rule is based on the premise that, in enforcing the Fourth Amendment, police are not to be trusted to restrain themselves; in other words, "courts must police the police" (Amsterdam 1974, 371).

Typically, when the prosecution's case is based, at least in part, on illegally obtained evidence, the defendant will, before or at trial, move to suppress the specified evidence. A suppression hearing then determines whether the evidence will be admitted. While the term "exclusionary rule" applies primarily to physical evidence obtained in violation of the Fourth Amendment, nonphysical evidence may be excluded if obtained in violation of other constitutional rights. For example, a confession from a suspect in custody who had not been read his *Miranda* rights might be excluded at trial as infringing upon the Fifth Amendment.

In *Weeks v. United States* (232 U.S. 383; 1914), the Supreme Court formally adopted the exclusionary rule, holding that evidence obtained by federal agents in violation of the Fourth Amendment could not be used against a criminal defendant in a federal trial. Because the police had no authority to seize the evidence, the prosecution had no right to introduce the evidence at trial. The *Weeks* decision clearly marked the start of a suppression of evidence doctrine that had not previously existed in the common law.

Fremont Weeks was convicted in federal district court on the basis of evidence seized from his home in two warrantless searches. Before the trial, Weeks filed a petition requesting that his private property be returned to him. The right to recover illegally seized property existed in English common law and, some would say, was implicit in the Fourth Amendment (Wilson 1982, 1084). What made this case unique was the Court's consideration of the right in conjunction with a criminal proceeding. Historically, the right had been civil in nature, that is, it had never been attached to a criminal action. The petition was denied, and Weeks was charged, prosecuted, and convicted.

According to the high Court, the primary wrong was the warrantless searches and seizures. Although the justices had previously adopted the old common law maxim that a court would not look to the source of otherwise competent evidence, they had done so in a case where incidental seizure was made in the execution of a legal warrant (*Adams v. New York,* 192 U.S. 585; 1904). Here, because there was no incidental seizure made in the execution of a legal warrant, the justices departed from that premise, noting that it was very much the business of the judiciary, charged at all times with the support of the Constitution, to do so when confronted with a constitutional violation. Any other construction would be an abrogation of judicial duty. Furthermore, if private letters and documents could be seized and introduced into evidence against a citizen accused of a crime, the protection of the Fourth Amendment was "of no value, and [the amendment] might as well be stricken from the Constitution" (232 U.S. at 393).

The *Weeks* decision interpreted the Fourth Amendment as more than "a mere admonition of good behaviour on the part of police, the absence of which brings forth no attendant consequences." Rather, it interpreted the Fourth Amendment as "one of a body of rights within whose framework government officials must operate" (Landynski 1966, 64). And to allow the admission of evidence seized in violation of the Fourth Amendment would reduce it "to an unenforceable right." The exact scope and significance of the decision in *Weeks,* however, have been subjects of much discussion and controversy. This is in large part because the opinion in *Weeks,* though unanimous, was ambiguous about whether the exclusionary rule was a constitutional requirement or simply a judicially created remedy to deter constitutional violations. On the one hand, the opinion written by Justice William Day observed that to allow the use of illegally seized evidence would be to affirm "a manifest neglect if not an open defiance . . . of the Constitution" (232 U.S. at 394). Yet the opinion also suggested that the exclusion of illegally seized evidence was necessary to deter further police misconduct. Since the case against the defendant would be harmed by the exclusion of relevant evidence, police would be less likely to violate the prohibition against unreasonable searches and seizures. Justice Day further noted that the integrity of trial courts would be undermined if they permitted the introduction of illegally obtained evidence. This point he emphasized:

> The efforts of the courts and their officials to bring the guilty to punishment, praise-worthy as they are, are not to be aided by the sacrifice of those great principles established by years of endeavor and suffering which have resulted in their embodiment in the fundamental law of the land. (232 U.S. at 393)

In brief, the courts could not become accomplices in willful disobedience of the law.

Almost a century after the adoption of the exclusionary rule, the Supreme Court remains divided on its purpose. Some justices maintain that the Fourth Amendment implicitly requires the exclusion of all illegally seized evidence. Others insist that the exclusionary rule is necessary to preserve judicial integrity. Still others believe the rule to be simply a judicially created remedy applicable only in those situations in which the exclusion of evidence would deter further police misconduct. If the last interpretation is accurate, and it clearly appears to be the interpretation of choice among the majority of the justices today, then exceptions to the rule are possible.

Equally important, the *Weeks* decision explicitly stated that the exclusionary rule did not apply to searches conducted by state police officers. As a result, states were not required to exclude evidence obtained by an unreasonable search and seizure. Some states chose to do so; most did not. In *Wolf v. Colorado* (338 U.S. 25; 1949), the Supreme Court faced the question of whether the Fourth Amendment, and by extension the exclusionary rule, should be applied to the states through the Due Process Clause of the Fourteenth Amendment. While making the Fourth Amendment applicable to the states—or at least the "core of the Fourth Amendment"—the justices specifically rejected the notion that the exclusionary rule should be binding upon the states. Writing for the majority in a five-to-four decision, Justice Felix Frankfurter noted that the rule was a "judicial implication" without foundation in the Fourth Amendment. The justices granted that exclusion of illegally obtained evidence would be an effective way of deterring unreasonable searches. It was not the only way, however; other equally effective methods were available, or so they said. Accordingly, states remained free to adopt or ignore the exclusionary rule in state criminal proceedings. Federalism issues aside, the *Wolf* decision was also significant because it indicated that deterring police misconduct was the primary purpose of the exclusionary rule. It also foreshadowed the more modern view of the subject taken by the Rehnquist Court, that the exclusionary rule is nothing more than a judicially created rule of evidence.

Throughout the 1950's, evidence seized illegally by federal law enforcement agents was inadmissible in federal trials. But because the exclusionary rule was not binding on the states, evidence seized illegally by state law enforcement agents was admissible at trial. This double standard gave rise to the "silver platter" doctrine. This doctrine permitted federal prosecutors to introduce at trial evidence obtained illegally by state law enforcement agents. State agents, often at the request of federal officers, conducted illegal seizures. The evidence obtained was then served up to federal authorities on a "silver platter," and was admissible in federal court because federal officers had not participated in its seizure. In *Elkins v. United States* (364 U.S. 206; 1960), the Court repudiated this doctrine, claiming that it undermined federalism, rewarded police misconduct, and encouraged disobedience to the Constitution. "The [exclusionary] rule is calculated to prevent, not to repair," the *Elkins* Court said. "Its purpose it to deter—to compel respect for the constitutional guaranty in the only effectively available way—by removing the incentive to disregard it" (364 U.S. at 217). In other words, by disallowing illegally obtained evidence, the rule deterred police misconduct.

*Elkins* disallowed the admission of illegally obtained evidence in federal court, regardless of the source of the evidence. But *Wolf* still governed prosecutions in state court, where the exclusionary rule was not applicable. In *Mapp v. Ohio* (367 U.S. 643; 1961) the Supreme Court, again dividing five to four, overruled this aspect of the *Wolf* decision and extended the federal exclusionary rule to state criminal prosecutions. The justices were "compelled" to reach this conclusion, Justice Tom Clark said for the majority, because other remedies had completely failed to secure compliance with constitutional provisions on the part of police officers. As a result of that failure, the courts had been constantly required to participate in, and in effect condone, the lawless activities of law enforcement officers. Justice Clark's opinion emphasized both the constitutional foundations and the practical necessities of the rule: The exclusion doctrine was an "essential ingredient" of the Fourth Amendment *and* necessary to discourage police misconduct and maintain judicial integrity. To hold otherwise would be "to grant the right but in reality . . . withhold its privilege and enjoyment" (367 U.S. at 656). Accordingly, all evidence obtained by searches in violation of the Fourth Amendment was inadmissible in state criminal proceedings. The *Mapp* majority then concluded:

> Our decision, founded on reason and truth, gives to the individual no more than that which the Constitution guarantees him, to the police officer no less than that to which honest law enforcement is entitled, and, to the courts, the judicial integrity so necessary in the true administration of justice. (367 U.S. at 660)

Concurring Justice Hugo Black insisted that, while the Fourth Amendment did not itself contain any provision expressly precluding the use of illegally obtained evidence, when the Fourth Amendment was considered in conjunction with the Fifth Amendment's ban against forced self-incrimination, a constitutional basis emerged that not only justified but actually required the exclusionary rule. (This was the same argument initially advanced by Justice Joseph Bradley in *Boyd* [1886]; see Chapter Two.) Though the rule was constitutionally required, four years later the justices declined to apply retroactively the holding in *Mapp* (*Linkletter v. Walker*, 381 U.S. 618; 1965).

*Mapp* formally linked the exclusionary rule to the Fourth Amendment. Subsequent decisions of the Burger and Rehnquist Courts, however, have deconstitutionalized the rule, redefined its purpose, and limited its application. This has resulted in the significant curtailment of the operation of the exclusionary rule. In *United States v. Calandra* (414 U.S. 338; 1974), for example, the Court rejected the notion that the rule was a personal constitutional right. Instead, the six-member majority declared that the exclusionary rule was merely a preventive measure designed to deter future police misconduct. The justices then adopted a "cost-benefit approach," concluding that the rule was only to be applied in those settings in which the exclusion of evidence would result in the significant deterrence of future police misconduct. In all other settings, the social costs of excluding relevant evidence far outweighed any potential benefits from its application. *Stone v. Powell* (428 U.S. 465; 1976) confirmed the restricted purpose and limited application of the exclusionary rule:

> Although our decisions often have alluded to the "imperative of judicial integrity," they demonstrate the limited role of this justification in the determination of whether to apply the rule in a particular context. . . . While courts, of course, must ever be concerned with preserving the integrity of the judicial process, this concern has limited force as a justification for the exclusion of highly probative evidence. (428 U.S. at 485)

Both *Calandra* and *Powell* are clear in announcing the primary purpose of the judicially created exclusionary rule to be the deterrence of police misconduct, with application of the rule not absolute but rather dependent upon the social costs of excluding the relevant evidence. (*Calandra* held that the exclusionary rule did not apply to questions asked of a grand jury witness that were based on evidence obtained by an illegal search and seizure. *Powell* ruled that state prisoners could not petition for a writ of *habeas corpus* in federal district court to review their convictions, when they already argued on direct appeal that their Fourth Amendment rights were violated.)

### Exceptions to the Exclusionary Rule

Although the Burger and Rehnquist Courts have not expressly overturned *Mapp* or abandoned the exclusionary rule, they have been willing to carve out exceptions to it. The most notable of these include (1) inevitable discovery; (2) independent source; and (3) good faith (with all of its multiple permutations). These exceptions are not without their critics. Numerous courts and commentators have expressed the fear that these exceptions encourage police misconduct and threaten judicial integrity and thus collide with the fundamental purposes of the exclusionary rule.

**Inevitable Discovery.**    The first exception, announced in *Nix v. Williams* (467 U.S. 431; 1984), does not require the suppression of evidence that has been seized illegally if the prosecution can establish that the evidence inevitably would have been discovered by lawful means in the course of a continuing investigation. This is known as the "inevitable discovery" exception. On Christmas Eve, 1968, a ten-year-old girl disappeared from a Des Moines, Iowa, YMCA. Authorities soon focused their attention on Robert Williams, a recent escapee from a Missouri mental hospital who had been a resident at the YMCA. The following day, authorities found Williams in Davenport, Iowa, 160 miles east of Des Moines. They also discovered articles belonging to Williams and the young girl's clothing at a rest area on Interstate 80, which connected Des Moines and Davenport. Authorities, with the assistance of hundreds of volunteers, mounted an intensive search for the girl in the countryside between Des Moines and the rest area. Williams was arrested and arraigned in Davenport, and then transported back to Des Moines. Prior to the trip, authorities promised Williams's legal counsel that they would not question him during the trip. Nevertheless, one of the officers transporting Williams struck up a conversation with him, pleading with him to provide the location of the body so that she might receive a proper Christian burial. Williams ultimately provided incriminating statements about the murder and directed the officers to the body.

Before trial, Williams moved unsuccessfully to suppress the incriminating statements and evidence of the body, contending that both were the result of statements that had been illegally obtained in the absence of counsel, as guaranteed by the Sixth Amendment. Following the affirmance of his conviction by the Iowa Supreme

Court, Williams filed a petition for *habeas corpus* in the U.S. District Court. All three federal courts—the district court, the court of appeals, and the Supreme Court—held that the detective's conversation with Williams amounted to an "interrogation" without counsel, in violation of the Sixth Amendment. The Supreme Court noted, however, that even though the statements could not be admitted at a second trial, evidence of the body's location and condition might be admissible on the theory that the body would have been discovered even if the incriminating statements had not been elicited from Williams. At the second trial, prosecutors did not offer into evidence his incriminating statements, nor did they offer evidence that Williams had guided the police to the body. They did introduce evidence concerning the body's location and condition. Williams was convicted again, and that conviction was affirmed, again, by the Iowa Supreme Court. In subsequent federal proceedings, the district court denied relief, on the grounds that the body inevitably would have been found. The Court of Appeals for the Eighth Circuit reversed, finding that the police had acted in "bad faith" in eliciting the statements from Williams. The state then petitioned the Supreme Court for review.

Writing for a seven-member majority, Chief Justice Burger noted that the primary rationale for the exclusionary rule was the need to deter police from violations of constitutional privacy, notwithstanding the incredibly high cost of permitting obviously guilty persons to go free. That said, illegally obtained evidence could still be admitted if the prosecution established, by a mere preponderance of the evidence, that the evidence "ultimately or inevitably would have been discovered by lawful means" (467 U.S. at 444). The majority justified this exception to the exclusionary rule by asserting that the purpose of the rule was to restore the "status quo" that existed in the absence of a constitutional violation. Because it was accepted that the search party inevitably would have discovered the body, excluding the physical evidence would have placed the prosecution in a worse position than they would have occupied had there been no violation. Excluding the evidence added nothing either to the integrity or fairness of the criminal trial. The two dissenters agreed that the exception was justifiable under certain circumstances. They dissented only on the question of the appropriate standard of proof. In their view, the prosecution should be required to establish, by "clear and convincing evidence," that the evidence would have been discovered as a matter of course if an independent investigation were allowed to proceed. This, the dissenters believed, the prosecution could not do.

**Independent Source.**    In a companion ruling to *Williams, Segura v. United States* (468 U.S. 796; 1984), the justices announced an "independent source" exception to the exclusionary rule. This exception allows the admission of evidence that has been discovered "by means wholly independent of any constitutional violation." In *Segura,* police officers, after conducting surveillance of four persons suspected of trafficking in cocaine from their apartment, executed lawful arrests of two of them. The officers were advised that, because of "administrative delay," a search warrant for the apartment could not be obtained until the following day; nevertheless, they were instructed to "secure the apartment" to prevent the destruction of evidence. When arriving at the apartment, the officers encountered the other two suspects. Because this encounter took place in a home, the officers conducted a limited security check of the premises. During the course of that check, they observed, in plain view, drug paraphernalia. When the warrant arrived, some nineteen hours later, the agents discovered cocaine and records of narcotics transactions. Those items were seized, along with the drug paraphernalia observed during the initial security check. The trial court suppressed all the evidence. The appellate court suppressed only the evidence discovered in plain view on the initial entry, but not the evidence seized during the warrant-authorized search. The suspects were subsequently convicted. The Supreme Court held that, because the information on which the warrant was secured came from sources wholly unconnected with the initial entry and was known to the officers well before the entry, the legality or illegality of the initial entry was not relevant to the admissibility of evidence. This exception reflects the notion that while the government should not profit from official misconduct, neither should it be made worse off than it would have been absent the misconduct.

The independent source exception is similar to the inevitable discovery exception, with one notable difference. The inevitable discovery exception demands only that the evidence hypothetically would have been seized through some legal means; it thus allows evidence obtained illegally to be admitted. By contrast, the independent source exception requires that the evidence actually be obtained legally; it is, therefore, somewhat less controversial, because it does no violence to the constitutional protections that the exclusionary rule was meant to enforce. To prevail under this exception, the prosecution must prove that the evidence later would have been found as a result of other independent sources.

**Good Faith (Judicial Error).** In *United States v. Leon* (468 U.S. 897; 1984), the Supreme Court legitimized a "good faith" exception to the exclusionary rule. This exception, arguably the most controversial, permits the use of illegally obtained evidence when police possess an objectively reasonable belief that their warrant is valid, even though the warrant is later found to be unsupported by probable cause or technically deficient. In this situation, because the magistrate erred, declaring the evidence inadmissible would not advance the primary goal of the exclusionary rule—deterring police misconduct.

The facts of *Leon* are remarkable. In 1981 an anonymous informant of unproven reliability disclosed to officers of the Burbank, California, police department that two individuals known only to him as "Armando" and "Patsy" were selling cocaine and other illegal drugs out of their residence at 620 Price Drive. The informant also told the police that the drug dealers kept only small quantities at their residence, storing the larger quantities at another unknown Burbank residence. On that information, police initiated an extensive investigation of the occupants of the 620 Price Drive residence—Armando Sanchez, who had previously been arrested for possession of marijuana, and Patsy Stewart, who had no known criminal record. During the surveillance of the residence, Cyril Rombach, an experienced narcotics officer, observed the frequent visits of a vehicle that belonged to Ricardo Del Castillo, who also had previously been arrested for possession of marijuana. As a standard practice, the driver of the vehicle would enter the residence empty-handed, remain at the residence for only a short period, and depart carrying a small paper bag. From Del Castillo, police were led to Alberto Leon, who had previously been arrested on drug charges and was suspected of being heavily involved in the importation of drugs into the United States. Police also observed Sanchez and Stewart boarding separate flights to Miami, Florida. Upon their return to Los Angeles, Sanchez and Stewart were stopped at the request of the police and consented to a search of their luggage. A small amount of marijuana was discovered. Based on these and other observations, Rombach prepared an affidavit for a search warrant for the residences of Sanchez, Stewart, and Leon. This even though Leon had never been seen at the 620 Price Drive residence and was only linked to Sanchez and Stewart by the testimony of Del Castillo! The affidavit specified a long list of items related to drug trafficking. After several district attorneys viewed the affidavit, a facially valid search warrant was issued. During the search, large quantities of drugs and other paraphernalia were found at all three residences. Sanchez, Stewart, and Leon were all indicted by a grand jury and charged with conspiracy to possess and distribute cocaine and other drugs.

Leon filed a motion to suppress the evidence seized pursuant to the warrant. He asserted that the police had failed to establish probable cause in the application for the warrant. A district court judge agreed. Because Leon's home was searched under a warrant that was unsupported by probable cause, the evidence obtained was inadmissible. Although conceding that Rombach had not engaged in any misconduct, the judge rejected the government's argument that the exclusionary rule should not apply when evidence was seized by police who reasonably acted in good faith on a facially valid search warrant. A divided panel of the Court of Appeals for the Ninth Circuit affirmed, holding that the affidavit was inadequate to support a search warrant because the investigation failed to corroborate the informant's statement. Because there was no probable cause, the search was unconstitutional.

The Supreme Court, at the request of the Reagan administration, granted certiorari to decide whether the exclusionary rule should be modified so as not to bar the admission of evidence seized in reasonable, good-faith reliance on a search warrant that was subsequently held to be defective. The Reagan administration did not request review of the Ninth Circuit's holding that the affidavit had failed to establish probable cause. In *Leon,* the justices allowed the evidence to be admitted in the prosecution's case-in-chief on the grounds that Rombach had reasonably relied on the issuance of the warrant by a neutral and detached magistrate. (The case-in-chief is the part of the trial in which the party with the initial burden of proof—here, the prosecution—presents its evidence as to the defendant's guilt, after which it rests.) The majority in *Leon* rejected early and outright the argument that the Fourth Amendment required the exclusion of illegally obtained evidence: The exclusionary rule was not an individual right, but a "remedial device" justified *only* by its deterrent effect on law enforcement officials. As such, courts should decide whether to apply the rule on a case-by-case basis, balancing the costs of excluding the evidence against the probable deterrent effect of that exclusion on police misconduct. When applied in a situation, as here, where police had an objectively reasonable belief that the warrant was valid and the search constitutional, the costs of excluding the evidence were far too "substantial." Guilty persons went unpunished or received lighter sentences, and the citizenry lost its respect for the law to the great detriment of society. By contrast the benefits of exclusion under these circumstances were tenuous at best. The exclusion of evidence could not possibly deter police misconduct, for there was no police misconduct. Rombach acted as any reasonable law enforcement officer would; he requested from a magistrate a warrant; and when he received it, he executed the search. It was the magistrate's responsibility to decide whether the allegations offered in the affidavit established probable cause and, if so, to issue the warrant. The officer could not be expected to question the magistrate's determination of probable cause; after all, police officers are not trained in the law. The majority also pointed out that Rombach's affidavit provided evidence sufficient to create disagreement among the thoughtful and competent judges of the panel of the Ninth Circuit, one of whom believed probable cause existed.

Additionally, the majority dismissed the "judicial integrity" rationale for the exclusionary rule, concluding that no evidence suggested that judges or magistrates were inclined to ignore the law or would be deterred by the exclusion of illegally obtained evidence. Moreover, the rule was never designed "to punish the errors of judges and magistrates" (468 U.S. at 916).

Under *Leon,* a judge should admit all evidence obtained by a law enforcement officer acting in objectively reasonable reliance on a facially valid search warrant. *Leon* also held that appellate courts could consider the "good faith" issue prior to, or without, deciding the probable cause issue. If "good faith" were present, the probable cause issue was moot. The Court did clarify, however, that exclusion was the proper remedy when an officer had no reasonable grounds for believing that the warrant was properly issued—if, for example, it should have been obvious that the magistrate had "wholly abandoned" his neutral role; or if the warrant was obviously deficient on its face; or if the issuing magistrate had been intentionally misled by information; or if the officer was dishonest or reckless in preparing the affidavit.

In *Leon,* the search warrant had not been supported by probable cause. In *Massachusetts v. Sheppard* (468 U.S. 981; 1984), a companion case to *Leon,* the search warrant had not specified the items to be seized; it was thus technically deficient. During a murder investigation, the police sought a warrant to search a suspect's home. The affidavit presented to the judge included a detailed list of the items to be seized during the search. The police, though, were unable to locate a correct warrant form. Instead, they used a form designed primarily for drug searches. In doing so, they made a number of corrections on the form, but failed to change the list of items to be seized to reflect accurately the evidence they hoped to discover. After determining that the police had established probable cause, a judge approved the search and promised the police that he would make the necessary changes in the warrant. That did not happen, nor did the judge attach the detailed affidavit. After the search uncovered incriminating evidence, the suspect was arrested and charged with murder. The trial judge, though finding the warrant defective, admitted the evidence because the search had been carried out in good faith. The Massachusetts Supreme Judicial Court reversed, concluding that the search violated the Fourth Amendment.

Employing the *Leon* standard, the *Sheppard* Court modified the exclusionary rule to permit evidence seized by police officers acting in objectively reasonable reliance on a technically defective warrant. The police had reasonably concluded that the search was authorized by a valid warrant. They informed the judge of the defects in the warrant and received his assurances that those defects would be corrected. It was the magistrate's responsibility to determine whether the application was technically deficient. The officers could not be expected to question the magistrate's judgment that the form of the warrant was technically sufficient. Moreover, any exclusion of evidence would not deter future police misconduct—the primary goal of the exclusionary rule—because in this case there was no police misconduct.

The dissenters in *Leon* and *Sheppard* criticized the majority for its narrow interpretation of the exclusionary rule. To Justices William Brennan and Thurgood Marshall, the rule was not a judicially created remedy, but a constitutional right, implicit in the Fourth Amendment. Because searches and seizures were conducted primarily to secure evidence to be introduced against a defendant at trial, the use of illegally obtained evidence at trial was as much a constitutional violation and equally egregious as the initial search and seizure. With any other construction, the judiciary "becomes part of what is in fact a single governmental action prohibited by the terms of the [Fourth] Amendment" (468 U.S. at 933). Justice Stevens dissented in *Leon*, but concurred in *Sheppard*. In *Leon*, the absence of probable cause rendered the search unreasonable. He also feared that police officers might engage in "judge shopping," hoping to find a judge willing to sign off on a warrant that may not be supported by probable cause, on the assumption that the evidence could be admitted nonetheless. In *Sheppard*, however, probable cause existed. Thus, the search, even if based on an invalid warrant, was reasonable.

The holdings in *Leon* and *Shephard* confirmed that the exclusionary rule was outside the realm of guaranteed Fourth Amendment rights: "The Fourth Amendment contains no provision expressly precluding the use of evidence obtained in violation of its commands" (468 U.S. at 913). Instead, the exclusionary rule was an evidentiary rule, to be used or not depending upon the social costs of excluding the relevant evidence. Additionally, with these decisions the Court announced that the exclusionary rule was applicable only in those cases of police misconduct, not judicial error. As such, when a defective warrant was the fault of the magistrate, nothing of value was gained from excluding the evidence seized.

The Supreme Court has extended the "good faith" exception, and thus limited the application of the exclusionary rule further, in a number of contexts. The exception applies when police obtain evidence by making an honest mistake in the execution of a warrant (police error); when police conduct a warrantless search pursuant to a state statute that is later declared unconstitutional (legislative error); and when police obtain evidence in reliance on an erroneous police record indicating the presence of an outstanding warrant (clerical error).

**Good Faith (Police Error).**  In *Maryland v. Garrison* (1987), mentioned earlier, police officers possessed a search warrant for Lawrence McWebb—who had been under police surveillance for some time—and his place of residence, listed on the warrant as the "2036 Park Avenue third floor apartment." When the officers applied for the warrant and when they conducted the search pursuant to the warrant, they believed that there was only one apartment on the premises described in the warrant. In fact, however, the third floor was divided into two apartments, one occupied by McWebb and one by Harold Garrison. The police inadvertently entered the apartment belonging to Garrison, who was not the target of the search warrant, and found drugs and drug paraphernalia. Unapologetic for this simple mistake, the *Garrison* majority concluded that the search warrant was valid and the execution of the warrant was also valid because the officers' lack of knowledge of the overly broad description in the warrant was objectively reasonable. Additionally, while the police had erred, they had not engaged in any misconduct. The dissent argued vigorously that the police knew the building was a multifamily dwelling and thus unreasonably assumed there was only one apartment on the third floor.

**Good Faith (Legislative Error).**  Most of the Fourth Amendment issues decided by the Supreme Court have not required its review of legislative judgments, but rather executive actions. That was not true, however, in *Illinois v. Krull* (480 U.S. 340; 1987). Here, the justices extended the "good faith" exception holding that the exclusionary rule did not apply to evidence obtained by police who acted in objectively reasonable reliance upon a state statute authorizing warrantless searches, but which was subsequently found to violate the Fourth Amendment. As part of its vehicle code, Illinois regulated the sale of motor vehicles and motor vehicle parts. Any person engaged in the sale of motor vehicle parts had to permit state officials to examine records "at any reasonable time during the night or day." The regulatory scheme also allowed for a warrantless examination of the premises to determine the accuracy of the records. In 1981 state officials, inspecting an automobile wrecking yard in Chicago, determined that a number of vehicles were stolen. The officer seized the vehicles and arrested Albert Krull, one of the operators of the wrecking yard, and his partners. At trial the evidence was suppressed, the state court holding that the statute in question provided state officials with too much unbridled discretion in conducting warrantless searches. Eventually, the Illinois Supreme Court affirmed, and the U.S. Supreme Court granted certiorari.

The *Krull* majority, mindful of precedent and fond of the cost-benefit approach, refused to exclude the evidence unless it could be shown that doing so would effectively deter future police misconduct. This the respondents could not show. The Justices thus could not distinguish this case in any meaningful way from *Leon.* The application of the exclusionary rule to suppress evidence obtained by an officer acting in objectively reasonable reliance on a statute would have no more deterrent effect on an officer than it would when the officer reasonably relied on an invalid warrant. The only remaining inquiry was whether excluding the evidence would deter legislative error. The Court reasoned that just as excluding evidence obtained by judicial error would not deter judicial error (*Leon* and *Sheppard*), excluding evidence obtained by legislative error would not deter legislators from passing constitutionally infirm statutes.

But even if one were found unconstitutional, as this one was, the evidence obtained as a result could still be admitted at trial. The Court also noted that neither Congress nor state legislatures had attempted to apply this type of administrative search statute. In other words, since it was not occurring often, the justices would afford this type of statute a presumption of constitutionality.

The four dissenters, in an opinion by Justice O'Connor, compared the statute to the acts of the British Parliament authorizing indiscriminate general searches by writs of assistance. (See Chapter Two.) To them the very purpose of the Fourth Amendment was to deny to the government the power to conduct warrantless searches. Accordingly, all evidence seized pursuant to a modern-day writ of assistance should be inadmissible at trial.

**Good Faith (Clerical Error).** Finally, *Arizona v. Evans* (514 U.S. 1; 1995) held that the exclusionary rule did not require the suppression of evidence seized pursuant to mistaken information resulting from clerical errors of court employees. After stopping a vehicle going in the wrong direction on a one-way street, police learned from their squad car computer that the driver, Isaac Evans, had an outstanding arrest warrant. Based on that information, the police searched the vehicle and discovered marijuana. The police later learned that the arrest warrant had been canceled seventeen days previously, but that cancellation had not yet been entered into the police department's computerized database. Subsequently, the Arizona Supreme Court, in *State v. Evans,* held that the marijuana could not be introduced as evidence and refused to apply the "good faith" exception to the exclusionary rule. In the state supreme court's words, "As automation increasingly invades modern life, the potential for Orwellian mischief grows. Under such circumstances, the exclusionary rule is a 'cost' we cannot afford to be without" (177 Ariz. 201, 204; [Ariz. 1994]). The state subsequently appealed that ruling, and the Supreme Court granted review.

The issue before the Court was whether the exclusionary rule required the suppression of evidence seized incident to an arrest resulting from an inaccurate computer record, regardless of whether police personnel or court personnel were responsible. Relying upon *Leon* and its progeny, the Court, in an opinion by Chief Justice Rehnquist, held that the exclusionary rule did not apply. The exclusionary rule was designed to deter police misconduct—not judicial errors, not police errors, not legislative errors, and, most assuredly, not errors by court employees. Because the exclusion here would not result in any appreciable deterrence, either by police or court employees, its use was unwarranted. Like judges and legislators, clerks are "adjuncts to the law enforcement team; they have no stake in the outcome of particular criminal prosecutions" (514 U.S. at 15). Two dissenters—Justices Stevens and Ginsburg—lambasted the majority for its dubious conclusion that the Fourth Amendment's sole purpose was the deterrence of police misconduct. Rather, it served as a fundamental check on all official invasions of the individual's right to privacy.

The good faith exception remains controversial. Opponents of the exception point to four adverse consequences (La Fave 1996, 330–332). First, it halts the judicial development of Fourth Amendment rights. If evidence is to be admitted in a criminal trial in the absence of clear precedent declaring the search to be unconstitutional, then the courts will, as a matter of priority, deny the accused's motion to suppress. Second, the exception imposes an "exceedingly difficult" burden on the judge hearing the motion to suppress. Because the good faith test is subjective, it is necessary for the suppression judge to probe the subjective knowledge of the officer executing the search. Third, it results in a distinct anti–Fourth Amendment bias in suppression rulings. Appellate courts defer to trial courts; and trial courts defer to police officers. And fourth, admitting illegally seized evidence creates a perception among police officers and the public at large that police officers have broad license to engage in the same kind of conduct in the future.

On the other hand, supporters of the rule submit that because the law of search and seizure is so complex (and often conflicting), police officers, untrained in the law, cannot always differentiate between what is permissible and what is prohibited (Carrington 1982, 115–118). Moreover, judicial bodies render decisions in "very pleasant and relaxed surroundings," whereas police officers on the street must make decisions in a fraction of a second, and in situations where indecision may result in danger to self and others. Because of these realities, supporters of the good faith exception are willing more often than not to give law enforcement authorities the benefit of the doubt.

In *each* of the aforementioned cases in this section, the justices concluded that no basis existed for believing that the exclusion of evidence would have any deterrent effect upon police misconduct, or judicial, police, legislative, or clerical error. In addition, unconstitutionally seized evidence is admissible in grand jury proceedings (*United States v. Calandra*; 1974); in federal civil tax proceedings (*United States v. Janis*, 428 U.S. 433; 1976); in habeas corpus proceedings (*Stone v. Powell*; 1976); in deportation hearings (*United States v. Lopez-Mendoza*, 468 U.S. 1032; 1984); to impeach a defendant's testimony at trial (*Michigan v. Harvey*, 494 U.S. 344; 1990); at a defendant's sentencing hearing (*United States v. Torres*, 926 F.2d 321; [3d Cir. 1991]); and at parole revocation hearings (*Pennsylvania Board of Probation and Parole v. Scott*, 524 U.S. 357; 1998). *Michigan v. Harvey* is particularly interesting, for it could prevent a defendant who has successfully moved for suppression of evidence from testifying at his or her own trial.

### Summary

The exclusionary rule is a shell of what was envisioned in *Weeks* (1914) and affirmed in *Mapp* (1961). In *Mapp*, the Supreme Court was clear: The exclusion doctrine was an "essential ingredient" of the Fourth Amendment, necessary to discourage police misconduct *and* maintain judicial integrity. Post-*Mapp* adjudication, however, has been built on the premise that the exclusionary rule is not a constitutional requirement, but a judicially created remedy to deter police misconduct.

Almost a century after its adoption, the exclusionary rule continues to generate controversy. Few constitutional debates, if any, are as sustained and as bitter as those over the exclusionary rule (Dripps 2001, 1). Supporters of the exclusionary rule argue that without the rule the protection of the Fourth Amendment is of no value. In the words of Justice Frank Murphy, dissenting in *Wolf,* the rule is the only means of "giving content to the commands of the Fourth Amendment" (338 U.S. at 41). Without it, nothing will deter the police from heavy-handed tactics and clear violations of individual constitutional rights. Opponents assert that the rule is contrary to justice and leads to the withholding of valuable evidence that could help establish truth in judicial proceedings. Much of the opposition to the exclusion of relevant evidence was distilled in a single sentence in *People v. Defore* (150 N.E. 585, 587; [NY 1926]), where Judge (later Justice) Benjamin N. Cardozo critically observed the possible consequences of such a practice: "The criminal is to go free because the Constable has blundered."

## CONCLUSION

From its inception, the Fourth Amendment has been "indispensable to the full enjoyment of the rights of personal security, personal liberty, and private property" (Story 1851, 608–609). Its purpose, in part, has been to reject the notion of "police government," in which an officer of the law, acting without a warrant, could enter any room or house at any time, break any drawer, and seize any papers or other items (Lieber 1853, 44–47); in short, to protect against the bane of general searches and seizures. More directly than any other amendment, the Fourth Amendment seeks to strike an appropriate balance between two equally legitimate interests—society's need for order and public safety, on the one hand, and the individual's desire for liberty and privacy, on the other hand. Fourth Amendment jurisprudence in the twentieth century has reflected this tension.

In attempting to protect the constitutional rights of individuals suspected of crimes, the Supreme Court has confronted established law enforcement practices in the area of search and seizure. The effort to "police the police" reached its heyday during the Warren era, with the landmark decisions in *Mapp, Katz,* and *Chimel.* This expansion of the rights of criminal defendants became a source of tremendous conservative dissatisfaction with the Warren Court (Maltz 2000, 151). By the late 1960s, the justices faced great scorn for these and other decisions, scorn exacerbated no doubt by the "coincidence in timing between the rise in crime, violence, and racial tension and the Supreme Court's campaign to strengthen the rights of criminal suspects" (Graham 1970, 4).

Reflecting public frustration with the Warren Court's expansion of the rights of criminal defendants, as well as the impact of the Republican Presidents Nixon, Reagan, and George H. W. Bush appointees, the Supreme Court since the 1970's has been decidedly less protective of the rights of criminal suspects. While only a few of the Warren Court precedents have been overturned, many have been seriously curtailed by the subsequent Burger and Rehnquist Courts. The formerly "few specifically established and well-delineated exceptions" to the warrant requirement are now many in number. Police only need "reasonable suspicion"—some minimal level of objective justification, something more than a hunch, but less than probable cause—to stop and detain a person for investigatory purposes. And the exclusionary rule has been reduced to a preventive device, not required by the Fourth Amendment and applicable only where law enforcement officers have engaged in misconduct.

One more thing is clear: Fourth Amendment jurisprudence in the twentieth century underscores the severe limitations on what the Supreme Court can accomplish in the "police practices" phase of criminal procedure. It is inherently difficult for the judiciary to define and protect the constitutional rights of criminal suspects. Doing so may well be beyond the power of the judiciary, even in the best of times. For the most part, the Court lacks supervisory powers over police practices. Because the Court can only hear a handful of cases a year involving police treatment of criminal suspects, it is "uniquely unable to take a comprehensive view of the subject of suspects' rights" (Amsterdam 1970, 788). And when the Court does announce some constitutional right, that right "filters down to the level of flesh and blood suspects only through the refracting layers of lower courts, trial judges, magistrates, and police officials" (Amsterdam 1970, 792). Protecting the constitutional rights of criminal suspects is made more difficult by the fact that virtually the only law relating to rights of criminal defendants in the entire twentieth century has been the law that the Court has created. This haphazard and unstable approach to law invites confusion. Judge-made law is not optimal in this field, "where police need clear guidelines and where the penalty for police mistakes is high."

A problem with the case method is that, in theory at least, it is not forward looking. As a leading observer of the Court has noted, the Court is not always able to:

> anticipate future cases and craft its rules, and the exceptions to those rules, with such cases in mind. Thus the Court is invariably left in the position of declaring a partial rule . . . that fails to deal adequately with the majority of subsequent cases that present related issues. Few, if any, would deny that in the field of criminal procedure legislative rulemaking has advantages over constitutional decision making. But are the courts supposed to do nothing in the absence of legislative rulemaking? A legislature never has to act, but a court does; it must decide the case at hand. (Kamisar 1995, 53–54)

If there is to be protection for criminal suspects, judge-made law, even if poorly made, is preferable to no law at all. "It is silly to ask whether the courts are doing an optimal job," observed Herbert Packer. "One might well ask whether surgery is optimally undertaken with a carving knife without revealing that on the particular occasion the surgeon has no other instruments at his disposal" (Packer 1965, 17).

## References and Further Reading

Allen, Francis. 1996. *The Habits of Legality: Criminal Justice and the Rule of Law.* New York: Oxford University Press.

Amar, Akhil Reed. 1997. *The Constitution and Criminal Procedure: First Principles.* New Haven, CT: Yale University Press.

Amsterdam, Anthony. 1970. "The Supreme Court and the Rights of Suspects in Criminal Cases." *New York University Law Review* 45: 785–815.

———. 1974. "Perspectives on the Fourth Amendment." *Minnesota Law Review* 58: 349–477.

Bernardi, Frederick A. 1980. "The Exclusionary Rule: Is a Good Faith Standard Needed to Preserve a Liberal Interpretation of the Fourth Amendment?" *De Paul Law Review* 30: 51–108.

Blackstone, Sir William. 1765–1769. *Commentaries on the Laws of England.* Four volumes. Oxford, England: Clarendon Press.

Bloom, Robert M., and Mark S. Brodin. 2004. *Criminal Procedure: Examples and Explanations.* 4th ed. New York: Aspen Publishers, Inc.

Cammack, Mark E., and Norman Garland. 2001. *Advanced Criminal Procedure.* St. Paul, MN: West Group.

Carrington, Frank. 1982. Hearings before the Subcommittee of Criminal Law, Committee on the Judiciary Senate, 97th Congress, 1st and 2nd Sessions, March 16 and 25, 115–118.

Commager, Henry Steele. 1958. *Documents of American History.* 6th ed. New York: Appleton-Century-Crofts, Inc.

Cooke, Jennifer Ison. 2002. "Discretionary Warrantless Searches and Seizures and the Fourth Amendment: A Need for Clearer Guidelines." *South Carolina Law Review* 53: 641–659.

Cray, Ed. 1997. Chief Justice: *A Biography of Earl Warren.* New York: Simon and Schuster.

Diffie, Whitfield, and Susan Landau. 1998. *Privacy on the Line: The Politics of Wiretapping and Encryption.* Boston: M.I.T. Press.

Dripps, Donald. 2001. "The Case for the Contingent Exclusionary Rule." *American Criminal Law Review* 38: 1–46.

Dudley, Eric C., Jr. 1998. "Terry v. Ohio, the Warren Court and the Fourth Amendment: A Law Clerk's Perspective." *St. John's Law Review.* 72: 891–903.

Dworkin, Ronald. 1973. "Fact Style Adjudication and the Fourth Amendment: The Limits of Lawyering." *Indiana Law Journal* 48: 329–368.

Foote, Caleb. 1960. "The Fourth Amendment: Obstacle or Necessity in the Law of Arrest?" *Journal of Criminal Law, Criminology & Political Science* 51: 402–408.

Friedman, Paul R. 1969. "Scope Limitations for Searches Incident to Arrest." *Yale Law Journal.* 78: 433–447.

Gilliom, John. 1994. *Surveillance, Privacy, and the Law: Employee Drug Testing and the Politics of Social Control.* Ann Arbor: University of Michigan Press.

Graham, Fred P. 1970. *The Self-Inflicted Wound.* New York: Macmillan.

Holcomb, Jayme Walker. 2002. "Consent Searches: Factors Courts Consider in Determining Voluntariness." *FBI Law Enforcement Bulletin.*

Kamisar, Yale. 1984. "Gates, 'Probable Cause,' 'Good Faith,' and Beyond." *Iowa Law Review.* 69: 551–615.

———. 1995. "The Warren Court and Criminal Justice: A Quarter-Century Retrospective." *Tulsa Law Journal.* 31: 1–55.

Kamisar, Yale, Wayne R. LaFave, and Jerold H. Israel. 1999. *Basic Criminal Procedure: Cases, Comments, and Questions.* St. Paul, MN: West Group.

———. 2002. *Advanced Criminal Procedure: Cases, Comments, and Questions.* St. Paul, MN: West Group.

Kaplan, John. 1974. "The Limits of the Exclusionary Rule." *Stanford Law Review.* 26: 1027–1055.

Kuras, Jeffrey Haningan, Catherine Kreindler Levy, Jennifer L. Burns, and Scott A. Lowry. 2002. "Thirty-First Annual Review of Criminal Procedure: I. Investigation and Police Practices: Warrantless Searches and Seizures." *Georgetown Law Review.* 90: 1130–1209.

LaFave, Wayne R. 1966. "Search and Seizure: 'The Course of the True Law . . . Has Not . . . Run Smooth.'" *University of Illinois Law Forum.* 1966: 255–389.

———. 1981. Hearings before the Subcommittee of Criminal Law, Committee on the Judiciary Senate, 97th Congress, 1st and 2nd Sessions, October 5 and 11, pp. 330–332.

————. 1984. "'The Seductive Call of Expediency': *United States v. Leon, Its Rationale and Ramifications.*" *University of Illinois Law Review.* 1984: 895–931.

————. 1995. *Search and Seizure: A Treatise on the Fourth Amendment.* 3rd ed. Four volumes. St. Paul, MN: West Publishing.

Landynski, Jacob W. [1968] 1978. *Search and Seizure and the Supreme Court.* Baltimore, MD: Johns Hopkins Press.

Lasson, Nelson B. 1937. *The History and Development of the Fourth Amendment to the United States Constitution.* Baltimore, MD: Johns Hopkins Press. Reprint Edition, New York: Da Capo Press.

Lehmann, Nicole J. 1994. "Note: The 'Plain Feel' Exception in *Minnesota v. Dickerson:* A Further Erosion of the Fourth Amendment." *Campbell Law Review.* 16: 257–274.

Levy, Leonard W. 1974. *Against the Law: The Nixon Court and Criminal Justice.* New York: Harper and Row.

Lieber, Francis. 1853. *On Civil Liberty and Self Government.* London: Trubner & Co.

Love, Brian S. 2004. "Comment: Beyond Police Conduct: Analyzing Voluntary Consent to Warrantless Searches by the Mentally Ill and Disabled." *St. Louis Law Journal.* 48: 1469–1500.

Maltz, Earl M. 2000. *The Chief Justiceship of Warren Burger.* Columbia: University of South Carolina Press.

Mason, Alpheus Thomas, and Donald Grier Stephenson, Jr. 2005. *American Constitutional Law: Introductory Essays and Selected Cases.* 14th ed. Upper Saddle River, NJ: Prentice Hall.

Mericli, Kemal Alexander. 1989. "The Apprehension of Peril Exception to the Knock and Announce Rule." *Search and Seizure Law Report.* 16: 129–136.

Moenssens, Andre. 2003. "Police Procedures: Some Problems With Warrants." *Forensic Evidence Newsletter,* available at www.forensic-evidence.com (last visited January 15, 2005).

Note. 1967. "The Supreme Court 1966 Term." *Harvard Law Review.* 81: 69–262.

Oaks, Dallin. 1970. "Studying the Exclusionary Rule in Search and Seizure." *University of Chicago Law Review.* 37: 665–757.

O'Brien, David M. 2005. *Constitutional Law and Politics: Civil Rights and Civil Liberties.* 6th ed. New York: W. W. Norton.

Packer, Herbert L. 1965. "Policing the Police." *The New Republic.* September 4, 1965, 17–21.

Persico, Deborah A. 1997. Mapp v. Ohio: *Evidence and Search Warrants.* Springfield, NJ: Enlsow Publishers.

Powe, Lucas A., Jr. 2000. *The Warren Court and American Politics.* Cambridge, MA: The Belknap Press of Harvard University Press.

Scheb, John M., and John M. Scheb, II. 2005. *Criminal Law and Procedure.* 5th ed. Belmont, CA: West Wadsworth.

Schlesinger, Stephen. 1977. *Exclusionary Injustice: The Problem of Illegally Obtained Evidence.* New York: Dekker.

Shapiro, B. J. 1991. *"Beyond Reasonable Doubt" and "Probable Cause": Historical Perspectives on the Anglo-American Law of Evidence.* Berkeley: University of California Press.

Story, Joseph. 1851. *Commentaries on the Constitution of the United States.* 2nd ed. Boston: C. C. Little and J. Brown.

Wallin, Howard E. 1987. "The Uncertain Scope of the Plain View Doctrine." *University of Baltimore Law Review.* 16: 266–286.

———. 2002. "Plain View Revisited." *Pace Law Review* 22: 307–345.

Way, H. Frank, Jr. 1959. "Increasing Scope of Search Incidental to Arrest." *Washington University Law Quarterly* 1959: 261–280.

———. 1980. *Criminal Justice and the American Constitution.* Belmont, CA: Duxbury Press.

Westin, Alan F. 1966. "Science, Privacy, and Freedom: Issues and Proposals for the 1970's." *Columbia Law Review.* 66: 1003–1050.

Wetterer, Charles M. 1998. *The Fourth Amendment: Search and Seizure.* Springfield, NJ: Enslow Publishers.

White, G. Edward. 1982. *Earl Warren: A Public Life.* New York: Oxford University Press.

White, Theodore H. 1969. *The Making of the President, 1968.* New York: Atheneum Publishers.

Wilkey, Malcolm R. 1982. *Enforcing the Fourth Amendment by Alternatives to the Exclusionary Rule.* Washington, DC: National Legal Center for Public Interest.

Wilson, Bradford. 1982. "The Origin and Development of the Federal Rule of Exclusion." *Wake Forest Law Review.* 18: 1073–1109.

Zalman, Marvin and Larry J. Siegel. 1997. *Criminal Procedure.* 2nd ed. Belmont, CA: West/Wadsworth.

# 4

# The Twenty-first
# Century

## Introduction

As noted in the previous chapter, by the year 2000—the final year of the twentieth century—the U.S. Supreme Court had substantially narrowed many of the Fourth Amendment protections once afforded criminal defendants. This narrowing process was precipitated by changes in Supreme Court membership resulting from Republican President Richard Nixon's fulfillment of a 1968 presidential campaign promise to "restore the balance" on the courts between "peace forces" and "criminal forces." During the campaign Nixon, along with third-party presidential candidate George Wallace, attempted to link controversial Supreme Court decisions of the 1960s to an increase in reported crime and with urban violence that they attributed largely to the civil rights movement and opposition to the war in Vietnam. The controversy swirling around the Supreme Court had been compounded in the summer of 1968 by President Lyndon Johnson's announcement of Chief Justice Earl Warren's intention to retire at the end of that year's Supreme Court term. Johnson nominated Associate Justice

Abe Fortas as Warren's successor and federal judge Homer Thornberry to fill the vacancy expected to be created by the Fortas promotion. Following three months of intense partisan opposition in the Senate, Fortas asked Johnson to withdraw his nomination and Warren withdrew his resignation. As such, the Senate took no action on the abortive Thornberry nomination. (For a full and informative account of this and other controversies surrounding Supreme Court nominations and appointments, see Abraham 1999. The unsuccessful nominations of Fortas for Chief Justice and Thornberry for Associate Justice are discussed in Chapters Two and Three of that book.) Historians and political scientists generally agree that the anti-Court strategies of Nixon and Wallace were among the factors that contributed to the defeat of the Democratic Party's candidate, Vice President Hubert Humphrey, and to the close election victory of Richard Nixon in 1968.

After Chief Justice Earl Warren announced unequivocally in May 1969 that he would retire at the close of that year's Supreme Court term, the new president had an opportunity to make good on the above-mentioned campaign promise. He promptly nominated and the Senate overwhelmingly confirmed Court of Appeals Judge Warren E. Burger, a vocal critic of the Fourth Amendment exclusionary rule, to succeed Chief Justice Warren, one of the rule's strong proponents. Burger also had serious reservations about Supreme Court decisions on other Fourth Amendment issues and in such related areas as police interrogation. (Compare, for example, Chief Justice Warren's majority opinion requiring warnings and waiver prior to police interrogation in the landmark case of *Miranda v. Arizona* (384 U.S. 436; 1966) with Chief Justice Burger's majority opinion narrowing the breadth of *Miranda* in *Harris v. New York* (401 U.S. 222; 1971). For background on the *Miranda* and *Harris* cases, see Stephens 1973, Chapter Six.) President Nixon's three additional Supreme Court appointees, Justices Harry A. Blackmun, Lewis F. Powell, and William H. Rehnquist, were all regarded at the time of their nominations as basically supportive of Burger's views in the field of criminal procedure. With these new judicial appointments in place, the Supreme Court began in the 1970s to restrict the procedural rights of criminal defendants. The specific curtailment of Fourth Amendment rights, including adoption of the "good faith" exception to the exclusionary rule, was discussed in Chapter Three. In this chapter we will examine Fourth Amendment cases decided between 2001 and the early spring of 2005 in an effort to assess the extent to which the trend of the 1970s, 1980s, and 1990s has continued.

Before turning to the central theme of this chapter, however, it may be helpful to the reader to provide a brief review of late-twentieth-century developments regarding domestic surveillance in the field of national security. Recall from Chapter Three that, beginning in *Olmstead v. United States* (1928), the U.S. Supreme Court held that the Fourth Amendment was not applicable to electronic wiretapping devices because such devices did not constitute a physical search of a suspect's premises, nor did they seize a suspect's property. In *Katz v. United States* (1967), however, the Court overruled *Olmstead* and extended Fourth Amendment protection to electronic surveillance, in this case wiretapping of a public telephone line, where individuals had a reasonable expectation of privacy. Notably, though, the justices declined to extend this holding to cases "involving the national security" (389 U.S. at 358 n. 23). Accordingly, federal courts have been reluctant to apply Fourth Amendment protections to foreign intelligence surveillance, preferring instead to defer to the Congress and the president on matters of national security. Numerous federal courts even adopted foreign intelligence exceptions to the Fourth Amendment. Prior to the early 1970s, executive agencies were largely unrestrained in conducting foreign intelligence surveillance.

In *United States v. United States District Court for the Eastern District of Michigan* (1972), however, the Supreme Court held that, to comply with customary Fourth Amendment requirements, judicial approval was necessary before initiation of searches or surveillance in domestic security cases. Writing for a six-member majority, Justice Powell emphasized that this case involved "only the domestic aspects of national security." He noted that the Court "[had] not addressed, and express[ed] no opinion as to, the issues which may be involved with respect to the activities of foreign powers or their agents" (407 U.S. at 321–322). The Court was careful to note that domestic security surveillance involved different policy and practical considerations from ordinary criminal surveillance. The majority even suggested that Congress consider different protective standards for surveillance concerning national security and criminal investigation: "Different standards may be compatible with the Fourth Amendment if they are reasonable both in relation to the legitimate need of Government for intelligence information and the protected rights of our citizens" (407 U.S. at 322–323). This invitation to distinguish between national security surveillance and criminal investigation, and its subsequent abuses by the Nixon administration, gave rise to the Foreign Intelligence Surveillance Act (FISA) (Pub. L. No. 95–511, 92 Stat. 1783; 1978).

In 1978, Congress passed FISA. Signed into law by President Jimmy Carter on October 25 of that year, this Act sought to strike an appropriate balance between the government's need for national security and an individual's constitutional rights. FISA set out the procedures for the government to follow when conducting surveillance in foreign intelligence investigations. The probable cause standard required by FISA differed from that required in a run-of-the-mill criminal investigation. In the latter, probable cause existed "where the facts and circumstances within [the government's] knowledge . . . [are] sufficient in themselves to warrant a man of reasonable caution in the belief that an offense has been or is being committed" (*Brineger,* 338 U.S. at 175–176; 1949). FISA, however, allowed for wiretapping of permanent residents in the United States on a showing of probable cause to believe that the target of the investigation was a "foreign power" or an "agent of a foreign power" and that the acquisition of such information was "necessary to national defense or security or the conduct of foreign affairs."

FISA did not require any showing of criminal activity on behalf of the target of the surveillance, unless the communications intercepted belonged to a "United States person." Where a "United States person" was involved, the courts required only a minimal standard of probable cause that the target be engaged in activity that "may involve" a criminal violation. Additionally, if the target were a "United States person," officials had to stipulate that the target was not being considered "solely upon the basis of activities protected by the first amendment to the Constitution."

FISA also created the Foreign Intelligence Surveillance Court (FISC), staffed by seven (now eleven) federal district court judges appointed by the chief justice of the United States for nonrenewable terms of up to seven years, to hear applications for foreign-intelligence surveillance orders and warrants. If a warrant application were denied by the FISC, it was immediately forwarded to a three-judge court of appeal, the Foreign Intelligence Surveillance Court of Review (FISCR). If denied there, the government could petition the Supreme Court for a writ of certiorari, although the Supreme Court has never heard a FISA application case. Between 1978 and 2002, the FISC, which meets *in camera* and hears cases on an expedited basis, considered roughly 15,000 applications, summarily approving the requests in all but a few instances, and denying none until May 2002.

Despite a number of constitutional challenges under the First and Fourth Amendments, courts have consistently upheld FISA, concluding that it effectively balances two competing interests: individual liberty and national security. Additionally, courts have permitted evidence obtained under FISA to be admitted in criminal prosecutions, so long as foreign intelligence gathering was the "primary purpose" of the surveillance.

## SEPTEMBER 11, 2001: POTENTIAL IMPACT ON THE FOURTH AMENDMENT

For the United States, the horrendous terrorist attacks launched against the World Trade Center and the Pentagon on September 11, 2001, constituted the defining event of the early twenty-first century. Three days later, on September 14, President George W. Bush responded by declaring a state of national emergency (*Proclamation 7463*). Congress immediately passed a resolution authorizing the president to use "all necessary and appropriate force" against the 9/11 terrorists and those who harbored them ("Sense of Congress Regarding Terrorist Attacks," Pub L. No. 107–140, 115 Stat. 224; 2001). In October, President Bush initiated military operations in Afghanistan "resulting a few months later in the overthrow of the Taliban regime and the destruction of many of the Al Qaeda cells and training camps operating in that country" (Stephens 2004, 71).

Meanwhile, eight days after the attacks, President Bush and Attorney General John Ashcroft proposed comprehensive legislation that Congress—with limited modifications, little debate, and only token opposition—passed as the USA PATRIOT Act (an acronym for Uniting and Strengthening America by Providing Appropriate Tools Required to Intercept and Obstruct Terrorism). The president signed the USA PATRIOT Act into law on October 26, 2001. A "sunset" clause, perhaps the most significant concession that the Senate and House of Representatives were able to obtain from the Bush administration, called for expiration of most of the statute's provisions on December 31, 2005, unless reenacted by Congress. As of this writing (August 2005) both the House of Representatives and the Senate have passed revised versions of the Act. A conference committee will attempt to resolve differences between the House and Senate versions. Both versions would retain and extend many, but not all, of the more controversial provisions. The USA PATRIOT Act took the form of amendments to a number of existing federal statutes and was spread piecemeal over some 342 pages of the United States Code. Few, if any, members of Congress had the opportunity to read this legislation in full before voting on it. Proponents of the hastily passed law sought to justify its enactment by claiming that it strengthened national security in several vulnerable areas. (For a comprehensive analysis of this aspect of this statute, see Banks 2004, 29–70.) The USA PATRIOT Act immediately threatened to erode a number of protections under the Bill of Rights, including those of the First, Fourth, Fifth, Sixth, and Eighth Amendments. We are primarily concerned here with the possible adverse impact of the USA PATRIOT Act on Fourth Amendment protections against unreasonable searches and seizures.

Several provisions of this Act expand the power of government to monitor private telephone, E-mail, and Internet communications. (See, for example, Section 214, "Pen Register and Trap and Trace Authority under FISA.") This expanded surveillance authority does not require the government to establish probable cause and, in fact, imposes only minimal warrant requirements. In addition, the "sneak-and-peek" provision of Section 213 permits the government to obtain a warrant, secretly enter a person's private property, and seize potential evidence before informing that person of the warrant's existence.

Section 215 of the Act relaxes the probable cause requirements and expands the reach of FISA. Under this section, the FBI may obtain an order from the FISC requiring the production of "any tangible things (including books, records, papers, documents, and other items) sought for an investigation . . . to protect against international terrorism or clandestine intelligence activities." Probable cause is not required. All the FBI needs to articulate is that the items requested are "sought for" an authorized investigation. The target of the investigation need not be suspected of any criminal wrongdoing. And the extension of the physical searches is not limited to foreign powers and their agents. Anyone, including U.S. citizens, may be investigated. If targeting a U.S. citizen, however, the investigation cannot be conducted "solely on the basis of activities protected by the first amendment to the Constitution." Procedurally, a judge presented with a Section 215 application must grant the order if he or she "finds that the application meets the requirements of this section." Those who are ordered to relinquish their records are prohibited from disclosing to any other person that federal law enforcement authorities had sought or obtained such information.

At this writing (Summer 2005), none of the surveillance provisions of the USA PATRIOT Act has reached the United States Supreme Court for review. Challenges to various aspects of the law have, however, been initiated. (See, for example, *In Re Sealed Case,* No. 02–001, United States Foreign Intelligence Surveillance Court (2002); and *Humanitarian Law Project v. Ashcroft,* 309 F.Supp. 2d 1185 [C. D. Cal. 2004].)

The American Civil Liberties Union brought the first constitutional challenge to the USA PATRIOT Act in July 2003 in the case of *Muslim Community Association* (MCA) *et al. v. Ashcroft and Mueller* (No. 03–72913, E.D. Mich., filed July 30, 2003). The plaintiffs specifically alleged that Section 215 was violative of their freedom of speech, right of privacy, and right to be free from unreasonable searches and seizures. The six Muslim advocacy groups represented by the ACLU contended that:

> while they [had] no way of knowing that the FBI [had] used its surveillance powers against them, their members [had] been unfairly singled out, questioned, accused, deported, and imprisoned by the FBI because of their ethnicity; religion; and political beliefs, activities, and associations (and those of their friends). (quoted in Glenn 2004, 23)

These groups, composed mostly of Muslim Arab-Americans, continue to be outspoken critics of the war in Iraq and of the "wide net that has been cast over the Muslim community" since 9/11. According to the plaintiffs, the oppressive tactics of the FBI, coupled with its freedom to operate with very little judicial oversight and in virtual secrecy, had sharply curtailed a wide range of their First and Fourth Amendment rights. (For a detailed account of the issues raised in this case, see Glenn 2004.)

Because Section 215 does not require individualized suspicion, the plaintiffs maintained that the FBI could demand from a bookstore or library a list of individuals who had purchased or checked out a book on Islamic fundamentalism; from a health clinic a list of patients who had received medical care; from a publisher a list of subscribers to a particular magazine; from an Internet provider a list of persons who had visited a particular Web site; from a church, mosque, or synagogue a list of members; or from a charity a list of clients and contributors. At a June 2003 hearing before the House Judiciary Committee, Attorney General John Ashcroft conceded that Section 215 could be used to obtain, among other things, education records and genetic information. The plaintiffs contended that granting such unfettered power to the government endangers personal privacy.

The plaintiffs' Fourth Amendment objection pointed to the FISA court's lack of authority to make an independent probable cause determination. As previously noted, if the FBI director or his designee meets the minimal standards of Section 215, the court lacks discretion to deny the application and must issue the order. Thus, the FBI may search and seize records or personal belongings without a conventional warrant, without showing probable cause, and without giving notice of the searches. In short, the plaintiffs argued that without meaningful judicial oversight, Section 215 will render the Fourth Amendment impotent as a guardian of civil liberty.

On December 3, 2003, Judge Denise Page Hood of the U.S. District Court for the Eastern District of Michigan heard a motion from the Department of Justice to dismiss *MCA v. Ashcroft and Mueller.* According to a February 25, 2005, article in the *Detroit Free Press,* Judge Hood, although promising an early ruling in this case, had yet to respond to the motion. The *Free Press* observed that "the need for a decision has grown more acute, with

Congress set to debate which sections of the [PATRIOT Act] should be allowed to expire this year and which should be renewed" (*Detroit Free Press*, February 25, 2005). As of May 10, 2005, Judge Hood still had the motion to dismiss under consideration.

The U.S. Supreme Court, in June 2004, surprised many observers by ruling on the constitutionality of the federal government's indefinite detention of citizen and noncitizen enemy combatants. In *Hamdi v. Rumsfeld* (542 U.S. 507; 2004), a badly fractured majority decided that, although Congress had authorized the detention of enemy combatants captured in Afghanistan, due process of law requires that an American citizen thus detained must be given a meaningful opportunity to contest the detention before a neutral decision-maker. In the companion case of *Rasul v. Bush* (542 U.S. 466; 2004), the Court, by a six-three margin, held, among other things, that "the federal courts have jurisdiction to determine the legality of the Executive's potentially indefinite detention of individuals who claim to be wholly innocent of wrongdoing."

If the Court is thus willing to consider challenges to the government's exercise of military power against enemy combatants, it is not unreasonable to speculate that the Court may ultimately rule on the constitutionality of Fourth Amendment restrictions embodied in the USA PATRIOT Act. Further speculation about the possible application of the Fourth Amendment to antiterrorist measures must give way at this point to an examination of the Supreme Court's most recent review of search and seizure issues.

## THE WARRANT CLAUSE

As made clear in the previous chapters, most arrests and many police searches in the United States are conducted without warrants.

Nevertheless, the warrant requirement remains an important component of Fourth Amendment law. In this section we will examine the Supreme Court's most recent pronouncements on the nature and extent of this requirement.

## Probable Cause

In dissenting from the denial of certiorari in *Overton v. Ohio* (534 U.S. 982; 2001), Justice Stephen Breyer, joined by Justices John Paul Stevens, Sandra Day O'Connor, and David Souter, restated the well-established requirements for an arrest warrant. Whether probable cause exists as a basis for the issuance of an arrest warrant must be determined "by a neutral magistrate in order 'to insure that the deliberate, impartial judgment of a judicial officer will be interposed between the citizen and the police, to assess the weight and credibility of the information which the complaining officer adduces as probable cause'" (534 U.S. at 982, quoting *Wong Sun v. United States,* 371 U.S. 471, 481–82; 1963).

Justice Breyer then explained why the efforts of the police were insufficient to support the issuance of a valid arrest warrant. The only evidence offered to the magistrate to show probable cause was a previously prepared "form complaint" listing Overton's name, the date of the offense, the designation of the offense, and the relevant statutory reference. The complaint merely described the alleged crime in general terms. Because the complaint did not "indicate *how* [the police officer] *knows, or why he believes, that Overton committed the crime,* the Magistrate could not 'assess independently the probability that [the] petitioner committed the crime charged'" (534 U.S. at 982, quoting *Giordenello v. United States,* 357 U.S. 480, 487; 1958). In other words, Justice Breyer believed that the complaint was inadequate because it contained nothing more than "the complainant's conclusion" that the named persons "perpetrated the offense described in the complaint" (534 U.S. at 982). Certiorari was denied "because [the] Court [had] already answered directly the basic legal question presented in this case."

Justice Breyer and three of his colleagues would have reversed the conviction summarily but, of course, their views did not carry the day.

## Particularity

Two questions were presented to the Supreme Court in the 2004 case of *Groh v. Ramirez* (540 U.S. 551). First, was the challenged search warrant invalid because it failed to meet the particularity requirement of the Fourth Amendment? Second, was the officer who conducted the search entitled to qualified immunity in a subsequent suit for damages? A resident of Butte–Silver Bow County, Montana, informed Jeff Groh, an agent of the Bureau of Alcohol, Tobacco, and Firearms (ATF), that he had visited the ranch of Joseph Ramirez and, on several occasions, had seen a large arsenal of illegal weapons. Groh prepared and signed a search warrant application, which specifically listed the types of weapons for which he intended to search, and a detailed affidavit explaining why he believed the weapons were at Ramirez's ranch. Groh provided these documents and a warrant form to the local magistrate. The portion of the warrant form used to describe the "persons or things to be seized" did not list the weapons; instead it described Ramirez's house. The warrant subsequently issued by the magistrate did not specifically refer to the application or affidavit, but it did state that the magistrate believed that the affidavit satisfied the probable cause requirement. On the day following issuance of the warrant, Groh led a team of federal and local law enforcement officers in a search of the house. Groh later claimed that he informed Ramirez of the types of weapons for which the officers were searching. Ramirez insisted, however, that Groh said he was only searching for "an explosive device in a box." After finding no incriminating evidence in the house, Groh gave Ramirez a copy of the warrant form. He failed, however, to provide Ramirez with the page of the warrant application containing the list of weapons to be seized. Ramirez's attorney requested and received this information on the following day.

Ramirez sued Groh and the other officers, claiming, among other things, that his Fourth Amendment rights had been violated by a search warrant that failed to describe with particularity the persons or things to be seized. The federal district court entered judgment for Groh and his fellow officers, and the court of appeals affirmed except as to the Fourth Amendment claim. The Supreme Court, in an opinion written by Justice Stevens, held that the search warrant was invalid. Justice Stevens noted that the Fourth Amendment unambiguously requires that warrants "particularly describe the place to be searched, and the persons to be seized" (540 U.S. at 556). The particularity requirement is not satisfied merely because another document beyond the purview of the person whose property is to be seized happens to list the items in question.

Additionally, Groh's search of the ranch was not reasonable even though the magistrate examined the application before issuing the warrant. The warrant did not merely make a minor mistake but completely failed to describe the items to be seized. Accordingly, "the warrant was so obviously deficient that [the Court] regard[ed] the search as 'warrantless'." Justice Stevens reiterated the "firmly established . . . basic principle of Fourth Amendment law that searches and seizures inside a home without a warrant are presumptively unreasonable" (540 U.S. at 559, quoting *Payton v. New York*, 445 U.S. 573, 586; 1980, discussed in Chapter Three). This basic principle, as previously noted, applies to search warrants that do not meet the particularity requirement. Therefore Groh's search of Ramirez's house for "contraband" was unconstitutional unless consent was given or exigent circumstances were present, even if a felony had been committed and probable cause existed. The facts before the Court indicated neither consent nor exigent circumstances.

Justice Stevens added that since the items listed on the application did not appear on the warrant, "there [could] be no written assurance that the magistrate actually found probable cause to search for, and to seize, every item mentioned in the affidavit" (540 U.S. at 560, citing *McDonald v. United States,* 335 U.S. 451, 455; 1948). The fact that Groh and the other officers limited their search to those items listed on the application did not render the search constitutional. Moreover, "even if the magistrate was aware of the deficiency," it would be unreasonable for Groh to rely on a warrant "that was so patently defective" (540 U.S. at 561, note 4, citing *United States v. Leon,* 468 U.S. 897, 915, 922, note 23; 1984). The Court's decision does not create a duty for officers to proofread the warrant, but instead requires them to "ensure that the warrant conforms to constitutional requirements" (540 U.S. at 563, note 6). Justice Stevens explained that the particularity requirement is essential so that the person whose property is to be searched knows what the investigating officer has a right to search, the officer's reason for conducting the search, and the limits within which the search must be conducted. While recognizing that the Fourth Amendment does not specifically require that the warrant be shown to the person before beginning the search, Justice Stevens expressed a strong preference for doing so unless it would be "impractical or imprudent" (540 U.S. at 562, note 5). No such circumstances existed in this case.

With respect to the other claims brought by Ramirez, the Court ruled that Groh was not entitled to qualified immunity. The standard that the Court applied was "whether it would be clear to a reasonable officer that his conduct was unlawful in the situation he confronted" (540 U.S. at 563, quoting *Saucier v. Katz,* 533 U.S. 194, 202; 2001). Since public officials should know the clearly established laws governing their conduct, any reasonable officer would know of the Fourth Amendment's particularity requirement and that the warrant in this case did not satisfy that requirement. Groh had prepared the warrant application himself and was thus responsible for the glaring errors that "even a cursory reading ... would have revealed." (540 U.S. at 564). Moreover, a reasonable officer would have known that, because of the invalidity of the warrant, he could not search Ramirez's house without consent or the existence of exigent circumstances. Since neither of these exceptions to the warrant requirement were present, a reasonable officer would not have performed the search.

Justice Anthony Kennedy, joined by Chief Justice Rehnquist, agreed with the majority that the search warrant violated the Fourth Amendment's particularity requirement, but dissented from its holding on the qualified immunity issue. Justice Kennedy adhered to the same "reasonable officer" standard that the majority applied, but would have invoked a "good faith" exception similar to that developed in exclusionary rule cases. Justice Kennedy contended that Groh's failure to detect the warrant's lack of particularity was reasonable. The clerical error was not made on the application and supporting affidavit. No one else noted the error and Groh did not rely on it. Given the numerous responsibilities confronting Groh in preparing for the search, some "latitude for honest mistakes" should be allowed "in the dangerous and difficult process of making arrests and executing search warrants" (540 U.S. 568, quoting *Maryland v. Garrison*, 480 U.S. 79, 87; 1987).

Justice Clarence Thomas, joined by Justice Antonin Scalia, dissented on both issues, maintaining that the warrant was constitutional and that Groh was protected by qualified immunity. Chief Justice Rehnquist joined this opinion with respect to the qualified immunity issue. Thomas noted that the Court's "warrantless search" cases generally "involve situations in which the officers neither sought nor obtained a warrant" (540 U.S. at 574). Justice Thomas insisted that when an objective and neutral magistrate issues a search warrant, that warrant is not presumptively unreasonable. The search was reasonable because Groh explained its scope to the other officers, stayed within that scope, gave Ramirez and other members of his family a copy of the warrant at the end of the search, and sent them the more detailed warrant application the following day.

According to Justice Thomas, Groh was entitled to qualified immunity because of his objectively reasonable belief that the search warrant was valid. Finally, Groh was entitled to the protection afforded by qualified immunity. Groh had no reason to believe the search warrant was invalid after it had been approved by the magistrate.

In summation, seven of the nine justices found that the search warrant was invalid because of the agent's error. Unlike the Court in *United States v. Leon* (1984), the *Ramirez* Court exhibited little patience with innocent mistakes that infringe on an individual's Fourth Amendment rights. The most surprising aspect of this case was the Court's conclusion that Agent Groh was not entitled to qualified immunity. Again, the justices did not imply that the agent was acting in bad faith. Instead the Court found that the mistake made the warrant so facially deficient that no officer could believe it was still valid. Since Groh was presumably unaware of the defect in the warrant, however, and was preparing his team to execute it, he had little incentive to double-check and make sure that he had completed the forms correctly.

## Execution of the Warrant

At about 2:00 p.m. on a Wednesday in Las Vegas, Nevada, local police and FBI agents went to the apartment of LaShawn Lowell Banks to execute a search warrant and seize evidence of drug dealing. They knocked on the front door and called out "police search warrant" loud enough to be heard by officers on the other side of Banks's apartment. After waiting fifteen to twenty seconds, the officers used a battering ram to knock down the front door. Banks later testified that he was in the shower and did not hear the officers until they rammed the door. The officers seized weapons, cocaine, and other drug paraphernalia, later used to convict Banks. Banks moved to suppress the evidence, contending that the officers had not waited a reasonable amount of time before breaking into his apartment. The District Court denied the motion, but the Court of Appeals for the Ninth Circuit reversed. The Supreme Court granted certiorari and in turn reversed the decision of the Ninth Circuit.

Writing for a unanimous Court, Justice David Souter discussed the prevailing "totality of the circumstances" approach used to determine the constitutional validity of a search. According to Justice Souter, the Court has tended to avoid "categories and protocols" because they tend to "play down important facts while emphasizing trivialities" (540 U.S. 31, 36; 2003). Generally, before searching closed premises, police have an obligation to "knock and announce." They are not required to do so, however, when they are reasonably suspicious that doing so "would be dangerous or futile or . . . would [allow] the destruction of evidence" (540 U.S. at 36, quoting *Richards v. Wisconsin,* 520 U.S. 385 at 394; 1997).

Referring to the facts of this case, Justice Souter asserted that exigent circumstances arose during the fifteen-to-twenty-second period after officers knocked and announced their intent to search Banks' apartment. During that time, Banks could "flush away the easily disposable cocaine." But was it reasonable for the officers to believe that the evidence might be destroyed if they waited any longer than fifteen to twenty seconds? The Court answered this question in the affirmative, citing a long line of federal appellate court cases that considered "the risk of disposal of drug evidence as a factor in evaluating the reasonableness of waiting time" (540 U.S. at 38). What counted were the facts known to the police. Accordingly, it did not matter whether Banks was in the shower at the time the officers knocked and announced their intent to search his apartment. It also did not matter that it would have taken more than fifteen to twenty seconds to answer the door. What mattered was how long it would have taken to dispose of the drug evidence. "We think," Justice Souter concluded, "that after 15 or 20 seconds without a response, police could fairly suspect that [the] cocaine would be gone if they were reticent any longer" (540 U.S. at 38). The Court clarified the scope of its decision by noting that it did not apply to warrantless entry cases or cases involving the risk of losing evidence of a minor offense.

The *Banks* case added content to other Supreme Court rulings that refer only in general terms to the requirement that the police make their presence known before entering a residence to execute a search warrant. One commentator observed that this decision was not a complete victory for the government. The totality of circumstances, including the fragility of the evidence being sought, should always be considered. "Police seeking a stolen piano, may be able to spend more time to make sure they really need the battering ram" (Greenhouse 2003).

For a recent discussion of the scope of the power of the police to detain, handcuff, and question the occupant of a house, *pursuant* to a search warrant, see *Muehler v. Mena*, 125 S.Ct. 1465; decided March 22, 2005. In this case, the Supreme Court foun no Fourth Amendment violation.

## EXCEPTIONS TO THE WARRANT REQUIREMENT

### Consent Searches

In the 2002 case of *United States v. Drayton* (536 U.S. 194), the Supreme Court applied the "consent search" exception to police questioning of Greyhound passengers Christopher Drayton and Clifton Brown, Jr. They were traveling on a bus that made a scheduled stop in Tallahassee, Florida. After Drayton and Brown reboarded the bus with other passengers, the driver allowed three local police officers, in plain clothes but with visible badges, to board the bus and perform a routine drug and weapons interdiction. One officer stood at the back of the bus, another knelt against the bus driver's seat, while the third walked down the aisle and began speaking to passengers. The officers did not inform the passengers that they were not required to answer the officers' questions and could leave at any time.

An officer approached Drayton and Brown, told them he was conducting a drug and weapon interdiction, and asked them if he could search their bags. They consented to the search and no illegal drugs were found in their bags. Noting that Drayton and Brown were wearing baggy clothes, the officer first asked Brown for consent to search his person, to which Brown agreed. The officer patted him down and found what he believed to be packages of drugs. The officer then arrested Brown and had him taken off the bus. After obtaining Drayton's consent to a pat-down search of his person, the officer found packages similar to those he had identified on Brown's person. After Drayton was arrested and removed from the bus, both suspects were searched more thoroughly. It turned out that they had "duct taped plastic bundles of powder cocaine between several pairs of their boxer shorts" (536 U.S. at 199). The cocaine was later introduced as evidence against them.

The trial judge rejected Drayton and Brown's motions to suppress the cocaine, concluding that they had voluntarily consented to the search of their persons. They were convicted of conspiring to distribute cocaine and possession with intent to distribute. The Court of Appeals for the Eleventh Circuit reversed and remanded, holding that the search was coerced, not voluntary. The Supreme Court granted certiorari and reversed, holding that the consent to search was voluntary.

In his majority opinion, Justice Kennedy expressed the view that police coercion of an individual does not occur so long as "a reasonable person would feel free to terminate the encounter" (536 U.S. at 202, quoting *Florida v. Bostick*, 501 U.S. at 436; 1991, discussed in Chapter Three). The Court used a "totality of the circumstances" test to determine how an objective reasonable person would feel. This test was qualified, however, by the Court's presumption that the reasonable person was "an *innocent* person" (536 U.S. at 202, quoting 501 U.S. at 437–438; emphasis in original).

Adhering to the analysis in *Bostick,* Kennedy found that since a reasonable person would have felt free under the circumstances to decline to cooperate or leave the bus, Drayton and Brown had voluntarily consented to the search. The officer "did not brandish a weapon[,] make any intimidating movements" or use any force (536 U.S. at 203–204). These same circumstances would be constitutional if they occurred on a street corner; the fact that they took place on a bus did not make the officer's questioning an illegal seizure. It did not follow that a seizure occurred merely because the officers wore badges and were stationed at the doors of the bus. The fact that most passengers cooperated with the police in such situations did not mean "that a reasonable person would not feel free to terminate the bus encounter" (536 U.S. at 205). While the officers' failure to inform Drayton and Brown that they need not consent was a factor to be weighed in considering the totality of the circumstances, that factor was not dispositive.

In dissent Justice Souter, joined by Justices Ginsburg and Stevens, discounted various precedents that the majority had cited in its opinion. One of these involved airport searches and another concerned federal immigration agents who were posted at the entrance to a factory (see *Florida v. Rodriguez,* 469 U.S. 1; 1984; and *INS v. Delgado,* 466 U.S. 210; 1984). For Justice Souter, the only issue before the Court was whether the police officers' drug and weapon interdiction was a "suspicionless seizure" (536 U.S. at 208). If it was, the consent of Drayton and Brown was automatically invalid. The dissenters, like the majority, relied on the *Bostick* test, but viewed the facts of the case from an entirely different perspective. Justice Souter described how the circumstances in the instant case might appear if they had taken place on the street. His vivid description merits quoting at length:

Now consider three officers, one of whom stands behind the pedestrian, another at his side toward the open sidewalk, with the third addressing questions to the pedestrian a foot or two from his face. Finally, consider the same scene in a narrow alley. On such barebones facts, one may not be able to say a seizure occurred, even in the last case, but one can say without qualification that the atmosphere of the encounters differed significantly from the first to the last examples. In the final instance there is every reason to believe that the pedestrian would have understood, to his considerable discomfort, what Justice Potter Stewart described as the "threatening presence of several officers." (536 U.S. at 210, quoting in part from *United States v. Mendenhall*, 446 U.S. 544 at 554; 1980)

Justice Souter continued: With the driver absent, the officers effectively took control of the bus, positioning themselves at the exits during the investigation. The officers did not inform the passengers that they did not have to answer their questions and that they could leave the bus at any time. They thus created "an atmosphere of obligatory participation" (536 U.S. at 212).

The majority believed that because pedestrians are not coerced by the police when approached in the street, bus passengers should not feel coerced. But, as the dissent asserted, the bus passengers in *Drayton* were not merely approached; they were effectively cornered and surrounded in a tight and restrictive space by three officers. Such circumstances should be considered coercive. Instead, officers receive substantial leeway when performing unwarranted searches on buses, especially in connection with the ongoing "war on drugs." There is reason to believe that the same wide latitude would be accorded to searches on trains, subways, and possibly airplanes.

**Probation and Consent Searches.**   The Supreme Court has not limited the consent exception to the warrant requirement to preliminary investigations of suspected criminal activity. This exception also applies to conditions of a convicted defendant's probation, as the Supreme Court's decision in *United States v. Knights* (534 U.S. 112; 2001) makes clear. One of the conditions for Mark

James Knights's probation following his conviction for a drug offense was his consent to a police search of his person, property,
residence, and automobile at any time without probable cause. By
signing the probation order, Knights agreed to this condition.
Three days after he was placed on probation, a Pacific Gas and
Electric (PG&E) transformer was vandalized, causing damage
amounting to $1.5 million. PG&E had previously sued Knights
for theft-of-services; and since the filing of the lawsuit he had been
suspected of numerous acts of vandalism of the company's facilities. After viewing suspicious behavior outside Knights's residence, a detective searched his driveway and apartment, finding
explosives and related material. The detective was aware, prior to
the search, of the consent condition in Knights's probation order.

Knights moved to suppress the potential evidence obtained in
the search of the apartment. A district court granted the motion,
holding that Knights had only agreed to searches for probationary, as distinguished from investigatory, purposes. The Court of
Appeals for the Ninth Circuit affirmed, but the U.S. Supreme
Court reversed.

In an opinion for a unanimous Court, Chief Justice Rehnquist
clearly stated the issue: "whether the Fourth Amendment limits
searches pursuant to [the California] probation condition to those
with a 'probationary' purpose" (534 U.S. at 116). In addressing
this issue the Court relied on its 1987 decision in *Griffin v. Wisconsin* (discussed in Chapter Three). There the Court upheld a
Wisconsin statute allowing probation officers to conduct warrantless searches of probationers' residences with supervisor approval
so long as the searches were based on reasonable grounds. While
the Court took note of the "special need" of law enforcement to
ensure that probation restrictions were being followed, it did not
limit such searches solely to probationary purposes.

In determining whether a search was reasonable, the Court
looked at the totality of the circumstances, balancing the government's interest in rehabilitation and protection of society from fu-

ture criminal violations against the privacy rights of the probationer. While not as severe as incarceration, probation is a court's criminal sanction entered into "after verdict, finding, or plea of guilty" (534 U.S. at 119, quoting *Griffin v. Wisconsin*, 483 U.S. at 874). Probationers have a lesser liberty interest than the law-abiding citizen and "a court . . . may impose reasonable conditions that deprive [a probationer] of some freedoms" (534 U.S. at 119). The balance between the interests of the government and the probationer "requires no more than reasonable suspicion to conduct a search of [the] probationer's house . . ." (534 U.S. at 121). Chief Justice Rehnquist maintained that a warrantless search is reasonable if there is "a sufficiently high probability that criminal conduct is occurring." Finally, because the Court considered the totality of the circumstances when determining whether the search was reasonable, there was no need to examine "the actual motivation of individual officers" conducting the search (534 U.S. at 122, quoting *Whren v. United States*, 517 U.S. at 814; 1996).

Because the search was reasonable, the Court did not decide whether Knights's "acceptance of the search condition constituted consent [and] a complete waiver of Fourth Amendment rights" (534 U.S. at 118). The Court also avoided deciding whether Knights's consent would allow law enforcement officers to perform searches without any individualized suspicion.

Justice Souter concurred, stating that *Whren* made it clear that the subjective motivations of the investigating officer should not be considered when performing an "ordinary, probable-cause Fourth Amendment analysis." Justice Souter preferred to reserve the question of whether these subjective motivations ought to be considered in "searches based only upon reasonable suspicion" (534 U.S. at 123).

The important question left unanswered in the *Knights* ruling is whether a probationer's consent would allow a suspicionless search. Could a probationer in fact waive a reasonable suspicion requirement completely? The answer to this question would probably be determined by the Court's assessment of whether conditional consent to a search would meet the requirements of a truly voluntary waiver.

### International Border Searches

As noted in the previous chapter, the government's power to conduct warrantless searches at international borders is very broad. In *United States v. Flores-Montano* (541 U.S. 149; 2004), the Supreme Court reaffirmed the federal authority to conduct suspicionless inspections of automobiles at the border. Here the Court ruled that this power included the authority to remove, disassemble, and reassemble the fuel tank of a privately owned automobile.

The chain of events leading up to this case can be traced to Manuel Flores-Montano's attempt to enter the United States from Mexico through the Otay Mesa Port of Entry. After inspecting Flores-Montano's station wagon, a customs agent decided that the vehicle should go through a more thorough search at a secondary station. Another agent inspected the gas tank by tapping it, noticed that it sounded solid, and called a mechanic to examine it. Within an hour, the mechanic had removed the gas tank from the underside of the car. The inspector then "hammered off" a putty-like substance that concealed an access plate, and on removing the plate discovered 37 kilograms (81 pounds) of marijuana inside the tank. Flores-Montano was charged with unlawful importation of marijuana and possession with intent to distribute.

The U.S. District Court for the Southern District of California granted Flores-Montano's motion to suppress the marijuana evidence. The district court agreed with the defendant that the case was controlled by a Court of Appeals for the Ninth Circuit precedent, *United States v. Molina-Tarazon* (279 F.3d 709; [9th Cir. 2002]), holding that the removal of a gas tank required reasonable suspicion in order to comply with the Fourth Amendment. The government, rather than attempting to prove reasonable suspicion under *Molina-Tarazon,* attempted to discredit this precedent, but the trial court was not persuaded by the argument. Not surprisingly, the Court of Appeals for the Ninth Circuit summarily affirmed the decision of the district court. Given the running battle between the Supreme Court and the Ninth Circuit in this and other areas of constitutional interpretation, it also comes as no surprise that the Supreme Court in turn reversed this decision.

In his opinion for the majority, Chief Justice Rehnquist noted that the Court had discussed the constitutionality of searches at international borders almost two decades earlier. In the present case the Court was undivided in holding that while "highly intrusive [border] searches of the person" might require a level of suspicion, searches of vehicles are "routine" and constitutional without any suspicion for the simple reason that such searches occur at the border. He pointed out that the Court was suggesting "no view on what level of suspicion, if any, is required for nonroutine border searches such as strip, body-cavity or involuntary X-ray searches" (541 U.S. at 152, quoting from *United States v. Montoya de Hernandez,* 473 U.S. 531, 541; 1985). The chief justice added that "reasons that might support a requirement of some level of suspicion in the case of highly intrusive searches of the person— dignity and privacy interests of the person being searched—simply do not carry over to vehicles" (541 U.S. at 152).

The opinion made some additional points. First, at the international border, "[t]he Government's interest in preventing the entry of unwanted persons and effects is at its zenith" (541 U.S. at 149). Second, Congress has continuously recognized that this governmental interest outweighs an individual's privacy interest, which "is less at the border than it is in the interior" (541 U.S. at 154, quoting from *Montoya de Hernandez,* 473 U.S. at 538). And third, the search merely involved the dismantling and reassembly of a gas tank—a brief procedure that rarely damages the vehicle. The chief justice concluded by observing that, "While it may be true that some searches of property are so destructive as to require a different result, this was not one of them" (541 U.S. at 155–156). Justice Breyer concurred, adding that the Customs administrative procedures prevent gas tank searches from being performed abusively. The unanimity of the *Flores-Montano* decision supports the conclusion that in the post-9/11 era the Supreme Court is not prepared to apply significant Fourth Amendment standards to searches at international borders.

## Investigatory Detentions: Stop and Identify Statutes

On June 21, 2004, the Supreme Court decided *Hiibel v. Sixth Judicial District Court of Nevada* (542 U.S. 177; 124 S.Ct. 2451; 2004), recognizing the constitutionality of Nevada's stop-and-identify statute. Although the Court had reviewed such statutes on three previous occasions, *Hiibel* was the first decision in which the Court had upheld such a statute. Nevada's stop-and-identify statute creates an affirmative duty upon citizens detained by a police officer during a *Terry* stop to give their names if asked by the officer. Refusal to give one's name establishes probable cause to arrest that individual. The holding in *Hiibel* departed from past dicta stating that since a *Terry* stop requires only reasonable suspicion, individuals were under no obligation to provide any information to police officers. Despite objections grounded in the Fourth and Fifth Amendments, the Court held that forced compulsion to state one's name in a *Terry* stop is not an unreasonable search and seizure, and does not violate the Self-Incrimination Clause of the Fifth Amendment.

The sequence of events leading up to this case began when Lee Dove, a sheriff's deputy in Humboldt County, Nevada, investigated a telephone report that a man in a silver and red pickup truck had been seen striking a female passenger. When Dove arrived on the scene, he found Larry D. Hiibel standing beside a parked red truck on the roadside and a young woman (Hiibel's minor daughter with whom he had earlier had an altercation over her choice of boyfriends) sitting inside the vehicle. Observing that Hiibel appeared to be drunk, Dove asked him whether he had "any identification on him." Hiibel refused to answer this question and asked in turn why Dove wanted to see his identification. Dove explained that he was conducting an investigation and needed to see some identification. Hiibel again refused to comply with the request and became agitated, insisting that he had done nothing wrong. After continued refusals to comply with Dove's request for identification, Hiibel began to taunt the officer. When Hiibel refused Dove's eleventh request to identify himself, the officer warned him that he would be arrested if he continued refusing to comply. Dove then placed Hiibel under arrest.

Hiibel was subsequently prosecuted for impeding an officer's right to obtain his name and obstructing an officer in discharging his legal duty in violation of Nevada law. Hiibel was tried and convicted in the Justice Court of Union Township and fined $250. The Sixth Judicial District Court affirmed, rejecting Hiibel's argument that the stop-and-identify statute violated his Fourth and Fifth Amendment rights. The Supreme Court of Nevada affirmed, holding that Hiibel's conviction did not violate the Fourth Amendment. The Supreme Court of Nevada denied Hiibel's motion for rehearing on the Fifth Amendment issue. The U.S. Supreme Court granted Hiibel's petition for certiorari, and Justice Kennedy wrote the five-four majority opinion.

He began by noting that "stop and identify statutes often combine elements of traditional vagrancy laws with provisions intended to regulate police behavior in the course of investigatory stops." After an extensive review of history and precedent, Kennedy concluded the search and seizure analysis, holding that "the stop, the request, and the State's requirement of a response did not contravene the guarantees of the Fourth Amendment." Justice Kennedy reasoned that "knowledge of identity may inform an officer that a suspect is wanted for another offense, or has a record of violence or mental disorder. On the other hand, knowing identity may help clear a suspect and allow the police to concentrate their efforts elsewhere." The Court also rejected Hiibel's Fifth Amendment argument, but claimed to leave open a window of opportunity for an as-applied challenge to a conviction under a stop-and-identify statute.

Justice Stevens wrote a dissenting opinion, taking issue only with the Court's self-incrimination holding. He concluded that as a target of the investigation, Hiibel "acted well within his rights when he opted to stand mute" (124 S.Ct. at 2464). Justice Breyer, joined by Justices Souter and Ginsburg, also dissented. He maintained that under the *Terry* precedent an officer is permitted to ask a detainee a moderate number of questions and to confirm or dispel the officer's suspicions. Justice Bryon White's concurring opinion in *Terry*, however, recognized that a detainee was not compelled to answer police questions. The Court had long accepted this *Terry* condition, and Justice Breyer saw no reason for departing from it in this case. Justice Breyer concluded by asserting that "the majority [had presented] no evidence that the rule enunciated by Justice White . . . which for nearly a generation [had] set forth a settled Terry stop condition has significantly interfered with law enforcement." Justice Breyer was unwilling to "begin to erode a clear rule with special exceptions." According to a recent commentary:

> exercising constitutional rights does not necessarily render a citizen irresponsible. Now that *Hiibel* has rejected a Fourth Amendment interest in refusal to self-identify, no rational person, under the Court's test, would refuse to disclose his name. Any rational citizen who refuses to identify himself must have committed a crime with a potential

punishment more serious than that imposed by the stop-and-identify statute. (*Harvard Law Review Editors* 2004, 296)

Viewed from this perspective, the *Hiibel* decision seriously erodes rights traditionally protected by the Fourth Amendment.

## Warrantless Arrests

In the 2003 case of *Maryland v. Pringle* (540 U.S. 366) a unanimous Supreme Court, speaking through Chief Justice Rehnquist, found that police officers had probable cause to arrest the three occupants of an automobile when a large roll of money and illegal drugs were found following a routine stop for speeding. A Baltimore County Police officer had stopped the automobile at 3:16 a.m. and asked the driver, Donte Partlow, for his license and registration. Partlow opened the glove compartment, revealing a large roll of bills. Although the license and registration check indicated no legal violations, the officer called for reinforcements and had the driver step out of the car. He then asked Partlow if he had any weapons or drugs in the car, to which Partlow answered in the negative. The officer then obtained Partlow's consent to search the vehicle, whereupon the officer seized the roll of money (amounting to $763) and found "five plastic glassine baggies containing cocaine." Partlow and each of his two passengers, Joseph Pringle and Otis Smith, initially offered no information regarding the ownership of the drugs or money. At this point, Partlow, Pringle, and Smith were placed under arrest and taken to the police station. Later that morning, Pringle waived his *Miranda* rights (the right to remain silent and the right to have counsel present during questioning) and confessed that the cocaine was his. Partlow and Smith were released after Pringle indicated that they had no knowledge of the cocaine.

At trial, Pringle moved unsuccessfully for suppression of his confession as the "fruit of an illegal arrest." He was subsequently convicted of possession with intent to distribute cocaine and possession of cocaine. The Maryland Court of Special Appeals affirmed his conviction and ten-year prison sentence, but the Maryland Court of Appeals reversed. On certiorari, the U.S. Supreme Court, in turn, reversed the decision of Maryland's highest appellate court. Because the offense in this case was felony drug possession, the only question before the Court was whether the officer had probable cause to believe that Pringle, and not the other two men, committed the crime. Chief Justice Rehnquist acknowledged that the "probable-cause standard is incapable of precise definition or quantification into percentages because it deals with probabilities and depends on the totality of the circumstances" (540 U.S. at 371). After examining the facts leading up to the arrest, the Court found that probable cause did exist. Chief Justice Rehnquist maintained that "a reasonable officer could conclude that there was probable cause to believe Pringle committed the crime of possession of cocaine, either solely or jointly" (540 U.S. at 372).

The Court distinguished the *Pringle* case from *Ybarra v. Illinois* (444 U.S. 85; 1979), which held that officers did not have probable cause to search Ybarra and other patrons of a bar because their propinquity to the bar was not related to the search warrant; therefore, the search was not particularized with respect to them. By contrast, Pringle, as one of the three occupants of the car in which the police discovered illegal drugs, was readily identifiable with their possession.

## Reasonable Suspicion

Two terms before *Pringle*, the Supreme Court considered *United States v. Arvizu* (534 U.S. 266; 2002), a very similar drug arrest case that raised related issues regarding the totality of the circumstances test. In January 1998, magnetic sensors were triggered on a seldom-used road in southeastern Arizona near the Mexican border, alerting a federal border patrol agent, Clinton Stoddard, to the possibility that an automobile might be attempting to evade the border checkpoint. Additional sensors indicated the direction in which the vehicle was traveling. According to Agent Stoddard's account, he pulled his vehicle over to the side of the road and closely watched the first car that he had seen since the alert. He noted that this was a minivan, a vehicle that drug smugglers commonly use. He also observed that the minivan slowed dramatically and that the driver, later to be identified as Ralph Arvizu, was stiff and rigid. Once Stoddard began following the minivan, children in the backseat started waving to him in an abnormal fashion, as if ordered to do so. Stoddard noticed that the minivan's registered address was in an area notorious for drug trafficking. After the minivan abruptly turned off the road leading to the checkpoint, Stoddard pulled it over and obtained Arvizu's consent to search the vehicle. Stoddard's search revealed over $99,000 worth of marijuana.

At his trial in a federal court, Arvizu moved to suppress the marijuana, but the court rejected this motion, citing numerous facts that gave Stoddard reasonable suspicion to stop the minivan. The Court of Appeals for the Ninth Circuit reversed the trial court's denial of Arvizu's motion, and the U.S. Supreme Court agreed to review the question on certiorari.

Writing for a unanimous Court, Chief Justice Rehnquist explained that a law enforcement officer needs only reasonable suspicion, not probable cause, to conduct a valid search and seizure during "brief investigatory stops of persons or vehicles that fall short of traditional arrest" (534 U.S. at 272). Justice Scalia filed a brief concurring opinion: The Court looks to the "totality of circumstances" to determine whether the officer "has a 'particularized and objective basis' for suspecting legal wrongdoing" (534 U.S. at 273, quoting *United States v. Cortez,* 449 U.S. 411, 417; 1981) Officers may "draw on their own experience and specialized training," but a hunch does not constitute reasonable suspicion. (534 U.S. at 274).

Chief Justice Rehnquist criticized the Ninth Circuit for what he called its "divide and conquer analysis" of the facts. Instead of considering the totality of the circumstances, the Ninth Circuit looked at Stoddard's observations separately and found that most of them were easily and innocently explainable. Chief Justice Rehnquist pointed out, however, that Supreme Court precedent has held that actions that are relatively innocuous by themselves may collectively "warrant further investigation" (534 U.S. at 274–275, quoting *Terry v. Ohio,* 392 U.S. 1, 22; 1968). In addition, it was unnecessary for the Ninth Circuit to attempt to reduce case law "uncertainty" by limiting certain factors that an officer may consider (534 U.S. at 275). On the basis of the totality of circumstances, including officer Stoddard's various observations of the minivan driver and the waving children inside the vehicle, as well as the triggered sensors and the registration check, the agent had reasonable suspicion of criminal activity. In view of the sharp differences in constitutional interpretation between the Ninth Circuit and the Supreme Court, it is likely that the justices chose to grant certiorari in this case for the purpose of "instructing" their lower court colleagues on the preferability of the totality of circumstances test in making a "reasonable suspicion" determination.

## Searches Incident to a Lawful Arrest

The scope of a police officer's authority to conduct a search incident to a valid arrest has been at issue in a number of cases since the seminal decision in *Chimel v. California* (1969) (discussed in Chapter Three). In *New York v. Belton* (1981) (also discussed in Chapter Three), an important post-*Chimel* decision, the Supreme Court held that when a police officer has made a valid custodial arrest of an occupant of an automobile, the Fourth Amendment permits a search of the passenger compartment of that vehicle as a contemporaneous incident of arrest. For many years, it was unclear whether the rule announced in *Belton* was limited to situations in which the police officer makes contact with the occupant of the car while the latter is inside the vehicle. That was in fact the situation in *Belton*. But suppose the arrestee steps outside the car before the initial contact is made. This question was raised but left unanswered in two cases—*Florida v. Thomas* (532 U.S. 774; 2001) and *Arizona v. Gant* (540 U.S. 1096; 2003). In *Thornton v. United States* (541 U.S. 615; 2004), the Court addressed and finally resolved the question. Writing for a fractured five-member majority, Chief Justice Rehnquist concluded that the *Belton* rule "governs even when an officer does not make contact until the person arrested has left the vehicle" (541 U.S. at 619).

In this case, Officer Deion Nichols of the Norfolk, Virginia, Police Department, while in uniform but driving an unmarked car, noticed that another driver, Marcus Thornton, had slowed down to avoid driving next to him. Nichols surmised that Thornton recognized him as a police officer and for some reason was trying to avoid his attention. Nichols then pulled off into a side street, ran a check on Thornton's license tags, and learned that the plates had been issued to a 1982 Chevy two-door, not to the Lincoln Town Car that Thornton was driving. Nichols then drove in pursuit of Thornton, but the latter pulled into a parking lot and got out of his car before Nichols reached him. Nichols parked his car and accosted Thornton, who appeared nervous and evasive. Fearing for his own safety, Nichols asked Thornton if he had narcotics or weapons on his person or in his car. Thornton answered in the negative and then consented to a "pat-down" search of his person. Detecting a bulge in Thornton's left front pocket, Nichols again asked about narcotics. This time, Thornton admitted possession and produced from his pocket bags containing marijuana and crack cocaine. Nichols informed Thornton that he was under arrest and placed him, handcuffed, in the backseat of the patrol car. Nichols then proceeded to search Thornton's car, where he found a 9-millimeter handgun under the driver's seat.

At his trial in a district court, Thornton sought to suppress, among other things, the firearm as the fruit of an unconstitutional search. In denying this motion, the trial court held that the search of Thornton's car was valid under the rule announced in *Belton.* After his conviction on federal gun and drug charges, Thornton appealed the denial of his suppression motion. In rejecting this appeal, the Court of Appeals for the Fourth Circuit noted that Thornton was admittedly in "close proximity" to his car at the time of his arrest. From this admission, the court concluded that Thornton's car was within his immediate control and that Nichols's search was therefore reasonable under the *Belton* rule. This conclusion is open to question since Thornton was handcuffed and placed in the patrol car at the time of his arrest and was thus in no position to retrieve the weapon found under the front seat of his car.

In affirming Thornton's conviction, the U.S. Supreme Court majority attempted to place this case in historical perspective. Chief Justice Rehnquist noted that in *Chimel* the Court had held that, in removing weapons that the arrestee might use and preventing the concealment or destruction of evidence, the police could search "the person of the arrestee and the area immediately surrounding him" (395 U.S. at 763). As previously noted, *Belton* applied the *Chimel* principle to the passenger compartment of an automobile occupied by the arrestee. In the *Thornton* case, the fact that the automobile was within the arrestee's immediate control did not depend on whether the officer accosted the arrestee while he was in his automobile or just after he had exited it. The same "concerns regarding officer safety and the destruction of evidence" existed under both circumstances (541 U.S. at 621). Chief Justice Rehnquist drew the logical conclusion that police officers needed a bright-line rule based on the arrestee's proximity to his car, not on whether the officer approached him before or after he exited the vehicle. Although Chief Justice Rehnquist succeeded in clarifying the *Belton* rule, it did not fit the facts of the *Thornton* case. Thornton might have been in "close proximity" to his car at the time of his arrest, but, as a practical matter, there was no risk of danger to the officer or of the destruction of evidence once Thornton was physically restrained and removed to the patrol car.

Justice Scalia emphasized this point in a separate opinion, joined by Justice Ginsburg, concurring in the judgment but rejecting the reasoning of the majority opinion. In his view, the majority stretched the *Belton* rule "beyond its breaking point" (541 U.S. at 625). The possibility that Thornton might break free of his restraints and regain access to his car was too remote to justify Nichols's search. "If *Belton* searches are justifiable," Justice Scalia argued, "it is not because the arrestee might grab a weapon or evidentiary item from his car, but simply because the car might contain evidence relevant to the crime for which he was arrested." Thus Justice Scalia concluded that the *Belton* case could not "reasonably be explained as a mere application of *Chimel.*" He regarded *Belton* as "a return to the broader sort of search incident to arrest . . . allowed before *Chimel*—limited, of course, to searches of motor vehicles, a category of 'effects' which give rise to a reduced expectation of privacy . . . and heightened law enforcement needs. . . ." He would therefore limit searches governed by the *Belton* rule to "cases where it is reasonable to believe evidence relevant to the crime of arrest might be found in the vehicle" (541 U.S. at 631). Since Thornton was lawfully arrested for a drug offense, it was reasonable for Nichols to believe that related evidence was in "the vehicle from which he had just alighted and was still within his vicinity at the time of arrest" (541 U.S. at 632).

Justice Stevens, joined by Justice Souter, dissented, contending that the *Chimel* rule, not the *Belton* rule, should have been used by the Court. "The *Chimel* rule should provide the same protection to a 'recent occupant' of a vehicle as to a recent occupant of a house." In response to Justice Scalia, the dissent added that "the interest in uncovering potentially valuable evidence" does not outweigh "the citizen's constitutionally protected interest in privacy." Finally, Justice Stevens criticized the majority for "extend[ing] *Belton's* reach without supplying any guidance for the future application of its swollen rule." According to the majority, police may search a vehicle incident to arrest "[s]o long as [the] arrestee is the sort of 'recent occupant' of a vehicle" that Thornton was. But the majority failed to specify "how recent is recent" or indicate how close the arrestee must be to his vehicle (541 U.S. at 636).

## Arrests for Non-Jailable Offenses

In *Atwater v. City of Lago Vista* (532 U.S. 318; 2001), a five-four majority of the Supreme Court, speaking through Justice Souter, upheld the warrantless arrest of Gail Atwater on a misdemeanor, "fine-only" traffic violation. The Court rejected the argument that the only misdemeanor for which a person could be arrested under the Fourth Amendment was a breach of the peace. Because the officer had probable cause against Atwater for the traffic violation, her arrest was reasonable.

When the arresting officer pulled Atwater's pickup truck over, neither she nor her three-year-old son and five-year-old daughter were wearing seatbelts. Under Texas law, an officer may make an arrest on a minor traffic violation such as this. The Court accepted Atwater's allegations that the officer was needlessly hostile, threatening to take her two children into custody along with her and refusing to allow Atwater to drop the children off before taking her to the station. (A friend of Atwater's who happened to be in the neighborhood arrived and took charge of the children.) The officer then handcuffed Atwater, placed her in his squad car, and drove her to the police station. There, booking officers "had her remove her shoes, jewelry, and eyeglasses, and empty her pockets." She was then photographed, jailed for an hour, released on a $310 bond, and eventually fined $50 for the seatbelt offense. She subsequently filed a federal civil rights suit against the officer, the chief of police, and the city for compensatory and punitive damages.

A district court granted the city's summary judgment motion. The Court of Appeals for the Fifth Circuit initially reversed the decision, but later affirmed it after an *en banc* hearing. (Typically, appellate decisions come from three-judge panels. An *en blanc* hearing is a session of an appellate court in which a larger number of judges assigned to the court participate. These hearings are usually reserved for cases of extraordinary importance.) The *en banc* opinion relied on *Whren v. United States* (517 U.S. 806; 1996), which stated that probable cause was generally justification enough for any arrest. And since Atwater did not suffer any harm beyond that normally associated with custodial arrest, her arrest was valid under the Fourth Amendment.

Before the Supreme Court, Atwater argued that at the time of the Fourth Amendment's drafting, common law did not permit the warrantless arrest of non-breach of the peace misdemeanor offenders. Atwater's chief support for this contention came from *Carroll v. United States* (1925; discussed in Chapter Three). Justice Souter's opinion held that Atwater had taken her quotation out of context, and found the whole passage to be much less supportive. Also, Justice Souter asserted that at the time the Fourth Amendment was drafted, English law permitted night watchmen to arrest pedestrians just for being out after dark. After examining the historical record of the Founding Era, including the debates over general warrants and writs of assistance, the Court found that Atwater's argument was undermined by many contradictory decisions. Justice Souter asserted that arrest authority for minor offenses was virtually unlimited when the Fourth Amendment was adopted. This conclusion has been seriously challenged by recent scholarship on the origins of the Fourth Amendment. (For a detailed critique of Justice Souter's interpretation of Fourth Amendment history, see Davies 2002. Professor Davies maintains that "Souter's claims bear little resemblance to authentic framing-era arrest doctrine. Indeed . . . his supposed historical analysis consist[s] almost entirely of rhetorical ploys and distortions of the historical sources.")

Atwater's second argument was that freedom from arrest for non-violent misdemeanors had become part of the contemporary concept of liberty, and that the Court should have recognized modern standards by deciding in her favor. The Court conceded that there was no good reason for Atwater's arrest, the particulars of which were "gratuitous humiliations" (532 U.S. at 346). The Court was unwilling, however, to create rules separating unarrestable from arrestable misdemeanors. Such rules would, for example, place an undue burden on officers in the field trying to gauge by eye whether a suspect had more or less than one gram of marijuana in his plastic bag.

The Court held that being too sensitive to the plight of people in Atwater's position would open the floodgates of frivolous constitutional claims on every misdemeanor arrest. The Court wanted police officers to have substantial discretion in choosing who gets arrested. The opinion suggested that because cases like Atwater's are so rare, it is not worthwhile to rethink the boundaries of police power (532 U.S. at 353).

Justice O'Connor wrote a powerful dissent, joined by Justices Stevens, Ginsburg, and Breyer. The dissenters believed that an arrest without a good reason behind it is by definition unreasonable, and thus violates the Fourth Amendment. Because the language of the Amendment so clearly invalidates unreasonable arrests, it was not necessary to consider whether they were allowed prior to the Amendment's adoption. The dissenters would have given a narrow reading to the holding in *Whren* that probable cause can justify an arrest even when the officer has an ulterior motive. The higher meaning of the Fourth Amendment is that warrantless searches and seizures must be reasonable, and having probable cause to believe a minor offense has been committed is not the same as having reasonable grounds to arrest a person. Justice O'Connor dismissed the majority's fear about limiting the effectiveness of field officers by pointing out that those officers would be protected from liability for damages by qualified immunity in civil suits. She was dismayed by the idea of putting administrative convenience before personal liberty. The *Atwater* case is an important reminder of the relevance of Fourth Amendment history to contemporary issues.

## Exigent Circumstances

In the 2002 case of *Kirk v. Louisiana* (536 U.S. 635), the Supreme Court revisited the elusive "exigent circumstances" issue. In this case, local police received an anonymous tip that drugs were being sold at Kennedy D. Kirk's apartment. Without a warrant, the police went to Kirk's apartment and observed from outside what appeared to be several drug purchases. After stopping one of the suspected buyers a block away on the street, the officers hastened to Kirk's apartment and conducted a search in an effort to prevent the destruction of potential evidence. They found cocaine and money from the drug sales in the apartment and on Kirk's person. Only after completing the search did the police obtain a warrant.

At trial, Kirk moved unsuccessfully to suppress the evidence gathered during the warrantless search. He was convicted of possession with intent to distribute and given a prison sentence of fifteen years at hard labor. The Louisiana Court of Appeal affirmed the trial court decision and by a vote of four to three, the State Supreme Court denied review. In a powerful dissenting opinion, Louisiana Supreme Court Chief Justice Pascal Calogero asserted that the police had clearly violated Kirk's Fourth Amendment rights. The defendant "was arrested inside an apartment, without a warrant, and the state has not demonstrated that exigent circumstances were present. Consequently, [his] arrest was unconstitutional, and his motion to suppress should have been granted" (536 U.S. at 637, quoting from Kirk's application to petition the U.S. Supreme Court for review on certiorari).

In a *per curiam* opinion the Supreme Court explicitly endorsed Chief Justice Calogero's view of the case. (A *per curiam* opinion is an unsigned opinion "by the court.")The Court reiterated the rule in *Payton v. New York* that "'[a]bsent exigent circumstances,' the 'firm line at the entrance to the house . . . may not reasonably be crossed without a warrant'" (536 U.S. at 636, quoting *Payton*, 445 U.S. 573 at 590; 1980; discussed in Chapter Three). The Louisiana Court of Appeal had ruled in favor of the state, concluding that the officers had probable cause to conduct the search. Since that court did not address the exigent circumstances issue, the U.S. Supreme Court reversed and remanded with instructions to consider this issue. The Court's *per curiam* decision served to clarify the lower courts' confusion in this area and did not affect existing Supreme Court precedent.

## Automobile Searches

In *Illinois v. Lidster* (540 U.S. 419; 2004), the Supreme Court addressed the question of whether the police violated the Fourth Amendment by stopping a motorist at a checkpoint established to investigate an unrelated crime and then arresting him when he failed a sobriety test. The specific purpose was to ask motorists for information about a fatal hit-and-run accident that occurred a week earlier at the same time and place as the checkpoint. Each stop lasted about fifteen seconds, with officers briefly questioning drivers and handing out a flyer describing and requesting information about the accident. As Robert S. Lidster approached the checkpoint in his minivan, he swerved, almost hitting an officer. Detecting alcohol on Lidster's breath, the officer directed Lidster to a side street. There another officer, after administering a sobriety test, arrested Lidster. At his trial, Lidster argued unsuccessfully that the checkpoint was unconstitutional and that the sobriety test evidence had been obtained unlawfully. An intermediate appellate court reversed the conviction, however, and the Illinois Supreme Court affirmed this decision.

Granting the state's petition for certiorari, the U.S. Supreme Court reversed, holding that the checkpoint stop did not violate the Fourth Amendment. Writing for the majority, Justice Stephen

Breyer first distinguished the instant case from the Court's previous ruling in *City of Indianapolis v. Edmond* (2000), another checkpoint stop case, discussed in Chapter Three.) In *Edmond,* the police set up a checkpoint to search for evidence of drug crimes. They typically looked inside the vehicles and walked drug-sniffing dogs around them. After finding that "the police had set up the checkpoint primarily for general 'crime control' purposes, i.e., 'to detect evidence of ordinary criminal wrongdoing,'" the Court in *Edmond* held that the arrests were unconstitutional for failing to meet the Fourth Amendment's "individualized suspicion" requirement.

By contrast, the officers in *Lidster* were not performing a general crime search. Instead they were seeking information about a specific crime that had occurred a week earlier. The officers intended to ask questions about another individual's criminal acts, not search motorists' vehicles for evidence of their own illegal activity. The *Edmond* opinion limits unconstitutional checkpoints to situations in which police attempt to use "interrogation and inspection [to] reveal that any given motorist has committed some crime" (540 U.S. at 424).

Justice Breyer further maintained that the "individualized suspicion" requirement of the Fourth Amendment does not render checkpoints automatically unconstitutional. Sobriety and border checkpoints, for example, are valid because of special law enforcement concerns. An "information-seeking stop" does not normally involve individualized suspicion and is "less likely to provoke anxiety or to prove intrusion" (540 U.S. at 425). Justice Breyer observed that the Fourth Amendment does not prohibit police from approaching pedestrians and asking questions about particular crimes. While involuntarily stopping an automobile, as opposed to a pedestrian, is a seizure, "the motorist stop will likely be brief," so the burden placed on the public is minimal when compared to the government's interest in solving a crime involving a human death (540 U.S. at 426). Finally Justice Breyer surmised that limits in police resources and public displeasure with traffic tie-ups would prevent the proliferation of unreasonable check-points.

Because the checkpoint was not presumptively unconstitutional under *Edmond,* the Court considered whether the stop was reasonable. Justice Breyer found that the checkpoint was reasonable and therefore constitutional. The police were warranted in speculating that motorists using the road around the time of the accident might be driving there at about the same time a week later. Most importantly, the checkpoint stops were systematic, nondiscriminatory, short, and minimally intrusive, lasting only a few seconds.

Justice Stevens, joined by Justices Souter and Ginsburg, concurred in part and dissented in part. Justice Stevens agreed with the majority that the *Edmond* rule did not apply to the instant case because the police, instead of performing a general crime search, were seeking information about a particular crime committed a week earlier. He preferred, however, that the case be remanded to the Illinois state courts for a determination of the reasonableness of the checkpoint stop. "We should be especially reluctant," Justice Stevens cautioned, "to abandon our role as a court of review in a case in which the constitutional inquiry requires analysis of local conditions and practices more familiar to judges closer to the scene" (540 U.S. at 429).

First of all, checkpoints may create longer wait periods than the majority recognized. Also it is reasonable to believe that some drivers might be apprehensive about "find[ing] an unpublicized roadblock at midnight . . ." (540 U.S. at 429). It was at best speculative whether the police would gather better information about the week-old accident by questioning motorists as opposed to placing flyers on vehicles parked at nearby businesses. Because the Illinois appellate courts found that the roadblock was *per se* unconstitutional and did not determine whether it was reasonable, Justice Stevens maintained that the case should be remanded with instructions to apply the correct test.

In appraising the majority opinion of Justice Breyer and the separate opinion of Justice Stevens, it is noteworthy that all nine justices agreed that a reasonableness standard was appropriate. Unlike the situation in *Edmond,* the police in *Lidster* had set up a checkpoint to gather information about a specific crime, not to perform a general crime search. If, however, the police had set up a sobriety checkpoint, Lidster's DUI arrest would undoubtedly have been constitutional under the law enforcement "special needs" exception.

## Administrative Searches/"Special Needs"

In Chapter Three, we discussed the origins and early development of the "special needs exception" to the Fourth Amendment, commenting on its first appearance in the Court's administrative search decisions of the late 1960s. (See, for example, *Camara v. Municipal Court* [1967]; and *See vs. Seattle* [1966].) We noted that this exception was extended in 1995 to sustain the constitutionality of random drug testing of high school athletes in *Vernonia v. Acton* (1995). (For early recognition of the potential scope of the special needs exception, see Buffaloe 1997, 529.) Emboldened by the *Vernonia* decision, a number of school districts began to test the outer limits of warrantless drug testing of students. The Pottawatomie School District in Tecumseh, Oklahoma, adopted a policy of testing all students engaged in extracurricular activities. Specifically, this policy required students to consent to drug testing as a precondition for participating in such activities as band, choir, academic teams, athletic teams, and the Future Farmers of America. High school students Lindsey Earls and Daniel James, who wished to participate in a number of extracurricular activities, filed suit against the school board, alleging that the policy violated the Fourth Amendment in several respects. They contended, for example, that the testing violated their privacy by permitting teachers to stand outside the restroom stall and "'listen for the normal sounds of urination in order to guard against tampered specimens and to insure an accurate chain of custody'" (536 U.S. at 823, quoting from the respondents' brief). They also maintain that the school district showed little regard for confidentiality in its careless handling of personal information collected under the policy.

The district court, citing the Supreme Court's decision in *Vernonia,* rejected the plaintiff's Fourth Amendment claim. The Court of Appeals for the Tenth Circuit reversed, holding that the Fourth Amendment was violated because the school had failed to demonstrate "that there is some identifiable drug abuse problem among a sufficient number of those subject to the testing, such that testing that group of students will actually redress its drug problem" (*Earls v. Board of Education of Independent School District No. 92 of Pottawatomie County,* 242 F. 3d 1264, 1270; 2001).

Relying heavily on the reasoning in *Vernonia,* the Supreme Court reversed in *Board of Education of Independent School District No. 92 of Pottawatomie County v. Earls* (537 U.S. 822; 2002). Writing for a five-member majority, Justice Clarence Thomas concluded that students affected by the policy had only a limited expectation of privacy because they "voluntarily subject themselves to many of the same intrusions on their privacy as do athletes" (536 U.S. at 831). Moreover, the urine sample collection procedure followed in this case was less intrusive than the procedure in *Vernonia.* Justice Thomas maintained that the invasion of the students' privacy was not significant since the test results were not turned over to the police, nor could they result in disciplinary action or adverse academic consequences. He found that the policy was an effective means of accomplishing the government's objectives. In addition, Thomas noted that the court had not previously "required a particularized or pervasive drug problem before allowing the government to conduct suspicionless drug testing" (537 U.S. at 824). Nevertheless, he emphasized the seriousness of the problem by observing that "the nationwide drug epidemic makes the war against drugs a pressing concern in every school" (537 U.S. at 832).

Justices O'Connor and Souter filed a one-paragraph dissent contending that *Vernonia* was wrongly decided in the first place. In addition, they fully supported the dissenting opinion of Justice Ginsburg, which was also joined by Justice Stevens. Justice Ginsburg maintained that *Earls* did not fit the circumstances of *Vernonia.* She pointed out that Pottawatomie County's drug problem was less severe and that the risk of drug abuse for nonathletes was less clear. Justice Ginsburg thus concluded that "special needs" did not exist with respect to the students tested by the Pottawatomie school district. The health risks faced by students participating in nonathletic activities were no greater than those confronting "*all* children" (537 U.S. at 844) (emphasis in original). Justice Ginsburg rejected the majority's characterization of extracurricular activities as "voluntary." She pointed out that such activities are "a key component of school life, essential . . . for students applying to college, and . . . a significant contributor to the breadth and quality of the educational experience" (537 U.S. at 845).

The Supreme Court has by no means limited its consideration of the "special needs" exception to the public school setting. Over a year before the *Earls* decision, the justices in *Ferguson v. City of Charleston,* (532 U.S. 67, 70; 2001) addressed the specific question of whether "the interest in using the threat of criminal sanctions to deter pregnant women from using cocaine can justify a departure from the general rule that an official nonconsensual search is unconstitutional if not authorized by a valid warrant."

Staff members at The Medical University of South Carolina had become concerned about an increase in the number of infants who, at birth, tested positive for cocaine. With police cooperation, the hospital developed a policy for the drug testing of maternity patients who were suspected of using cocaine. If the tests revealed drug use, the police were notified and the expectant mother was arrested. Crystal Ferguson and nine other pregnant women who were arrested pursuant to the policy, after receiving obstetrical care at the hospital, alleged that the warrantless, nonconsensual drug tests were unconstitutional because they were conducted for criminal investigatory purposes. The city of Charleston responded by arguing that the tests were consensual, but even if nonconsensual, they were justified by a "special" non–law enforcement need—in this instance, the obvious health benefit to mother and child—and were thus reasonable. The trial court found the searches unreasonable in the absence of consent. The Court of Appeals for the Fourth Circuit reversed, declaring that "special needs" may, in exceptional circumstances, justify a search policy designed to serve non–law enforcement ends. That court thus did not reach the question of consent.

Dividing six-three, the Supreme Court, in an opinion by Justice Stevens, reversed the court of appeals and invalidated the search after concluding that it did not "fit within the closely guarded category" of permissible suspicionless searches. In other "special needs" cases regarding drug testing—*Skinner, National Treasury,* and *Vernonia*—the "special need" asserted was divorced from the general interest in law enforcement. (For further discussion, see Chapter Three.) By contrast, in the *Ferguson* case, the "central and indispensable feature" of the hospital's drug testing policy from its inception was the threat of criminal arrest and prosecution to force women into treatment. The extensive involvement of law enforcement officials at every stage of the policy's implementation confirmed this conclusion. Moreover, the invasion of privacy in this scenario was far more substantial than in the other "special needs" drug cases. In each of those cases, there was no misunderstanding about the purpose of the test or the potential use of the test results. Here, while the patients might have consented to the test, they clearly had a reasonable expectation that the test results would not be turned over to law enforcement for criminal prosecution.

Justice Scalia penned a dissent, joined in full by Chief Justice Rehnquist, and in part by Justice Thomas. Because the mothers voluntarily consented to the drug test—after all, the urine samples were not extracted forcibly—Justice Scalia insisted that no Fourth Amendment violation had occurred. As a long line of cases had established, a search based on consent was not unreasonable. (See the discussion of "Consent Searches" in Chapter Three, page 84.) That said, even if the drug testing constituted a nonconsensual search, the "special needs" exception was applicable. Coercing drug-abusing mothers to enter drug treatment, an obvious health benefit to both mother and child, provided a sufficient rationale for the program.

The "special needs" exception, previously applied to the drug testing of public employees and school children, is potentially applicable in other contexts. Even if it is limited to noncriminal investigations, the exception lends itself to ever-increasing governmental demands for private information sought in the name of such objectives as the maintenance of national security, environmental protection, and highway safety, to cite only a few examples. Important as such information gathering is, it is clear that such inquiries will, at some point, threaten legitimate liberty interests. It remains to be seen whether the Supreme Court will be able to strike an appropriate balance between competing interests in this area.

## ELECTRONIC SURVEILLANCE

### *The New Technology: Thermal Imaging*

In determining "reasonable expectations of privacy" in the twenty-first century, a challenging question was presented to the court in *Kyllo v. United States* (533 U.S. 27; 2001). In this case the Court decided whether police officers acting without a warrant violated the Fourth Amendment by using a thermal imaging device aimed at a private residence from a public street for the purpose of detecting relative amounts of heat within the residence.

Suspicious that marijuana was being grown inside Danny Kyllo's home, agents of the U.S. Department of the Interior used a thermal imaging device to scan the portion of the triplex owned by Kyllo. The scan took only a few minutes and was conducted from within a vehicle parked on a public street. The scan revealed that the garage roof and one side wall were relatively hot compared to the rest of the home and quite a bit warmer than neighboring homes. Based on tips from informants, an abnormally high rate of electrical consumption, and the thermal imaging scan, a federal magistrate issued a search warrant, which, upon execution, exposed a large, indoor marijuana-growing operation with a crop of over 100 plants and the "grow lights" necessary to sustain them. The thermal imaging procedure that the police employed in this case, although not in general public use, has been widely employed by law enforcement officers within the United States for a number of years as part of the national "war on drugs."

Prior to *Kyllo,* police and prosecutors typically took the view that the thermal scan was not a search within the meaning of the Fourth Amendment since it merely collected data on heat that was being released into the public space. Kyllo disagreed, however, and moved for the suppression of the evidence at his trial in a federal district court. The district court denied this motion, at which time Kyllo entered a conditional guilty plea. On appeal, the Court of Appeals for the Ninth Circuit remanded the case for an evidentiary hearing on the intrusiveness of thermal imaging. The district court then determined that thermal imaging was nonintrusive; it could not penetrate the structure of the residence or reveal intimate details of the home. Accordingly, the district court held that the use of the thermal imager did not constitute a search under the Fourth Amendment. The Ninth Circuit initially reversed, but eventually affirmed, that decision.

On the basis of *Katz,* the judges reasoned that Kyllo had no objective reasonable expectation of privacy because the thermal imaging did not expose intimate details of his life, but only measured the heat escaping from his home. Additionally, Kyllo had not taken any affirmative steps to conceal the heat emanating from his home. The majority compared the thermal scanning to the use of trained police dogs to detect the odor of illegal drugs, the non-intrusive outside observation by law enforcement officers of activities taking place within a home, and police searches of garbage left on the curb for pick-up—all of which had been upheld by the high Court.

In a five-four decision, the Supreme Court disagreed with this perspective. Writing for an unusually aligned majority, which included Justices Souter, Thomas, Ginsburg, and Breyer, Justice Scalia declared that:

> [w]here, as here, the government uses a device that is not in general public use, to explore details of the home that would previously have been unknowable without physical intrusion, the surveillance is a search and is presumptively unreasonable without a warrant." (533 U.S. at 31)

Justice Scalia began his analysis by recognizing and reaffirming that privacy expectations were most heightened in the home: "At the very core [of the Fourth Amendment] stands the right of a man to retreat into his home and there be free from unreasonable searches and seizures" (533 U.S. at 31). With few exceptions, warrants have traditionally been required for searches of the home.

Justice Scalia then addressed the level of intrusiveness posed by thermal imaging. Even the four dissenters, speaking through Justice Stevens, agreed with the majority that the use of a device disclosing what people were actually doing within the home would have constituted a search. The dissenters, however, drew a distinction between "off the wall" observations and "through the wall" surveillance. They regarded the reasonable observation of "off the wall" emissions as constitutional, even in the absence of a warrant. As Justice Stevens explained:

While the Court "takes the long view" and decides this case based largely on the potential of yet-to-be developed technology that might allow 'through-the-wall surveillance,' . . .this case involves nothing more than off-the-wall surveillance by law enforcement officers to gather information exposed to the general public from the outside of petitioner's home. (533 U.S. at 42)

Justice Stevens asserted, in short, that "the process of drawing inferences from data in the public domain (in this case heat emissions emanating from the outside wall of a house) should not be characterized as a search" (533 U.S. at 50). Justice Scalia rejected the off-the-wall/through-the-wall distinction, pointing out that "just as a thermal imager captures only heat emanating from a house, so also a powerful directional microphone picks up only sound emanating from a house—and a satellite capable of scanning from many miles away would pick up only visible light emanating from a house." He noted that the dissenters' "mechanical interpretation of the Fourth Amendment" had been rejected many years earlier in *Katz v. United States* (1967). Justice Scalia contended that "reversing" the *Katz* approach "would leave the homeowner at the mercy of advancing technology—including imaging technology that could discern all human activity in the home" (533 U.S. at 35–36). The majority was careful to point out that mere warrantless *visual* surveillance of a home did not constitute a search. They recognized, however, a fundamental difference between naked eye observation and thermal imaging, in large part because thermal imaging, as an investigatory technique, was not widely available to the general public. Finally, the Court rejected the government's argument that thermal imaging was constitutional because it did not reveal intimate details of the home. The majority insisted that "*all* details [within the home were] intimate details" and that the distinction suggested by the government was thus uncertain and confusing (533 U.S. at 37). In any event, the secret cultivation of marijuana inside the home would certainly qualify as an "intimate detail."

Because the thermal imaging only gathered information already exposed to the general public, the dissenters maintained that it did not invade any constitutionally protected interest in privacy. Comparable information could have been obtained by observation from outside the curtilage of the home—by examining the rate at which rainwater or snow evaporated or by looking through the contents of discarded garbage. The dissenters also contended that the police officers should not be required to avert their senses or their equipment from detecting emissions in the public domain. The dissenters suggested a new standard for evaluating warrantless electronic surveillance: whether the technology offered the "functional equivalent of actual presence" in the area being searched (533 U.S. at 44). Applying this standard, they maintained that thermal imaging differed qualitatively from wiretapping. The latter was the "functional equivalent of actual presence." The former was not, since it disclosed only the relative amounts of heat radiating from the home; "it would be as if, in *Katz,* the listening device disclosed only the relative volume of sound leaving the [phone] booth" (533 U.S. at 49–50). In short, observation did not become unreasonable simply because it was obtained by an unconventional device. By comparison, the dissenters pointed out that the Court had permitted a dog sniff that disclosed only the presence or absence of narcotics. They maintained that it was therefore implausible, and damaging to legitimate privacy interests, to conclude that an individual had a subjective expectation of privacy in the heat waves leaving his home. And even if he did, society was not prepared to recognize such an expectation as reasonable. The dog-sniff analogy, however, did not match the thermal imaging surveillance used in this case. Justice Scalia found no "necessary connection between the sophistication of the surveillance equipment and the 'intimacy' of the details that it observes. . . ." A trained narcotics detection dog is very unlikely to alert the police to anything other than narcotics, whereas the thermal imaging device detects only changes in the heat level inside a house. Rather than suggesting the presence of marijuana plants, those changes might just as easily indicate "at what hour each night the lady of the house takes her daily sauna and bath—a detail that many would consider 'intimate'. . . ." (533 U.S. at 38).

The most convincing argument that the dissenters presented was that the rule announced by the majority would become obsolete once similar technology came into general public use. (For a detailed critique of this aspect of the *Kyllo* decision, see Hull 2005). The *Kyllo* decision is clearly vulnerable on this point. The ruling is significant, however, because it reaffirms the Court's commitment to heightened Fourth Amendment protection associated with the home and because it recognized the power of technology to shrink the realm of guaranteed privacy.

## The Old Technology: Narcotics Detection Dogs

As previously noted, the Supreme Court held in *United States v. Place* (462 U.S. 696; 1983) that while exposure of a traveler's luggage to a trained narcotics detection dog was not a search for Fourth Amendment purposes, a ninety-minute delay in arranging such a search was unreasonable. In the 2005 case of *Illinois v. Caballes* (125 S.Ct. 834; 2005), the Court held that a dog sniff performed on the exterior of a car a few minutes after the driver was stopped for speeding did not violate the Fourth Amendment. Here Illinois State Trooper Daniel Gillette stopped Roy I. Caballes, who was driving his car in excess of the speed limit on an interstate highway. A second state trooper, Craig Graham, overheard Gillette's radio report to the police dispatcher and immediately headed for the scene with a trained narcotics detection dog. Graham presumably had no information about Caballes other than that he had been stopped for speeding. While Gillette was writing a warning ticket for Caballes, Graham arrived and walked his dog around the car. At the rear of the car, the dog signaled an "alert," whereupon the troopers searched the trunk, found marijuana, and arrested Caballes. Less than ten minutes elapsed between the stop and Caballes's arrest for possession of an illegal drug. The marijuana was introduced into evidence against Caballes, and the trial judge rejected his motion to suppress the seized evidence and quash the arrest. Caballes was convicted of cannabis trafficking, was sentenced to twelve years' imprisonment, and was fined $256,136. Illinois' intermediate appellate court affirmed the conviction, but the Supreme Court of Illinois reversed. That court concluded that, because the canine sniff had been performed without any specific and articulable facts to suggest drug activity, the use of the dog had unjustifiably enlarged the scope of a routine traffic stop into a drug investigation. The U.S. Supreme Court vacated this decision and remanded the case for further proceedings.

A six-member majority, speaking through Justice Stevens, held that the dog sniff did not violate the Fourth Amendment under the circumstances presented in this case. (Chief Justice Rehnquist did not participate in this decision.) It was conceded that the "initial seizure" of Caballes was lawful since it was based on probable cause. Justice Stevens maintained that the duration of the stop was fully justified by the traffic offense and the ordinary inquiries arising in such a situation: "A seizure that is justified solely by the interest in issuing a warning ticket to the driver can become unlawful if it is prolonged beyond the time reasonably required to complete that mission." Nevertheless, "conducting a dog sniff would not change the character of a traffic stop that is lawful at its inception and otherwise executed in a reasonable manner, unless the dog sniff itself infringed respondent's constitutionally protected interest in privacy. Our cases hold that it did not" (125 S.Ct. at 837). The majority thus concluded that "A dog sniff conducted during a concededly lawful traffic stop that reveals no information other than the location of a substance that no individual has any right to possess does not violate the Fourth Amendment" (125 S.Ct. at 838).

In a separate dissenting opinion, Justice Souter asserted that "using the dog for the purposes of determining the presence of marijuana in the car's trunk was a search unauthorized as an incident of the speeding stop and unjustified on any other ground" (125 S.Ct. at 838). Thus he would have repudiated the holding in *Place* that a dog sniff is not a search for Fourth Amendment purposes. Justice Souter also joined the dissenting opinion of Justice Ginsburg who insisted that "[e]ven if the drug sniff is not characterized as a Fourth Amendment 'search,' . . . the sniff surely broadened the scope of the traffic-violation-related seizure." Justice Ginsburg further maintained that "injecting" a narcotics detection dog "into a routine traffic stop changes the character of the encounter between the police and the motorist." As far as the troopers knew, Caballes was guilty of nothing more than "driving six miles per hour over the speed limit." This exposed him "to the embarrassment and intimidation of being investigated, on a public thoroughfare, for drugs" (125 S.Ct. at 845).

## CONCLUSION

The greatest expansion and erosion of Fourth Amendment rights occurred in the twentieth century. The expansion began with the 1914 announcement of the federal exclusionary rule in *Weeks v. United States.* It continued as the Court applied the Fourth Amendment and the exclusionary rule to the states via the Fourteenth Amendment, in *Wolf v. Colorado* (1949) and *Mapp v. Ohio* (1961), respectively. This expansion reached its zenith toward the end of the Warren Court era with the Court's decisions in *Katz v. United States* (1967) and *Chimel v. California* (1969). In *Katz* the Court placed Fourth Amendment restrictions on illegal wiretapping. And in *Chimel* the Court limited the area within which police could conduct a search incident to a valid arrest.

The erosion of Fourth Amendment rights began during the chief justiceship of Warren E. Burger and continued into the Rehnquist Court era with cases that gradually cut back on the scope of the exclusionary rule. See, for example, *United States v.*

*Calandra* (1974), *Stone v. Powell* (1976), *United States v. Leon* (1984), and decisions that expanded the investigatory latitude of the police in such areas as automobile and airport searches— *United States v. Ross* (1982); *United States v. Montoya de Hernandez* (1985); *United States v. Sokolow* (1989); and *Alabama v. White* (1990); *California v. Acevedo* (1991). This trend in Fourth Amendment interpretation has extended without a discernible cut-off point well into the twenty-first century. It is true, of course, that during this period the Court has occasionally affirmed the Fourth Amendment rights of criminal defendants. See, for example, *Kyllo v. United States* (2001), the thermal imaging case; *Kirk v. Louisiana* (2002); and *Groh v. Ramirez* (2004). The Court in recent years might be displaying a few sober second thoughts about the implications of its earlier concessions to law enforcement in deference to the "war on drugs." It is still too early to determine whether the Court is undergoing a significant change in this area.

Currently, the most serious threat to Fourth Amendment rights is posed by legislation adopted by Congress in the aftermath of the terrorist attacks of September 11, 2001. Critics of the USA PATRIOT Act maintain that this statutory expansion of search and surveillance power poses a potential threat to essential Fourth Amendment values. At this writing, the Supreme Court has yet to interpret Fourth Amendment aspects of the USA PATRIOT Act. We await its decisions in this area with great interest, but with confidence that the Court will maintain the appropriate balance between the values of liberty and order in a democratic society.

Looking to the future, one of the most difficult challenges to the continuing relevance of the Fourth Amendment as a significant check on arbitrary law enforcement authority is presented by the rapid growth of computer-related crime. As we move further into the digital age, crimes such as bank robbery no longer require that the perpetrator physically enter the bank, confront bank employees, and attempt to escape with the loot in hand. The job can now be performed electronically by a skilled computer "hacker" who, without leaving home, could transfer a sum of money from a corporate account into his own account and from there to a bank account in another country. (For background, see Kerr 2005.) Could the Fourth Amendment's restrictions against unreasonable searches and seizures or its traditional warrant requirement be brought to bear on police investigations of such crimes? Are the limitations imposed by the Fourth Amendment workable, as a practical matter, in a digital age with its emphasis on paperless transactions?

No doubt similar concerns regarding the time- and space-bound characteristics of the Fourth Amendment were raised early in the automobile age almost a century ago. The Supreme Court found a way to address such concerns with the development of the "automobile exception" to the warrant requirement. It will take even more inventiveness to apply the Fourth Amendment meaningfully to computer-related crime. Nevertheless, through the intricate process of constitutional interpretation, Fourth Amendment law has exhibited a dynamic quality. It remains to be seen whether the adaptability of this amendment is sufficient to ensure its survival or whether an as yet unknown alternative may be created to protect individuals against unreasonable searches and seizures in the Information Age.

## REFERENCES AND FURTHER READING

Abraham, Henry J. 1999. *Justices, Presidents, and Senators: A History of the U.S. Supreme Court Appointments from Washington to Clinton.* Lanham, MD: Rowman and Littlefield Publishers.

Banks, Christopher P. 2004. "Protecting (or Destroying) Freedom through Law: The USA PATRIOT Act's Constitutional Implications." In *American National Security and Civil Liberties in an Era of Terrorism*, edited by David Cohen and John Wells. New York: Palgrave MacMillan.

Buffaloe, Jennifer Y. 1997. "'Special Needs' and the Fourth Amendment: An Exception Poised to Swallow the Warrant Preference Rule." *Harvard Civil Rights–Civil Liberties Law Review.* 32: 529–564.

Bush, President George W. 2001. *Proclamation 7463.* "Declaration of National Emergency by Reason of Certain Terrorist Attacks." Available at http://www.whitehouse.gov/news/releases/2001/09/20010914-4.html.

Davies, Thomas Y. 2002. "The Fictional Character of Law-and-Order Originalism: A Case Study of the Distortions and Evasions of Framing-Era Arrest Doctrine in *Atwater v. Lago Vista.*" *Wake Forest Law Review* 37: 239–437.

Editorial. 2005. "PATRIOT ACT: Court ruling on key section is long overdue," *Detroit Free Press,* February 25, 2005, 10A.

Glenn, Richard A. 2004. "Civil Liberties in an Age of Terrorism." *Trial: Journal of the Association of Trial Lawyers of America* 40, No. 4: 18–28.

Greenhouse, Linda. 2003. "Knock, Wait 15 Seconds, and then Break In, Justices Rule." *New York Times,* December 2: A1.

Harvard Law Review Editors. 2004. "The Supreme Court, 2003 Term: LEADING CASES: 3. Fourth and Fifth Amendments—Stop-and-Identify Statutes." *Harvard Law Review.* 118: 286–296.

Hull, Daniel. 2004. *Memorandum on the Fourth Amendment.* On file in the Law Library, University of Tennessee College of Law.

Kerr, Orrin S. 2005. "Digital Evidence and the New Criminal Procedure." *Columbia Law Review* 105: 279–318.

Stephens, Otis H. 1973. *The Supreme Court and Confessions of Guilt.* Knoxville: University of Tennessee Press.

———. 2004. "Presidential Power, Judicial Deference, and the Status of Detainees in an Age of Terrorism." In *American National Security and Civil Liberties in an Era of Terrorism,* edited by David B. Cohen and John W. Wells. New York: Palgrave MacMillan.

United States Congress. 2001. "Sense of Congress Regarding Terrorist Attacks," Pub L. N. 107–140, 115 Stat. 224.

# 5

# KEY CASES,
# CONCEPTS, PERSONS,
# LAWS, AND TERMS

### "Abandoned Property" Exception

This exception to the warrant requirement holds that a person who voluntarily abandons his or her property forfeits any reasonable expectation of privacy in that property. The Fourth Amendment is not violated when government appropriates abandoned property. Abandoned property is property over which the owner has given up control with no intention of reclaiming it. *California v. Greenwood* (1988) is demonstrative of the "abandoned property" exception.

### *Adams v. Williams* (1972)

In this six-to-three decision of the U.S. Supreme Court, the justices held that information obtained from a reliable informant established reasonable suspicion. When an informant is used, police are required to demonstrate the reliability of the information received, either by corroborating the details independently or establishing the credibility of the informant.

## Administrative Searches/"Special Needs" Exception

Inspections or searches conducted as part of a general regulatory scheme, often but not exclusively to ensure compliance with laws and regulations, are called administrative searches. One of the fundamental principles of administrative searches is that they may not be used as a pretext to search for evidence of criminal activity. Because these searches are justified by "special needs" beyond the normal need for law enforcement, they do not merit the same constitutional protections. See, for example, *Camara v. Municipal Court* (1967). In the last twenty years, courts have broadened the "special needs" exception to permit a variety of warrantless, suspicionless searches, including mandatory drug testing of certain segments of the population. See, for example, *Skinner v. Railway Labor Executives' Association* (1989); *National Treasury Employees Union v. Von Raab* (1989); *Vernonia School District v. Acton* (1995); and *Board of Education of Independent School District No. 92 of Pottawatomie County v. Earls* (2002).

### *Alabama v. White* (1990)

In the ordinary course of police work, law enforcement officers often rely upon anonymous tips to further their investigation. In this decision, the Supreme Court, dividing six to three, determined that if officers were able to corroborate independently parts of an anonymous telephone tip, then the information in that tip pertaining to criminal activity could be presumed reliable and used to provide reasonable suspicion. This decision is subject to criticism on two points. First, it makes it possible for anyone with sufficient knowledge about another person to formulate an anonymous tip justifying an investigatory detention of that person. Second, declaring constitutional an investigatory detention based on anonymous tips subjects every citizen to being stopped and questioned by any officer who is willing to attest that the warrantless stop was precipitated by an anonymous tip predicting whatever conduct the police officer had just witnessed for himself or herself.

## *Arizona v. Evans* (1995)

This seven-to-two decision of the U.S. Supreme Court established the "clerical error" exception to the exclusionary rule. Here, the justices extended the "good faith" exception, holding that the exclusionary rule did not require the suppression of evidence seized pursuant to mistaken information resulting from clerical errors of court employees. After stopping a vehicle going in the wrong direction on a one-way street, police learned from their squad car computer that the driver had an outstanding arrest warrant. Based on that information, the police searched the vehicle and discovered marijuana. The police later learned that the arrest warrant had been canceled seventeen days previously, but that cancellation had not been entered into the police department's computerized database. Relying upon *United States v. Leon* (1984), the Court reaffirmed the conclusion that the exclusionary rule was designed to deter police misconduct—not judicial errors, not police errors, not legislative errors, and, most assuredly, not errors by court employees. Because the exclusion here would not result in any appreciable deterrence of misconduct (either by police or court employees), its use was unwarranted.

## *Atwater v. City of Lago Vista* (2001)

In this much publicized five-to-four decision, the U.S. Supreme Court confirmed that police officers have broad latitude to make warrantless arrests when criminal behavior occurs in their presence. This general grant of authority extends even to misdemeanors. Here, Gail Atwater was arrested—handcuffed, photographed, jailed, and later released on bond—for not wearing a safety belt and failing to secure her children in safety belts, in violation of a state law. The justices held that if a police officer has probable cause to believe that a person has committed even a minor criminal offense, then the officer *may* make a custodial arrest. Obviously, the Fourth Amendment does not require an arrest in these circumstances; it simply does not prohibit one.

## Automobile Exception

Shortly after the first mass production of combustion engine automobiles, the Supreme Court created an exception to the warrant requirement for automobile searches. The initial justification for this exception was the inherent mobility of automobiles, which made obtaining a warrant to search one often impracticable. See, for example, *Carroll v. United States* (1925). A half-century later, the Supreme Court announced a second reason for distinguishing between automobiles and other private property—a lesser expectation of privacy in a motor vehicle.

### *Barron v. Baltimore* (1833)

This unanimous decision of the U.S. Supreme Court held that the Just Compensation Clause of the Fifth Amendment, and by extension the entire Bill of Rights, was a limitation of power on the federal government, not on the state governments. This clause was eventually applied to the states in 1987. Save this notable exception, the Bill of Rights did not limit the powers of the state governments until well into the twentieth century, following the Supreme Court's selective incorporation of the Bill of Rights.

## Bill of Rights

The first ten amendments to the U.S. Constitution, collectively ratified in December 1791, is a list of individuals' rights, protected from encroachment by the government. The absence of a comprehensive list of individual rights in the original, unamended Constitution is not an indication that such rights were unimportant to the framers. They apparently thought it was unnecessary to include a more detailed list of rights, in part because they were well aware that most of the state constitutions adopted during the American Revolution contained fairly detailed bills of rights placing limits on state and local government. Because the framers anticipated a limited role for the national government exercising enumerated powers, they envisioned no critical need for a federal bill of rights. The Bill of Rights was adopted later largely because of the Antifederalists' fears that the Constitution would destroy the sovereignty and autonomy of the states.

## Board of Education of Independent School District No. 92 of Pottawatomie County v. Earls (2002)

In this case, a narrowly divided U.S. Supreme Court sustained a public school district policy that required suspicionless drug testing of all students who participated in any extracurricular activity. Relying heavily on the logic of *Vernonia v. Acton* (1995), the justices found that a "special need" existed (the need to prevent the harm of childhood drug use); the individual privacy interests were diminished because those being tested were children in the temporary custody of the state who chose to participate in voluntary extracurricular activities; the character of the privacy intrusion was not significant (the tests were designed to detect only illegal drugs, and the actual testing process was minimally intrusive); and the policy was an effective means of accomplishing the government's interest. Accordingly, the interests of the school district outweighed the limited privacy expectations of the students.

## Bond v. United States (2000)

This seven-to-two decision by the U.S. Supreme Court held that an individual possesses a reasonable expectation of privacy in his carry-on luggage while traveling aboard a Greyhound bus. The Fourth Amendment is thus violated when a law enforcement officer, without a warrant, squeezes or otherwise manipulates personal luggage in an exploratory manner for the purpose of determining its contents (the squeezing and manipulating constitutes a search of a constitutionally protected "effect" under the Fourth Amendment). To reach this conclusion, the justices applied *United States v. Katz*'s (1967) two-pronged reasonable expectation of privacy test. The justices distinguished this case from *California v. Ciraolo* (1986) and *Florida v. Riley* (1989) by noting that those cases involved only visual, as opposed to tactile, observation, the latter being a more physically invasive and intrusive inspection than the purely visual inspection.

## Boyd v. United States (1886)

This landmark decision by the U.S. Supreme Court was the first extensive analysis of the meaning and scope of the Fourth Amendment. Here, the justices unanimously declared unconstitutional a part of the Federal Customs Act requiring a person to produce his business papers in court when his goods had been seized as contraband or else have the charges of fraudulent importing taken as "confessed," forfeiting the goods. In doing so, the justices specifically recognized protection for privacy interests under the Fourth and Fifth Amendments, laying the basis for a broad construction of the Fourth Amendment. Noting that a close and literal construction of the constitutional provisions for the security of person and property would deprive them of "half their efficacy, and lead to gradual depreciation," the Court held that the amendments applied "to all invasions on the part of government and its employees of the sanctity of a man's home and the privacies of his life." Justice Joseph Bradley wrote, "It is not the breaking of his doors, and the rummaging of his drawers, that constitutes the essence of the offence, . . . but it is the invasion of his indefeasible right of personal security, personal liberty and private property." In short, the Court linked the Fourth Amendment's protection against unreasonable searches and seizure to the Fifth Amendment's guarantee against self-incrimination: to provide protection to "the sanctity of a man's home and the privacies of his life." The Court also suggested here that evidence obtained in violation of the Fourth Amendment should be excluded at trial. Almost thirty years later, in *Weeks v. United States* (1914), the Court converted this suggestion into a formal requirement (at least in federal prosecutions). Justice William Brennan later called *Boyd* "part of the process by which the Fourth Amendment . . . has become more than a dead letter in the federal courts."

## Brandeis, Louis (1856–1941)

This associate justice of the U.S. Supreme Court from 1916 to 1939 argued against a narrow construction of the Fourth Amendment in *Olmstead v. United States* (1928). Justice Brandeis understood the amendment to bestow upon each individual a general right of privacy, one not confined to traditional categories of searches involving actual trespass on private property or seizures of tangible items. In *Katz v. United States* (1967), the Court adopted this broad construction of the Fourth Amendment.

## Burger Court

Warren Burger (1907–1995) was chief justice of the United States from 1969 until 1986. During that time, the Supreme Court reversed the Warren Court trend of expanding the criminal rights of defendants. Significant Fourth Amendment cases decided by the

Burger Court include *United States v. U.S. District Court for the Eastern District of Michigan* (1972), *Stone v. Powell* (1976), *Illinois v. Gates* (1983), *Nix v. Williams* (1984), and *United States v. Leon* (1984).

## California v. Acevedo (1991)

This six-to-three decision of the U.S. Supreme Court eliminated the warrant requirement for closed containers found in automobiles. Under *Acevedo*, law enforcement officers may conduct a warrantless search of all closed containers found in an automobile, so long as the search of the automobile is supported by probable cause.

## California v. Ciraolo (1986)

This five-to-four decision of the U.S. Supreme Court held that a warrantless, naked-eye aerial observation of an individual's fenced-in backyard was not a search within the meaning of the Fourth Amendment, even if the observation was directed at identifying marijuana plants growing in that yard. (Police officers had hired a private plane and flew over Ciraolo's home at an altitude of 1,000 feet.) The justices concluded that the respondent's expectation of privacy from all observations of his backyard was not an expectation that was reasonable. The fact that the respondent had taken measures to restrict some views of his activities "does not preclude an officer's observation from a public vantage point where he has a right to be and which renders the activities clearly visible." Compare with *Kyllo v. United States* (2001).

## California v. Greenwood (1988)

This six-to-two decision by the U.S. Supreme Court held that an individual who places his trash on the curb for the express purpose of having someone else pick it up forfeits any reasonable expectation of privacy in the contents of the trash. As such, the Fourth Amendment is not violated when law enforcement officers, without a warrant, rummage through discarded trash. To reach this conclusion, the justices applied *United States v. Katz's* (1967) two-pronged reasonable expectation of privacy test. Compare with *Bond v. United States* (2000).

## Camara v. Municipal Court (1967)

In this six-to-three decision by the U.S. Supreme Court, the justices held that administrative searches, because they were conducted as part of a general regulatory scheme and not to uncover evidence of criminal activity, benefited from a more relaxed Fourth Amendment standard. Unlike searches pursuant to a criminal investigation, which had to be based on probable cause, administrative searches required only "reasonableness," to be determined by balancing the intrusion on the individual's Fourth Amendment interests against the promotion of a legitimate governmental interest. So long as the intrusion is limited and the state's objective is a "special need" outside normal law enforcement, the reasonableness standard is satisfied.

## Carroll v. United States (1925)

In this seven-to-two decision by the U.S. Supreme Court, the justices recognized a necessary difference between a search of a store, dwelling house, or other structure—in which a proper official warrant may be readily obtained—and a search of an automobile, in which it was not practicable to secure a warrant because the vehicle could be quickly moved out of the locality or jurisdiction in which the warrant was requested. *Carroll* stipulated, however, that the "automobile exception" did not grant unfettered authority to law enforcement to search vehicles for any reason. Instead, vehicles could be searched without warrants only if the officer conducting the search had probable cause to believe that the vehicle was carrying illegal goods or was involved in criminal activity.

## Chandler v. Miller (1997)

This eight-to-one decision by the U.S. Supreme Court disallowed a state law that required candidates for designated state public offices to certify that they were drug-free. The justices distinguished this case from others in which mandatory drug-testing programs had been sustained. First, there was no evidence of a drug problem among the state's elected officials. Second, most elected officials did not perform high-risk, safety-sensitive tasks (as was the case in *Skinner v. Railway Labor Executives Association* [1989]). And third, most elected officials were directly involved in drug interdiction efforts (as in *National Treasury Employees Union v. Von Rabb* [1989]). Where such risks were present, blanket, suspicionless searches appropriately calibrated might be reasonable. It was not enough, the Court said, to compel a search of this sort and of these people solely for "public image" considerations (to be able to say that the state's candidates for public office were "drug-free").

## Checks and Balances

One of the four defining principles of the Constitution, checks and balances is a structure in which the legislative, executive, and judicial branches of the national government share certain powers so that no branch has exclusive domain over any activity. This way, each branch may "resist encroachment" by the others. For example, the legislature may check the executive by overriding a presidential veto, impeaching and removing the president, and rejecting presidential nominees, including federal judges. The legislature may check the judiciary by determining the jurisdiction of federal courts, and by rejecting, impeaching, and removing federal judges. The executive may check the legislature by rejecting bills passed by Congress, and check the judiciary by appointing all federal judges and by pardoning those accused or convicted of federal crimes. And the judiciary may check the legislative and executive through the exercise of judicial review.

## *Chimel v. California* (1969)

In this seven-to-two decision, the U.S. Supreme Court drew a distinction between, on the one hand, a search of the person arrested and the area within his or her reach and, on the other hand, more extensive searches. The justices declared that there is no constitutional justification, in the absence of a search warrant, for searching rooms other than the room in which the arrest occurs or, for that matter, for searching through closed or concealed areas even in the room where the arrest occurs. *Chimel* has been criticized for constraining police action.

## *City of Indianapolis v. Edmond* (2000)

Fixed road checkpoints staffed by law enforcement officers with drug-sniffing dogs violate the Fourth Amendment, said the U.S. Supreme Court in this six-to-three decision. Because these checkpoints were set up to detect ordinary criminal activity (to interdict unlawful drugs), individual suspicion was required.

## Confidential Informants

Individuals who refuse to cooperate with the police unless their anonymity is guaranteed are confidential informants. Police officers regularly rely upon these people to convince a judge or magistrate that probable cause exists. When information obtained from informants is used to establish probable cause, the officer has some convincing to do. The old standard for establishing probable cause based on information provided by an informant was established by the Warren Court (1954–1969) in *Aguilar v. Texas* (1964). In evaluating such information, the officer had to convince a judge or magistrate of the veracity of the informant (how it is that the informant knows what he or she claims to know) and the reliability of the informant's knowledge (why it is that the officer believes the information to be accurate). The two prongs had to be satisfied separately and independently. The more conservative Burger Court (1969–1986) abandoned the two-pronged test in *Illinois v. Gates* (1983). In its place, the justices adopted a "totality of the circumstances" approach. After acknowledging that an informant's veracity, reliability, and basis of knowledge were "all highly relevant" in determining probable cause, the justices held that those elements should not be understood as separate and independent requirements to be rigidly exacted in every case. Strength in one element could compensate for a deficiency in another. Additionally, the justices left open the possibility that other factors might have a bearing on the determination of probable cause when based on information obtained from secondhand sources.

## Consent Searches

These searches, among the exceptions to the warrant requirement, are justified on the grounds that individuals may waive their Fourth Amendment rights. For a consent search to be valid, the consent must be voluntarily given by the individual affected or someone authorized by that person to control access to the place to be searched or the things to be seized. The question whether consent to a search is voluntary is determined from the "totality of all the circumstances," including any coercive police tactics and the personal characteristics of the subject giving the consent. A prosecutor seeking to rely upon consent to justify a warrantless search has the burden of proving that the consent was, "in fact, freely and voluntarily given," and not the result of implicit or explicit coercion. More recently, the courts have asked, in determining voluntariness, if a reasonable person would feel free to refuse consent. Consent need not be given by the defendant in a criminal proceeding. For example, police may search a bedroom inhabited by two persons so long as they have consent from one of the inhabitants. In other words, the consent of one person who possesses common authority over the premises or effects is valid against the absent, nonconsenting person with whom that authority is shared. Additionally, a reasonable belief by an officer that a person has authority to consent to a search—regardless of whether that person actually possesses such authority—is all that is necessary for such a search to be binding on the defendant. A person who gives consent may withdraw that consent at any time. When consent is effectively withdrawn, police must discontinue searching.

## Constitution of 1787

Written in 1787 and put into effect in 1789, this document was designed to provide a structure, basic institutions, and a set of powers, principles, and prohibitions for the operations of government in the United States. The four defining principles of the Constitution are federalism, separation of powers, checks and balances, and individual rights.

## Coolidge v. New Hampshire (1971)

In this five-to-four decision of the U.S. Supreme Court, the justices held that in certain circumstances and in the absence of a warrant, a police officer may seize an item that is within his or her sight. See "Plain View" Exception.

## Declaration of Independence (1776)

Written in 1776 by Thomas Jefferson, this document explained why it was necessary for the colonies to sever all political ties with

Great Britain. The Declaration did not designate general warrants or writs of assistance among its long list of grievances against the Crown. By implication, however, general warrants and writs of assistance might have been included in the open-ended complaint that the king "has . . . sent hither swarms of Officers to harass our people."

### Delaware v. Prouse (1978)

In this case, the U.S. Supreme Court, dividing eight-to-one, declared unconstitutional random stops of motorists to check drivers' licenses and vehicle registrations, if not supported by probable cause or reasonable suspicion.

### Entick v. Carrington (1765)

In this decision, an English court ruled that a house search conducted pursuant to a general warrant violated English common law. Along with *Wilkes v. Wood* (1763), this decision was highly publicized in England and briefly reported in colonial newspapers. Among the most enthusiastic supporters of this decision were many American revolutionary leaders, many of whom had first-hand knowledge of the abuses that frequently accompanied these general warrants.

## Exceptions to the Exclusionary Rule

While the Burger and Rehnquist Courts have not expressly overturned *Mapp v. Ohio* (1961) or abandoned the exclusionary rule, they have been willing to carve out exceptions to it. The most notable of these exceptions include (1) inevitable discovery; (2) independent source; and (3) good faith (with all of its multiple permutations).

## Exceptions to the Warrant Requirement

As a general rule, searches and seizures conducted outside the judicial process, without prior approval by a judge or magistrate, are per se unreasonable under the Fourth Amendment, subject to only a few "jealously and carefully drawn" exceptions. (While the Court once referred to the exceptions to the warrant requirement as limited in number and "jealously and carefully drawn," the list of exceptions now seems to include much of what is characterized as routine police activity.) At present, these exceptions include consent searches; international border searches; investigatory detentions; warrantless arrests; searches incident to a lawful arrest; plain view searches; plain feel searches; exigent circumstances; automobile searches; administrative/"special needs" searches; container searches; inventory searches; airport searches; searches at sea; searches of abandoned property; and searches of property in foreign countries belonging to individuals jailed in the United States.

## Exclusionary Rule

Adopted in *Weeks v. United States* (1914), this rule is a judicially fashioned doctrine commanding the exclusion of evidence obtained from an unreasonable search and seizure at trial. It is the primary instrument for enforcing the Fourth Amendment, and is based on the premise that, in enforcing the Fourth Amendment, police are not to be trusted to restrain themselves; instead, the courts "must police the police." Almost a century after the adoption of the exclusionary rule, members of the high Court remain divided on its purpose. Some justices maintain that the Fourth Amendment implicitly requires the exclusion of all illegally seized evidence. Others insist that the exclusionary rule is necessary to preserve judicial integrity. Still others believe the rule to be simply a judicially created remedy applicable only in those situations in which the exclusion of evidence would deter further police misconduct. Much of the opposition to the exclusion of relevant evidence was distilled in a single sentence in *People v. Defore* (NY 1926), where Judge (later Justice) Benjamin N. Cardozo critically observed the possible consequences of such a practice—"The criminal is to go free because the Constable has blundered." See *Weeks v. United States* (1914), *Wolf v. Colorado* (1949), *Mapp v. Ohio* (1961) and *United States v. Leon* (1984).

## Exigent Circumstances

This type of police emergency justifies a warrantless, nonconsensual, and forcible entry into a home. In these circumstances, a rapidly developing situation makes obtaining a warrant impracticable; thus, law enforcement is excused from the procedural requirements of the Fourth Amendment. The quintessential exigent circumstance is immediate danger to the life or safety of a person. A more frequent type of exigent circumstance is the destruction or removal of contraband. A third danger satisfying the exigent circumstances doctrine is the imminent escape of a suspect. Courts have long held that exigent circumstances exist if police officers are in "hot pursuit" of a fugitive. Exigent circumstances may also exist if some other consequence improperly frustrates legitimate law enforcement efforts; to qualify, however, an exigency must exist. The "exigent circumstances" doctrine is also known as the "emergency doctrine" and the "necessity doctrine."

### Ex Parte Burford (1806)

In this first Fourth Amendment decision to reach the U.S. Supreme Court, the justices unanimously assumed, in an opinion by Chief Justice John Marshall, that the Fourth Amendment, which extended to "persons and things to be seized," was designed to protect against imprisonment without a criminal conviction as well as arbitrary searches. Although the amendment does not explicitly refer to arrests, Marshall took it for granted that this view of its scope was self-evident. He concluded that in the absence of "some good cause certain, supported by oath..." the prisoner had been improperly committed.

## *Ex Parte Jackson* (1878)

In this unanimous U.S. Supreme Court decision, the justices ruled that the U.S Post Office could not open sealed mail without a warrant.

## Federalism

One of the four defining principles of the U.S. Constitution, federalism is a system of government in which a constitution divides power between a national government and subnational governments. Neither the national government nor the state government receives its powers from the other. Instead, both governments derive their powers from the Constitution. The framers of the Constitution viewed the division of governmental authority as a means of checking power with power, and providing "double security" to the people. The national government would keep the state governments "in check," and the state governments would prevent excesses by the national government. In a federal system, both governments may act directly upon the people.

## Felony

This is a general name for a class of crimes regarded by the law as very serious; a misdemeanor is a less serious crime. Aggravated assault, arson, burglary, kidnapping, murder, and rape are commonly considered to be felonious crimes. Historically, felonies were crimes for which punishment included forfeiture of property, imprisonment, or death.

## Ferguson v. City of Charleston (2001)

This decision by the U.S. Supreme Court held that a state hospital could not test pregnant women to obtain evidence of cocaine use for law enforcement purposes if the pregnant women did not consent to the procedure with full knowledge of the purpose for the test. The justices, dividing six to three, concluded that the program did not fit within the "closely guarded category" of constitutionally permissible suspicionless searches. In the other "special needs" cases regarding drug testing (*Skinner v. Railway Labor Executives' Association* [1989]; *National Treasury Employees Union v. Von Raab* [1989]; *Vernonia v. Acton* [1995], for example) the "special need" asserted was divorced from the general interest in law enforcement. Here, the "central and indispensable feature" of the policy from its inception was the threat of criminal arrest and prosecution to force women into treatment.

## Florida v. Bostick (1991)

In this six-to-three decision of the U.S. Supreme Court, the justices held that a police officer's request that a bus passenger consent to a search of this luggage did not necessarily constitute a seizure for purposes of the Fourth Amendment.

## Florida v. J. L. (2000)

This unanimous decision by the U.S. Supreme Court disallowed a "stop and frisk" based solely on an anonymous tip that a person was carrying a gun. Because the anonymous tip left the police officers without means to corroborate the details or establish the trustworthiness of the informant, the tip alone did not exhibit sufficient indications of reliability to provide reasonable suspicion to make an investigatory detention. Though asked to do so, the justices refused to adopt a "firearms exception," under which an anonymous tip alleging the possession of an illegal gun would, by itself, justify a "stop and frisk."

## *Florida v. Riley* (1989)

This five-to-four decision of the U.S. Supreme court held that surveillance from a helicopter, at an altitude of 400 feet, of the interior of a residential greenhouse was not a search requiring a warrant under the Fourth Amendment.

## Fourteenth Amendment
## Due Process Clause

Provision of the Fourteenth Amendment that prohibits a state from depriving any person of "life, liberty, or property, without due process of law." Not until well into the twentieth century did the U.S. Supreme Court accept the argument that this clause "incorporated" most of the provisions of the Bill of Rights, thus making most of the provisions of the Bill of Rights binding upon state governments. In its most generic sense, due process of law refers to the methods by which governmental authority is exercised; this is commonly known as procedural due process. Due process of law has also been interpreted as imposing certain substantive limitations on governmental policies. This concept is often referred to as substantive due process.

## Fourth Amendment

This amendment affirms that

> [t]he right of the people to be secure in their persons, houses, papers, and effects, against unreasonable searches and seizures, shall not be violated, and no Warrants shall issue, but upon probable cause, supported by Oath or affirmation, and particularly describing the place to be searched, and the persons or things to be seized.

Prior to the Fourth Amendment, many states provided similarly worded constitutional guarantees against arbitrary governmental invasion of individual privacy and liberty. The core objectives of the amendment—safeguarding individual liberty, securing personal privacy, and protecting the rights of property against arbitrary governmental intrusion—remain the same today as when the amendment was ratified in 1791. The imperatives of maintaining security in the face of violent crime and the seemingly ubiquitous threat of international terrorism place constant pressure on law enforcement agencies to bypass Fourth Amendment protections of individual rights in furtherance of the demands for public order and stability.

## General Warrants

In the seventeenth and eighteenth centuries, agents of the English Crown, as a means of gathering evidence for the prosecution of a wide array of offenses, relied upon warrants that "lacked specificity as to whom to arrest or where to search." These general warrants authorized agents of the Crown to force their way into private residences in search of contraband, and resulted in gross invasions of privacy. As early as 1685, the English Parliament recognized that general warrants amounted to an exercise of arbitrary governmental authority. By the middle of the eighteenth century, English judges began to rule against general warrants. The colonial experience with general warrants is directly responsible for the Fourth Amendment.

## "Good Faith" Exception to the Exclusionary Rule

Announced in *United States v. Leon* (1984), this exception to the exclusionary rule permits the use of illegally obtained evidence where police possess an objectively reasonable belief that their warrant is valid, even though the warrant is later found to be unsupported by probable cause or is technically deficient. In this type of situation, because the magistrate erred, declaring the evidence inadmissible would not advance the primary goal of the exclusionary rule—deterring police misconduct. The Court has extended the "good faith" exception, and thus limited the application of the exclusionary rule, in a number of contexts. The exception applies when police obtain evidence by making an honest mistake in the execution of a warrant (police error); when police conduct a warrantless search pursuant to a state statute that is later declared unconstitutional (legislative error); and when police obtain evidence in reliance on an erroneous police record indicating the presence of an outstanding warrant (clerical error). See *Maryland v. Garrison* (1987), *Illinois v. Krull* (1987), and *Arizona v. Evans* (1995), respectively.

## *Groh v. Ramirez* (2004)

This five-to-four decision of the U.S. Supreme Court invalidated a home search pursuant to a warrant that failed to describe with particularity the persons or things to be seized. Additionally, the federal agent who completed the application and conducted the search was not entitled to qualified immunity in a subsequent suit for damages.

## Hiibel v. Sixth Judicial District Court of Nevada (2004)

This five-to-four decision of the U.S. Supreme Court addressed the question of whether a state "stop and identify" statute exceeded the constitutional boundaries established *Terry v. Ohio* (1968). When asked by a police officer investigating an alleged assault to identify himself, Larry Hiibel refused to disclose his identity, asserting that his identity was none of the officer's business. The justices upheld his conviction against a Fourth Amendment challenge, noting that the request for identity "has an immediate relation to the purpose, rationale, and practical demands of a *Terry* stop." So long as the request for identification is reasonably related to the circumstances justifying the stop—in this case, the assault investigation—the Fourth Amendment is not violated.

## "Hot Pursuit" Doctrine

Often listed as an exception to the warrant requirement, the "hot pursuit" doctrine is commonly defined as the immediate pursuit of a suspect from the location of a crime involving some sort of chase. This doctrine permits a warrantless, nonconsensual, and forcible entry into a residence. An entry based on "hot pursuit" requires four elements: probable cause (to make the arrest), an attempted arrest (in some public location), flight (from that location to a home or other private place), and chase (pursuit by a police officer).

## Illinois v. Caballes (2005)

This six-to-three decision of the U.S. Supreme Court upheld a dog sniff performed on the exterior of a car only a few minutes after the vehicle was stopped for speeding. So long as the traffic stop was lawful at its inception, the dog sniff did not change the character of the traffic stop nor did it infringe upon a constitutionally protected privacy interest, said the justices.

### *Illinois v. Gates (1983)*

This six-to-three decision of the U.S. Supreme Court established the totality of the circumstances approach for determining probable cause based on information obtained by an informant.

### *Illinois v. Krull* (1987)

This five-to-four decision of the U.S. Supreme Court established the "legislative error" exception to the exclusionary rule. Here, the justices extended the "good faith" exception holding that the exclusionary rule did not apply to evidence obtained by police who acted in objectively reasonable reliance upon a state statute authorizing warrantless searches, but that was subsequently found to violate the Fourth Amendment. The *Krull* majority refused to exclude the evidence unless it could be shown that doing so would effectively deter future police misconduct. The dissenters compared the statute to the acts of the British Parliament authorizing indiscriminate general searches by writs of assistance.

### *Illinois v. Lidster* (2004)

This six-to-three decision of the U.S. Supreme Court held that the police did not violate the Fourth Amendment by stopping a motorist at a checkpoint established to investigate an unrelated crime and then arresting the motorist when he failed a sobriety test. The checkpoint was reasonable, the majority said, because it advanced a "grave" public interest, was not set up primarily for general crime control purposes, and was not likely to provoke anxiety or prove overly intrusive. Compare with *City of Indi-*

*anapolis v. Edmond,* where the high Court disallowed a "crime control" checkpoint.

## *Illinois v. Wardlow* (2000)

This five-to-four decision by the U.S. Supreme Court determined that a police officer had reasonable suspicion to stop an individual who, upon seeing a police caravan patrolling an area known for heavy narcotics trafficking, fled. Instead of relying upon the *Terry v. Ohio* (1968) standard, the justices invoked the "totality of the circumstances" yardstick, concluding that law enforcement officers are not required to ignore relevant characteristics of a particular location (a high drug-trade area) or sufficiently suspicious activity ("headlong flight" being the consummate act of evasion and clearly suggestive of wrongdoing). In short, unprovoked flight in a high-crime area amounts to reasonable suspicion justifying an investigatory detention.

## Incorporation/Nationalization of the Bill of Rights

This is the process by which most of the provisions of the Bill of Rights have been brought within the scope of the Fourteenth Amendment Due Process Clause, thus making most of the provisions of the Bill of Rights binding upon the states. In *Palko v. Connecticut* (1937), the U.S. Supreme Court rationalized the selective application of the guarantees of the Bill of Rights. According to this theory, often known as selective incorporation, only fundamental rights are applied to the states. For a right to be fundamental, it either had to be "implicit in the concept of ordered liberty" or "deeply rooted in this Nation's history and tradition." The core of the Fourth Amendment was incorporated in *Wolf v. Colorado* (1949). Several provisions of the Bill of Rights—the Second Amendment, the Third Amendment, the Grand Jury Clause of the Fifth Amendment, the Seventh Amendment, and the Excessive Bail and Fines Clauses of the Eighth Amendment—have never been incorporated and are not applicable to the states.

## "Independent Source" Exception to the Exclusionary Rule

Announced in *Segura v. United States* (1984), this exception to the exclusionary rule allows the admission of evidence that has been discovered "by means wholly independent of any constitutional violation." This exception reflects the notion that while government should not profit from official misconduct, neither should it be made worse off than it would have been absent the misconduct. To prevail under this exception, the prosecution must prove that the evidence later would have been found as a result of other, independent sources.

## Individual Rights

One of the four defining principles of the Constitution, individual rights, often referred to as civil liberties, are the freedoms of all persons from governmental interference. The Bill of Rights lists specific freedoms—such as freedom of speech, press, and religion, and freedom from unreasonable searches and seizures; and may be properly viewed as a general expression of the framers' prevalent fear of fundamental rights being deprived by government. The driving force behind these grants of freedom was the memory of tyranny under the King of England.

## "Inevitable Discovery" Exception to the Exclusionary Rule

Announced in *Nix v. Williams* (1984), this exception to the exclusionary rule does not require the suppression of evidence that has been seized illegally if the prosecution can establish that the evidence inevitably would have been discovered by lawful means in the course of a continuing investigation. The Court has justified this exception by asserting that the purpose of the rule is to restore the "status quo" that existed in the absence of a constitutional violation.

## International Border Search Exception

This exception to the warrant requirement authorizes unconsented searches without either a warrant or any individual suspicion that the person or place to be searched is connected to criminal activity at international borders.

A variety of governmental officials may conduct such searches, including immigration officials, Coast Guard officers, and customs agents. In the interest of national security, courts have long authorized routine border stops and searches of persons, luggage, personal effects, and vehicles based on the sovereign authority of the United States to protect itself by controlling what persons and property cross into the country. Because it is within the power of the federal government to exclude aliens from the country, and because the Fourth Amendment's "balance of reasonableness is qualitatively different at the international border than in the interior," routine border searches of incoming or outgoing persons and property do not require reasonable suspicion, probable cause, or a warrant. The "border search" exception not only applies at the border, but also at its "functional equivalent." Such functional equivalents may include an established station near a border, a point marking the confluence of two or more roads that extend from the border, or an airport at which arriving passengers and cargo of an airplane are searched after a nonstop flight from a foreign country. Recognizing the importance in controlling the illegal entry of aliens into the United States, the Supreme Court has, in limited circumstances, permitted the use of roving border patrols to stop vehicles to question occupants as to their citizenship and immigration status. Because stops of this sort are typically brief, result in no search of the vehicle or its occupants, and require at most a response to a brief question or the production of certain documentation, probable cause is not required for the stop. Additionally, automotive travelers may be stopped at fixed checkpoints near the border without individualized suspicion; and boats on inland waters with ready access to the sea may be hailed and boarded with no suspicion whatsoever. Searches that occur at greater distances from the border (or the sea) require either consent or probable cause.

## Investigatory Detention

In the stop-detention-arrest process, this is the intermediate stage during which the law enforcement officer determines whether he or she has probable cause to make an arrest. This exception to the warrant requirement permits law enforcement officers to detain temporarily an individual to maintain the status quo while the officer obtains additional information. Unlike an arrest, an investigatory detention does not require probable cause. Instead, investigatory detention requires only that the officers have reasonable, articulable suspicion of criminal activity. The Supreme Court first addressed the legality of warrantless investigatory detentions in *Terry v. Ohio* (1968).

## Judicial Federalism

This term applies to the distribution of power between federal and state judiciaries. In the American legal system, the ultimate answers to questions arising from the U.S. Constitution are provided by the U.S. Supreme Court. Federal judicial power, however, is limited. Only certain decisional categories—cases "arising under this Constitution, [and] the Laws of the United States," for example—and controversies involving certain parties—states and citizens of different states, for example—come under the jurisdiction of the federal courts. Federal courts have no power to interpret state constitutions. Thus, state courts, construing their own constitutions—many of which contain similar search and seizure restrictions—play an important role in this and other areas of constitutional interpretation. On the basis of clearly stated "adequate and independent state grounds," a number of state courts have in recent years extended search and seizure rights beyond the requirements of the Fourth Amendment as interpreted by the U.S. Supreme Court. In establishing standards for state courts to follow in this complex area of constitutional jurisdiction, the justices concluded, "If the state court decision indicates clearly and expressly that it is . . . based on bona fide separate, adequate, and independent [state] grounds, we . . . will not undertake to review the decision." See *Michigan v. Long* (1983). Fourth Amendment requirements thus represent a uniform national minimum standard. The individual states may exceed this standard so long as they do not violate other provisions of the U.S. Constitution, but under our federal system, they cannot fall short of it. This basic feature of American federalism is important, since most criminal prosecutions raising search and seizure issues originate at the local level and are first addressed by state courts.

## Judicial Review

The power of American courts, most notably the United States Supreme Court, to declare unconstitutional the acts and proceedings of other branches and levels of government is known as judicial review. Federal and state courts, exercising judicial review, may determine the constitutionality of governmental action; and if that action should be deemed inconsistent with the U.S. Constitution, then the judiciary has the power to nullify the action. Over the years, Congress and state legislatures have enacted numerous statutes—and police departments numerous regulations—to spell out the broad requirements of the Fourth Amendment and its counterparts in state constitutions. In the course of deciding cases, courts are typically called upon to determine whether particular statutory provisions or police regulations are consistent with constitutional requirements, and whether they have been constitutionally applied. Sooner or later, the most difficult questions work their way up to the U.S. Supreme Court, presenting the nine justices of that tribunal with the formidable task of transforming general abstract constitutional values into tangible, practical requirements for law enforcement agencies to follow.

### *Katz v. United States* (1967)

Arguably the most important Fourth Amendment case of the last half-century, this seven-to-one decision by the U.S. Supreme Court overturned *Olmstead v. United States* (1928). Prior to 1967, the Court employed the concept of a "constitutionally protected area" to define the scope of searches of "persons, houses, papers, and effects" in a Fourth Amendment context. This restrictive standard for determining a search came to an end in *Katz.* Charles Katz was convicted in federal district court of placing bets and wagers in violation of federal law. The evidence used to convict Katz was obtained by an electronic listening device placed outside a public telephone booth in Los Angeles, California. The device was placed outside the booth by federal agents who did not have a warrant. In *Katz,* the justices decided that a search could occur without a physical intrusion into a "constitutionally protected area": "[T]he Fourth Amendment protects people not places. . . . What a person . . . seeks to preserve as private, even if in an area accessible to the public, may be constitutionally protected," wrote Justice Potter Stewart. Under the *Katz* standard, the touchstone of Fourth Amendment analysis is whether an individual has a constitutionally protected, reasonable expectation of privacy. A concurring opinion endeavored to clarify the majority's holding by proposing a two-part inquiry: first, that a person manifest a subjective expectation of privacy in the object of the challenged search; and second, that the expectation be one that society is prepared to recognize as reasonable. In pursuing the second inquiry, the test of legitimacy is not whether the individual chooses to conceal assertedly "private activity," but whether the government's intrusion infringes upon the personal and societal values protected by the Fourth Amendment. This concurrence has become the governing standard for determining whether a search has occurred in the absence of physical intrusion. This "reasonable expectation of privacy" standard has proved difficult to apply with consistency. Compare, for example, two Supreme Court decisions, one involving aerial surveillance of private property— *California v. Ciraolo* (1986)—and the other involving thermal imaging of a private residence—*Kyllo v. United States* (2001).

## *Kirk v. Louisiana* (2002)

This decision of the U.S. Supreme Court reiterated the bright-line rule announced in *Payton v. New York* (1980). In a per curiam opinion, the justices reaffirmed the view that police officers need either a warrant or probable cause plus exigent circumstances to make a lawful entry into a home.

## "Knock and Announce" Requirement

The Fourth Amendment incorporates the common law requirement that law enforcement officers knock and announce their presence, identity, authority, and purpose before forcibly entering a residence to execute a warrant. The so-called "knock-and-announce" rule requires police officers to notify the occupants of their presence, identify themselves as police officers, express their specific legal purpose for requesting entry, and to wait a reasonable amount of time to allow the occupants to admit the officers voluntarily or to refuse to do so, at which time the officers may enter the residence forcibly. While there is no "bright-line" rule for distinguishing between a reasonable and unreasonable amount of time for officers to wait after announcing their presence but before entering a residence forcibly, fifteen to twenty seconds has become the general standard employed by law enforcement officers and supported by numerous courts. Courts have recognized three exceptions to this general requirement. To justify a "no-knock" entry, police officers must have reasonable suspicion to believe that knocking and announcing their presence will (1) be perilously dangerous; (2) be useless; or (3) inhibit the effective investigation of the crime by, for example, allowing the destruction of evidence. The Supreme Court has held that these exceptions strike an appropriate balance between the legitimate needs of law enforcement at issue in the execution of warrants and the individual privacy concerns affected by "no-knock" entries.

### *Kyllo v. United States* (2001)

In this five-to-four decision of the U.S. Supreme Court, the justices squarely confronted the limits upon the power of technology to shrink the realm of guaranteed privacy. The specific issue addressed was whether law enforcement's warrantless use of a thermal imaging device—designed to detect relative amounts of heat within a residence—violated the Fourth Amendment when the device was aimed at a private residence from a public street. The justices held that the government's use of a device not in general public use to explore details of a private home that were previously unknowable without physical intrusion constituted a search under the Fourth Amendment and was presumptively unreasonable without a warrant. Writing for the majority, Justice Antonin Scalia identified a reasonable expectation of privacy in the interior of the home. "To withdraw protection of this minimum expectation would be to permit police technology to erode the privacy guaranteed by the Fourth Amendment," leaving the homeowner at the mercy of ever more sophisticated technology. All nine justices agreed that the use of a device disclosing what people were actually doing within the home would have constituted a search. The four dissenters, however, drew a distinction between "off the wall" observations and "through the wall" surveillance, the former being constitutional so long as reasonable, even if warrantless. Because the thermal imaging only gathered information already exposed to the general public, the dissenters maintained that it did not invade any constitutionally protected interest in privacy.

## Limited Government

This principle recognizes legal, written restraints on governmental authority. Limited government was a central assumption of American political thought at the time of the Constitutional Convention.

## Madison, James (1751–1836)

This forceful advocate for a strong national government at the Constitutional Convention and coauthor of *The Federalist* was present at nearly all of the deliberations and kept detailed notes of them, thus earning him the title "Father of the Constitution." Because he feared "the abuse of the powers of the General Government," Madison authored and introduced into the House of Representatives what became the Bill of Rights.

## "Malcom Affair"

In this 1766 affair, characterized as the "most famous search in colonial America," customs agents, searching for smuggled brandy and other liquors, ransacked the house of Daniel Malcom, a prominent Boston merchant. A fiery response from Malcom and other colonists forced the agents to withdraw. This event, precisely the kind of search the authors of the Fourth Amendment found so offensive, had the effect of fueling resentment and resistance to writs of assistance in the colonies.

## Mapp v. Ohio (1961)

In this landmark decision of the Warren Court, the justices extended the federal exclusionary rule to state criminal prosecutions. The majority opinion, supported by five justices, emphasized both the constitutional foundations and the practical necessities of the rule: The exclusion doctrine was both an "essential ingredient" of the Fourth Amendment and necessary to discourage police misconduct and maintain judicial integrity. Accordingly, all evidence obtained by searches in violation of the Fourth Amendment was inadmissible in state criminal proceedings. *Mapp* formally linked the exclusionary rule to the Fourth Amendment. Subsequent decisions of the Burger and Rehnquist Courts have deconstitutionalized the rule, redefined its purpose, and limited its application. This has resulted in the significant curtailment of the operation of the exclusionary rule. See "Exceptions to the Exclusionary Rule," page 258.

## Maryland v. Buie (1990)

In this seven-to-two decision, the U.S. Supreme Court ruled that, when making an arrest, police officers who have reason to believe that someone else may be present in another part of the house and that such person might pose a danger to them, may make a "protective sweep" for safety purposes. Probable cause for the search is not required.

## Maryland v. Garrison (1987)

This decision by the U.S. Supreme Court established the "police error" exception to the exclusionary rule. This exception applies when police make an honest mistake in the execution of a warrant. Here, the justices extended the "good faith" exception, declaring valid under the Fourth Amendment a search warrant that ambiguously described the place to be searched and resulted in a search of the wrong apartment. Police officers possessed a search warrant for Lawrence McWebb and his place of residence, listed on the warrant as the "2036 Park Avenue third floor apartment." The officers reasonably believed that there was only one apartment on the premises described in the warrant. In fact, however, the third floor was divided into two apartments. The police inadvertently entered the apartment belonging to Harold Garrison, who was not the target of the search warrant, and found drugs and drug paraphernalia. The six-person majority permitted the introduction of the evidence at trial against Garrison, concluding that the search warrant and execution of the warrant were valid because the officers' lack of knowledge of the overly broad description in the warrant was objectively reasonable. Additionally, while the police had erred, they had not engaged in any misconduct.

## Maryland v. Pringle (2003)

This unanimous decision of the U.S. Supreme Court ruled that law enforcement officers had probable cause to arrest three occupants of an automobile when a large roll of money and illegal drugs were found following a routine stop for speeding. Given all the circumstances, the justices determined that it was reasonable for the officers to conclude that the occupants committed the crime, either solely or jointly. By contrast, consider *Ybarra v. Illinois* (1979).

## Michigan v. Long (1983)

In this six-to-three decision of the U.S. Supreme Court, Justice O'Connor, writing for the Court, explained that through interpretation of their state constitutions, state courts remain free to provide broader protections against unreasonable searches and seizures than the protection afforded by the U.S. Supreme Court's interpretation of the Fourth Amendment. Fourth Amendment requirements thus represent a uniform national minimum standard. The individual states may exceed this standard, but may not fall short of it. See "Judicial Federalism," page 271.

## *Michigan State Police v. Sitz* (1990)

This six-to-three decision of the U.S. Supreme Court upheld fixed highway sobriety checkpoints, even in the absence of any individualized suspicion. In reaching this conclusion, the justices relied upon the magnitude of the drunken driving problem; the minimal intrusion resulting from the checkpoint (merely visual observation for signs of intoxication); the direct relation of the checkpoints to roadway safety; and the randomness of the stops.

## *Minnesota v. Dickerson* (1993)

In this case, a unanimous U.S. Supreme Court held that a police officer may seize nonthreatening contraband detected during a protective pat-down search of a person whom the officer has briefly and lawfully stopped based on the officer's reasonable conclusion that criminal activity may be afoot, where the officer is justified in believing that the person is armed and presently dangerous to the officer or to others nearby. The justices noted, however, that the search must be strictly limited to that which is necessary for the discovery of weapons that might be used to harm the officer or others.

## *Murray v. Hoboken Land Company* (1855)

This unanimous decision of the U.S. Supreme Court ruled that the Fourth Amendment did not apply to civil proceedings.

## National Treasury Employees Union v. Von Raab (1989)

This U.S. Supreme Court case was a challenge to a mandatory drug-screening program for agents of the U.S. Customs Service. Though conceding that the urine tests were searches within the meaning of the Fourth Amendment, the justices, dividing five-to-four, sustained the program. Because the "searches" were not part of a criminal investigation, they did not have to be supported by a warrant, probable cause, or individualized suspicion. Instead, reasonableness, to be determined by balancing the government's interest against the individual's privacy interest, was the touchstone. Whatever individual privacy interests were implicated came up short when measured against the compelling governmental interest in ensuring the drug-free Customs Service work force.

## Neutral and Detached Judge or Magistrate

Determining probable cause is the task of a judicial officer. Search warrants may be issued only by a "neutral and detached" judge or magistrate. If the issuing officer is not "neutral and detached"— that is, he or she has some personal interest in the matter to be prosecuted—then the resulting warrant cannot be objectively reasonable. The Supreme Court summed up the justification for this requirement well more than a half-century ago: "The point of the Fourth Amendment, which often is not grasped by zealous officers, is not that it denies law enforcement the support of the usual inferences which reasonable men draw from evidence. Its protection consists in requiring that those inferences be drawn by a neutral and detached magistrate instead of being judged by the officer engaged in the often competitive enterprise of ferreting out crime."

## *New York v. Belton* (1981)

This six-to-three decision of the U.S. Supreme Court upheld a warrantless search of a passenger compartment of an automobile and a "container" found within the passenger compartment as a contemporaneous search incident to a lawful arrest. Because the item was located inside the passenger compartment of the vehicle, it was "within the arrestee's immediate control."

## *Olmstead v. United States* (1928)

This five-to-four decision of the U.S. Supreme Court held that the use of evidence obtained through a warrantless wiretap in a federal criminal trial did not violate the Fourth Amendment's guarantee against unreasonable searches and seizures. Because the interception of the telephone conversations occurred without "trespass" on private property, there was no "search" of a constitutionally protected area; moreover, conversations were not tangible items that could be "seized." In dissent, Justice Louis Brandeis argued against this narrow construction of the Fourth Amendment, recognizing the necessity of interpreting the amendment in light of changing technological conditions: "Ways may someday be developed by which the government, without removing papers from secret drawers, can reproduce them in court, and by which it will be enabled to expose to a jury the most intimate occurrences of the home. . . . Can it be that the Constitution affords no protection against such invasions of individual security?" Justice Brandeis understood the amendment to bestow upon each individual a general right of privacy, one not confined to traditional categories of searches involving actual trespass on private property or seizures of tangible items. He then concluded, "The makers of our Constitution . . . conferred, as against the government, the right to be let alone—the most comprehensive of rights and the right most valued by civilized men." Four decades later, *Olmstead* was overruled in *Katz v. United States* (1967). No doubt the *Katz* Court was motivated by Justice Brandeis's dissent in *Olmstead*. It is also worth noting that in a separate dissenting opinion, Justice Oliver Wendell Holmes asserted that "We have to choose, and for my part I think it a less evil that some criminals should escape than that the government should play an ignoble part."

## Otis, James (1725–1783)

This prominent Boston lawyer delivered a rousing address condemning writs of assistance before the Superior Court in Boston on February 24, 1761. Otis denounced the writs as "the worst instrument[s] of arbitrary power, the most destructive of English liberty and the fundamental principles of law, that ever was found in an English law-book." John Adams, then a young member of the Boston Bar who was present in the courtroom that day, later spoke of the significance of the speech. "Then and there the child Independence was born," Adams said. Otis lost the case, commonly referred to as *Paxton's Case* (1761).

## *Paxton's Case* (1761)

In this case, prominent Boston lawyer James Otis, representing Charles Paxton, denounced writs of assistance as instruments of "slavery" and "villainy." Unconvinced, the Massachusetts Superior Court sustained the legality of the writs. This case is also known as the *Writs of Assistance* case.

## *Payton v. New York* (1980)

In this six-to-three decision, the U.S. Supreme Court held that the Fourth Amendment prohibits law enforcement authorities from making a warrantless and nonconsensual entry into a suspect's home to make a routine felony arrest. Here, the justices distinguished earlier pronouncements upholding warrantless arrests in public places on the ground that the physical entry of the home is the "chief evil" against which the wording of the Fourth Amendment was directed. It is fair to conclude from this and other decisions that a presumption of unreasonableness attaches to all warrantless entries into the home.

## "Plain Feel" Exception

This exception to the warrant requirement authorizes a police officer who is lawfully patting down a suspect's outer clothing (within the boundaries established by *Terry v. Ohio*) to seize any object—to include nonthreatening ones—whose shape or mass makes it immediately apparent as contraband. The "plain feel" exception is applicable under the following conditions. First, there must be a valid *Terry* stop. The police officer must be reasonably justified in believing that criminal activity is afoot. Second, the officer is justified in conducting a limited, protective search of the outer clothing. The officer must reasonably believe that the individual whose suspicious behavior the officer is investigating at close range is armed and presently dangerous to the officer and others. And third, the object discovered by feel must be immediately apparent to the officer as contraband. *Minnesota v. Dickerson* (1993) introduced this exception.

## "Plain View" Exception

This exception to the warrant requirement allows a police officer in certain circumstances, and in the absence of a warrant, to seize an item that is within his or her sight. Reliance on this exception requires the coalescence of four conditions: (1) a justified intrusion by police; (2) the items must be found in plain view; (3) it must be "immediately apparent" that the items are incriminating;

and (4) the discovery must be inadvertent. This exception was initially announced in *Coolidge v. New Hampshire* (1971).

## Probable Cause

The Fourth Amendment imposes on government the requirement that searches and seizures be based on probable cause. Probable cause, however, is not defined in the Fourth Amendment or elsewhere in the Constitution. The Supreme Court has observed that police officers have probable cause "where the facts and circumstances within their knowledge and of which they had reasonable and trustworthy information [are] sufficient in themselves to warrant a man of reasonable caution in the belief that an offense has been or is being committed." The justices have also referred to probable cause as the "accumulated wisdom of precedent and experience." In requesting a warrant, police officers are not required to prove their assertions. The Fourth Amendment demands "probability" not "certainty." To be certain, however, rumor, simple suspicion, and even a strong reason to suspect do not constitute probable cause.

## Rehnquist Court

William Rehnquist (1924–2005) was appointed to the chief justiceship in 1986 by President Ronald Reagan. During his tenure, the Supreme Court significantly curtailed many of the procedural rights of criminal defendants, consistently siding with the interests of law enforcement. Important Fourth Amendment cases decided by the Rehnquist Court include *United States v. Sokolow* (1990), *California v. Acevedo* (1991), *Atwater v. City of Lago Vista* (2001), *Kyllo v. United States* (2001) (over Rehnquist's dissent), *Board of Education of Independent School District No. 92 of Pottawatomie County v. Earls* (2002), and *Illinois v. Caballes* (2005).

## *Richards v. Wisconsin* (1997)

In this unanimous decision, the U.S. Supreme Court disallowed a blanket exception to the knock-and-announce requirement in drug felony investigations. The justices held that it was the duty of the court confronted with the question to determine whether the totality of the circumstances of the particular entry provided compelling reasons for disregarding the knock-and-announce requirement.

## "*Ross* Anomaly"

In *United States v. Ross* (1982), the Supreme Court held that if police have probable cause to search a vehicle lawfully stopped, they may search any portion of the vehicle in which the sought-after items might be located, including any closed containers and packages inside the car. This decision created what some have called the "*Ross* anomaly": With probable cause to search a closed container that happens to be in an automobile, a warrant is required. Yet if police have probable cause to search an automobile, no warrant is needed to search a closed container that just happens to be in the automobile. This anomaly was resolved in *California v. Acevedo* (1991).

## Search and Seizure Clause

The first part of the Fourth Amendment, which grants to certain persons certain freedoms against certain types of searches and seizures, is the Search and Seizure Clause. It does not guarantee to each individual freedom from all searches and seizures. Searches and seizures are not prohibited by the Fourth Amendment except insofar as they bear the requisite relationship to "persons, houses, papers, and effects." Even then, searches and seizures affecting those areas are prohibited only if they are "unreasonable"; reasonable searches and seizures, even if affecting those areas, are not proscribed. Similarly, law enforcement practices may be unreasonable—incredibly unreasonable—and still be constitutional, as long as those practices do not constitute searches and seizures within the meaning of the Fourth Amendment.

## Searches Incident to a Lawful Arrest

Because there is no way for an arresting officer to predict reliably if a suspect being arrested poses a serious threat to the arresting officer, courts have historically permitted police some leeway in conducting searches that are incident to lawful arrests. Under this "search incident to lawful arrest" principle, whenever an arrest is made, the arresting officer may search the person being arrested to remove any weapons that may be used against the officer to effect an escape and to seize evidence on the arrestee's person to prevent its concealment or destruction. Additionally, the officer may search the area within the arrestee's "immediate control" to prevent the individual being arrested from grabbing a weapon or other evidence. Courts have construed the phrase "within the immediate control" as the area from within which the arrestee might reach to gain possession of a weapon or destructible evidence. Lower courts have referred to the area within the suspect's immediate control as the "grabbing area." The leading case on searches incident to lawful arrests is *Chimel v. California* (1969).

## Separation of Powers

One of the four defining principles of the Constitution, separation of powers is a way of parceling out power among the three branches of the national government. The Constitution assigns the legislative, executive, and judicial powers of the national government to three separate, independent branches of government.

This separation, James Madison maintained, provided an "essential precaution in favor of liberty."

### *Skinner v. Railway Labor Executives' Association* (1989)

This seven-to-two decision by the U.S. Supreme Court upheld a mandatory drug testing policy for employees of the Federal Railroad Administration involved in serious train accidents. Applying a balancing test adopted in *Camara v. Municipal Court* (1967), the justices reasoned that the regulation of railroad employees to ensure safety constituted a "special need" beyond normal law enforcement justifying the departure from the usual warrant and probable cause requirements. In doing so, the majority affirmed that individualized suspicion was not a prerequisite for all drug testing.

### "Stop and Frisk" Exception

See *Terry v. Ohio* (1968).

### *Terry v. Ohio* (1968)

This eight-to-one decision of the U.S. Supreme Court noted:

> where a police officer observes unusual conduct which leads him reasonably to conclude in light of his experience that criminal activity may be afoot and that the persons with whom he is dealing may be armed and presently dangerous, . . . he is entitled for the protection of himself and others in the area to conduct a limited search of the outer clothing of such persons in an attempt to discover weapons which might be used to assault him.

In short, certain governmental interests—in this case, public safety—may justify a brief investigatory detention on less than probable cause. This so-called "stop and frisk" exception quickly came to stand for the proposition that a citizen on the street could be legally stopped and frisked if a police officer had "reasonable suspicion." While the primary bases for reasonable suspicion in *Terry* were the personal observations, and rational conclusions drawn from those observations and other experience and special knowledge of a trained police officer, subsequent decisions of the Burger and Rehnquist Courts have enlarged the bases for reasonable suspicion and extended the rationale for investigatory detentions. See, for example, *United States v. Sokolow* (1990).

## Thornton v. United States (2004)

This five-to-four decision of the U.S. Supreme Court resolved a long-unanswered question regarding searches and seizures of occupants of automobiles. In *New York v. Belton* (1981), the high Court ruled that the Fourth Amendment permitted a warrantless search of the passenger compartment of an automobile validly stopped. For many years, it was unclear whether the rule announced in *Belton* was limited to situations in which the police officer made contact with the occupant of the car while the latter was inside the vehicle. *Thornton* clarified that *Belton* governed even when initial contact took place after the occupant left the vehicle.

## United States v. Arvizu (2002)

This unanimous decision of the U.S. Supreme Court reaffirmed that law enforcement officers need only reasonable suspicion, not probable cause, to conduct searches and seizures during brief investigatory stops of vehicles. The justices applied the "totality of the circumstances" test, concluding that even though each of the factors involved—(1) a nervous-looking driver and passengers; (2) in a type of vehicle commonly used by drug smugglers, with a registered address in an area notorious for drug trafficking; and (3) traveling on a seldom-used road near the Mexican border—was by itself susceptible to innocent explanation, taken together the factors sufficed to form a "a particularized and objective basis for suspecting legal wrongdoing." Consider along with *United States v. Sokolow* (1990).

## United States v. Banks (2003)

In this unanimous decision, the U.S. Supreme Court held that police officers, in possession of a warrant to search for cocaine in a relatively small apartment, could enter the home forcibly after knocking on the apartment door, calling out "police search warrant," and waiting fifteen to twenty seconds without a response. The justices concluded that the officers could fairly have suspected that the cocaine would be destroyed if the officers were reticent any longer. Lower courts have permitted even shorter wait times in cases involving easily disposable evidence.

## United States v. Calandra (1974)

In this U.S. Supreme Court decision, the justices rejected the notion that the exclusionary rule was a personal constitutional right. Instead, the six-member majority declared that the exclusionary rule was merely a preventive measure designed to deter future police misconduct. The justices then adopted a "cost-benefit approach," concluding that the rule was only to be applied in those settings where the exclusion of evidence would result in the significant deterrence of future police misconduct. In all other settings, the social costs of excluding relevant evidence far outweighed any potential benefits from its application.

## United States v. Drayton (2002)

This six-to-three decision of the U.S. Supreme Court reaffirmed the holding in *Florida v. Bostick* (1991) that police coercion of an individual does not occur so long as a "reasonable person" would feel free to terminate the encounter. To determine how a reasonable person would feel, the justices used the "totality of the circumstances" test. This test was qualified, however, by the majority's presumption that a reasonable person was an "innocent" person.

## United States v. Flores-Montano (2004)

This unanimous decision of the U.S. Supreme Court reaffirmed federal authority to conduct suspicionless inspections of automobiles at the border. Here the justices ruled that this power included the authority to remove, disassemble, and reassemble the fuel tank of a privately owned automobile.

## United States v. Knights (2001)

This unanimous decision of the U.S. Supreme Court held that the consent exception to the warrant requirement applied to conditions of a convicted defendant's probation. Here, one of the conditions of the convicted defendant's probation was his consent to a police search without probable cause. In upholding the probation condition, the justices noted that probationers had a lesser liberty interest than the law-abiding citizen and that a court could impose reasonable conditions that deprive the probationer of some freedoms.

## United States v. Leon (1984)

In this decision, the U.S. Supreme Court modified the exclusionary rule so as not to bar the admission of evidence seized in reasonable, good-faith reliance on a search warrant that was subsequently held to be defective. (Here, a magistrate had issued a warrant that was later found to be unsupported by probable cause.) The justices rejected the argument that the Fourth Amendment required the exclusion of illegally obtained evidence: The exclusionary rule was not an individual right, the six-person majority said, but a "remedial device" justified *only* by its deterrent effect on law enforcement officials. Thus, courts should decide whether to apply the rule on a case-by-case basis, balancing the costs of excluding the evidence against the probable deterrent effect of that exclusion on police misconduct. The benefits of exclusion in circumstances in which police possess an objectively reasonable belief that the warrant is valid and the search is constitutional are nonexistent. Here, the exclusion of evidence could not possibly deter police misconduct, for there had been no police misconduct. The error belonged to the magistrate; as such, the evidence, though seized without probable cause, was admissible. *Leon* confirmed that the exclusionary rule was outside of the realm of guaranteed Fourth Amendment rights. Instead, the exclusionary rule was an evidentiary rule, to be used or not used dependent upon the social costs of excluding the relevant evidence.

### United States v. Robinson (1973)

Citing an arresting officer's need to protect himself by disarming a suspect, this six-to-three decision of the U.S. Supreme Court confirmed that once a police officer had lawfully placed a suspect under arrest, the officer could conduct a "full" search of the arrestee.

### United States v. Sokolow (1990)

In this seven-to-two decision, the U.S. Supreme Court held that agents of the Drug Enforcement Administration had reasonable suspicion to detain an airline passenger matching six characteristics common to drug couriers. At the time of the detention, the agents knew that the passenger paid $2,100 for two round-trip airplane tickets from a roll of $20 bills; traveled under an alias; had an original destination of Miami, a major source city for illicit drugs; stayed in Miami for only forty-eight hours, even though his round-trip flight from Honolulu to Miami took approximately twenty hours; appeared nervous during his trip; and checked none of his luggage. Even though any one of the factors considered alone was insufficient proof of illegal conduct and was consistent with innocent travel, all of the factors, considered collectively, amounted to reasonable suspicion, the justices concluded. This case underscores the holding in *Terry v. Ohio:* Despite the textual commands of the Fourth Amendment, law enforcement officers do not need probable cause to stop and frisk suspicious individuals. Taking a cue from *Sokolow,* numerous lower courts have held that law enforcement officers acted reasonably when detaining persons on the basis of several apparently innocent activities. See the subsequent application of this "totality of the circumstances" approach in *United States v. Arvizu* (2002).

## USA PATRIOT Act (2001)

This federal law, passed following the terrorist attacks of September 11, 2001, broadened the power of the federal government to conduct surveillance, and may ultimately represent the most far-reaching challenge to Fourth Amendment values in American history. As of this writing, none of the surveillance provisions of the USA PATRIOT Act have reached the U.S. Supreme Court for review.

### *Vernonia School District v. Acton* (1995)

This case was the first challenge to mandatory drug-testing for student athletes to reach the high Court. Dividing six to three, the justices found that the drug-testing scheme fit squarely within the "special needs" analysis. Accordingly, neither warrant nor individualized suspicion was required as long as the search was a reasonable one. To determine reasonableness, the majority considered the individual privacy interests of the students, ruling that public school students, because they were in the temporary custody of the state as "schoolmaster," had a lesser expectation of privacy than did adults. Additionally, privacy expectations were lower than for students who did not participate in athletics than for student athletes. The justices then considered the government's interest in the drug testing, concluding that the nature of the concern was "important—indeed perhaps compelling." Having balanced the intrusion on the individual's Fourth Amendment privacy interests against the promotion of a legitimate governmental interest, the Court held the policy to be reasonable and, therefore, constitutional. This case marked the first time the Court had sustained a random, suspicionless drug-testing program outside of the public employment context.

## *Warden v. Harden* (1967)

This eight-to-one decision by the U.S. Supreme Court recognized the "hot pursuit" exception to the warrant requirement.

## Warrant Clause

The second part of the Fourth Amendment, which announces three prerequisites for obtaining a warrant, is the Warrant Clause. First, the warrant must be based upon probable cause. Second, it must be signed by a neutral and detached judge or magistrate. Third, the warrant must state with specificity the place to be searched and the persons or items to be seized.

## Warrantless Arrests

While police occasionally obtain arrest warrants, most arrests are conducted in the absence of such warrants. If a police officer has firsthand knowledge—say, for example, the offense occurs in the presence of an officer—the officer may make a warrantless arrest. Additionally, if a police officer has probable cause to believe that a felony has been committed, the officer may make a warrantless arrest. The Fourth Amendment does not require that a judge or magistrate review the factual justification for an arrest *prior* to the arrest. This would undoubtedly constitute a sufficient handicap for legitimate law enforcement. An officer's on-the-scene determination of probable cause provides the legal justification both for the arrest and the subsequent brief detention necessary to take the administrative steps incident to the arrest. The officer's on-the-scene determination, however, is subject to judicial review *ex post*. As soon as is practicable after the arrest, the officer must secure a judicial determination of whether probable cause in fact existed at the time of the arrest. In certain circumstances, a warrantless arrest, even if based on probable cause, is unconstitutional. See, for example, *Payton v. New York* (1980).

## Warren Court

Earl Warren (1891–1974) was chief justice of the United States from 1953 until 1969. During the 1960s, the Supreme Court, under the leadership of Warren, significantly expanded the procedural rights of criminal defendants. This expansion, especially in the areas of search and seizure and police interrogation, became a source of tremendous conservative dissatisfaction with the Warren Court. In 1968, two presidential candidates, Republican Richard Nixon and Democrat George Wallace, in effect ran "against the Court" and aimed pointed criticism at its criminal procedure decisions. Nixon particularly vowed to reverse the trend of the Warren Court in this area through judicial appointments; when elected, he promptly proceeded to make good on this promise. Landmark Fourth Amendment cases decided by the Warren Court include *Mapp v. Ohio* (1961), *Katz v. United States* (1967), *Terry v. Ohio* (1968), and *Chimel v. California* (1969).

## Weeks v. United States (1914)

In this unanimous decision, the U.S. Supreme Court formally adopted the exclusionary rule, holding that evidence obtained by police in violation of the Fourth Amendment could not be used against a criminal defendant in a federal trial. Because the police had no authority to seize the evidence, the prosecution had no right to introduce the evidence at trial. If such evidence could be introduced against a citizen accused of a crime, the protection of the Fourth Amendment was "of no value, and [the amendment] might as well be stricken from the Constitution." The exact scope and significance of *Weeks* have been subjects of much discussion and controversy. This is in large part because the opinion in *Weeks,* though unanimous, was ambiguous about whether the exclusionary rule was a constitutional requirement or simply a judicially created remedy to deter constitutional violations. On the one hand, the Court observed that to allow the use of illegally seized evidence would be to affirm "a manifest neglect if not an open defiance . . . of the Constitution." On the other hand, the opinion suggested that the exclusion of illegally seized evidence was necessary to deter further police misconduct. Either way, the *Weeks* decision clearly marked the start of a suppression of evidence doctrine that had not previously existed in the common law. Equally important, *Weeks* explicitly stated that the exclusionary rule did not apply to searches conducted by state police officers. As a result, states were not required to exclude evidence obtained by an unreasonable search and seizure. See, also, *Wolf v. Colorado* (1949), *Mapp v. Ohio* (1961), and *United States v. Leon* (1984).

## Welsh v. Wisconsin (1984)

This six-to-three decision of the U.S. Supreme Court held that an important factor to be considered when determining whether any exigency existed is the gravity of the underlying offense for which the arrest is made. *Welsh* indicates that exigent circumstances for a warrantless arrest can be dependent on the state's asserted level of interest in making an arrest. Where the gravity of the underlying offense is high—indicating the state's high interest in making an arrest—it may be easier to satisfy the exigent circumstances requirements. Where the gravity of the underlying offense is low—indicating the state's low interest in making an arrest—it may be more difficult to convince a court that the circumstances are legitimately exigent.

## Wilkes v. Wood (1763)

In this decision, an English court ruled that a house search conducted pursuant to a general warrant violated English common law. Along with *Entick v. Carrington* (1765), this decision was publicized both in England and the American colonies. Among the most enthusiastic supporters of this decision were a number of American revolutionary leaders, many of whom had firsthand knowledge of the abuses that frequently accompanied these general warrants.

## Wilson v. Arkansas (1995)

In this unanimous decision, the U.S. Supreme Court held that the Fourth Amendment did not require police officers in all circumstances to knock and announce their presence prior to entering the residence to execute a warrant. In some situations, police officers could enter a home to execute a warrant unannounced. Declining to fashion a "bright-line" remedy, the justices left it up to the lower courts to determine the circumstances under which an unannounced entry was reasonable under the Fourth Amendment. See "'Knock and Announce' Requirement."

## *Wolf v. Colorado* (1949)

In this case, the U.S. Supreme Court faced the question of whether the Fourth Amendment, and by extension the exclusionary rule, should be applied to the states. While making the "core of the Fourth Amendment" applicable to the states, the majority, speaking through Justice Frankfurter, specifically rejected the notion that the exclusionary rule should be binding upon the states. In a five-to-four decision, the justices noted that the rule was a "judicial implication" without foundation in the Fourth Amendment. Accordingly, states remained free to adopt or ignore the exclusionary rule in state criminal proceedings. The *Wolf* decision is significant because it indicated that deterring police misconduct was the primary, perhaps only, purpose of the exclusionary rule. It also foreshadowed the more modern view of the subject taken by the Rehnquist Court, that the exclusionary rule is nothing more than a judicially created rule of evidence. Contrast with *Mapp v. Ohio* (1961).

## Writs of Assistance

Similar to general warrants, writs of assistance authorized customs officers in the colonies to search any house or business at their whim to uncover imports smuggled illegally into the country. Since these writs were even more arbitrary and subject to abuse than general warrants, they were particularly offensive to the colonists.

## Wyoming v. Houghton (1999)

This six-to-three decision of the U.S. Supreme Court held that if police have probable cause for a warrantless search of a vehicle, they can search *all* of the personal belongings that are capable of concealing contraband of *all* passengers in the car.

## Ybarra v. Illinois (1979)

This six-to-three decision of the U.S. Supreme Court disallowed a warrantless search of patrons in a bar, which was itself subject to a search warrant, because the patron's propinquity to the bar was not related to the search warrant. As such, the search was not particularized to the patrons. By contrast, consider *Maryland v. Pringle* (2003).

# 6

## DOCUMENTS

This chapter presents twenty primary documents. Because virtually the only law relating to search and seizure has been the law created by the courts, eleven of these documents are excerpts from cases decided by the U.S. Supreme Court. Preceding the cases is a 1749 general customs warrant from the British government; a 1761 writ of assistance from the British government; and an abridged reprint of James Otis's 1761 speech arguing against the colonial writs of assistance. Following the cases are copies of present day warrants and warrant-related materials. From Pennsylvania, an "APPLICATION FOR SEARCH WARRANT AND AUTHORIZATION," an "AFFIDAVIT OF PROBABLE CAUSE," a "RECEIPT/INVENTORY OF SEIZED PROPERTY," and a "RETURN OF SERVICE AND INVENTORY"; from the federal government, an "APPLICATION AND AFFIDAVIT FOR SEARCH WARRANT" and an "APPLICATION AND AFFIDAVIT FOR SEIZURE WARRANT."

As a general rule, searches and seizures conducted outside the judicial process—that is, without prior approval by a judge or magistrate—are per se unreasonable under the Fourth Amendment. Nevertheless, the Supreme Court has articulated some exceptions. Four of the cases presented here concern these exceptions. *Terry v. Ohio* (1968) deals with the investigatory practice commonly referred to as a "stop and frisk," in which a police officer stops a suspicious person for purposes of interrogation, often accompanied by a "pat-down" search of the individual's clothing to make certain that the individual is not armed. *City of Indianapolis v. Edmond* (2000) and *Illinois v. Caballas* (2005) involve questions about the types of searches police officers may not and may conduct during a lawful traffic stop. And *Board of Education of Pottawatomie County v. Earls* (2002) affirms the authority of public school officials to conduct suspicionless drug testing of public school students.

Technological developments over the last century have heightened threats to individual privacy and Fourth Amendment values. These developments set the stage for the Supreme Court to consider whether the Fourth Amendment protects individuals from electronic surveillance by government officials. Four of the cases excerpted in this chapter deal with electronic surveillance. *Olmstead v. United States* (1928) established the trespass doctrine, which holds that for a search to occur, government officials had to trespass on private property. Also important, *Olmstead* held that conversations were not tangible items that could be "seized." *Katz v. United States* (1967) overruled *Olmstead;* since *Katz,* the Court has consistently held that the Fourth Amendment extends to any place or any thing in which an individual has an expectation of privacy. Of particular interest in a post–September 11, 2001, world is the Court's decision in *United States v. United States District Court for the Eastern District of Michigan* (1972), in which the justices suggested that there was a distinct justification for treating electronic surveillance for national security purposes differently from electronic surveillance for basic criminal purposes. And, *Kyllo v. United States* (2001) demonstrates well the inherent difficulty in applying the Fourth Amendment, written more than two centuries ago, to a modern world in which surveillance technology is ubiquitous.

Finally, three cases involve the exclusionary rule. In *Weeks v. United States* (1914), the Supreme Court adopted the exclusionary rule. In *Mapp v. Ohio* (1961), the justices "constitutionalized" the rule, applying it to the states in the process. And in *United States v. Leon* (1984), the Court created one of the more controversial exceptions to the rule—the "good faith" exception.

The excerpts are divided into three sections: exceptions to the warrant requirement; electronic surveillance; and the exclusionary rule. Within each section, the excerpts appear, for the most part, chronologically. This will allow the reader to trace the evolution and, in some cases, devolution of certain liberties under the Fourth Amendment. Where two or more cases within a specific section deal with a particular issue, as with the automobile cases, all of the cases raising similar issues will be presented together. Each case is preceded by a "headnote," a brief statement of the circumstances that brought about the case, identifying the parties and the holding of the lower courts, stating concisely the holding of the U.S. Supreme Court, and explaining the significance of the case. To appreciate better the various sides of the argument, selected separate opinions, both concurring and dissenting, are excerpted.

## ORIGINS

### General Customs Warrant (1749)

*Customs search warrant from* Conductor Generalis
   *Warrant to search for goods (for which Customs ought to be paid) which are privately conveyed away and concealed.*
   *To the Constables of the Parish of* Stepney, *in the County of* Middlesex
   *Midd.* ss. WHEREAS *Andrew Bull,* of *Woodbridge,* in the said County, Gent. hath this Day made Oath before me, that on *Monday* last past, about the Hour of Ten at night, *John Badblood* of *Stepney* aforesaid, landed at the *New Dock,* from the Ship *Union,* lately arrived from *Coracoa,* two Casks of Liquor, about the Size of Quarter Barrels, and conveyed them to his House "Shoate" in *Stephney* aforesaid; and the

said *Andrew Bull,* having searched the Custom-House Books, and finding no Entry made of the said Barrels of Liquor, or any agreement made with the Collectors for the Customs thereof; and the said *John Badblood* being no way concerned by Profession, or otherwise, in foreign Liquors, and the said *Andrew Bull,* having produced a Witness to prove that he drank Brandy and Red Wine, on *Wednesday* last, at the House of the said *John Badblood,* who hath proved the same accordingly; all which being considered, there is good Reason to suspect that the said *John Badblood* hath concealed Liquors, for which Duties are payable to the Crown, with intent to defraud his Majesty, and contrary to the Statutes in that Case made: These are therefore in his Majesty's Name, to require and authorize you to assist the said *Andrew Bull* in the entering of the said House, and to enter with him into the House of the said *John Badblood,* and search for the said Barrels of Liquor, or any other foreign Liquors, for which Customs ought to be paid, which may be concealed there; and in Case you meet with any Resistance, that you do enter the said House by Force; and if you find any such Liquors, that you do seize the same as forfeited, &c. Given under my hand and Seal, *etc.*

Reproduced in *Conductor Generalis: or the Office, Duty and Authority of Justices of the Peace, etc.:* New York, 1749. Copied from M. H. Smith, *The Writs of Assistance Case.* Berkeley: University of California Press, 1978: 529–530.

## Writ of Assistance (1761)

*Writ of assistance (English) of George III, 1761*
  *George the Third* by the Grace of God of Great Britain France & Ireland King Defender of the Faith and so forth To all & every the Officers and Ministers who now are or hereafter shall have any Office Power or Authority from or under the Jurisdiction of the Lord High Admiral of our Admiralty of England to all & every our Vice Admirals Justices of the Peace Mayors Sheriffs Constables Bailiffs Headboroughs And all other Our Officers Ministers & Subjects within every City Borough Town and County of England the Dominion of Wales & Town of Berwick upon Tweed And to every of you *Greeting Know Ye That Whereas We* by our Letters patent under our Great Seal of Great Britain bearing date the Eighteenth Day of August in the Sixth Year of our Reign *Have* Constituted Appointed & Assigned our Trusty and Well

beloved Saml. Mead, Edwd. Hooper, Henry Pelham, Jno. Frederick, Henry Bankes Esqrs., Sir Wm. Musgrave Baront., Joseph Pennington, Corbyn Morris & Jas. Jeffreys Esqrs. Commissrs. For Managing & causing to be collected & Levied our Customs Subsidies & other Duties in the sd. Ltrs Paten mentd. during our Pleasure And by our Commissn. afsd. *We* have Given & Granted to our sd. Commissrs. or any four or more of them full power & Authority to Manage or Cause to be Levied & Collected all & every the Customs Subsidies Duties of Tonnage & Poundage and all other Sums Growing & Becoming due & payable to us for or by Reason of any Goods Wares & Town of Berwick upon Tweed or Exported out of England the Dominion of Wales of Town of Berwick upon Tweed by way of Merchandize according to the Tenor & Effect of a certain Act of Reputed Act of Parliament made at Westminster the Twentyfifth Day of April in the Twelfth Year of the Reign of the late King Charles the Second Ratified & Confirmed in & by anor. Act of Parliamt. made at Westmr. the Eighth Day of May in the Thirteenth Year of the Reign of the sd. late King Charles the Second & according to the sevl. partlar. Rates & Values of the sd. Goods Wares marchandizes mentd. & Engrossed in a certain Book of Rates and certain Rules Orders Directions & Allowances to the sd. Book of Rates annexed And in & by the sd. Acts or one of them Enacted Approved Ratified and Confirmed and according to the Tenor & Effect of anor. Act of Parliament made in the first Year of the late King James the Second Intitd. an Act fro the Settling the Revenue on his Maty. for his Life wch. was settled on his late Maty. for his Life *And Also* full power and Authority to Manage & Cause to be Levied & Collected all &every the Customs Rates Subsidies Duties Paymts. & Sums of Money Arising & Growing due & Payable to us according to the Tenor & Effect of sevl. Acts of Parliamt. in the sd. Letters Paten mented. As also full Pow'r & Authority to Manage & Cause to be Collected & Levied all other the Customs Rates Duties & Paymts. wch are or shall be in any wise due or payable to us for or upon the Importation or Exportation of the same Goods Wares or Town of Berwick upon Tweed *And Further* by our sd. Letters Paten We have Given & Granted to our sd. Comissrs. or any four or more of them during our Pleasure afsd. full Pow'r & Authority to Cause to be put into Execution all & every the Clauses in the same or in any other Act or Acts of Parliamt. contained touching or Concerning the Collecting Levying Receiving or Securing of the Dutys therein mentd. or any of them or any part or parts

thereof And to do all othr. Mrs. Or Things wtsoever or wch by any the
Commissrs. for the time being Intrusted wth. the Rect. & Management
of our Customs can or may be Lawfully done *And Further* by our
Commissn. afsd. We have given full pow'r & Authority to our sd. Commissrs. or any four or moure of them from time to time to Constitute &
Appoint by any Writing undr. the Hands & Seals of them or any four or
more of them such Inferiour Officers in all & every the Ports of England
the Dominion of Wales or Town of Berwick upon Tweed as by Nomination Warrt. & Direccon from the Commissrs. of the Treasy then or for
the time being or from the Lord Trear. for the time being as our said
Commissrs. shall Direct And them from time to time to Suspend Remove & displace as to our said Commissrs. or any four or more of them
shall seem necessary or Expedient for our Service in the Premises *And
Further* Tha all & every the Customs & Subsidies of Tonnage &
Poundage & all & Singular the Sums of Money & other the Premises
may be duly paid to us And we may be truly & faithfully Answered the
Same We have given & Granted to our sd. Commissrs. or any four or
more of them And to all & every the Collectors Dpty Collectors Ministers Servts. or other Officers serving & Attending in all & every the Ports
of England the Dominion of Wales or Town of Berwick upon Tweed full
pow'r & Authority from time to time at their & every of their Wills &
Pleasure as well by Night as by Day to Enter & go on Board any Ship
Boat or other Vessl. Ryding Lying or Being within & Coming to any
Port Creek or Haven of England the Dominion of Wales or Town of
Berwick upon Tweed And Such Ship Boat & Vessl. then & there found
to Search & Look into And the Psons therein being strictly to Examine
touching or concerng. the Premes. afsd. As also in the day Time to Enter
into the Vaults Cellars Warehouses Shops & other places where any
Goods Wares or Merchandizes Lye Concealed or are Suspected to be
Concealed for wch the Customs & Subsidies & other the Duties & Sums
of Money afsd. are not or shall not be duly & truly Answd. Satisfied &
Paid to the Collectors Dpty Collectors Ministers Servts. & other Officers afsd. respively or otherwise agreed for according to the true Intent
of the Law And the same Vaults Cellars Warehouses Shops & other
Places afsd. to Search & Look into And all & every the Trunks Chests
Boxes & Packs then & there found to break open And to do all other
Mrs. wch shall be found necessary for our Services in such Cases agree-

able to the Laws & Statutes of England as in the sd. Commissn. among othr. Things is more fully Contained *Therefore We strictly Injoin and Command* You and every one of You That all Excuses apart You & every one of You permit the sd. Saml. Mead, Edwd. Hooper, Henry Pelham, Jno. Frederick, Henry Bankes Esqrs, Sir Wm. Musgrve Baront., Josph. Pennington, Corbyn Morris & Jas. Jeffreys Esqrs. and the Deptys Ministers Servts. & other Officers of the sd. Commissrs. & every one of them from time to time as they think proper as well by Night as by Day to Enter & go on Board any Ship Boat or Vessl. Ryding Lying or being within & coming to any Port Creek or haven of England the Dominion of Wales & Town of Berwick upon Tweed & such Ship Boat & Vessl. then & there found to Search & and the Psons. Therein being strictly to Examine touching & concerning the Premes. afsd. according to the Tenor & Effect & true Intent of our Commissn. & the Laws & Statutes of England in the Behalf made & provided And in the day time to Enter & Go into the Vaults Cellars Warehouses Shops & other Places where any Goods Wares or Merchandizes lye Concealed, or are Suspected to be Concealed for which the Customs & Subsidies of Tonnage & Poundage & other the Sums of Money are not or shall not be duly & truly Answd. Satisfied & paid to our Collectors Dpty Collectors Ministrs. Servts. & other Officrs. respively or otherwise Agreed for accordg. to the true Intent of the Law to Inspect & Oversee & Search for the sd. Goods Wares or Merchandizes *And further* to do & Execute all Things wch of Right accordg. to the Laws & Statutes of England *And We further strictly Injoyn and Command* You and every one of You That to the sd. Saml. Mead, Edwd. Hooper, Henry Pelham, Jno. Frederick Henry Bankes Esqrs. Sir Wm. Musgrave Baront. Josph. Pennignton Corbyn Morris & Jas. Jeffreys Esqrs. Our Commissrs. & their Dptys Ministers Servts. And other Officers & every one of them You & every one of You from Time to Time be Aiding Assisting & Helping in the Execution of the Premes. as is Meet And this You or any of You in no wise Omit at Your perils. *Witness* Sir Thos. Parker Knt. At Westmr. the Fourteenth Day of April in the First Year of Our Reign by the Remembrance Rolls & so forth And the Barons.

Copied from M. H. Smith, *The Writs of Assistance Case.* Berkeley: University of California Press, 1978: 524–528.

## James Otis's Speech Against
## Writs of Assistance

February 24, 1761

*This famous case involved the constitutionality of writs of assis-*
*tance (general warrants giving agents of the Crown in the Ameri-*
*can colonies the authority to search for smuggled goods without*
*any limitations). A group of Boston merchants, opposed to the*
*granting of these writs, engaged Oxenbridge Thatcher and James*
*Otis to argue against their issuance. No formal record of Otis's ar-*
*gument, delivered before the Superior Court in Boston on Febru-*
*ary 24, 1761, exists. John Adams, however, was present at the ar-*
*gument and took extensive notes of the five-hour speech. Those*
*notes were later expanded into a version of the argument by G. R.*
*Minot in his* History of Massachusetts, 1748–1765. *The expanded*
*version, abridged, is reprinted below. Both the notes and expanded*
*version are reproduced in Henry Steele Commager's* Documents
of American History *(1958, 45–47). Although Otis lost the case,*
*Adams later spoke of the significance of the speech*

> *Otis was a flame of fire! . . . American independence was then and*
> *there born; the seeds of patriots and heroes were then and there*
> *sown, to defend the vigorous youth. . . . Every man of a crowded*
> *audience appeared to me to go away, as I did, ready to take arms*
> *against writs of assistance. Then and there was the first scene of the*
> *first act of opposition to the arbitrary claims of Great Britain. Then*
> *and there the child Independence was born. (Nelson B. Lasson*
> *1937, 59)*

May it please your Honors: I was desired by one of the court to look
into the [law] books, and consider the question now before them concerning Writs of Assistance. I have accordingly considered it, and now
appear not only in obedience to your order, but likewise in behalf of the
inhabitants of this town, who have presented another petition, and out
of regard to the liberties of the subject. And I take this opportunity to

declare that whether under a fee or not (for in such a cause as this I despise a fee) I will to my dying day oppose, with all the powers and faculties God has given me, all such instruments of slavery on the one hand and villainly on the other, as this Writ of Assistance is.

It appears to me the worst instrument of arbitrary power, the most destructive of English liberty and the fundamental principles of law that ever was found in an English lawbook. I must therefore beg your Honors' patience and attention to the whole range of an argument that may perhaps appear uncommon in many things, as well as to points of learning that are more remote and unusual, that the whole tendency of my design may the more easily be perceived, the conclusions better descend, and the force of them be better felt. I shall not think much of my pains in this cause, as I engaged in it from principle. I was solicited to argue this case as Advocate-General; and, because I would not, I have been charged with desertion from my office. To this charge I can give a very sufficient answer. I renounced that office and I argue this cause from the same principle; and I argue it with the greatest pleasure, as it is in favour of British liberty, at a time when we hear the greatest monarch upon earth declaring from his throne that he glories in the name of Briton and that the privileges of his people are dearer to him than the most valuable prerogatives of his crown; and as it is in opposition to a kind of power, the exercise of which in former periods of history cost one king of England his head and another his crown, I have taken more pains in this cause than I ever will take again, although my engaging in this and another popular cause has raised much resentment. But I think I can sincerely declare that I cheerfully submit myself to every odious name for conscience' sake; and from my soul I despise all those whose guilt, malice, or folly has made them my foes. Let the consequences be what they will, I am determined to proceed. The only principles of public conduct that are worthy of a gentleman or a man are to sacrifice estate, ease, health, and applause, and even life, to the sacred calls of his country. These manly sentiments, in private life, make good citizens; in public life, the patriot and the hero. I do not say that, when brought to the test, I shall be invincible. I pray God I may never be brought to the melancholy trial; but if ever I should, it will then be known how far I can reduce to practice principles which I know to be founded in truth. In the meantime, I will proceed to the subject of this writ.

In the first place, may it please your Honors, I will admit that writs of one kind may be legal; that is, special writs, directed to special officers, and to search certain houses, etc., specially set forth in the writ, may be granted by the Court of Exchequer at home, upon oath made before the Lord Treasurer by the person who asks it, that he suspects such goods to be concealed in those very places he desires to search. The Act of 14 Charles II., which Mr. Gridley mentions, proves this. And in this light the writ appears like a warrant from a Justice of the Peace to search for stolen goods. Your Honors will find in the old books concerning the office of a Justice of the Peace, precedents of general warrants to search suspected houses. But in more modern books you will find only special warrants to search such and such houses, specially named, in which the complainant has before sworn that he suspects his goods are concealed; and will find it adjudged that special warrants only are legal. In the same manner I rely on it, that the writ prayed for in this petition is illegal. It is a power that places the liberty of every man in the hands of every petty officer. I say, I admit that special Writs of Assistance, to search special places, may be granted to certain persons on oath; but I deny that the writ now prayed for can be granted, for I beg leave to make some observations on the writ itself, before I proceed to other Acts of Parliament. In the first place, the writ is universal, being directed "to all and singular justices, sheriffs, constables, and all other officers and subjects"; so that, in short, it is directed to every subject in the King's domains. Every one with this writ may be a tyrant; if this commission be legal, a tyrant in a legal manner, also, may control, imprison, or murder any one within the realm. In the next place, it is perpetual; there is no return. A man is accountable to no person for his doings. Every man may reign secure in his petty tyranny, and spread terror and desolation around him [until the trump of the Archangel shall excite different emotions in his soul]. In the third place, a person with this writ, in the daytime, may enter all houses, shops, etc., at will, and command all to assist him. Fourthly, by this writ not only deputies, etc., but even their menial servants, are allowed to lord it over us. [What is this but to have the curse of Canaan with a witness on us: to be the servants of servants, the most despicable of God's creation?] Now one of the most essential branches of English liberty is the freedom of one's house. A man's house is his castle; and whilst he is quiet, he is as well guarded as a prince in his castle. This writ, if it should be declared legal, would totally annihilate this privilege. Custom-house officers may enter our houses when they please; we are commanded to permit their entry. Their menial servants may enter, may break locks, bars, and everything in their way; and whether they break through malice or revenge, no man, no court can inquire. Bare suspicion without oath is sufficient. This wanton exercise of this power is not a chimerical suggestion of a heated brain. I will mention some facts. Mr. Pew had one of these writs, and when Mr. Ware succeeded him, he endorsed this writ over to Mr. Ware, so that these writs are negotiable from one officer to another; and so your Honors have no opportunity of judging the persons to whom this vast power is delegated. Another instance is this: Mr. Justice Walley had called this same Mr. Ware before him, by a constable, for a breach of the Sabbath-day Acts, or that of profane swearing. As soon as he had finished, Mr. Ware asked him if he had done. He replied, "Yes." "Well, then," said Mr. Ware, "I will show you a little of my power. I command you to permit me to search your house for uncustomed goods," and went on to search the house from garret to cellar; and then served the constable in the same manner! But to show another absurdity in this writ, if it should be established, I insist upon it every person, by the 14 Charles II., has this power as well as the Custom-house officers. The words are, "it shall be lawful for any person or persons authorized, etc." What a scene does this open! Every man prompted by revenge, ill-humor or wantonness to inspect the inside of his neighbour's house, may get a Writ of Assistance. Others will ask it from self defence; one arbitrary exertion will provoke another, until society be involved in tumult and in blood!

Again, these writs are not returned. Writs, in their nature, are temporary things. When the purposes for which they are issued are answered, they exist no more; but these live forever; no one can be called to account. Thus reason and the constitution are both against this writ. Let us see what authority there is for it. Not more than one instance can be found of it in all our law-books; and that was in the zenith of arbitrary power, namely, in the reign of Charles II., when star-chamber powers were pushed to extremity by some ignorant clerk of the exchequer. But had this writ been in any book whatever, it would have been illegal. All precedents are under the control of the principles of law. Lord Talbot [the Earl of Shrewsbury, an English peer of the era of William and Mary] says it is better to observe these than any precedents, though in the House of Lords the last resort of the subject. No Acts of Parliament can establish such a writ; though it should be made in the very words of the petition, it would be void. An act against the constitution is void. But this proves no more than what I before observed, that special writs may be granted on oath and probable suspicion. The act of 7 and 8 William III. that the officers of the plantations shall have the same powers, etc., is confined to this sense; that an officer should show probable ground; should take his oath of it; should do this before a magistrate; and that such magistrate, if he think proper, should issue a special warrant to a constable to search the places. That of 6 Anne can prove no more.

## EXCEPTIONS TO THE WARRANT REQUIREMENT

### *Terry v. Ohio*

392 U.S. 1 (1968)

*The Supreme Court first addressed the legality of warrantless investigatory detentions in this case. John W. Terry was convicted of carrying a concealed weapon. The evidence used to convict Terry was seized by a detective, who, after observing the unusual behavior of Terry and two other men, suspected that they were contemplating a robbery. The detective stopped the individuals, identified himself as a police officer, and conducted a pat-down search of their outer clothing, thereby discovering the concealed weapon. The trial court rejected Terry's motion to suppress the seized evidence, drawing a distinction between a "frisk" of the outer clothing for weapons and a full-fledged search for evidence of a crime. Terry's conviction was affirmed by the state appellate courts. A brief excerpt from Justice Harlan's concurring opinion is included because it has become perhaps the most memorable statement from this case. The lone dissenter, Justice Douglas, angrily dismissed the majority's reliance on "reasonableness," as opposed to probable cause, as the touchstone of constitutionality.*

Argued December 12, 1967; Decided June 10, 1968.

MR. CHIEF JUSTICE WARREN delivered the opinion of the Court. This case presents serious questions concerning the role of the

Fourth Amendment in the confrontation on the street between the citizen and the policeman investigating suspicious circumstances. Our first task is to establish at what point in this encounter the Fourth Amendment becomes relevant. That is, we must decide whether and when Officer McFadden "seized" Terry and whether and when he conducted a "search." There is some suggestion in the use of such terms as "stop" and "frisk" that such police conduct is outside the purview of the Fourth Amendment because neither action rises to the level of a "search" or "seizure" within the meaning of the Constitution. We emphatically reject this notion. It is quite plain that the Fourth Amendment governs "seizures" of the person which do not eventuate in a trip to the station house and prosecution for crime—"arrests" in traditional terminology. It must be recognized that whenever a police officer accosts an individual and restrains his freedom to walk away, he has "seized" that person. And it is nothing less than sheer torture of the English language to suggest that a careful exploration of the outer surfaces of a person's clothing all over his or her body in an attempt to find weapons is not a "search." Moreover, it is simply fantastic to urge that such a procedure performed in public by a policeman while the citizen stands helpless, perhaps facing a wall with his hands raised, is a "petty indignity." It is a serious intrusion upon the sanctity of the person, which may inflict great indignity and arouse strong resentment, and it is not to be undertaken lightly. The danger in the logic which proceeds upon distinctions between a "stop" and an "arrest," or "seizure" of the person, and between a "frisk" and a "search" is twofold. It seeks to isolate from constitutional scrutiny the initial stages of the contact between the policeman and the citizen. And by suggesting a rigid all-or-nothing model of justification and regulation under the Amendment, it obscures the utility of limitations upon the scope, as well as the initiation, of police action as a means of constitutional regulation. . . .

The distinctions of classical "stop-and-frisk" theory thus serve to divert attention from the central inquiry under the Fourth Amendment—the reasonableness in all the circumstances of the particular governmental invasion of a citizen's personal security. "Search" and "seizure" are not talismans. We therefore reject the notions that the Fourth Amendment does not come into play at all as a limitation upon police conduct if the officers stop short of something called a "technical arrest" or a "full-blown search."

In this case there can be no question, then, that Officer McFadden "seized" petitioner and subjected him to a "search" when he took hold of him and patted down the outer surfaces of his clothing. We must decide whether at that point it was reasonable for Officer McFadden to have interfered with petitioner's personal security as he did. And in determining whether the seizure and search were "unreasonable" our inquiry is a dual one—whether the officer's action was justified at its inception, and whether it was reasonably related in scope to the circumstances which justified the interference in the first place. . . .

The crux of this case . . . is not the propriety of Officer McFadden's taking steps to investigate petitioner's suspicious behavior, but rather, whether there was justification for McFadden's invasion of Terry's personal security by searching him for weapons in the course of that investigation. We are now concerned with more than the governmental interest in investigating crime; in addition, there is the more immediate interest of the police officer in taking steps to assure himself that the person with whom he is dealing is not armed with a weapon that could unexpectedly and fatally be used against him. Certainly it would be unreasonable to require that police officers take unnecessary risks in the performance of their duties. American criminals have a long tradition of armed violence, and every year in this country many law enforcement officers are killed in the line of duty, and thousands more are wounded. Virtually all of these deaths and a substantial portion of the injuries are inflicted with guns and knives.

In view of these facts, we cannot blind ourselves to the need for law enforcement officers to protect themselves and other prospective victims of violence in situations where they may lack probable cause for an arrest. When an officer is justified in believing that the individual whose suspicious behavior he is investigating at close range is armed and presently dangerous to the officer or to others, it would appear to be clearly unreasonable to deny the officer the power to take necessary measures to determine whether the person is in fact carrying a weapon and to neutralize the threat of physical harm. . . .

We conclude that the revolver seized from Terry was properly admitted in evidence against him. At the time he seized petitioner and searched him for weapons, Officer McFadden had reasonable grounds to believe that petitioner was armed and dangerous, and it was necessary for the protection of himself and others to take swift measures to discover the true facts and neutralize the threat of harm if it materialized. The policeman carefully restricted his search to what was appropriate to the discovery of the particular items which he sought. Each case of this sort will, of course, have to be decided on its own facts. We merely hold today that where a police officer observes unusual conduct which leads him reasonably to conclude in light of his experience that criminal activity may be afoot and that the persons with whom he is dealing may be armed and presently dangerous, where in the course of investigating this behavior he identifies himself as a policeman and makes reasonable inquiries, and where nothing in the initial stages of the encounter serves to dispel his reasonable fear for his own or others' safety, he is entitled for the protection of himself and others in the area to conduct a carefully limited search of the outer clothing of such persons in an attempt to discover weapons which might be used to assault him.

Such a search is a reasonable search under the Fourth Amendment, and any weapons seized may properly be introduced in evidence against the person from whom they were taken.

*Affirmed.*

MR. JUSTICE HARLAN, concurring.

Where such a stop is reasonable, . . . the right to frisk must be immediate and automatic if the reason for the stop is, as here, an articulable suspicion of a crime of violence. Just as a full search incident to a lawful arrest requires no additional justification, a limited frisk incident to a lawful stop must often be rapid and routine. There is no reason why an officer, rightfully but forcibly confronting a person suspected of a serious crime, should have to ask one question and take the risk that the answer might be a bullet.

MR. JUSTICE DOUGLAS, dissenting.

The opinion of the Court disclaims the existence of "probable cause." If loitering were in issue and that was the offense charged, there would be "probable cause" shown. But the crime here is carrying concealed weapons; and there is no basis for concluding that the officer had "probable cause" for believing that that crime was being committed. Had a warrant been sought, a magistrate would, therefore, have been unauthorized to issue one, for he can act only if there is a showing of "probable cause." We hold today that the police have greater authority to make a "seizure" and conduct a "search" than a judge has to authorize such action. We have said precisely the opposite over and over again. . . .

The infringement on personal liberty of any "seizure" of a person can only be "reasonable" under the Fourth Amendment if we require the police to possess "probable cause" before they seize him. Only that line draws a meaningful distinction between an officer's mere inkling and the presence of facts within the officer's personal knowledge which would convince a reasonable man that the person seized has committed, is committing, or is about to commit a particular crime. . . .

To give the police greater power than a magistrate is to take a long step down the totalitarian path. Perhaps such a step is desirable to cope with modern forms of lawlessness. But if it is taken, it should be the deliberate choice of the people through a constitutional amendment. . . .

## City of Indianapolis v. Edmond

531 U.S. 32 (2000)

*In 1998, the city of Indianapolis established a checkpoint program under which the police, acting without individualized suspicion, stopped a predetermined number of vehicles at roadblocks in various locations on city roads for the primary purpose of the discovery and interdiction of illegal narcotics. Under the program, at least one officer would (1) approach each vehicle, (2) advise the driver that he or she was being stopped briefly at a drug checkpoint, (3) ask the driver to produce a driver's license and the vehicle's registration, (4) look for signs of impairment, and (5) conduct an open-view examination of the vehicle from the outside. In addition, a narcotics-detection dog would walk around the outside of each stopped vehicle. Two motorists who had been stopped at such a checkpoint filed suit in federal district court asserting that the checkpoint program violated the Fourth Amendment. The district court concluded that the program did not violate the Fourth Amendment, but the U.S. Court of Appeals for the Seventh Circuit reversed on the grounds that there was neither probable cause nor articulable suspicion to stop any given driver. The Supreme Court affirmed the appellate court's de-*

*cision. (The reader may want to review the discussion of* Michigan Department of State Police v. Sitz *(1990) and the entry on* Sitz *in Chapter Five prior to reading this excerpt.)*

Argued October 3, 2000; Decided November 28, 2000.

JUSTICE O'CONNOR delivered the opinion of the Court. In *Michigan Department of State Police v. Sitz* (1990), . . . we held that brief, suspicionless seizures at highway checkpoints for the purposes of combating drunk driving and intercepting illegal immigrants were constitutional. We now consider the constitutionality of a highway checkpoint program whose primary purpose is the discovery and interdiction of illegal narcotics. . . .

The Fourth Amendment requires that searches and seizures be reasonable. A search or seizure is ordinarily unreasonable in the absence of individualized suspicion of wrongdoing. While such suspicion is not an "irreducible" component of reasonableness, we have recognized only limited circumstances in which the usual rule does not apply. For example, we have upheld certain regimes of suspicionless searches where the program was designed to serve "special needs, beyond the normal need for law enforcement." We have also allowed searches for certain administrative purposes without particularized suspicion of misconduct, provided that those searches are appropriately limited.

We have also upheld brief, suspicionless seizures of motorists at a fixed Border Patrol checkpoint designed to intercept illegal aliens, and at a sobriety checkpoint aimed at removing drunk drivers from the road. In addition, in *Delaware v. Prouse* (1979), we suggested that a similar type of roadblock with the purpose of verifying drivers' licenses and vehicle registrations would be permissible. In none of these cases, however, did we indicate approval of a checkpoint program whose primary purpose was to detect evidence of ordinary criminal wrongdoing. . . .

In *Sitz,* we evaluated the constitutionality of a Michigan highway sobriety checkpoint program. The *Sitz* checkpoint involved brief suspicionless stops of motorists so that police officers could detect signs of intoxication and remove impaired drivers from the road. Motorists who exhibited signs of intoxication were diverted for a license and registration check and, if warranted, further sobriety tests. This checkpoint program was clearly aimed at reducing the immediate hazard posed by the presence of drunk drivers on the highways, and there was an obvious connection

between the imperative of highway safety and the law enforcement practice at issue. The gravity of the drunk driving problem and the magnitude
of the State's interest in getting drunk drivers off the road weighed heavily
in our determination that the program was constitutional. In *Prouse*, we
invalidated a discretionary, suspicionless stop for a spot check of a motorist's driver's license and vehicle registration. The officer's conduct in
that case was unconstitutional primarily on account of his exercise of
"standardless and unconstrained discretion." We nonetheless acknowledged the States' "vital interest in ensuring that only those qualified to do
so are permitted to operate motor vehicles, that these vehicles are fit for
safe operation, and hence that licensing, registration, and vehicle inspection requirements are being observed." Accordingly, we suggested that
"questioning of all oncoming traffic at roadblock-type stops" would be a
lawful means of serving this interest in highway safety. . . .

Not only does the common thread of highway safety thus run
through *Sitz* and *Prouse*, but *Prouse* itself reveals a difference in the
Fourth Amendment significance of highway safety interests and the
general interest in crime control. . . .

We have never approved a checkpoint program whose primary purpose was to detect evidence of ordinary criminal wrongdoing. Rather,
our checkpoint cases have recognized only limited exceptions to the
general rule that a seizure must be accompanied by some measure of individualized suspicion. . . .

The primary purpose of the Indianapolis narcotics checkpoints is in
the end to advance "the general interest in crime control." We decline to
suspend the usual requirement of individualized suspicion where the police seek to employ a checkpoint primarily for the ordinary enterprise of
investigating crimes. We cannot sanction stops justified only by the generalized and ever-present possibility that interrogation and inspection
may reveal that any given motorist has committed some crime. Of
course, there are circumstances that may justify a law enforcement
checkpoint where the primary purpose would otherwise, but for some
emergency, relate to ordinary crime control. For example, as the Court
of Appeals noted, the Fourth Amendment would almost certainly permit an appropriately tailored roadblock set up to thwart an imminent
terrorist attack or to catch a dangerous criminal who is likely to flee by
way of a particular route. The exigencies created by these scenarios are

far removed from the circumstances under which authorities might simply stop cars as a matter of course to see if there just happens to be a felon leaving the jurisdiction. . . .

It goes without saying that our holding today does nothing to alter the constitutional status of the sobriety and border checkpoints that we approved in *Sitz* and *Martinez-Fuerte,* or of the type of traffic checkpoint that we suggested would be lawful in *Prouse.* The constitutionality of such checkpoint programs still depends on a balancing of the competing interests at stake and the effectiveness of the program. When law enforcement authorities pursue primarily general crime control purposes at checkpoints such as here, however, stops can only be justified by some quantum of individualized suspicion. . . .

Because the primary purpose of the Indianapolis checkpoint program is ultimately indistinguishable from the general interest in crime control, the checkpoints violate the Fourth Amendment. The judgment of the Court of Appeals is accordingly affirmed. *It is so ordered.*

CHIEF JUSTICE REHNQUIST, with whom JUSTICE THOMAS joins, and with whom JUSTICE SCALIA joins as to Part I, dissenting. Petitioners acknowledge that the "primary purpose" of these roadblocks is to interdict illegal drugs, but this fact should not be controlling. . . . The use of roadblocks to look for signs of impairment was validated by *Sitz,* and the use of roadblocks to check for driver's licenses and vehicle registrations was expressly recognized in . . . *Prouse.* . . .

Because of the valid reasons for conducting these roadblock seizures, it is constitutionally irrelevant that petitioners also hoped to interdict drugs. . . . [T]he roadblocks here are objectively reasonable because they serve the substantial interests of preventing drunken driving and checking for driver's licenses and vehicle registrations with minimal intrusion on motorists. . . .

The seizure is objectively reasonable as it lasts, on average, two to three minutes and does not involve a search. The subjective intrusion is likewise limited as the checkpoints are clearly marked and operated by uniformed officers who are directed to stop every vehicle in the same manner. The only difference between this case and *Sitz* is the presence of the dog. We have already held, however, that a "sniff test" by a trained narcotics dog is not a "search" within the meaning of the Fourth Amendment because it does not require physical intrusion of the object being sniffed and it does not expose anything other than the contraband items. And there is nothing in the record to indicate that the dog sniff lengthens the stop. Finally, the checkpoints' success rate—49 arrests for offenses unrelated to drugs—only confirms the State's legitimate interests in preventing drunken driving and ensuring the proper licensing of drivers and registration of their vehicles.

These stops effectively serve the State's legitimate interests; they are executed in a regularized and neutral manner; and they only minimally intrude upon the privacy of the motorists. They should therefore be constitutional.

## Illinois v. Caballes

125 S.Ct. 834 (2005)
*After an Illinois state trooper stopped Roy Caballes for speeding, a second trooper, overhearing the radio transmission of the stop, drove to the scene with his narcotics-detection dog and walked the dog around Caballes's vehicle while the first trooper wrote Caballes a warning ticket. When the dog alerted at the trunk of Caballes's vehicle, the officers searched the trunk, found marijuana, and arrested Caballes. The trial court determined that the dog's alerting provided sufficient probable cause to conduct the search. Caballes was convicted, but the Illinois Supreme Court reversed, finding that because there were no specific and articulable facts to suggest drug activity, use of the dog unjustifiably enlarged a routine traffic stop into a drug investigation. The U.S. Supreme Court reversed the Illinois Supreme Court, holding that a dog sniff conducted during a lawful traffic stop that revealed no information other than the location of a substance that no individual had any right to possess did not violate the Fourth Amendment. Two dissenting opinions are included.*

Argued November 10, 2004; Decided January 24, 2005.
JUSTICE STEVENS delivered the opinion of the Court. The question on which we granted certiorari is narrow: "Whether the Fourth

Amendment requires reasonable, articulable suspicion to justify using a drug-detection dog to sniff a vehicle during a legitimate traffic stop." Thus, we proceed on the assumption that the officer conducting the dog sniff had no information about respondent except that he had been stopped for speeding. . . .

Here, the initial seizure of respondent when he was stopped on the highway was based on probable cause, and was concededly lawful. It is nevertheless clear that a seizure that is lawful at its inception can violate the Fourth Amendment if its manner of execution unreasonably infringes interests protected by the Constitution. A seizure that is justified solely by the interest in issuing a warning ticket to the driver can become unlawful if it is prolonged beyond the time reasonably required to complete that mission. . . .

[W]e accept the state court's conclusion that the duration of the stop in this case was entirely justified by the traffic offense and the ordinary inquiries incident to such a stop. Despite this conclusion, the Illinois Supreme Court held that the initially lawful traffic stop became an unlawful seizure solely as a result of the canine sniff that occurred outside respondent's stopped car. That is, the court characterized the dog sniff as the cause rather than the consequence of a constitutional violation. In its view, the use of the dog converted the citizen-police encounter from a lawful traffic stop into a drug investigation, and because the shift in purpose was not supported by any reasonable suspicion that respondent possessed narcotics, it was unlawful. In our view, conducting a dog sniff would not change the character of a traffic stop that is lawful at its inception and otherwise executed in a reasonable manner, unless the dog sniff itself infringed respondent's constitutionally protected interest in privacy. Our cases hold that it did not. Official conduct that does not "compromise any legitimate interest in privacy" is not a search subject to the Fourth Amendment. We have held that any interest in possessing contraband cannot be deemed "legitimate," and thus, governmental conduct that only reveals the possession of contraband "compromises no legitimate privacy interest." . . . In *United States v. Place* (1983), we treated a canine sniff by a well-trained narcotics-detection dog as "sui generis" because it "discloses only the presence or absence of narcotics, a contraband item.". . .

Accordingly, the use of a well-trained narcotics-detection dog—one that "does not expose noncontraband items that otherwise would remain hidden from public view,"—during a lawful traffic stop, generally does not implicate legitimate privacy interests. In this case, the dog sniff was performed on the exterior of respondent's car while he was lawfully seized for a traffic violation. Any intrusion on respondent's privacy expectations does not rise to the level of a constitutionally cognizable infringement. This conclusion is entirely consistent with our recent decision that the use of a thermal-imaging device to detect the growth of marijuana in a home constituted an unlawful search [*Kyllo v. United States* (2001)]. Critical to that decision was the fact that the device was capable of detecting lawful activity. . . . The legitimate expectation that information about perfectly lawful activity will remain private is categorically distinguishable from respondent's hopes or expectations concerning the nondetection of contraband in the trunk of his car. A dog sniff conducted during a concededly lawful traffic stop that reveals no information other than the location of a substance that no individual has any right to possess does not violate the Fourth Amendment. The judgment of the Illinois Supreme Court is vacated. . . .

*It is so ordered.*

JUSTICE SOUTER, dissenting. I would hold that using the dog for the purposes of determining the presence of marijuana in the car's trunk was a search unauthorized as an incident of the speeding stop and unjustified on any other ground.

In . . . *Place* (1983), we categorized the sniff of the narcotics-seeking dog as "sui generis" under the Fourth Amendment and held it was not a search. The classification rests not only upon the limited nature of the intrusion, but on a further premise that experience has shown to be untenable, the assumption that trained sniffing dogs do not err. . . .

At the heart both of *Place* and the Court's opinion today is the proposition that sniffs by a trained dog are sui generis because a reaction by the dog in going alert is a response to nothing but the presence of contraband. Hence, the argument goes, because the sniff can only reveal the presence of items devoid of any legal use, the sniff "does not implicate legitimate privacy interests" and is not to be treated as a search.

The infallible dog, however, is a creature of legal fiction. [T]heir supposed infallibility is belied by judicial opinions describing well-trained animals sniffing and alerting with less than perfect accuracy, whether owing to errors by their handlers, the limitations of the dogs themselves, or even the pervasive contamination of currency by cocaine. In practical terms, the evidence is clear that the dog that alerts hundreds of times will be wrong dozens of times. Once the dog's fallibility is recognized, however, that ends the justification claimed in *Place* for treating the sniff as sui generis under the Fourth Amendment: the sniff alert does not necessarily signal hidden contraband, and opening the container or enclosed space whose emanations the dog has sensed will not necessarily reveal contraband or any other evidence of crime. This is not, of course, to deny that a dog's reaction may provide reasonable suspicion, or probable cause, to search the container or enclosure; the Fourth Amendment does not demand certainty of success to justify a search for evidence or contraband. The point is simply that the sniff and alert cannot claim the certainty that *Place* assumed, both in treating the deliberate use of sniffing dogs as sui generis and then taking that characterization as a reason to say they are not searches subject to Fourth Amendment scrutiny. . . .

It makes sense, then, to treat a sniff as the search that it amounts to in practice, and to rely on the body of our Fourth Amendment cases, including *Kyllo,* in deciding whether such a search is reasonable. As a general proposition, using a dog to sniff for drugs is subject to the rule that the object of enforcing criminal laws does not, without more, justify suspicionless Fourth Amendment intrusions. Since the police claim to have had no particular suspicion that Caballes was violating any drug law, this sniff search must stand or fall on its being ancillary to the traffic stop that led up to it. It is true that the police had probable cause to stop the car for an offense committed in the office's presence, which Caballes concedes could have justified his arrest. There is no occasion to consider authority incident to arrest, however, for the police did nothing more than detain Caballes long enough to check his record and write a ticket. As a consequence, the reasonableness of the search must be assessed in relation to the actual delay the police chose to impose. . . .

The Court today does not go so far as to say explicitly that sniff searches by dogs trained to sense contraband always get a free pass under the Fourth Amendment, since it reserves judgment on the constitutional significance of sniffs assumed to be more intrusive than a dog's walk around a stopped car. For this reason, I do not take the [decision] as actually signaling recognition of a broad authority to conduct suspicionless sniffs for drugs in any parked car . . . or on the person of any pedestrian minding his own business on a sidewalk. But the Court's stated reasoning provides no apparent stopping point short of such excesses. For the sake of providing a workable framework to analyze cases on facts like these, which are certain to come along, I would treat the dog sniff as the familiar search it is in fact, subject to scrutiny under the Fourth Amendment.

JUSTICE GINSBURG, with whom JUSTICE SOUTER joins, dissenting. . . . In my view, the Court diminishes the Fourth Amendment's force by abandoning the second *Terry* inquiry (was the police action "reasonably related in scope to the circumstances [justifying] the [initial] interference"). A drug-detection dog is an intimidating animal. Injecting such an animal into a routine traffic stop changes the character of the encounter between the police and the motorist. The stop becomes broader, more adversarial, and (in at least some cases) longer. Caballes—who, as far as [the] Troopers knew, was guilty solely of driving six miles per hour over the speed limit—was exposed to the embarrassment and intimidation of being investigated, on a public thoroughfare, for drugs. Even if the drug sniff is not characterized as a Fourth Amendment "search," the sniff surely broadened the scope of the traffic-violation-related seizure. . . .

The dog sniff in this case, it bears emphasis, was for drug detection only. A dog sniff for explosives, involving security interests not presented here, would be an entirely different matter. . . .

This Court has distinguished between the general interest in crime control and more immediate threats to public safety.

The use of bomb-detection dogs to check vehicles for explosives without doubt has a closer kinship to the sobriety checkpoints in *Sitz* than to the drug checkpoints in *Edmond*. . . .

## Board of Education of Pottawatomie County v. Earls

536 U.S. 822 (2002)
*A policy adopted by the Tecumseh, Oklahoma, School District required all middle and high school students to consent to urinalysis testing for drugs in order to participate in any extracurricular activity. Lindsay Earls and others challenged the policy as contravening Fourth Amendment principles. On the basis of* Vernonia

School Dist. 47J v. Acton *(1995), the district court upheld the policy. (The reader may want to review the discussion of* Vernonia *in Chapter Three and the entry on* Vernonia *in Chapter Five prior to reading this excerpt.) The United States Court of Appeals for the Tenth Circuit reversed, holding that the policy violated the Fourth Amendment. It concluded that before imposing a suspicionless drug testing program a school had to demonstrate some identifiable drug abuse problem among a sufficient number of those tested, so that testing the group would actually redress the drug problem. The U.S. Supreme Court, dividing five to four, reversed the appellate court, upholding the program. Justice Ginsburg, who had concurred in* Vernonia, *dissented here; her dissent draws distinctions between the two policies.*

Argued March 19, 2002; Decided June 27, 2002.

JUSTICE THOMAS delivered the opinion of the Court. Because this Policy reasonably serves the School District's important interest in detecting and preventing drug use among its students, we hold that it is constitutional. . . .

Searches by public school officials, such as the collection of urine samples, implicate Fourth Amendment interests. We must therefore review the School District's Policy for "reasonableness," which is the touchstone of the constitutionality of a governmental search. In the criminal context, reasonableness usually requires a showing of probable cause. The probable-cause standard, however, "is peculiarly related to criminal investigations" and may be unsuited to determining the reasonableness of administrative searches where the "Government seeks to *prevent* the development of hazardous conditions." . . .

Given that the School District's Policy is not in any way related to the conduct of criminal investigations, respondents do not contend that the School District requires probable cause before testing students for drug use. Respondents instead argue that drug testing must be based at least on some level of individualized suspicion. . . . But we have long held that "the Fourth Amendment imposes no irreducible requirement of [individualized] suspicion." . . . Therefore, in the context of safety and administrative regulations, a search unsupported by probable cause may be reasonable "when 'special needs, beyond the normal need for law enforcement, make the warrant and probable-cause requirement impracticable.'"

Significantly, this Court has previously held that "special needs" inhere in the public school context. While schoolchildren do not shed their constitutional rights when they enter the schoolhouse, "Fourth Amendment rights . . . are different in public schools than elsewhere; the 'reasonableness' inquiry cannot disregard the schools' custodial and tutelary responsibility for children." In particular, a finding of individualized suspicion may not be necessary when a school conducts drug testing. In *Vernonia*, this Court held that the suspicionless drug testing of athletes was constitutional. The Court, however, did not simply authorize all school drug testing, but rather conducted a fact-specific balancing of the intrusion on the children's Fourth Amendment rights against the promotion of legitimate governmental interests. Applying the principles of *Vernonia* to the somewhat different facts of this case, we conclude that Tecumseh's Policy is also constitutional.

We first consider the nature of the privacy interest allegedly compromised by the drug testing. . . .

A student's privacy interest is limited in a public school environment where the State is responsible for maintaining discipline, health, and safety. Schoolchildren are routinely required to submit to physical examinations and vaccinations against disease. Securing order in the school environment sometimes requires that students be subjected to greater controls than those appropriate for adults.

Respondents argue that because children participating in nonathletic extracurricular activities are not subject to regular physicals and communal undress, they have a stronger expectation of privacy than the athletes tested in *Vernonia*. This distinction, however, was not essential to our decision in *Vernonia*, which depended primarily upon the school's custodial responsibility and authority.

In any event, students who participate in competitive extracurricular activities voluntarily subject themselves to many of the same intrusions on their privacy as do athletes. Some of these clubs and activities require occasional off-campus travel and communal undress. All of them have their own rules and requirements for participating students that do not apply to the student body as a whole. . . . This regulation of extracurricular activities further diminishes the expectation of privacy among schoolchildren.

Next, we consider the character of the intrusion imposed by the Policy. Urination is "an excretory function traditionally shielded by great privacy." But the "degree of intrusion" on one's privacy caused by collecting a urine sample "depends upon the manner in which production of the urine sample is monitored."

Under the Policy, a faculty monitor waits outside the closed restroom stall for the student to produce a sample and must "listen for the normal sounds of urination in order to guard against tampered specimens and to insure an accurate chain of custody." The monitor then pours the sample into two bottles that are sealed and placed into a mailing pouch along with a consent form signed by the student. This procedure is virtually identical to that reviewed in *Vernonia,* except that it additionally protects privacy by allowing male students to produce their samples behind a closed stall. Given that we considered the method of collection in *Vernonia* a "negligible" intrusion, the method here is even less problematic. In addition, the Policy clearly requires that the test results be kept in confidential files separate from a student's other educational records and released to school personnel only on a "need to know" basis. . . .

Moreover, the test results are not turned over to any law enforcement authority. Nor do the test results here lead to the imposition of discipline or have any academic consequences. Rather, the only consequence of a failed drug test is to limit the student's privilege of participating in extracurricular activities. Indeed, a student may test positive for drugs twice and still be allowed to participate in extracurricular activities. . . .

Given the minimally intrusive nature of the sample collection and the limited uses to which the test results are put, we conclude that the invasion of students' privacy is not significant. Finally, this Court must consider the nature and immediacy of the government's concerns and the efficacy of the Policy in meeting them. This Court has already articulated in detail the importance of the governmental concern in preventing drug use by schoolchildren. The drug abuse problem among our Nation's youth has hardly abated since *Vernonia* was decided in 1995. In fact, evidence suggests that it has only grown worse. . . . The health and safety risks identified in *Vernonia* apply with equal force to Tecumseh's children. Indeed, the nationwide drug epidemic makes the war against drugs a pressing concern in every school. Additionally, the School District in this case has presented specific evidence of drug use at Tecumseh schools. Teachers testified that they had seen students who appeared to be under the influence of drugs and that they had heard students speaking openly about using drugs. A drug dog found marijuana cigarettes near the school parking lot. Police officers once found drugs or drug paraphernalia in a car driven by a Future Farmers of America member. And the school board president reported that people in the community were calling the board to discuss the "drug situation." . . .

Respondents consider the proffered evidence insufficient and argue that there is no "real and immediate interest" to justify a policy of drug testing nonathletes. We have recognized, however, that "[a] demonstrated problem of drug abuse . . . [is] not in all cases necessary to the validity of a testing regime," but that some showing does "shore up an assertion of special need for a suspicionless general search program." The School District has provided sufficient evidence to shore up the need for its drug testing program. Furthermore, this Court has not required a particularized or pervasive drug problem before allowing the government to conduct suspicionless drug testing. For instance, in [*National Treasury Employees Union v.*] *Von Raab* the Court upheld the drug testing of customs officials on a purely preventive basis, without any documented history of drug use by such officials. . . . Likewise, the need to prevent and deter the substantial harm of childhood drug use provides the necessary immediacy for a school testing policy. Indeed, it would make little sense to require a school district to wait for a substantial portion of its students to begin using drugs before it was allowed to institute a drug testing program designed to deter drug use. Given the nationwide epidemic of drug use, and the evidence of increased drug use in Tecumseh schools, it was entirely reasonable for the School District to enact this particular drug testing policy. We reject the Court of Appeals' novel test that "any district seeking to impose a random suspicionless drug testing policy as a condition to participation in a school activity must demonstrate that there is some identifiable drug abuse problem among a sufficient number of those subject to the testing, such that testing that group of students will actually redress its drug problem." Among other problems, it would be difficult to administer such a test. As we cannot articulate a threshold level of drug use that would suffice to justify a drug testing program for schoolchildren, we refuse to fashion what would in effect be a constitutional quantum of drug use necessary to show a "drug problem." . . .

We also reject respondents' argument that drug testing must presumptively be based upon an individualized reasonable suspicion of wrongdoing because such a testing regime would be less intrusive. In this context, the Fourth Amendment does not require a finding of individualized suspicion, and we decline to impose such a requirement on schools attempting to prevent and detect drug use by students. Moreover, we question whether testing based on individualized suspicion in fact would be less intrusive. Such a regime would place an additional burden on public school teachers who are already tasked with the difficult job of maintaining order and discipline. A program of individualized suspicion might unfairly target members of unpopular groups. The fear of lawsuits resulting from such targeted searches may chill enforcement of the program, rendering it ineffective in combating drug use. . . .

Finally, we find that testing students who participate in extracurricular activities is a reasonably effective means of addressing the School District's legitimate concerns in preventing, deterring, and detecting drug use. . . . In upholding the constitutionality of the Policy, we express no opinion as to its wisdom. Rather, we hold only that Tecumseh's Policy is a reasonable means of furthering the School District's important interest in preventing and deterring drug use among its schoolchildren. Accordingly, we reverse the judgment of the Court of Appeals. *It is so ordered.*

JUSTICE GINSBURG, with whom JUSTICE STEVENS, JUSTICE O'CONNOR, and JUSTICE SOUTER join, dissenting. Seven years ago, in *Vernonia School Dist. 47J v. Acton,* this Court determined that a school district's policy of randomly testing the urine of its student athletes for illicit drugs did not violate the Fourth Amendment. In so ruling, the Court emphasized that drug use "increased the risk of sports-related injury" and that Vernonia's athletes were the "leaders" of an aggressive local "drug culture" that had reached "'epidemic proportions.'" Today, the Court relies upon *Vernonia* to permit a school district with a drug problem its superintendent repeatedly described as "not . . . major," to test the urine of an academic team member solely by reason of her participation in a nonathletic, competitive extracurricular activity—participation associated with neither special dangers from, nor particular predilections for, drug use. . . . The particular testing program upheld today is not reasonable, it is capricious, even perverse: Petitioners' policy targets for testing a student population least likely to be at risk from illicit drugs and their damaging effects. I therefore dissent. . . . This case presents circumstances dispositively different from those of *Vernonia.* True, as the Court stresses, Tecumseh students participating in competitive extracurricular activities other than athletics share two relevant characteristics with the athletes of *Vernonia.* First, both groups attend public schools. . . . Concern for student health and safety is basic to the school's caretaking, and it is undeniable that "drug use carries a variety of health risks for children, including death from overdose."

Those risks, however, are present for *all* schoolchildren. *Vernonia* cannot be read to endorse invasive and suspicionless drug testing of all students upon any evidence of drug use, solely because drugs jeopardize the life and health of those who use them. Many children, like many adults, engage in dangerous activities on their own time; that the children are enrolled in school scarcely allows government to monitor all such activities. If a student has a reasonable subjective expectation of privacy in the personal items she brings to school, surely she has a similar expectation regarding the chemical composition of her urine. Had the *Vernonia* Court agreed that public school attendance, in and of itself, permitted the State to test each student's blood or urine for drugs, the opinion in *Vernonia* could have saved many words.

The second commonality to which the Court points is the voluntary character of both interscholastic athletics and other competitive extracurricular activities. . . .

The comparison is enlightening. While extracurricular activities are "voluntary" in the sense that they are not required for graduation, they are part of the school's educational program; for that reason, the petitioner (hereinafter School District) is justified in expending public resources to make them available. Participation in such activities is a key component of school life, essential in reality for students applying to college, and, for all participants, a significant contributor to the breadth and quality of the educational experience. Students "volunteer" for extracurricular pursuits in the same way they might volunteer for honors classes: They subject themselves to additional requirements, but they do so in order to take full advantage of the education offered them. . . .

Voluntary participation in athletics has a distinctly different dimension: Schools regulate student athletes discretely because competitive school sports by their nature require communal undress and, more important, expose students to physical risks that schools have a duty to mitigate. For the very reason that schools cannot offer a program of competitive athletics without intimately affecting the privacy of students, *Vernonia* reasonably analogized school athletes to "adults who choose to participate in a closely regulated industry." Interscholastic athletics similarly require close safety and health regulation; a school's choir, band, and academic team do not. *Vernonia* initially considered "the nature of the privacy interest upon which the search [there] at issue intruded." The Court emphasized that student athletes' expectations of privacy are necessarily attenuated. . . . Competitive extracurricular activities other than athletics, however, serve students of all manner: the modest and shy along with the bold and uninhibited. Activities of the kind plaintiff-respondent Lindsay Earls pursued—choir, show choir, marching band, and academic team—afford opportunities to gain self-assurance, to "come to know faculty members in a less formal setting than the typical classroom," and to acquire "positive social supports and networks [that] play a critical role in periods of heightened stress."

On "occasional out-of-town trips," students like Lindsay Earls "must sleep together in communal settings and use communal bathrooms." But those situations are hardly equivalent to the routine communal undress associated with athletics; the School District itself admits that when such trips occur, "public-like restroom facilities," which presumably include enclosed stalls, are ordinarily available for changing, and that "more modest students" find other ways to maintain their privacy.

Finally, the "nature and immediacy of the governmental concern," faced by the Vernonia School District dwarfed that confronting Tecumseh administrators. Vernonia initiated its drug testing policy in response to an alarming situation: "[A] large segment of the student body, particularly those involved in interscholastic athletics, was in a state of rebellion . . . fueled by alcohol and drug abuse as well as the student[s'] misperceptions about the drug culture." Tecumseh, by contrast, repeatedly reported to the Federal Government during the period leading up to the adoption of the policy that "types of drugs [other than alcohol and tobacco] including controlled dangerous substances, are present [in the schools] but have not identified themselves as major problems at this time." . . .

Not only did the Vernonia and Tecumseh districts confront drug problems of distinctly different magnitudes, they also chose different

solutions: Vernonia limited its policy to athletes; Tecumseh indiscriminately subjected to testing all participants in competitive extracurricular activities. Urging that "the safety interest furthered by drug testing
is undoubtedly substantial for all children, athletes and nonathletes
alike," the Court cuts out an element essential to the *Vernonia* judgment. Citing medical literature on the effects of combining illicit drug
use with physical exertion, the *Vernonia* Court emphasized that "the
particular drugs screened by [Vernonia's] Policy have been demonstrated to pose substantial physical risks to athletes." . . .

Notwithstanding nightmarish images of out-of-control flatware, live-
stock run amok, and colliding tubas disturbing the peace and quiet of
Tecumseh, the great majority of students the School District seeks to test
in truth are engaged in activities that are not safety sensitive to an unusual degree. . . .

Nationwide, students who participate in extracurricular activities
are significantly less likely to develop substance abuse problems than
are their less-involved peers. Even if students might be deterred from
drug use in order to preserve their extracurricular eligibility, it is at
least as likely that other students might forgo their extracurricular involvement in order to avoid detection of their drug use. Tecumseh's
policy thus falls short doubly if deterrence is its aim: It invades the
privacy of students who need deterrence least, and risks steering students at greatest risk for substance abuse away from extracurricular
involvement that potentially may palliate drug problems. To summarize, this case resembles *Vernonia* only in that the School Districts in
both cases conditioned engagement in activities outside the obligatory
curriculum on random subjection to urinalysis. The defining characteristics of the two programs, however, are entirely dissimilar. The
Vernonia district sought to test a subpopulation of students distinguished by their reduced expectation of privacy, their special suscepti-
bility to drug-related injury, and their heavy involvement with drug
use. The Tecumseh district seeks to test a much larger population associated with none of these factors. It does so, moreover, without
carefully safeguarding student confidentiality and without regard to
the program's untoward effects. A program so sweeping is not shel-
tered by *Vernonia;* its unreasonable reach renders it impermissible under the Fourth Amendment.

# ELECTRONIC SURVEILLANCE

## *Olmstead v. United States*

277 U.S. 438 (1928)

*Roy Olmstead was convicted in federal district court of transporting and selling liquor in violation of the National Prohibition Act. The evidence used to convict Olmstead was secured by a warrantless wiretap placed by federal agents on telephone lines between Olmstead's home and office. Olmstead challenged the admission of this evidence on the grounds that it was obtained in violation of the Fourth Amendment's guarantee against unreasonable searches and seizures. The U.S. Supreme Court held that because the interception of telephone conversations occurred without "trespass" on private property there was no "search" of a constitutionally protected area. Moreover, conversations were not tangible items that could be "seized." In dissent, Justice Brandeis argued for a broader construction of the Fourth Amendment. He contended, in one of the most forward-looking opinions ever written, that the amendment conferred upon each individual a general right to privacy, one not confined to traditional categories of searches involving actual trespass on private property or seizures of tangible items. This dissent foreshadowed the Court's holding in* Katz v. United States *(1967), which overturned* Olmstead.

Argued February 20–21, 1928; Decided June 4, 1928.
MR. CHIEF JUSTICE TAFT delivered the opinion of the Court.
. . . The information which led to the discovery of the conspiracy and its nature and extent was largely obtained by intercepting messages on the telephones of the conspirators by four federal prohibition officers. Small wires were inserted along the ordinary telephone wires from the residences of four of the petitioners and those leading from the chief office. The insertions were made without trespass upon any property of the defendants. They were made in the basement of the large office building. The taps from house lines were made in the streets near the houses. . . .

The well known historical purpose of the Fourth Amendment, directed against general warrants and writs of assistance, was to prevent the use of governmental force to search a man's house, his person, his papers and his effects; and to prevent their seizure against his will. . . .

The Amendment itself shows that the search is to be of material things—the person, the house, his papers or his effects. The description of the warrant necessary to make the proceeding lawful, is that it must specify the place to be searched and the person or *things* to be seized. . . .

The [Fourth] Amendment does not forbid what was done here. There was no searching. There was no seizure. The evidence was secured by the use of the sense of hearing and that only. There was no entry of the houses of offices of the defendants.

By the invention of the telephone, fifty years ago, and its application for the purpose of extending communications, one can talk with another at a far distant place. The language of the Amendment can not be extended and expanded to include telephone wires reaching to the whole world from the defendant's house o[r] office. The intervening wires are not part of his house of office any more than are the highways along which they are stretched. . . .

Congress may of course protect the secrecy of telephone messages by making them, when intercepted, inadmissible in evidence in federal criminal trials, by direct legislation, and thus depart from the common law of evidence. But the courts may not adopt such a policy by attributing an enlarged and unusual meaning to the Fourth Amendment. The reasonable view is that one who installs in his house a telephone instrument with connecting wires intends to project his voice to those quite outside, and that the wires beyond his house and messages while passing over them are not within the protection of the Fourth Amendment. Here those who intercepted the projected voices were not in the house of either party to the conversation. Neither the cases we have cited nor any of the many federal decisions brought to our attention hold the Fourth Amendment to have been violated as against a defendant unless there has been an official search and seizure of his person, or such a seizure of his papers or his tangible material effects, or an actual physical invasion of his house "or curtilage" for the purpose of making a seizure.

We think, therefore, that the wire tapping here disclosed did not amount to a search or seizure within the meaning of the Fourth Amendment. . . .

Our general experience shows that much evidence has always been receivable although not obtained by conformity to the highest ethics. The history of criminal trials shows numerous cases of prosecutions of oathbound conspiracies for murder, robbery, and other crimes, where officers of the law have disguised themselves and joined the organizations, taken the oaths and given themselves every appearance of active members engaged in the promotion of crime, for the purpose of securing evidence. Evidence secured by such means has always been received. A standard which would forbid the reception of evidence if obtained by other than nice ethical conduct by government officials would make society suffer and give criminals greater immunity than has been known heretofore. In the absence of controlling legislation by Congress, those who realize the difficulties in bringing offenders to justice may well deem it wise that the exclusion of evidence should be confined to cases where rights under the Constitution would be violated by admitting it. . . .

*Affirmed.*

MR. JUSTICE BRANDEIS, dissenting. . . . When the Fourth and Fifth Amendments were adopted, "the form that evil had theretofore taken," had been necessarily simple. Force and violence were then the only means known to man by which a Government could directly effect self-incrimination. It could compel the individual to testify—a compulsion effected, if need be, by torture. It could secure possession of his papers and other articles incident to his private life—a seizure effected, if need be, by breaking and entry. Protection against such invasion of "the sanctities of a man's home and the privacies of life" was provided in the Fourth and Fifth Amendments by specific language. . . . Subtler and more far-reaching means of invading privacy have become available to the Government. Discovery and invention have made it possible for the Government, by means far more effective than stretching upon the rack, to obtain disclosure in court of what is whispered in the closet. . . . The progress of science in furnishing the Government with means of espionage is not likely to stop with wire-tapping. Ways may some day be developed by which the Government, without removing papers from secret drawers, can reproduce them in court, and by which it will be enabled to expose to a jury the most intimate occurrences of the home. . . . Can it be that the Constitution affords no protection against such invasions of individual security? . . .

Time and again, this court, in giving effect to the principle underlying the Fourth Amendment, has refused to place an unduly literal construction upon it. . . .

The protection guaranteed by the Amendments is much broader in scope. The makers of our Constitution undertook to secure conditions favorable to the pursuit of happiness. They recognized the significance of man's spiritual nature, of his feelings and of his intellect. They knew that only a part of the pain, pleasure and satisfactions of life are to be found in material things. They sought to protect Americans in their beliefs, their thoughts, their emotions and their sensations. They conferred, as against the Government, the right to be let alone—the most comprehensive of rights and the right most valued by civilized men. To protect that right, every unjustifiable intrusion by the Government upon the privacy of the individual, whatever the means employed, must be deemed a violation of the Fourth Amendment. . . .

. . . It is . . . immaterial where the physical connection with the telephone wires leading into the defendants's premises was made. And it is also immaterial that the intrusion was in aid of law enforcement. Experience should teach us to be most on our guard to protect liberty when the Government's purposes are beneficent. Men born to freedom are naturally alert to repel invasion of their liberty by evil-minded rulers. The greatest dangers to liberty lurk in insidious encroachment by men of zeal, well-meaning but without understanding. . . .

Decency, security and liberty alike demand that government officials shall be subjected to the same rules of conduct that are commands to the citizen. In a government of laws, existence of the government will be imperilled if it fails to observe the law scrupulously. Our Government is the potent, the omnipresent teacher. For good or for ill, it teaches the whole people by its example. Crime is contagious. If the Government becomes a lawbreaker, it breeds contempt for law; it invites every man to become a law unto himself; it invites anarchy. To declare that in the administration of the criminal law the end justifies the means—to declare that the Government may commit crimes in order to secure the conviction of a private criminal—would bring terrible retribution. Against that pernicious doctrine this Court should resolutely set its face.

## *Katz v. United States*

389 U.S. 347 (1967)

*Charles Katz was convicted in federal district court of placing bets and wagers in violation of federal law. The evidence used to convict Katz was obtained by an electronic listening device placed outside a public telephone booth in Los Angeles, California. The device was placed outside the booth by agents of the Federal Bureau of Investigation, who did not have a warrant. Katz unsuccessfully challenged the admission of this evidence on the grounds that it was obtained in violation of the Fourth Amendment. A federal appellate court affirmed his conviction. Inarguably the most important Fourth Amendment case of the last half-century, the* Katz *majority rejected* Olmstead's *trespass doctrine, deciding that a search could occur without physical intrusion into a "constitutionally protected area." In the now memorable phrase, Justice Stewart wrote, "[T]he Fourth Amendment protects people, not places." Justice Harlan's concurrence is included because it established the two-part inquiry that has become the governing standard for determining whether a search has occurred despite the absence of physical intrusion. Under* Katz, *the touchstone of Fourth Amendment analysis is whether an individual has a constitutionally protected reasonable expectation of privacy. Justice Black's dissent is also excerpted, for in it he takes up the broader question of the role of history in interpreting the Fourth Amendment, concluding that the amendment was not intended to prohibit eavesdropping of a public telephone booth, even if done electronically. By distorting the amendment "to bring it into harmony with the times," Justice Black asserted, the Court had assumed the improper role of a "continuously functioning constitutional convention."*

Argued October 17, 1967; Decided December 18, 1967.

MR. JUSTICE STEWART delivered the opinion of the Court. . . . [T]he parties have attached great significance to the characterization of the telephone booth from which the petitioner placed his calls. The petitioner has strenuously argued that the booth was a "constitutionally protected area." The Government has maintained with equal vigor that it was not. But this effort to decide whether or not a given "area," viewed in the abstract, is "constitutionally protected" deflects attention from the problem presented by this case. For the Fourth Amendment protects people, not places. What a person knowingly exposes to the public, even in his own home or office, is not a subject of Fourth Amendment protection. But what he seeks to preserve as private, even in an area accessible to the public, may be constitutionally protected. . . .

The Government stresses the fact that the telephone booth from which the petitioner made his calls was constructed partly of glass, so that he was as visible after he entered it as he would have been if he had remained outside. But what he sought to exclude when he entered the booth was not the intruding eye—it was the uninvited ear. He did not shed his right to do so simply because he made his calls from a place where he might be seen. No less than an individual in a business office, in a friend's apartment, or in a taxicab, a person in a telephone booth may rely upon the protection of the Fourth Amendment. One who occupies it, shuts the door behind him, and pays the toll that permits him to place a call is surely entitled to assume that the words he utters into the mouthpiece will not be broadcast to the world. To read the Constitution more narrowly is to ignore the vital role that the public telephone has come to play in private communication. The Government contends, however, that the activities of its agents in this case should not be tested by Fourth Amendment requirements, for the surveillance technique they employed involved no physical penetration of the telephone booth from which the petitioner placed his calls. It is true that the absence of such penetration was at one time thought to foreclose further Fourth Amendment inquiry. . . . Thus, although a closely divided Court supposed in *Olmstead* that surveillance without any trespass and without the seizure of any material object fell outside the ambit of the Constitution, we have since departed from the narrow view on which that decision rested. Indeed, we have expressly held that the Fourth Amendment governs not only the seizure of tangible items, but extends as well to the recording of oral statements, overheard without any "technical trespass under . . . local property law." Once this much is acknowledged, and once it is recognized that the Fourth Amendment protects people—and not simply "areas"—against unreasonable searches and seizures, it becomes clear that the reach of that Amendment cannot turn upon the presence or absence of a physical intrusion into any given enclosure. We conclude that the underpinnings of *Olmstead* and *Goldman* have been so eroded by our subsequent decisions that the "trespass" doctrine there enunciated can no longer be regarded as controlling. The Government's activities in electronically listening to and recording the petitioner's words violated the privacy upon which he justifiably relied while using the telephone booth and thus constituted a "search and seizure" within the meaning of the Fourth Amendment. The fact that the electronic device employed to achieve that end did not happen to penetrate the wall of the booth can have no constitutional significance. The question remaining for decision, then, is whether the search and seizure conducted in this case complied with constitutional standards. In that regard, the Government's position is that its agents acted in an entirely defensible manner: They did not begin their electronic surveillance until investigation of the petitioner's activities had established a strong probability that he was using the telephone in question to transmit gambling information to persons in other States, in violation of federal law. Moreover, the surveillance was limited, both in scope and in duration, to the specific purpose of establishing the contents of the petitioner's unlawful telephonic communications. The agents confined their surveillance to the brief periods during which he used the telephone booth, and they took great care to overhear only the conversations of the petitioner himself.

Accepting this account of the Government's actions as accurate, it is clear that this surveillance was so narrowly circumscribed that a duly authorized magistrate, properly notified of the need for such investigation, specifically informed of the basis on which it was to proceed, and clearly apprised of the precise intrusion it would entail, could constitutionally have authorized, with appropriate safeguards, the very limited search and seizure that the Government asserts in fact took place. . . .

It is apparent that the agents in this case acted with restraint. Yet the inescapable fact is that this restraint was imposed by the agents themselves, not by a judicial officer. They were not required, before commencing the search, to present their estimate of probable cause for detached scrutiny by a neutral magistrate. They were not compelled, during the conduct of the search itself, to observe precise limits established in advance by a specific court order. Nor were they directed, after the search had been completed, to notify the authorizing magistrate in detail of all that had been seized. In the absence of such safeguards, this Court has never sustained a search upon the sole ground that officers reasonably expected to find evidence of a particular crime and voluntarily confined their activities to the least intrusive means consistent with that end. . . .

The Government . . . argues that surveillance of a telephone booth should be exempted from the usual requirement of advance authorization by a magistrate upon a showing of probable cause. We cannot agree. Omission of such authorization "bypasses the safeguards provided by an objective predetermination of probable cause, and substitutes instead the far less reliable procedure of an after-the-event justification for the . . . search, too likely to be subtly influenced by the familiar shortcomings of hindsight judgment." . . .

And bypassing a neutral predetermination of the *scope* of a search leaves individuals secure from Fourth Amendment violations "only in the discretion of the police." . . .

Wherever a man may be, he is entitled to know that he will remain free from unreasonable searches and seizures. The government agents here ignored "the procedure of antecedent justification . . . that is central to the Fourth Amendment," a procedure that we hold to be a constitutional precondition of the kind of electronic surveillance involved in this case. Because the surveillance here failed to meet that condition, and because it led to the petitioner's conviction, the judgment must be reversed. *It is so ordered.*

MR. JUSTICE HARLAN, concurring. . . . As the Court's opinion states, "the Fourth Amendment protects people, not places." The question, however, is what protection it affords to those people. Generally, as here, the answer to that question requires reference to a "place." My understanding of the rule that has emerged from prior decisions is that there is a twofold requirement, first that a person have exhibited an actual (subjective) expectation of privacy and, second, that the expectation be one that society is prepared to recognize as "reasonable." Thus a man's home is, for most purposes, a place where he expects privacy, but objects, activities, or statements that he exposes to the "plain view" of outsiders are not "protected" because no intention to keep them to himself has been exhibited. On the other hand, conversations in the open would not be protected against being overheard, for the expectation of privacy under the circumstances would be unreasonable.

MR. JUSTICE BLACK, dissenting. . . . My basic objection is twofold: (1) I do not believe that the words of the Amendment will bear the meaning given them by today's decision, and (2) I do not believe that it is the proper role of this Court to rewrite the Amendment in order "to bring it into harmony with the times" and thus reach a result that many people believe to be desirable. . . . [T]he language of the [Fourth] Amendment is the crucial place to look in construing a written document such as our Constitution. . . .

The first clause protects "persons, houses, papers, and effects, against unreasonable searches and seizures. . . ." These words connote the idea of tangible things with size, form, and weight, things capable of being searched, seized, or both. The second clause of the Amendment still further establishes its Framers' purpose to limit its protection to tangible things by providing that no warrants shall issue but those "particularly describing the place to be searched, and the persons or things to be seized." A conversation overheard by eavesdropping, whether by plain snooping or wiretapping, is not tangible and, under the normally accepted meanings of the words, can neither be searched nor seized. In addition the language of the second clause indicates that the Amendment refers not only to something tangible so it can be seized but to something already in existence so it can be described. Yet the Court's interpretation would have the Amendment apply to overhearing future conversations which by their very nature are nonexistent until they take place. How can one "describe" a future conversation, and, if one cannot, how can a magistrate issue a warrant to eavesdrop [*sic*] one in the future? It is argued that information showing what is expected to be said is sufficient to limit the boundaries of what later can be admitted into evidence; but does such general information really meet the specific language of the Amendment which says "particularly describing"? Rather than using language in a completely artificial way, I must conclude that the Fourth Amendment simply does not apply to eavesdropping. Tapping telephone wires, of course, was an unknown possibility at the time the Fourth Amendment was adopted. But eavesdropping (and wiretapping is nothing more than eavesdropping by telephone) was. . . .

There can be no doubt that the Framers were aware of this practice, and if they had desired to outlaw or restrict the use of evidence obtained by eavesdropping, I believe that they would have used the appropriate language to do so in the Fourth Amendment. They certainly would not have left such a task to the ingenuity of language-stretching judges. . . .

Since I see no way in which the words of the Fourth Amendment can be construed to apply to eavesdropping, that closes the matter for me. In interpreting the Bill of Rights, I willingly go as far as a liberal construction of the language takes me, but I simply cannot in good conscience give a meaning to words which they have never before been thought to have and which they certainly do not have in common ordinary usage. I will not distort the words of the Amendment in order to "keep the Constitution up to date" or "to bring it into harmony with the times." It was never meant that this Court have such power, which in effect would make us a continuously functioning constitutional convention. . . .

### United States v. United States District Court for the Eastern District of Michigan

407 U.S. 297 (1972)

*The United States charged three defendants with conspiring to destroy, and one of them with destroying, government property. The government claimed that the electronic surveillances of the defendants, though warrantless, were lawful as a reasonable exercise of presidential power to protect the national security. The district court, holding the surveillances violative of the Fourth Amendment, issued an order for disclosure of the overheard conversations, which the U.S. Court of Appeals for the Sixth Circuit upheld. Title III of the Omnibus Crime Control and Safe Streets Act, which authorized court-approved electronic surveillance for specified crimes, contained a provision in 18 U.S.C. § 2511 (3) that nothing in that law limited the president's constitutional power to protect against the overthrow of the government or against "any other clear and present danger to the structure or existence of the Government." The government relied on § 2511 (3) in support of its contention that "in excepting national security surveillances from the Act's warrant requirement, Congress recognized the President's authority to conduct such surveillances without prior judicial approval." The U.S. Supreme Court disagreed. In this case, however, the justices suggested that there were good reasons for distinguishing between electronic surveillance for national security purposes and electronic surveillance for basic criminal purposes.*

Argued February 24, 1972; Decided June 19, 1972.

MR. JUSTICE POWELL delivered the opinion of the Court. The issue before us is an important one for the people of our country and their Government. It involves the delicate question of the President's power, acting through the Attorney General, to authorize electronic surveillance in internal security matters without prior judicial approval. Successive Presidents for more than one-quarter of a century have authorized such surveillance in varying degrees, without guidance from the Congress or a definitive decision of this Court. This case brings the issue here for the first time. Its resolution is a matter of national concern, requiring sensitivity both to the Government's right to protect itself from unlawful subversion and attack and to the citizen's right to be secure in his privacy against unreasonable Government intrusion. . . .

Title III of the Omnibus Crime Control and Safe Streets Act authorizes the use of electronic surveillance for classes of crimes carefully specified. . . . The Act represents a comprehensive attempt by Congress to promote more effective control of crime while protecting the privacy of individual thought and expression. . . .

Together with the elaborate surveillance requirements in Title III, there is the following proviso, 18 U. S. C. § 2511 (3): Nothing contained in this chapter or in section 605 of the Communications Act of 1934 shall limit the constitutional power of the President to take such measures as he deems necessary to protect the Nation against actual or potential attack or other hostile acts of a foreign power, to obtain foreign intelligence information deemed essential to the security of the United States, or to protect national security information against foreign intelligence activities. *Nor shall anything contained in this chapter be deemed to limit the constitu-*

*tional power of the President to take such measures as he deems necessary to protect the United States against the overthrow of the Government by force or other unlawful means, or against any other clear and present danger to the structure or existence of the Government.* The contents of any wire or oral communication intercepted by authority of the President in the exercise of the foregoing powers may be received in evidence in any trial hearing, or other proceeding only where such interception was reasonable, and shall not be otherwise used or disclosed except as is necessary to implement that power." (Emphasis supplied [by Justice Powell].) The Government relies on § 2511 (3). It argues that "in excepting national security surveillances from the Act's warrant requirement Congress recognized the President's authority to conduct such surveillances without prior judicial approval." The section thus is viewed as a recognition or affirmance of a constitutional authority in the President to conduct warrantless domestic security surveillance such as that involved in this case. We think the language of § 2511 (3), as well as the legislative history of the statute, refutes this interpretation. . . . At most, this is an implicit recognition that the President does have certain powers in the specified areas. Few would doubt this, as the section refers—among other things—to protection "against actual or potential attack or other hostile acts of a foreign power." But so far as the use of the President's electronic surveillance power is concerned, the language is essentially neutral.

Section 2511 (3) certainly confers no power, as the language is wholly inappropriate for such a purpose. It merely provides that the Act shall not be interpreted to limit or disturb such power as the President may have under the Constitution. In short, Congress simply left presidential powers where it found them. . . .

[N]othing in § 2511 (3) was intended to expand or to contract or to define whatever presidential surveillance powers existed in matters affecting the national security. If we could accept the Government's characterization of § 2511 (3) as a congressionally prescribed exception to the general requirement of a warrant, it would be necessary to consider the question of whether the surveillance in this case came within the exception and, if so, whether the statutory exception was itself constitutionally valid. But viewing § 2511 (3) as a congressional disclaimer and expression of neutrality, we hold that the statute is not the measure of the executive authority asserted in this case. Rather, we must look to the constitutional powers of the President. It is important at the outset to emphasize the limited nature of the question before the Court. . . . [There is no] question or doubt as to the necessity of obtaining a warrant in the surveillance of crimes unrelated to the national security interest. Further, the instant case requires no judgment on the scope of the President's surveillance power with respect to the activities of foreign powers, within or without this country. . . . There is no evidence of any involvement, directly or indirectly, of a foreign power. . . .

Our present inquiry, though important, is therefore a narrow one. It addresses a question left open by *Katz*, "Whether safeguards other than prior authorization by a magistrate would satisfy the Fourth Amendment in a situation involving the national security. . . ."

Though the Government and respondents debate their seriousness and magnitude, threats and acts of sabotage against the Government exist in sufficient number to justify investigative powers with respect to them. It would be contrary to the public interest for Government to deny to itself the prudent and lawful employment of those very techniques which are employed against the Government and its law-abiding citizens. . . .

But a recognition of these elementary truths does not make the employment by Government of electronic surveillance a welcome development—even when employed with restraint and under judicial supervision. There is, understandably, a deep-seated uneasiness and apprehension that this capability will be used to intrude upon cherished privacy of law-abiding citizens. . . .

History abundantly documents the tendency of Government—however benevolent and benign its motives—to view with suspicion those who most fervently dispute its policies. Fourth Amendment protections become the more necessary when the targets of official surveillance may be those suspected of unorthodoxy in their political beliefs. The danger to political dissent is acute where the Government attempts to act under so vague a concept as the power to protect "domestic security." Given the difficulty of defining the domestic security interest, the danger of abuse in acting to protect that interest becomes apparent. . . . The price of lawful public dissent must not be a dread of subjection to an unchecked surveillance power. Nor must the fear of unauthorized official eavesdropping deter vigorous citizen dissent and discussion of Government action in private conversation. For private dissent, no less than open public discourse, is essential to our free society.

As the Fourth Amendment is not absolute in its terms, our task is to examine and balance the basic values at stake in this case: the duty of Government to protect the domestic security, and the potential danger posed by unreasonable surveillance to individual privacy and free expression. If the legitimate need of Government to safeguard domestic security requires the use of electronic surveillance, the question is whether the needs of citizens for privacy and free expression may not be better protected by requiring a warrant before such surveillance is undertaken. We must also ask whether a warrant requirement would unduly frustrate the efforts of Government to protect itself from acts of subversion and overthrow directed against it.

. . . Fourth Amendment freedoms cannot properly be guaranteed if domestic security surveillances may be conducted solely within the discretion of the Executive Branch. The Fourth Amendment does not contemplate the executive officers of Government as neutral and disinterested magistrates. Their duty and responsibility are to enforce the laws, to investigate, and to prosecute. . . .

The Fourth Amendment contemplates a prior judicial judgment, not the risk that executive discretion may be reasonably exercised. This judicial role accords with our basic constitutional doctrine that individual freedoms will best be preserved through a separation of powers and division of functions among the different branches and levels of Government. The independent check upon executive discretion is not satisfied, as the Government argues, by "extremely limited" post-surveillance judicial review. Indeed, post-surveillance review would never reach the surveillances which failed to result in prosecutions. Prior review by a neutral and detached magistrate is the time-tested means of effectuating Fourth Amendment rights. . . .

The Government argues that the special circumstances applicable to domestic security surveillances necessitate a further exception to the warrant requirement. It is urged that the requirement of prior judicial review would obstruct the President in the discharge of his constitutional duty to protect domestic security. We are told further that these surveillances are directed primarily to the collecting and maintaining of intelligence with respect to subversive forces, and are not an attempt to gather evidence for specific criminal prosecutions. It is said that this type of surveillance should not be subject to traditional warrant requirements which were established to govern investigation of criminal activity, not ongoing intelligence gathering. . . .

The Government further insists that courts "as a practical matter would have neither the knowledge nor the techniques necessary to determine whether there was probable cause to believe that surveillance was necessary to protect national security." These security problems, the Government contends, involve "a large number of complex and subtle factors" beyond the competence of courts to evaluate. . . .

But we do not think a case has been made for the requested departure from Fourth Amendment standards. The circumstances described do not justify complete exemption of domestic security surveillance from prior judicial scrutiny. . . .

We cannot accept the Government's argument that internal security matters are too subtle and complex for judicial evaluation. Courts regularly deal with the most difficult issues of our society. There is no reason to believe that federal judges will be insensitive to or uncomprehending of the issues involved in domestic security cases. Certainly courts can recognize that domestic security surveillance involves different considerations from the surveillance of "ordinary crime." If the threat is too subtle or complex for our senior law enforcement officers to convey its significance to a court, one may question whether there is probable cause for surveillance. . . .

Thus, we conclude that the Government's concerns do not justify departure in this case from the customary Fourth Amendment requirement of judicial approval prior to initiation of a search or surveillance. Although some added burden will be imposed upon the Attorney General, this inconvenience is justified in a free society to protect constitutional values. Nor do we think the Government's domestic surveillance powers will be impaired to any significant degree. A prior warrant establishes presumptive validity of the surveillance and will minimize the burden of justification in post-surveillance judicial review. By no means of least importance will be the reassurance of the public generally that indiscriminate wiretapping and bugging of law-abiding citizens cannot occur.

We emphasize, before concluding this opinion, the scope of our decision. As stated at the outset, this case involves only the domestic aspects of national security. We have not addressed, and express no opinion as to, the issues which may be involved with respect to activities of foreign powers or their agents. . . .

Moreover, we do not hold that the same type of standards and procedures prescribed by Title III are necessarily applicable to this case. We recognize that domestic security surveillance may involve different policy and practical considerations from the surveillance of "ordinary crime." . . .

Given these potential distinctions between Title III criminal surveillances and those involving the domestic security, Congress may wish to consider protective standards for the latter which differ from those already prescribed for specified crimes in Title III. Different standards may be compatible with the Fourth Amendment if they are reasonable both in relation to the legitimate need of Government for intelligence information and the protected rights of our citizens. . . .

*Affirmed.*

## Kyllo v. United States

533 U.S. 27 (2001)

*Suspicious that marijuana was being grown inside Danny Kyllo's home, agents of the U.S. Department of the Interior used a thermal imaging device to scan the portion of the triplex owned by Kyllo. The purpose of the scan was to determine whether the amount of heat emanating from the home was consistent with the use of high-intensity halide lamps typically required for growing marijuana indoors. The scan was conducted from within a vehicle parked on a public street, and revealed that the garage roof and one side wall were relatively hot compared to the rest of the home and quite a bit warmer than neighboring homes. Based on tips from informants, an abnormally high rate of electrical consumption, and the thermal imaging scan, a federal magistrate issued a search warrant, which, upon execution, exposed a large, indoor marijuana growing operation. The district and appellate courts held that the use of the thermal imager did not constitute a search under the Fourth Amendment. On the basis of* Katz, *the judges reasoned that Kyllo had no objectively reasonable expectation of privacy because (1) the thermal imaging did not expose intimate details of Kyllo's life; and (2) Kyllo had not taken any affirmative steps to conceal the heat emanating from his home. The Supreme Court reversed, in a five-to-four opinion. A strongly worded dissenting opinion from Justice Stevens is included. This case demonstrates well the difficulty of applying the Fourth Amendment to modern conditions.*

Argued February 20, 2001; Decided June 11, 2001.

JUSTICE SCALIA delivered the opinion of the Court. This case presents the question whether the use of a thermal-imaging device aimed at a private home from a public street to detect relative amounts of heat within the home constitutes a "search" within the meaning of the Fourth Amendment. . . . "At the very core" of the Fourth Amendment "stands the right of a man to retreat into his own home and there be free from unreasonable governmental intrusion." With few exceptions, the question whether a warrantless search of a home is reasonable and hence constitutional must be answered no.

On the other hand, the antecedent question of whether or not a Fourth Amendment "search" has occurred is not so simple under our precedent. The permissibility of ordinary visual surveillance of a home used to be clear because, well into the 20th century, our Fourth Amendment jurisprudence was tied to common-law trespass. . . . We have since decoupled violation of a person's Fourth Amendment rights from trespassory violation of his property, but the lawfulness of warrantless visual surveillance of a home has still been preserved. . . .

The present case involves officers on a public street engaged in more than naked-eye surveillance of a home. We have previously reserved judgment as to how much technological enhancement of ordinary perception from such a vantage point, if any, is too much. While we upheld enhanced aerial photography of an industrial complex in *Dow Chemical*, we noted that we found "it important that this is *not* an area immediately adjacent to a private home, where privacy expectations are most heightened."

It would be foolish to contend that the degree of privacy secured to citizens by the Fourth Amendment has been entirely unaffected by the advance of technology. . . . The question we confront today is what limits there are upon this power of technology to shrink the realm of guaranteed privacy.

The *Katz* test—whether the individual has an expectation of privacy that society is prepared to recognize as reasonable—has often been criticized as circular, and hence subjective and unpredictable. While it may be difficult to refine *Katz* when the search of areas such as telephone booths, automobiles, or even the curtilage and uncovered portions of residences are at issue, in the case of the search of the interior of homes—the prototypical and hence most commonly litigated area of protected privacy—there is a ready criterion, with roots deep in the common law, of the minimal expectation of privacy that *exists,* and that is acknowledged to be *reasonable.* To withdraw protection of this minimum expectation would be to permit police technology to erode the privacy guaranteed by the Fourth Amendment. We think that obtaining by sense-enhancing technology any information regarding the interior of the home that could not otherwise have been obtained without physical "intrusion into a constitutionally protected area," constitutes a search—at least where (as here) the technology in question is not in general public use. This assures preservation of that degree of privacy against government that existed when the Fourth Amendment was adopted. On the basis of this criterion, the information obtained by the thermal imager in this case was the product of a search.

The Government maintains, however, that the thermal imaging must be upheld because it detected "only heat radiating from the external surface of the house." The dissent makes this its leading point, contending that there is a fundamental difference between what it calls "off-the-wall" observations and "through-the-wall surveillance." But just as a thermal imager captures only heat emanating from a house, so also a powerful directional microphone picks up only sound emanating from a house—and a satellite capable of scanning from many miles away would pick up only visible light emanating from a house. We rejected such a mechanical interpretation of the Fourth Amendment in *Katz,* where the eavesdropping device picked up only sound waves that reached the exterior of the phone booth. Reversing that approach would leave the homeowner at the mercy of advancing technology—including imaging technology that could discern all human activity in the home. While the technology used in the present case was relatively crude, the rule we adopt must take account of more sophisticated systems that are already in use or in development. . . .

The Government also contends that the thermal imaging was constitutional because it did not "detect private activities occurring in private areas." . . . [But] [t]he Fourth Amendment's protection of the home has never been tied to measurement of the quality or quantity of information obtained. . . . In the home, our cases show, *all* details are intimate details, because the entire area is held safe from prying government eyes. . . .

Limiting the prohibition of thermal imaging to "intimate details" would not only be wrong in principle; it would be impractical in application, failing to provide "a workable accommodation between the needs of law enforcement and the interests protected by the Fourth Amendment." To begin with, there is no necessary connection between the sophistication of the surveillance equipment and the "intimacy" of the details that it observes—which means that one cannot say (and the police cannot be assured) that use of the relatively crude equipment at issue here will always be lawful. The Agema Thermovision 210 might disclose, for example, at what hour each night the lady of the house takes her daily sauna and bath—a detail that many would consider "intimate"; and a much more sophisticated system might detect nothing more intimate than the fact that someone left a closet light on. We could not, in other words, develop a rule approving only that through-the-wall surveillance which identifies objects no smaller than 36 by 36 inches, but would have to develop a jurisprudence specifying which home activities are "intimate" and which are not. And even when (if ever) that jurisprudence were fully developed, no police officer would be able to know *in advance* whether his through-the-wall surveillance picks up "intimate" details—and thus would be unable to know in advance whether it is constitutional. . . .

We have said that the Fourth Amendment draws "a firm line at the entrance to the house." That line, we think, must be not only firm but also bright—which requires clear specification of those methods of surveillance that require a warrant. . . . Where, as here, the Government uses a device that is not in general public use, to explore details of the home that would previously have been unknowable without physical intrusion, the surveillance is a "search" and is presumptively unreasonable without a warrant. Since we hold the Thermovision imaging to have been an unlawful search, it will remain for the District Court to determine whether, without the evidence it provided, the search warrant issued in this case was supported by probable cause—and if not, whether there is any other basis for supporting admission of the evidence that the search pursuant to the warrant produced.

The judgment of the Court of Appeals is reversed; the case is remanded for further proceedings consistent with this opinion. *It is so ordered.*

JUSTICE STEVENS, with whom THE CHIEF JUSTICE, JUSTICE O'CONNOR, and JUSTICE KENNEDY join, dissenting. There is, in my judgment, a distinction of constitutional magnitude between "through-the-wall surveillance" that gives the observer or listener direct access to information in a private area, on the one hand, and the thought processes used to draw inferences from information in the public domain, on the other hand. The Court has crafted a rule that purports to deal with direct observations of the inside of the home, but the case before us merely involves indirect deductions from "off-the-wall" surveillance, that is, observations of the exterior of the home. Those observations were made with a fairly primitive thermal imager that gathered data exposed on the outside of petitioner's home but did not invade any constitutionally protected interest in privacy. Moreover, I believe that the supposedly "bright-line" rule the Court has created in response to its concerns about future technological developments is unnecessary, unwise, and inconsistent with the Fourth Amendment. There is no need for the Court to craft a new rule to decide this case, as it is controlled by established principles from our Fourth Amendment jurisprudence. One of those core principles, of course, is that "searches and seizures *inside a home* without a warrant are presumptively unreasonable." But it is equally well settled that searches and seizures of property in plain view are presumptively reasonable. . . . That is the principle implicated here. While the Court "takes the long view" and decides this case based largely on the potential of yet-to-be-developed technology that might allow "through-the-wall surveillance," this case involves nothing more than off-the-wall surveillance by law enforcement officers to gather information exposed to the general public from the outside of petitioner's home. All that the infrared camera did in this case was passively measure heat emitted from the exterior surfaces of petitioner's home; all that those measurements showed were relative differences in emission levels, vaguely indicating that some areas of the roof and outside walls were warmer than others.

Indeed, the ordinary use of the senses might enable a neighbor or passerby to notice the heat emanating from a building, particularly if it is vented, as was the case here. Additionally, any member of the public might notice that one part of a house is warmer than another part or a nearby building if, for example, rainwater evaporates or snow melts at different rates across its surfaces. Such use of the senses would not convert into an unreasonable search if, instead, an adjoining neighbor allowed an officer onto her property to verify her perceptions with a sensitive thermometer. Nor, in my view, does such observation become an unreasonable search if made from a distance with the aid of a device that merely discloses that the exterior of one house, or one area of the house, is much warmer than another. Nothing more occurred in this case. Thus, the notion that heat emissions from the outside of a dwelling is a private matter implicating the protections of the Fourth Amendment . . . is not only unprecedented but also quite difficult to take seriously. Heat waves, like aromas that are generated in a kitchen, or in a laboratory or opium den, enter the public domain if and when they leave a building. A subjective expectation that they would remain private is not only implausible but also surely not "one that society is prepared to recognize as 'reasonable.'"

To be sure, the homeowner has a reasonable expectation of privacy concerning what takes place within the home, and the Fourth Amendment's protection against physical invasions of the home should apply to their functional equivalent. But the equipment in this case did not penetrate the walls of petitioner's home, and while it did pick up "details of the home" that were exposed to the public, it did not obtain "any information regarding the *interior* of the home." . . .

Just as "the police cannot reasonably be expected to avert their eyes from evidence of criminal activity that could have been observed by any member of the public," so too public officials should not have to avert their senses or their equipment from detecting emissions in the public domain such as excessive heat, traces of smoke, suspicious odors, odorless gases, airborne particulates, or radioactive emissions, any of which could identify hazards to the community. In my judgment, monitoring such emissions with "sense-enhancing technology," and drawing useful conclusions from such monitoring, is an entirely reasonable public service. On the other hand, the countervailing privacy interest is at best trivial. After all, homes generally are insulated to keep heat in, rather than to prevent the detection of heat going out, and it does not seem to me that society will suffer from a rule requiring the rare homeowner who both intends to engage in uncommon activities that produce extraordinary amounts of heat, and wishes to conceal that production from outsiders, to make sure that the surrounding area is well insulated. The interest in concealing the heat escaping from one's house pales in significance to the "the chief evil against which the wording of the Fourth Amendment is directed," the "physical entry of the home," and it is hard to believe that it is an interest the Framers sought to protect in our Constitution. Since what was involved in this case was nothing more than drawing inferences from off-the-wall surveillance, rather than any "through-the-wall" surveillance, the officers' conduct did not amount to a search and was perfectly reasonable. . . .

Despite the Court's attempt to draw a line that is "not only firm but also bright," the contours of its new rule are uncertain because its protection apparently dissipates as soon as the relevant technology is "in general public use." Yet how much use is general public use is not even hinted at by the Court's opinion, which makes the somewhat doubtful assumption that the thermal imager used in this case does not satisfy that criterion. In any event, putting aside its lack of clarity, this criterion is somewhat perverse because it seems likely that the threat to privacy will grow, rather than recede, as the use of intrusive equipment becomes more readily available. . . . The two reasons advanced by the Court as justifications for the adoption of its new rule are both unpersuasive. First, the Court suggests that its rule is compelled by our holding in *Katz,* because in that case, as in this, the surveillance consisted of nothing more than the monitoring of waves emanating from a private area into the public domain. Yet there are critical differences between the cases. In *Katz,* the electronic listening device attached to the outside of the phone booth allowed the officers to pick up the content of the conversation inside the booth, making them the functional equivalent of intruders because they gathered information that was otherwise available only to someone inside the private area; it would be as if, in this case, the thermal imager presented a view of the heat-generating activity inside petitioner's home. By contrast, the thermal imager here disclosed only the relative amounts of heat radiating from the house; it would be as if, in *Katz,* the listening device disclosed only the relative volume of sound leaving the booth, which presumably was discernible in the public domain. . . . It is pure hyperbole for the Court to suggest that refusing to extend the holding of *Katz* to this case would leave the homeowner at the mercy of "technology that could discern all human activity in the home."

Second, the Court argues that the permissibility of "through-the-wall surveillance" cannot depend on a distinction between observing "intimate details" such as "the lady of the house [taking] her daily sauna and bath," and noticing only "the nonintimate rug on the vestibule floor" or "objects no smaller than 36 by 36 inches." This entire argument assumes, of course, that the thermal imager in this case could or did perform "through-the-wall surveillance" that could identify any detail "that would previously have been unknowable without physical intrusion." In fact, the device could not, and did not, enable its user to identify either the lady of the house, the rug on the vestibule floor, or anything else inside the house. . . .

Although the Court is properly and commendably concerned about the threats to privacy that may flow from advances in the technology available to the law enforcement profession, it has unfortunately failed to heed the tried and true counsel of judicial restraint. Instead of concentrating on the rather mundane issue that is actually presented by the case before it, the Court has endeavored to craft an all-encompassing rule for the future. It would be far wiser to give legislators an unimpeded opportunity to grapple with these emerging issues rather than to shackle them with prematurely devised constitutional constraints.

## THE EXCLUSIONARY RULE

### Weeks v. United States

232 U.S. 383 (1914)

*Fremont Weeks was convicted in federal district court on the basis of evidence seized from his home in two warrantless searches. Before the trial, Weeks filed a petition requesting that his private property be returned to him. The petition was denied, and Weeks was charged, prosecuted, and convicted. The U.S. Supreme Court reversed his conviction. In doing so, the justices established the*

*Fourth Amendment exclusionary rule, although the ruling applied only to criminal trials in federal courts.*

Argued December 2–3, 1913; Decided February 24, 1914.

MR. JUSTICE DAY delivered the opinion of the Court. . . .It is . . .apparent that the question presented involves the determination of the duty of the court with reference to the motion made by the defendant for the return of certain letters, as well as other papers, taken from his room by the United States Marshal, who, without authority of process, if any such could have been legally issued, visited the room of the defendant for the declared purpose of obtaining additional testimony to support the charge against the accused, and having gained admission to the house took from the drawer of a chiffonier there found certain letters written to the defendant, tending to show his guilt. These letters were placed in the control of the District Attorney and were subsequently produced by him and offered in evidence against the accused at the trial. The defendant contends that such appropriation of his private correspondence was in violation of rights secured to him by the Fourth and Fifth Amendments to the Constitution of the United States. We shall deal with the Fourth Amendment. . . .The history of this Amendment is given with particularity in the opinion of Mr. Justice Bradley, speaking for [*390] the court in *Boyd* v. *United States* [1886]. . . . As was there shown, it took its origin in the determination of the framers of the Amendments to the Federal Constitution to provide for that instrument a Bill of Rights, securing to the American people, among other things, those safeguards which had grown up in England to protect the people from unreasonable searches and seizures, such as were permitted under the general warrants issued under authority of the Government by which there had been invasions of the home and privacy of the citizens and the seizure of their private papers in support of charges, real or imaginary, made against them. Such practices had also received sanction under warrants and seizures under the so-called writs of assistance, issued in the American colonies. Resistance to these practices had established the principle which was enacted into the fundamental law in the Fourth Amendment, that a man's house was his castle and not to be invaded by any general authority to search and seize his goods and papers. . . .

The effect of the Fourth Amendment is to put the courts of the United States and Federal officials, in the exercise of their power and authority, under limitations and restraints as to the exercise of such power and authority, and to forever secure the people, their persons, houses, papers and effects against all unreasonable searches and seizures under the guise of law. This protection reaches all alike, whether accused of crime or not, and the duty of giving to it force and effect is obligatory upon all entrusted under our Federal system with the enforcement of the laws. The tendency of those who execute the criminal laws of the country to obtain conviction by means of unlawful seizures and enforced confessions, the latter often obtained after subjecting accused persons to unwarranted practices destructive of rights secured by the Federal Constitution, should find no sanction in the judgments of the courts which are charged at all times with the support of the Constitution and to which people of all conditions have a right to appeal for the maintenance of such fundamental rights. What then is the present case? Before answering that inquiry specifically, it may be well by a process of exclusion to state what it is not. It is not an assertion of the right on the part of the Government, always recognized under English and American law, to search the person of the accused when legally arrested to discover and seize the fruits or evidences of crime. . . .Nor is it the case of testimony offered at a trial where the court is asked to stop and consider the illegal means by which proofs, otherwise competent, were obtained—of which we shall have occasion to treat later in this opinion. Nor is it the case of burglar's tools or other proofs of guilt found upon his arrest within the control of the accused. The case in the aspect in which we are dealing with it involves the right of the court in a criminal prosecution to retain for the purposes of evidence the letters and correspondence of the accused, seized in his house in his absence and without his authority, by a United States Marshal holding no warrant for his arrest and none for the search of his premises. The accused, without awaiting his trial, made timely application to the court for an order for the return of these letters, as well as other property. This application was denied, the letters retained and put in evidence, after a further application at the beginning of the trial, both applications asserting the rights of the accused under the Fourth and Fifth Amendments to the Constitution. If letters and private documents can thus be seized and held and used in evidence against a citizen accused of an offense, the protection of the Fourth Amendment declaring his right to be secure against such searches and seizures is of no value, and, so far as those thus placed are concerned, might as well be stricken from the Constitution. The efforts of the courts and their officials to bring the guilty to punishment, praiseworthy as they are, are not to be aided by the sacrifice of those great principles established by years of endeavor and suffering which have resulted in their embodiment in the fundamental law of the land. The United States Marshal could only have invaded the house of the accused when armed with a warrant issued as required by the Constitution, upon sworn information and describing with reasonable particularity the thing for which the search was to be made. Instead, he acted without sanction of law, doubtless prompted by the desire to bring further proof to the aid of the Government, and under color of his office undertook to make a seizure of private papers in direct violation of the constitutional prohibition against such action. Under such circumstances, without sworn information and particular description, not even an order of court would have justified such procedure, much less was it within the authority of the United States Marshal to thus invade the house and privacy of the accused. . . . To sanction such proceedings would be to affirm by judicial decision a manifest neglect if not an open defiance of the prohibitions of the Constitution, intended for the protection of the people against such unauthorized action. . . .

We therefore reach the conclusion that the letters in question were taken from the house of the accused by an official of the United States acting under color of his office in direct violation of the constitutional rights of the defendant; that having made a seasonable application for their return, which was heard and passed upon by the court, there was involved in the order refusing the application a denial of the constitutional rights of the accused, and that the court should have restored these letters to the accused. In holding them and permitting their use upon the trial, we think prejudicial error was committed. . . .

It results that the judgment of the court below must be reversed, and the case remanded for further proceedings in accordance with this opinion.

*Reversed.*


## Mapp v. Ohio

367 U.S. 643 (1961)

*Dollree Mapp was convicted in an Ohio state court for possession of obscene literature on the basis of evidence seized from her home in a warrantless search. Both the Ohio Court and Appeals*

*and Supreme Court of Ohio affirmed her conviction, the latter rul-*
*ing that under Ohio law, evidence obtained by an unlawful search*
*was admissible in a criminal prosecution, and that under* Wolf v.
Colorado *(1949), a state was not prevented by the U.S. Constitu-*
*tion from adopting the rule as it prevailed in Ohio. [The reader*
*may want to review the discussion of* Wolf *in Chapter Three and*
*the entry on* Wolf *in Chapter Five prior to reading this excerpt.]*
*The U.S. Supreme Court held that the exclusionary rule limited*
*the states as well as the federal government. The majority opinion*
*emphasized both the constitutional foundations and the practical*
*necessities of the rule. The dissenting opinion criticized the major-*
*ity for its failure to preserve a proper balance between state and*
*federal responsibility in the area of criminal justice.*

Argued March 29, 1961; Decided June 19, 1961.

MR. JUSTICE CLARK delivered the opinion of the Court. Appel-
lant stands convicted of knowingly having had in her possession and under her control certain lewd and lascivious books, pictures, and pho-
tographs in violation of [state law]. . . .[T]he Supreme Court of Ohio
found that her conviction was valid though "based primarily upon the
introduction in evidence of lewd and lascivious books and pictures unlawfully seized during an unlawful search of defendant's home. . . ."

The State says that even if the search were made without authority, or
otherwise unreasonably, it is not prevented from using the unconstitutionally seized evidence at trial, citing *Wolf* v. *Colorado* (1949), in which
this Court did indeed hold "that in a prosecution in a State court for a
State crime the Fourteenth Amendment does not forbid the admission
of evidence obtained by an unreasonable search and seizure." [I]t is
urged once again that we review that holding. . . .

Today we once again examine *Wolf's* constitutional documentation of
the right to privacy free from unreasonable state intrusion, and, after its
dozen years on our books, are led by it to close the only courtroom
door remaining open to evidence secured by official lawlessness in fla-
grant abuse of that basic right, reserved to all persons as a specific guarantee against that very same unlawful conduct. We hold that all evidence
obtained by searches and seizures in violation of the Constitution is, by
that same authority, inadmissible in a state court. Since the Fourth

Amendment's right of privacy has been declared enforceable against the States through the Due Process Clause of the Fourteenth, it is enforceable against them by the same sanction of exclusion as is used against the Federal Government. Were it otherwise, then just as without the *Weeks* rule the assurance against unreasonable federal searches and seizures would be "a form of words," valueless and undeserving of mention in a perpetual charter of inestimable human liberties, so too, without that rule the freedom from state invasions of privacy would be so ephemeral and so neatly severed from its conceptual nexus with the freedom from all brutish means of coercing evidence as not to merit this Court's high regard as a freedom "implicit in the concept of ordered liberty." . . . [T]he admission of the new constitutional right by *Wolf* could not consistently tolerate denial of its most important constitutional privilege, namely, the exclusion of the evidence which an accused had been forced to give by reason of the unlawful seizure. To hold otherwise is to grant the right but in reality to withhold its privilege and enjoyment. . . .

Indeed, we are aware of no restraint, similar to that rejected today, conditioning the enforcement of any other basic constitutional right. The right to privacy, no less important than any other right carefully and particularly reserved to the people, would stand in marked contrast to all other rights declared as "basic to a free society." This Court has not hesitated to enforce as strictly against the States as it does against the Federal Government the rights of free speech and of a free press, the rights to notice and to a fair, public trial, including, as it does, the right not to be convicted by use of a coerced confession, however logically relevant it be, and without regard to its reliability. And nothing could be more certain than that when a coerced confession is involved, "the relevant rules of evidence" are overridden without regard to "the incidence of such conduct by the police," slight or frequent. Why should not the same rule apply to what is tantamount to coerced testimony by way of unconstitutional seizure of goods, papers, effects, documents, etc.? . . .

There are those who say, as did Justice (then Judge) Cardozo, that under our constitutional exclusionary doctrine "the criminal is to go free because the constable has blundered." In some cases this will undoubtedly be the result. But, . . . "there is another consideration—the imperative of judicial integrity." The criminal goes free, if he must, but it is the law that sets him free. Nothing can destroy a government more quickly than its failure to observe its own laws, or worse, its disregard of the charter of its own existence. As Mr. Justice Brandeis, dissenting, said in *Olmstead* v. *United States* (1928): "Our Government is the potent, the omnipresent teacher. For good or for ill, it teaches the whole people by its example. . . . If the Government becomes a lawbreaker, it breeds contempt for law; it invites every man to become a law unto himself; it invites anarchy." Nor can it lightly be assumed that, as a practical matter, adoption of the exclusionary rule fetters law enforcement. Only last year this Court expressly considered that contention and found that "pragmatic evidence of a sort" to the contrary was not wanting. . . .

The ignoble shortcut to conviction left open to the State tends to destroy the entire system of constitutional restraints on which the liberties of the people rest. Having once recognized that the right to privacy embodied in the Fourth Amendment is enforceable against the States, and that the right to be secure against rude invasions of privacy by state officers is, therefore, constitutional in origin, we can no longer permit that right to remain an empty promise. Because it is enforceable in the same manner and to like effect as other basic rights secured by the Due Process Clause, we can no longer permit it to be revocable at the whim of any police officer who, in the name of law enforcement itself, chooses to suspend its enjoyment. Our decision, founded on reason and truth, gives to the individual no more than that which the Constitution guarantees him, to the police officer no less than that to which honest law enforcement is entitled, and, to the courts, that judicial integrity so necessary in the true administration of justice.

*Reversed and remanded.*

MR. JUSTICE HARLAN, whom MR. JUSTICE FRANKFURTER and MR. JUSTICE WHITTAKER join, dissenting. In overruling the *Wolf* case the Court, in my opinion, has forgotten the sense of judicial restraint which, with due regard for stare decisis, is one element that should enter into deciding whether a past decision of this Court should be overruled. Apart from that I also believe that the *Wolf* rule represents sounder Constitutional doctrine than the new rule which now replaces it. . . .

At the heart of the majority's opinion in this case is the following syllogism: (1) the rule excluding in federal criminal trials evidence which is the product of an illegal search and seizure is "part and parcel" of the Fourth Amendment; (2) *Wolf* held that the "privacy" assured against federal action by the Fourth Amendment is also protected against state action by the Fourteenth Amendment; and (3) it is therefore "logically and constitutionally necessary" that the *Weeks* exclusionary rule should also be enforced against the States.

This reasoning ultimately rests on the unsound premise that because *Wolf* carried into the States, as part of "the concept of ordered liberty" embodied in the Fourteenth Amendment, the principle of "privacy" underlying the Fourth Amendment, it must follow that whatever configurations of the Fourth Amendment have been developed in the particularizing federal precedents are likewise to be deemed a part of "ordered liberty," and as such are enforceable against the States. For me, this does not follow at all. . . .

I would not impose upon the States this federal exclusionary remedy. The reasons given by the majority for now suddenly turning its back on *Wolf* seem to me notably unconvincing. First, it is said that "the factual grounds upon which *Wolf* was based" have since changed, in that more States now follow the *Weeks* exclusionary rule than was so at the time *Wolf* was decided. While that is true, a recent survey indicates that at present one-half of the States still adhere to the common-law non-exclusionary rule, and one, Maryland, retains the rule as to felonies. . . . Our concern here, as it was in *Wolf*, is not with the desirability of that rule but only with the question whether the States are Constitutionally free to follow it or not as they may themselves determine, and the relevance of the disparity of views among the States on this point lies simply in the fact that the judgment involved is a debatable one. . . .

The preservation of a proper balance between state and federal responsibility in the administration of criminal justice demands patience on the part of those who might like to see things move faster among the States in this respect. Problems of criminal law enforcement vary widely from State to State. . . . For us the question remains, as it has always been, one of state power, not one of passing judgment on the wisdom of one state course or another. In my view this Court should continue to forbear from fettering the States with an adamant rule which may embarrass them in coping with their own peculiar problems in criminal law enforcement. . . .

## United States v. Leon

468 U.S. 897 (1984)

*Relying upon a confidential informant, police officers instigated surveillance of Alberto Leon and others for suspected drug trafficking activities. Based on an affidavit summarizing police observations, an officer prepared a warrant application to search the suspects' homes and automobiles. A state judge issued a warrant. The warrant was executed and large quantities of illegal drugs were discovered. Leon and others were indicted for violating federal drug laws. The federal district court suppressed some of the evidence because the affidavit was insufficient to establish probable cause to search all of the residences and automobiles. The U.S. Court of Appeals for the Ninth Circuit affirmed. The U.S. Supreme Court held that the exclusionary rule should be modified so as not to bar the admission of evidence seized in reasonable, good-faith reliance on a search warrant that was subsequently held to be defective. Equally important, the majority rejected outright the argument that the Fourth Amendment required the exclusion of illegally obtained evidence. The dissenters criticized the majority for its narrow interpretation of the exclusionary rule.*

Argued January 17, 1984; Decided July 5, 1984.

JUSTICE WHITE delivered the opinion of the Court.

This case presents the question whether the Fourth Amendment exclusionary rule should be modified so as not to bar the use in the prosecution's case in chief of evidence obtained by officers acting in reasonable reliance on a search warrant issued by a detached and neutral magistrate but ultimately found to be unsupported by probable cause. To resolve this question, we must consider once again the tension between the sometimes competing goals of, on the one hand, deterring official misconduct and removing inducements to unreasonable invasions of privacy and, on the other, establishing procedures under which criminal defendants are "acquitted or convicted on the basis of all the evidence which exposes the truth." . . .

The Fourth Amendment contains no provision expressly precluding the use of evidence obtained in violation of its commands, and an examination of its origin and purposes makes clear that the use of fruits of a past unlawful search or seizure "[works] no new Fourth Amendment wrong." The wrong condemned by the Amendment is "fully accomplished" by the unlawful search or seizure itself, and the exclusionary rule is neither intended nor able to "cure the invasion of the defendant's rights which he has already suffered." The rule thus operates as "a judicially created remedy designed to safeguard Fourth Amendment rights generally through its deterrent effect, rather than a personal constitutional right of the party aggrieved."

Whether the exclusionary sanction is appropriately imposed in a particular case, our decisions make clear, is "an issue separate from the question whether the Fourth Amendment rights of the party seeking to invoke the rule were violated by police conduct." Only the former question is currently before us, and it must be resolved by weighing the costs and benefits of preventing the use in the prosecution's case in chief of inherently trustworthy tangible evidence obtained in reliance on a search warrant issued by a detached and neutral magistrate that ultimately is found to be defective. The substantial social costs exacted by the exclusionary rule for the vindication of Fourth Amendment rights have long been a source of concern. . . . An objectionable collateral consequence of this interference with the criminal justice system's truth-finding function is that some guilty defendants may go free or receive reduced sentences as a result of favorable plea bargains. Particularly when law enforcement officers have acted in objective good faith or their transgressions have been minor, the magnitude of the benefit conferred on such guilty defendants offends basic concepts of the criminal justice system. Indiscriminate application of the exclusionary rule, therefore, may well "[generate] disrespect for the law and administration of justice." Accordingly, "[as] with any remedial device, the application of the rule has been restricted to those areas where its remedial objectives are thought most efficaciously served." Close attention to those remedial objectives has characterized our recent decisions concerning the scope of the Fourth Amendment exclusionary rule. The Court has, to be sure, not seriously questioned, "in the absence of a more efficacious sanction, the continued application of the rule to suppress evidence from the [prosecution's] case where a Fourth Amendment violation has been substantial and deliberate. . . ." Nevertheless, the balancing approach that has evolved in various contexts—including criminal trials—"forcefully [suggests] that the exclusionary rule be more generally modified to permit the introduction of evidence obtained in the reasonable good-faith belief that a search or seizure was in accord with the Fourth Amendment." . . .

Reasonable minds frequently may differ on the question whether a particular affidavit establishes probable cause, and we have thus concluded that the preference for warrants is most appropriately effectuated by according "great deference" to a magistrate's determination.

Deference to the magistrate, however, is not boundless. It is clear, first, that the deference accorded to a magistrate's finding of probable cause does not preclude inquiry into the knowing or reckless falsity of the affidavit on which that determination was based. Second, the courts must also insist that the magistrate purport to "perform his 'neutral and detached' function and not serve merely as a rubber stamp for the police." . . .

Third, reviewing courts will not defer to a warrant based on an affidavit that does not "provide the magistrate with a substantial basis for determining the existence of probable cause." . . . Even if the warrant application was supported by more than a "bare bones" affidavit, a reviewing court may properly conclude that, notwithstanding the deference that magistrates deserve, the warrant was invalid because the magistrate's probable-cause determination reflected an improper analysis of the totality of the circumstances, or because the form of the warrant was improper in some respect. . . .

Only in the first of these three situations, however, has the Court set forth a rationale for suppressing evidence obtained pursuant to a search warrant; in the other areas, it has simply excluded such evidence without considering whether Fourth Amendment interests will be advanced. To the extent that proponents of exclusion rely on its behavioral effects on judges and magistrates in these areas, their reliance is misplaced. First, the exclusionary rule is designed to deter police misconduct rather than to punish the errors of judges and magistrates. Second, there exists no evidence suggesting that judges and magistrates are inclined to ignore or subvert the Fourth Amendment or that lawlessness among these actors requires application of the extreme sanction of exclusion.

Third, and most important, we discern no basis, and are offered none, for believing that exclusion of evidence seized pursuant to a warrant will have a significant deterrent effect on the issuing judge or magistrate. . . . Judges and magistrates are not adjuncts to the law enforcement team; as neutral judicial officers, they have no stake in the outcome of particular criminal prosecutions. The threat of exclusion thus cannot be expected significantly to deter them. Imposition of the exclusionary sanction is not necessary meaningfully to inform judicial officers of their errors, and we cannot conclude that admitting evidence obtained pursuant to a warrant while at the same time declaring that the warrant was somehow defective will in any way reduce judicial officers' professional incentives to comply with the Fourth Amendment, encourage them to repeat their mistakes, or lead to the granting of all colorable warrant requests. . . .

If exclusion of evidence obtained pursuant to a subsequently invalidated warrant is to have any deterrent effect, therefore, it must alter the behavior of individual law enforcement officers or the policies of their departments. . . .

[E]ven assuming that the rule effectively deters some police misconduct and provides incentives for the law enforcement profession as a whole to conduct itself in accord with the Fourth Amendment, it cannot be expected, and should not be applied, to deter objectively reasonable law enforcement activity. . . .

This is particularly true, we believe, when an officer acting with objective good faith has obtained a search warrant from a judge or magistrate and acted within its scope. In most such cases, there is no police illegality and thus nothing to deter. It is the magistrate's responsibility to determine whether the officer's allegations establish probable cause and, if so, to issue a warrant comporting in form with the requirements of the Fourth Amendment. In the ordinary case, an officer cannot be expected to question the magistrate's probable-cause determination or his judgment that the form of the warrant is technically sufficient. . . . Penalizing the officer for the magistrate's error, rather than his own, cannot logically contribute to the deterrence of Fourth Amendment violations.

We conclude that the marginal or nonexistent benefits produced by suppressing evidence obtained in objectively reasonable reliance on a subsequently invalidated search warrant cannot justify the substantial costs of exclusion. We do not suggest, however, that exclusion is always inappropriate in cases where an officer has obtained a warrant and abided by its terms. . . .

Suppression therefore remains an appropriate remedy if the magistrate or judge in issuing a warrant was misled by information in an affidavit that the affiant knew was false or would have known was false except for his reckless disregard of the truth. . . .

*Reversed.*

JUSTICE BRENNAN, with whom JUSTICE MARSHALL joins, dissenting. The majority ignores the fundamental constitutional importance of what is at stake here. While the machinery of law enforcement and indeed the nature of crime itself have changed dramatically since the Fourth Amendment became part of the Nation's fundamental law in 1791, what the Framers understood then remains true today—that the task of combating crime and convicting the guilty will in every era seem of such critical and pressing concern that we may be lured by the temptations of expediency into forsaking our commitment to protecting individual liberty and privacy. It was for that very reason that the Framers of the Bill of Rights insisted that law enforcement efforts be permanently and unambiguously restricted in order to preserve personal freedoms. In the constitutional scheme they ordained, the sometimes unpopular task of ensuring that the government's enforcement efforts remain within the strict boundaries fixed by the Fourth Amendment was entrusted to the courts. . . .

At the outset, the Court suggests that society has been asked to pay a high price—in terms either of setting guilty persons free or of impeding the proper functioning of trials—as a result of excluding relevant physical evidence in cases where the police, in conducting searches and seizing evidence, have made only an "objectively reasonable" mistake concerning the constitutionality of their actions. But what evidence is there to support such a claim?

Significantly, the Court points to none, and, indeed, as the Court acknowledges, recent studies have demonstrated that the "costs" of the exclusionary rule—calculated in terms of dropped prosecutions and lost convictions—are quite low. Contrary to the claims of the rule's critics that exclusion leads to "the release of countless guilty criminals," these studies have demonstrated that federal and state prosecutors very rarely drop cases because of potential search and seizure problems. . . .

What then supports the Court's insistence that this evidence be admitted? Apparently, the Court's only answer is that even though the costs of exclusion are not very substantial, the potential deterrent effect in these circumstances is so marginal that exclusion cannot be justified. The key to the Court's conclusion in this respect is its belief that the prospective deterrent effect of the exclusionary rule operates only in those situations in which police officers, when deciding whether to go forward with some particular search, have reason to know that their planned conduct will violate the requirements of the Fourth Amendment. . . .

The flaw in the Court's argument, however, is that its logic captures only one comparatively minor element of the generally acknowledged deterrent purposes of the exclusionary rule. To be sure, the rule operates to some extent to deter future misconduct by individual officers who have had evidence suppressed in their own cases. But what the Court overlooks is that the deterrence rationale for the rule is not designed to be, nor should it be thought of as, a form of "punishment" of individual police officers for their failures to obey the restraints imposed by the Fourth Amendment. Instead, the chief deterrent function of the rule is its tendency to promote institutional compliance with Fourth Amendment requirements on the part of law enforcement agencies generally. . . .

After today's decisions, however, that institutional incentive will be lost. Indeed, the Court's "reasonable mistake" exception to the exclusionary rule will tend to put a premium on police ignorance of the law. Armed with the assurance provided by today's decisions that evidence will always be admissible whenever an officer has "reasonably" relied upon a warrant, police departments will be encouraged to train officers that if a warrant has simply been signed, it is reasonable, without more, to rely on it. Since in close cases there will no longer be any incentive to err on the side of constitutional behavior, police would have every reason to adopt a "let's-wait-until-it's-decided" approach in situations in which there is a question about a warrant's validity or the basis for its issuance. . . .

Although the Court brushes these concerns aside, a host of grave consequences can be expected to result from its decision to carve this new exception out of the exclusionary rule. A chief consequence of today's decisions will be to convey a clear and unambiguous message to magistrates that their decisions to issue warrants are now insulated from subsequent judicial review. Creation of this new exception for good-faith reliance upon a warrant implicitly tells magistrates that they need not take much care in reviewing warrant applications, since their mistakes will from now on have virtually no consequence: If their decision to issue a warrant was correct, the evidence will be admitted; if their decision was incorrect but the police relied in good faith on the warrant, the evidence will also be admitted. Inevitably, the care and attention devoted to such an inconsequential chore will dwindle. Although the Court is correct to note that magistrates do not share the same stake in the outcome of a criminal case as the police, they nevertheless need to appreciate that their role is of some moment in order to continue performing the important task of carefully reviewing warrant applications. Today's decisions effectively remove that incentive.

PRESENT DAY WARRANTS AND
WARRANT-RELATED MATERIALS

## Application for Search Warrant and Authorization (Pennsylvania)

| **Commonwealth of Pennsylvania** | | **SEARCH WARRANT** |
| --- | --- | --- |
| **COUNTY OF** | | **AND AUTHORIZATION** |

| Docket Number (Issuing Authority): | Police Incident Number: | Warrant Control Number: |
| --- | --- | --- |

| AFFIANT NAME | AGENCY | PHONE NUMBER | DATE OF APPLICATION |
| --- | --- | --- | --- |

IDENTIFY ITEMS TO BE SEARCHED FOR AND SEIZED  (Be as specific as possible):

SPECIFIC DESCRIPTION OF PREMISES AND/OR PERSON TO BE SEARCHED  (Street and No., Apt. No., Vehicle, Safe Deposit Box, etc.):

NAME OF OWNER, OCCUPANT OR POSSESSOR OF SAID PREMISES TO BE SEARCHED  (If proper name is unknown, give alias and/or description):

| VIOLATION OF  (Describe conduct or specify statute): | DATE(S) OF VIOLATION: |
| --- | --- |

☐ Warrant Application Approved by District Attorney – DA File No.
  (If DA approval required per Pa.R.Crim.P. 2002A with assigned File No. per Pa.R.Crim.P. 107)
☐ Additional Pages Attached (Other than Affidavit of Probable Cause)

☐ Probable Cause Affidavit(s) MUST be attached (unless sealed below)   Total number of pages: _____

TOTAL NUMBER OF PAGES IS SUM OF ALL APPLICATION, PROBABLE CAUSE AND CONTINUATION PAGES EVEN IF ANY OF THE PAGES ARE SEALED

The below named Affiant, being duly sworn (or affirmed) before the Issuing Authority according to law, deposes and says that there is probable cause to believe that certain property is evidence of or the fruit of a crime or is contraband or is unlawfully possessed or is otherwise subject to seizure, and is located at the particular premises or in the possession of the particular person as described above.

| Signature of Affiant | Agency or Address if private Affiant | Badge Number |
| --- | --- | --- |

Sworn to and subscribed before me this _____ day of _____ 19____. Mag. Dist. No. _____

(SEAL)

| Signature of Issuing Authority | Office Address |
| --- | --- |

**SEARCH WARRANT**
TO LAW ENFORCEMENT OFFICER:

WHEREAS, facts have been sworn to or affirmed before me by written affidavit(s) attached hereto from which I have found probable cause, I do authorize you to search the premises or person described, and to seize, secure, inventory and make return according to the Pennsylvania Rules of Criminal Procedure.

☐ This Warrant shall be served as soon as practicable and shall be served only between the hours of 6AM to 10PM but in no event later than:*

☐ This Warrant shall be served as soon as practicable and may be served any time during the day or night but in no event later than: **

_____ M, o'clock _____ 19____.

* The issuing authority should specify a date not later than two (2) days after issuance.  Pa.R.Crim.P. 2005(d).
** If the issuing authority finds reasonable cause for issuing a nighttime warrant on the basis of additional reasonable cause set forth in the accompanying affidavit(s) and wishes to issue a nighttime warrant, then this block shall be checked.  Pa.R.Crim.P. 2006(g).

Issued under my hand this _____ day of _____ 19____ at _____ M, o'clock.

(SEAL)

| Signature of Issuing Authority | Mag. Dist. or Judicial Dist. No. | Date Commission Expires: |
| --- | --- | --- |

Title of Issuing Authority: ☐ District Justice ☐ Common Pleas Judge ☐ _____

☐ For good cause stated in the affidavits(s) the Search Warrant Affidavit(s) are sealed for _____ days by my certification and signature.  (Pa.R.Crim.P. 2011)

_____     _____ (Date)  (SEAL)
Signature of Issuing Authority   (Judge of the Court of Common Pleas or Appellate Court Justice or Judge).

TO BE COMPLETED BY THE ISSUING AUTHORITY

# Affidavit of Probable Cause (Pennsylvania)

| **Commonwealth of Pennsylvania** | | **AFFIDAVIT OF PROBABLE CAUSE** |
|---|---|---|
| **COUNTY OF** | | |
| Docket Number | Police Incident Number: | Warrant Control Number: |
| (Issuing Authority): | | |

PROBABLE CAUSE BELIEF IS BASED UPON THE FOLLOWING FACTS AND CIRCUMSTANCES:

I, THE AFFIANT, BEING DULY SWORN ACCORDING TO LAW, DEPOSE AND SAY THAT THE FACTS SET FORTH IN THE AFFIDAVIT ARE TRUE AND CORRECT TO THE BEST OF MY KNOWLEDGE, INFORMATION AND BELIEF.

_____ (SEAL)

| Affiant Signature | Date | Issuing Authority Signature | Date |
|---|---|---|---|

Page _____ of _____ Pages

# Receipt/Inventory of Seized Propery
## (Pennsylvania)

| Commonwealth of Pennsylvania | | RECEIPT / INVENTORY |
|---|---|---|
| **COUNTY OF** | | OF SEIZED PROPERTY |

| Docket Number (Issuing Authority): | Police Incident Number: | Warrant Control Number: |
|---|---|---|

| Date of Search: | Time of Search: | Inventory Page Number: of Pages |
|---|---|---|

| | | |
|---|---|---|
| Affiant | Agency or Address if private affiant | Badge No. |

The following property was taken / seized and a copy of this Receipt / Inventory with a copy of the Search Warrant and affidavit(s)  (if not sealed) was

☐ personally served on (name of person) _____

☐ was left at (describe the location) _____

| Item Number | Quantity | Item Description | Make, Model, Serial No. Color, etc. |
|---|---|---|---|
| | | | |
| | | | |
| | | | |
| | | | |
| | | | |
| | | | |
| | | | |
| | | | |
| | | | |
| | | | |
| | | | |
| | | | |
| | | | |
| | | | |
| | | | |
| | | | |
| | | | |
| | | | |
| | | | |
| | | | |
| | | | |
| | | | |
| | | | |
| | | | |
| | | | |
| | | | |
| | | | |
| | | | |

I/we do hereby state that this inventory is to the best of my/our knowledge and belief a true and correct listing of all items seized, and that I/we sign this Receipt / Inventory subject to the penalties and provisions of Title 18 Pa.C.S. 4904 (b). Unsworn Falsification to Authorities.

| Signature of person Issuing Receipt / Inventory | Printed Name | Affiliation | Badge or Title |
|---|---|---|---|

| Signature of Witness | Printed Name | Affiliation | Badge or Title |
|---|---|---|---|

| Signature of person making Search | Printed Name | Affiliation | Badge or Title |
|---|---|---|---|

AOPC 413B-10-24-98

# Return of Service and Inventory
# (Pennsylvania)

| Commonwealth of Pennsylvania  | RETURN of SERVICE AND INVENTORY |
|---|---|
| **COUNTY OF** | |

| Docket Number (Issuing Authority): | Police Incident Number: | Warrant Control Number: |
|---|---|---|
| Date of Search: | Time of Search: | Property Seized as result of Search (Y/N): |

| Date of Return: | Time of Return: | Officer making Return: |
|---|---|---|

Signature of Person Seizing Property:

Other Officers Participating in Search:

### Pa.R.Crim.P. Chapter 2000. SEARCH WARRANTS

**Rule 2002A. Approval of Search Warrant Applications by Attorney for the Commonwealth – Local Option.**
(a) The District Attorney of any county may require that search warrant applications filed in the county have the approval of an attorney for ☐ the Commonwealth prior to filing.

**Rule 2004. Person To Serve Warrant.**
A search warrant shall be served by a law enforcement officer.

**Rule 2005. Contents of Search Warrant.**
Each search warrant shall be signed by the issuing authority and shall:
(a) specify the date and time of issuance;
(b) identify specifically the property to be seized;
(c) name or describe with particularity the person or place to be searched;
(d) direct that the search be executed within a specified period of time, not to exceed 2 days from the time of issuance;
(e) direct that the warrant be served in the daytime unless otherwise authorized on the warrant, PROVIDED THAT, for purposes of the Rules of Chapter 2000, the term "daytime" shall be used to mean the hours of 6 a.m. to 10 p.m.;
(f) designate by title the judicial officer to whom the warrant shall be returned;
(g) certify that the issuing authority has found probable cause based upon the facts sworn to or affirmed before the issuing authority by written affidavit(s) attached to the warrant; and
(h) when applicable, certify on the face of the warrant that for good cause shown the affidavit(s) is sealed pursuant to Rule 2011 and state ☐ the length of time the affidavit(s) will be sealed.

**Rule 2006. Contents of Application for Search Warrant.**
Each application for a search warrant shall be supported by written affidavit(s) signed and sworn to or affirmed before an issuing authority, which affidavit(s) shall:
(a) state the name and department, agency, or address of the affiant;
(b) identify specifically the items or property to be searched for and seized;
(c) name or describe with particularity the person or place to be searched;
(d) identify the owner, occupant, or possessor of the place to be searched;
(e) specify or describe the crime which has been or is being committed;
(f) set forth specifically the facts and circumstances which form the basis for the affiant's conclusion that there is probable cause to believe the items or property identified are evidence or the fruit of a crime, or are contraband, or are otherwise unlawfully possessed or subject to seizure and that these items or property are located on the particular person or at the particular place described;
(g) if a "nighttime" search is requested (i.e., 10 p.m. to 6 a.m.), state additional reasonable cause for seeking permission to search in the nighttime;
(h) when the attorney for the Commonwealth is requesting that the affidavit(s) be sealed pursuant to Rule 2011, state the facts and circumstances which are alleged to establish good cause for the sealing of the affidavit(s).

**Rule 2008. Copy of Warrant; Receipt for Seized Property**
(a) A law enforcement officer, upon taking property pursuant to a search warrant, shall leave with the person from whom or from whose premises the property was taken a copy of the warrant and affidavit(s) in support thereof, and a receipt for the property seized. A copy of the warrant and affidavit(s) must be left whether or not any property is seized.
(b) If no one is present on the premises when the warrant is executed, the officer shall leave the documents specified in paragraph (a) at a conspicuous location in the said premises. A copy of the warrant and affidavit(s) must be left whether or not any property is seized.
(c) Notwithstanding the requirements in paragraphs (a) and (b), the officer shall not leave a copy of an affidavit that has been sealed pursuant to Rule 2011.

**Rule 2009. Return with Inventory**
(a) An inventory of items seized shall be made by the law enforcement officer serving a search warrant. The inventory shall be made in the presence of the person from whose possession or premises the property was taken, when feasible, or otherwise in the presence of at least one witness. The officer shall sign a statement on the inventory that it is a true and correct listing of all items seized, and that the signer is subject to the penalties and provisions of 18 Pa.C.S. Section 4904(b) - Unsworn Falsification To Authorities. The inventory shall be returned to and filed with the issuing authority.
(b) The judicial officer to whom the return was made shall upon request cause a copy of the inventory to be delivered to the applicant for the warrant and to the person from whom, or from whose premises, the property was taken.
(c) When the search warrant affidavit(s) is sealed pursuant to Rule 2011, the return shall be made to the justice or judge who issued the warrant.

**THE LAW ENFORCEMENT OFFICER SHALL MAKE ALL RETURNS TO THE ISSUING AUTHORITY DESIGNATED ON THE SEARCH WARRANT.**

AOPC 412A 10-01

# Application and Affidavit for Search Warrant (Federal Government)

## UNITED STATES DISTRICT COURT

_____  DISTRICT OF  _____

| In the Matter of the Search of <br> (Name, address or brief description of person, property or premises to be searched) | APPLICATION AND AFFIDAVIT <br> FOR SEARCH WARRANT <br><br> Case Number: |

I, _____ being duly sworn depose and say:

I am a(n) _____ and have reason to believe
Official Title

that ☐ on the person of or ☐ on the property or premises known as (name, description and/or location)

in the _____ District of _____

there is now concealed a certain person or property, namely (describe the person or property to be seized)

which is (state one or more bases for search and seizure set forth under Rule 41(b) of the Federal Rules of Criminal Procedure)

concerning a violation of Title _____ United States code, Section(s) _____

The facts to support a finding of probable cause are as follows:

Continued on the attached sheet and made a part hereof:     ☐ Yes     ☐ No

_____
Signature of Affiant

Sworn to before me and subscribed in my presence,

_____ at  _____
Date                                        City                              State

_____    _____
Name of Judige        Title of Judge        Signature of Judge

# UNITED STATES DISTRICT COURT

District of _____

In the Matter of the Search of
(Name, address or brief description of the person or property to be searched)

### SEARCH WARRANT

Case Number:

TO: _____ and any Authorized Officer of the United States

Affidavit(s) having been made before me by _____ who has reason to believe
Affiant

that ☐ on the person of, or ☐ on the premises known as (name, description and/or location)

in the _____ District of _____ there is now
concealed a certain person or property, namely (describe the person or property)

I am satisfied that the affidavit(s) and any record testimony establish probable cause to believe that the person or property so described is now concealed pn the person or premises above-described and established grounds for the issuance of this warrant.

YOU ARE HEREBY COMMANDED to search on or before _____
Date

(not to exceed 10 days) the person or place named above for the person or property specified, serving this warrant and making the search ☐ in the day time — 6:00 AM to 10:00 P.M. ☐ at any time in the day or night as I find reasonable cause has been established and if the person or property be found there to seize same, leaving a copy of this warrant and receipt for the person or property taken, and prepare a written inventory of the person or property seized and promptly return this warrant to
_____ as required by law.
U.S. Magistrate Judge (Rule 41(f)(4))

_____ at _____
Date and Time Issued                         City and State

_____       _____
Name and Title of Judge                        Signature of Judge

# UNITED STATES DISTRICT COURT

District of _____

In the Matter of the Search of
(Name, address or brief description of person or property to be searched)

### SEARCH WARRANT UPON ORAL TESTIMONY

Case Number: _____

TO: _____ and any Authorized Officer of the United States

Sworn oral testimony has been communicated to me by _____
Affiant

that ☐ on the person of, or ☐ on the premises known as (name, description and/or location)

in the _____ District of _____ there is now
concealed a certain person or property, namely (describe the person or property)

I am satisfied that the circumstances are such as to make it reasonable to dispense with a written affidavit and that there is probable cause to believe that the property or person so described is concealed on the person or premises above described and that the grounds for application for issuance of the search warrant exist as communicated orally to me in a sworn statement which has been recorded electronically, stenographically, or in long-hand and upon the return of the warrant, will be transcribed, certified as accurate and attached hereto.

YOU ARE HEREBY COMMANDED to search on or before _____
Date

the person or place named above for the person or property specified, serving this warrant and making the search ☐ in the day-time— 6:00 AM to 10:00 PM ☐ at anytime in the day or night as I find reasonable cause has been established and if the property be found there to seize same, leaving a copy of this warrant and receipt for the person or property taken, and prepare a written inventory of the person or property seized and promptly return this warrant to as required by law. _____
U.S. Magistrate Judge (Rule 41 (f)(4))

_____   at   _____
Date and Time Issued                      City and State

_____   _____
Name and Title of Judge                    Signature of Judge

I certify that on _____ at _____
Date                                              Time

_____ orally authorized the
Judge

issuance and execution of a search warrant conforming to all the foregoing terms.

_____   _____   _____
Name of affiant                     Signature of affiant                     Exact time warrant

# Application and Affidavit for Seizure Warrant (Federal Government)

## UNITED STATES DISTRICT COURT

_____ District of _____

In the Matter of the Search of
(Address or brief description of property or premises to be seized)

**APPLICATION AND AFFIDAVIT
FOR SEIZURE WARRANT**

CASE NUMBER:

I, _____ , being duly sworn depose and say:

I am a(n) _____ and have reason to believe
Official Title

that in the _____ District of _____
there is now certain property which is subject to forfeiture to the United States, namely (describe the property to be seized)

which is (state one or more bases for seizure under the United States Code)

concerning a violation of a Title _____ United States Code, Section(s) _____ .
The facts to support a finding of probable cause for issuance of a Seizure Warrant are as follows:

Continued on the attached sheet and made a part hereof.  ☐ Yes  ☐ No

_____
Signature of Affiant

Sworn to before me, and subscribed in my presence

_____ at    _____
Date                                                             City                                State

_____      _____
Name of Judge          Title of Judge                 Signature of Judge

# UNITED STATES DISTRICT COURT

District of _____

In the Matter of the Seizure of
(Address or brief description of property or premises to be seized)

### SEIZURE WARRANT

CASE NUMBER:

TO: _____ and any Authorized Officer of the United States

Affidavit(s) having been made before me by _____ who has reason to

Affiant

believe that in the _____ District of _____ there is now

certain property which is subject to forfeiture to the United States, namely (describe the property to be seized)

I am satisfied that the affidavit(s) and any recorded testimony establish probable cause to believe that the property so described is subject to seizure and that grounds exist for the issuance of this seizure warrant.

YOU ARE HEREBY COMMANDED to seize within 10 days the property specified, serving this warrant and making the seizure ☐ (in the daytime—6:00 A.M. to 10:00 P.M.)    ☐ (at any time in the day or night as I find reasonable cause has been established), leaving a copy of this warrant and receipt for the property seized, and prepare a written inventory of the property seized and promptly return this warrant to _____

as required by law.

U.S. Magistrate Judge    (Rule 41(f)(4))

_____ at _____

Date and Time Issued            City                              State

_____    _____

Name of Judge        Title of Judge        Signature of Judge

# CHRONOLOGY

1538      English King Henry VIII introduces a licensing system as a means of regulating publications that are critical of the Crown. Under this system, which will remain in effect until the late 1700s, legislative, executive, and judicial authorities are empowered to authorize broad searches to identify and suppress objectionable publications.

1634      Seeking to enforce libel and sedition laws, agents of the Privy Council, possessing a general warrant, search the residence and law chambers of prominent English jurist and legal scholar Sir Edward Coke. The agents seize, among other items, his voluminous legal writings.

1685      The English Parliament impeaches Chief Justice William Scroggs, citing among other things his issuance of general warrants. Parliament recognizes for the first time that general warrants amount to an exercise of "arbitrary . . . governmental authority." Within a century, English judges begin to rule against general warrants.

1761      The Superior Court of Massachusetts decides *Paxton's Case*, more commonly known as the *Writs of Assistance Case*. Representing sixty-three Boston merchants, colonial lawyer James Otis denounces the writs of assistance as "the worst instrument of arbitrary power, the most destructive of English liberty and the fundamental principles of law, that ever was found in an English law-book." Although Otis loses the case, the continued oppressive use of writs of assistance have the effect of fueling the resentment and resistance in the colonies. John Adams, an observer to Otis's speech that day, later wrote of it: "Then and there the child Independence was born."

1760s    English courts decide *Wilkes v. Wood* (1763), declaring the use of a general warrant "as totally subversive of the liberty [and] the person and property of every man ... ," as well as *Entick v. Carrington* (1765), strongly condemning the use of general warrants. These cases are publicized both in England and in the American colonies.

1765    The English Parliament passes the Stamp Act, imposing additional taxes on the colonies and reawakening animosity toward writs of assistance. In August of that year a rampaging mob in Boston threatens to destroy the home of Charles Paxton, surveyor of the port of Boston and agent of the Crown who commonly has executed writs of assistance.

1767    The English Parliament reaffirms the legality of writs of assistance.

1767    Agents of the English Crown ransack the home of Daniel Malcom, a prominent Boston merchant, on the basis of a tip that he had recently smuggled brandy and other liquors into his cellar. A large crowd gathers to defend the home from additional intrusions. This "Malcom Affair" has been characterized as "the most famous search in colonial America."

1774    The First Continental Congress formally objects to writs of assistance as an abuse of governmental search power.

1776      Virginia adopts a Declaration of Rights, which provides a constitutional guarantee against arbitrary governmental invasion of individual and privacy. Six other states soon follow, condemning general warrants and prohibiting unreasonable searches and seizures.

1776      The Continental Congress approves the Declaration of Independence, which announces and justifies the colonies' separation from England. Although the Declaration does not designate writs of assistance among its long list of grievances against England, writs of assistance and general warrants might have been included in the open-ended complaint in the Declaration that the King "has . . . sent hither swarms of Officers to harass our people . . . ."

1787      The proposed Constitution is written and sent to the states for ratification.

1789      The U.S. Constitution is formally adopted.

1789      Congress proposes twelve amendments to the U.S. Constitution, calling them a Bill of Rights. They are sent to the states for ratification.

1791      On December 15, the states ratify ten of the proposed twelve amendments, thus adding to the U.S. Constitution a Bill of Rights. The Fourth Amendment reads:

> The right of the people to be secure in their persons, houses, papers, and effects, against unreasonable searches and seizures, shall not be violated, and no Warrants shall issue, but upon probable cause, supported by Oath or affirmation, and particularly describing the place to be searched, and the persons or things to be seized.

1806      The U.S. Supreme Court decides *Ex Parte Burford*, determining that the Fourth Amendment protects against arbitrary arrests as well as searches.

1833    The U.S. Supreme Court decides *Barron v. Baltimore*, holding that the Fifth Amendment—and by extension the other amendments—did not apply to the states.

1855    The U.S. Supreme Court decides *Murray v. Hoboken Land Company*, ruling that the Fourth Amendment does not apply to civil proceedings.

1868    The Fourteenth Amendment is added to the U.S. Constitution. The Due Process Clause of this amendment becomes the medium through which most of the Bill of Rights is applied to the states.

1878    The U.S. Supreme Court decides *In Ex Parte Jackson*, holding that the post office cannot open sealed mail without a warrant.

1886    The U.S. Supreme Court decides *Boyd v. United States*, the justices' first extensive analysis of the meaning and scope of the Fourth Amendment. In one of the more memorable passages from the opinion, Justice Joseph Bradley wrote: "It is not the breaking of [a man's] doors, and the rummaging of his drawers, that constitutes the essence of the offence; but it is the invasion of his indefeasible right of personal security, personal liberty, and private property. . . ."

1897    The U.S. Supreme Court "incorporates" the "just compensation" clause of the Fifth Amendment into the Due Process Clause of the Fourteenth Amendment, thus beginning the process of applying parts of the Bill of Rights to the states in *Chicago, Burlington, and Quincy Railroad Company v. Chicago.*

1914    In *Weeks v. United States*, the U.S. Supreme Court adopts the exclusionary rule, holding that evidence obtained by police in violation of the Fourth Amendment cannot be used against a criminal defendant in federal trial.

1925    In *Carroll v. United States*, the U.S. Supreme Court distinguishes automobile searches from searches of "persons, houses, papers, and effects."

1926    In *People v. Defore,* a case involving a motion to suppress illegally obtained evidence, New York court of appeals judge (a future justice of the U.S. Supreme Court) Benjamin N. Cardozo critically observes the possible consequences of excluding relevant evidence in a criminal prosecution: "The criminal is to go free because the Constable has blundered."

1928    The U.S. Supreme Court decides *Olmstead v. United States,* establishing the trespass doctrine. For a search to occur, government officials must trespass on private property. Also important, the majority holds that conversations are not tangible things that can be seized. In dissent, Justice Louis Brandeis argues that the Fourth Amendment confers upon each individual a general right to privacy, one not confined to the traditional categories of searches involving actual trespass on private property or seizures of tangible items.

1942    In *Goldman v. United States,* the U.S. Supreme Court extends *Olmstead's* (1928) trespass doctrine to surveillance utilizing a detectaphone, a device placed against a wall to hear conversations on the other side of the wall.

1949    In *Wolf v. Colorado,* the U.S. Supreme Court makes the Fourth Amendment applicable to the states, but rejects the notion that the exclusionary rule should be binding upon the states.

The U.S. Supreme Court announces in *Brinegar v. United States* that probable cause exists "where the facts and circumstances within [the government's] knowledge . . . [are] sufficient in themselves to warrant a man of reasonable caution in the belief that an offense has been or is being committed." This is the "textbook definition" of probable cause.

1959    In *Frank v. Maryland,* the U.S. Supreme Court holds that only those searches aimed at obtaining evidence of criminal activity require a judicially issued search warrant. Administrative searches, because they are not aimed so, do not require a warrant.

1960    The U.S. Supreme Court declares in *Abel v. United States* that the Fourth Amendment is not violated when the government appropriates abandoned property.

In *Elkins v. United States,* the U.S. Supreme Court abandons the "silver platter" doctrine, which allowed evidence seized illegally by state agents to be admitted at trial in federal court.

1961    In *Silverman v. United States,* the U.S. Supreme Court disallows evidence obtained via a "spike mike"—a listening device consisting of a foot-long spike attached to a microphone—because the "spike mike" made contact with a heating duct serving the suspect's apartment.

In *Mapp v. Ohio,* the U.S. Supreme Court extends the federal exclusionary rule to state criminal prosecutions.

1964    In *Aguilar v. Texas,* the U.S. Supreme Court establishes a two-pronged standard for determining probable cause that is based on information provided to the police by an informant.

1967    In *Camara v. Municipal Court,* the U.S. Supreme Court holds that administrative searches, because they are not aimed at uncovering evidence of criminal activity, benefit from a relaxed Fourth Amendment standard. The U.S. Supreme Court recognizes a "hot pursuit" exception to the warrant requirement in *Warden v. Hayden.*

The U.S. Supreme Court decision *Katz v. United States,* arguably the single most important Fourth

Amendment case of the second half of the twentieth century, decides that a "search" could occur without a physical intrusion into a "constitutionally protected area." In doing so, the justices overturn *Olmstead v. United States* (1928), replacing the trespass theory with the "reasonable expectation of privacy" standard.

1968    The U.S. Supreme Court decides *Terry v. Ohio*, authorizing a warrantless investigatory detention and a brief "pat down" search of the outer clothing—commonly called a "stop and frisk"—where a the police officer reasonably concludes that criminal activity may be afoot and that the persons with whom the officer is dealing may be armed and presently dangerous.

Republican presidential nominee Richard M. Nixon, frustrated with the revolution in criminal rights brought about by the Warren Court, campaigns on a promise to restore "law and order" to the nation.

1969    In *Chimel v. California*, the U.S. Supreme Court limits the scope of a warrantless search incident to a lawful arrest to that which is in "plain view" or in "the immediate area" surrounding the arrestee. Here, because the search went far beyond the arrestee's person and the area from within which the arrestee might have obtained either a weapon or something that could have been used as evidence against him, the justices declare it unconstitutional.

1971    The U.S. Supreme Court decides *Coolidge v. New Hampshire*, declaring unconstitutional the practice of permitting a state attorney general to issue a warrant during a murder investigation in which the attorney general is the chief prosecutor. In the same case, justices create the "plain view" exception to the Fourth

Amendment, allowing a police officer in certain circumstances and in the absence of a warrant to seize an item that is within his or her sight.

1972    The U.S. Supreme Court holds in *Adams v. Williams* that information obtained by the police from a reliable informant establishes reasonable suspicion.

In *United States v. United States District Court for the Eastern District of Michigan* the Supreme Court held that the Fourth Amendment requirement of judicial approval prior to a search or surveillance is applicable to domestic security cases.

1973    The U.S. Supreme Court decides *Schneckloth v. Bustamonte,* upholding warrantless searches based on "voluntary" consent.

In *United States v. Robinson,* the U.S. Supreme Court holds that once a police officer has lawfully placed a suspect under arrest, the officer may conduct a "full" search of the arrestee.

1974    In *United States v. Calandra,* the U.S. Supreme Court rejects the notion that the exclusionary rule is a personal constitutional right.  Instead, the justices hold that it is a preventive measure designed to deter future police misconduct.

The U.S. Supreme Court decides *United States v. Matlock,* holding that police officers may search a bedroom inhabited by two persons so long as they have consent from one of the inhabitants.

1977    In *United States v. Chadwick,* the U.S. Supreme Court holds that one has a lesser expectation of privacy in an automobile because its function is transportation and it seldom serves as one's residence.

1978    The U.S. Supreme Court decision in *Mincey v. Arizona* holds that when police come upon a homicide scene, they may make a prompt warrantless search of the area to see if there are other victims or if the killer is still on the premises.

1979      The U.S. Supreme Court declares in *Delaware v. Prouse* that random stops of motorists to check drivers' licenses and vehicle registrations are violative of the Fourth Amendment.

In *Ybarra v. Illinois*, the U.S. Supreme Court disallows a search of bar patrons because the search warrant was specific to the bar and not to the patrons.

1980      In *Payton v. New York*, the U.S. Supreme Court holds that the Fourth Amendment prohibits law enforcement officers from making a warrantless and nonconsensual entry into a suspect's home to make a routine felony arrest. The opinion is clearly based on the sanctity of the home, which has a long history in the common law.

1981      In *New York v. Belton*, the U.S. Supreme Court upholds a warrantless search—incident to a lawful arrest—of a passenger compartment of an automobile and a "container" found within the compartment because both are "within the arrestee's immediate control."

1982      In *United States v. Ross*, the U.S. Supreme Court holds that if police have probable cause to search an automobile that has been legally stopped, they may search any portion of the vehicle in which items might be located.

1983      The U.S. Supreme Court decides *Illinois v. Gates*, adopting the "totality of the circumstances" approach for determining probable cause based on information provided to the police by an informant.

In *United States v. Villamonte-Marquez*, the U.S. Supreme Court declares that customs agents may, without any suspicion of wrongdoing, hail and board any vessel on the high seas or in U.S. territorial waters for the purposes of examining documentation and conducting safety inspections.

In *United States v. Place,* the U.S. Supreme Court decides that police may, without a warrant, detain briefly an airline passenger's luggage upon a reasonable belief that the luggage contains illegal drugs.

In *Michigan v. Long,* the U.S. Supreme Court affirms that states may extend search and seizure rights beyond the requirements of the Fourth Amendment, so long as on the basis of clearly stated "adequate and independent state grounds."

The U.S. Supreme Court decides *Illinois v. Batchelder,* upholding an implied consent law, common in all fifty states, requiring automobile drivers to submit to breath-analysis tests or have their drivers' licenses automatically suspended.

1984   The U.S. Supreme Court decision *Oliver v. United States* holds that a warrantless search of a marijuana field is permissible under the "open fields" doctrine.

In *Welsh v. Wisconsin,* the U.S. Supreme Court disallows a warrantless home arrest for a minor, noncriminal, nonjailable, traffic offense.

In *Nix v. Williams,* the U.S. Supreme Court rules that unlawfully obtained evidence is admissible in a criminal prosecution if the evidence ultimately or inevitably would have been discovered by lawful means. This is known as the "inevitable discovery" exception to the exclusionary rule.

In *Segura v. United States,* the U.S. Supreme Court announces an "independent source" exception to the exclusionary rule. This exception allows the admission of evidence if it is discovered by means wholly independent of any constitutional violation.

In *United States v. Leon,* the U.S. Supreme Court legitimizes a "good faith" exception to the exclusionary rule, which permits the use of illegally obtained evidence where police possess an objectively reasonable belief that their warrant is valid, even though the warrant is later found to be unsupported by probable cause. In a companion case, *Massachusetts v. Sheppard,* the justices extend this exception to technically deficient warrants.

1985    In *New Jersey v. T. L. O.,* the U.S. Supreme Court upholds the legality of warrantless searches executed by public school officials. Such searches should be assessed under a standard that is less exacting than probable cause because of the "special needs" of maintaining an environment conducive to learning.

The U.S. Supreme Court decides *United States v. Montoya de Hernandez,* concluding that routine border searches of incoming or outgoing persons and property do not require reasonable suspicion, probable cause, or a warrant.

1986    The U.S. Supreme Court decides *California v. Ciraolo,* determining that warrantless aerial observation of an individual's fenced-in backyard does not violate the Fourth Amendment.

1987    In *Maryland v. Garrison,* the U.S. Supreme Court upholds the constitutionality of a search despite an ambiguous search warrant that results in police mistakenly searching the wrong apartment.

In *Illinois v. Krull,* the U.S. Supreme Court extends the "good faith" exception to the exclusionary rule, holding that the rule does not apply to evidence obtained by police who act in objectively reasonable reliance upon a state statute authorizing warrantless searches, even though the statute is later found to violate the Fourth Amendment.

In *O'Connor v. Ortega,* the U.S. Supreme Court rules that searches and seizures by government employees of the private property of their subordinates are subject to Fourth Amendment restraints.

1988     The U.S. Supreme Court holds in *California v. Greenwood* that the Fourth Amendment does not prohibit warrantless searches and seizures of garbage left for collection on the curb outside a home.

1989     In two cases—*Skinner v. Railway Labor Executives' Association* and *National Treasury Employees Union v. Von Raab*—the U.S. Supreme Court sustains warrantless drug and alcohol testing of certain public employees: railway workers involved in serious train accidents (in *Skinner*) and customs agents (in *National Treasury*).

1990     The U.S. Supreme Court decision in *United States v. Sokolow* redefines "reasonable suspicion" to include conducting an investigatory detention as more than a "inchoate and unparticularized suspicion or hunch" but less than probable cause.

In *United States v. Verdugo-Urquidez,* the U.S. Supreme Court holds that the Fourth Amendment is not applicable to searches and seizures conducted by U.S. agents or property owned by a nonresident alien and located in a foreign country.

In *Maryland v. Buie,* the U.S. Supreme Court holds that when police officers making an arrest have reason to believe that someone else may be present in another part of the home and that such person may pose a danger to them, the officers may make a "protective sweep" of the home for safety purposes.

The U.S. Supreme Court decides *Alabama v. White*, holding that if law enforcement officers are able to corroborate independently parts of an anonymous telephone tip, that information may be used to establish probable cause.

The U.S. Supreme Court decides *Michigan State Police v. Sitz*, upholding fixed sobriety highway checkpoints.

The U.S. Supreme Court decides *Illinois v. Rodriguez*, upholding a warrantless search based upon the consent of a third party who police officers mistakenly, but reasonably, believed to possess the authority to consent to the search.

1991    The U.S. Supreme Court decides *Florida v. Jimeno*, concluding that general consent to search a vehicle also includes consent to search containers within the vehicle.

In *California v. Acevedo*, the U.S. Supreme Court decides that the police may conduct a warrantless search of all containers within an automobile if the search is supported by probable cause.

The U.S. Supreme Court decides *Florida v. Bostick*, announcing that the appropriate inquiry in determining whether an encounter between an individual and a law enforcement officer is consensual is whether a reasonable person would feel free to decline the officers' requests and terminate the encounter.

1993    In *Minnesota v. Dickerson*, the U.S. Supreme Court adopts a "plain feel" exception to the Fourth Amendment: A police officer who is lawfully patting down a suspect's outer clothing may seize any object whose shape or mass makes it immediately apparent as contraband.

1995    In *Arizona v. Evans,* the U.S. Supreme Court holds that the exclusionary rule does not require the suppression of evidence seized pursuant to mistaken information resulting from clerical errors of court employees.

The U.S. Supreme Court decides *Wilson v. Arkansas,* adopting the long-standing common law requirement that, in most circumstances, law enforcement officers knock and announce their presence, identity, authority, and purpose before forcibly entering a residence to execute a warrant.

In *Vernonia School District v. Acton,* the U.S. Supreme Court upholds random, suspicionless drug testing for public school student-athletes.

1997    In *Maryland v. Wilson,* the U.S. Supreme Court allows police to order both the driver and passengers out of a vehicle that has been legally stopped, and to frisk both.

In *Chandler v. Miller,* the U.S. Supreme Court disallows blanket suspicionless searches of candidates for designated state public offices (including judgeships).

The U.S. Supreme Court decides *Richards v. Wisconsin,* disallowing a blanket exception to the knock and announce-requirement in drug felony investigations, but holding that the officers' failure to knock-and-announce is reasonable because the drugs are of an easily disposable nature.

1999    In *Wyoming v. Houghton,* the U.S. Supreme Court rules that if police have probable cause for a warrantless search of a vehicle, they may search all personal belongings of the passengers in the car that are capable of concealing contraband.

2000    In *Illinois v. Wardlow*, the U.S. Supreme Court holds that unprovoked flight from a police caravan patrolling a high-crime area amounts to reasonable suspicion justifying an investigatory detention.

In *Bond v. United States*, the U.S. Supreme Court holds that a law enforcement officer's physical manipulation of a bus passenger's carry-on luggage constituted a search under the Fourth Amendment.

The U.S. Supreme Court declares in *City of Indianapolis v. Edmond* that police may not set up highway checkpoints to detect ordinary criminal activity. In this case, police were stopping vehicles to allow drug-sniffing dogs the opportunity to "search" for controlled substances.

2001    In *Ferguson v. City of Charleston*, the U.S. Supreme Court declares that a state hospital cannot test pregnant women to obtain evidence of cocaine use for law enforcement purposes if the women do not consent to the test with full knowledge of the purpose for the test.

The U.S. Supreme Court decision in *Atwater v. City of Lago Vista* confirms that police ordinarily have broad latitude to make warrantless arrests when the criminal behavior—even if minor—occurs in their presence.

The U.S. Supreme Court decision *Kyllo v. United States* invalidates law enforcement's warrantless use of a thermal imaging device aimed at a private residence from a public street—the purpose of which was to detect relative amounts of heat within the residence.

In *United States v. Knights*, the U.S. Supreme Court rules that the consent exception to the warrant requirement applies to conditions of a convicted defendant's probation.

Congress passes the USA PATRIOT (Uniting and Strengthening America by Providing Appropriate Tools Required to Intercept and Obstruct Terrorism) Act shortly after and in response to the terrorist attacks of September 11, 2001. One of the Act's more controversial provisions—Section 215—enlarges the Federal Bureau of Investigation's (FBI) power to conduct surveillance on individuals living in the United States, including citizens and permanent residents. This legislation might ultimately represent the most far-reaching challenge to Fourth Amendment values in United States history.

2002    The U.S. Supreme Court, in *United States v. Arvizu,* holds that law enforcement officers need only reasonable suspicion, not probable cause, to conduct a search of a vehicle during a brief investigatory stop of that vehicle.

In *United States v. Drayton,* the U.S. Supreme Court holds that police coercion of an individual does not occur when the police question an individual, so long as a reasonable person would feel free to terminate the encounter.

In *Kirk v. Louisiana,* the U.S. Supreme Court reaffirms its long-standing disapproval of warrantless searches of homes absent exigent circumstances.

In *Board of Education of Independent School District No. 92 of Pottawatomie County v. Earls,* the U.S. Supreme Court upholds random, suspicionless drug testing for public school students who wish to participate in extracurricular activities.

2003    The U.S. Supreme Court decides *Maryland v. Pringle,* allowing the warrantless arrest of three occupants of a vehicle after a large roll of money and illegal drugs are found in the vehicle following a routine traffic stop.

**2004** In *Groh v. Ramirez,* the U.S. Supreme Court invalidates a search warrant because it fails the particularity requirement.

The U.S. Supreme Court holds in *United States v. Flores-Montano* that the federal government's authority to conduct a warrantless inspection of an automobile entering the United States from Mexico need not be based on suspicion and extends to removal, disassembly, and reassembly of the vehicle's gas tank.

In *Illinois v. Lidster,* the U.S. Supreme Court upholds the validity of a highway checkpoint set up to ask vehicle occupants for their help in providing information about a hit-and-run accident.

In *Thornton v. United States,* the U.S. Supreme Court rules that even when police make an arrest after a suspect has exited a vehicle, they may conduct a warrantless search of the passenger compartment of the vehicle.

In *Hiibel v. Sixth Judicial District Court of Nevada,* the U.S. Supreme Court sustains an arrest of an individual who refuses to identify himself to a police officer when asked to disclose his identity during a valid investigatory stop.

In *Hamdi v. Rumsfeld,* the U.S. Supreme Court surprises many by holding that due process of law requires that an American citizen detained as an enemy combatant captured in Afghanistan be given a meaningful opportunity to contest the detention before a neutral decision-maker. In a companion case, *Rasul v. Bush,* the justices hold that federal courts have jurisdiction to determine the legality of the president's potentially infinite detention of individuals who claim to be wholly innocent of wrongdoing.

2005    In *Illinois v. Caballes*, the U.S. Supreme Court holds that a dog sniff performed on the exterior of a car a few minutes after the driver was stopped for speeding does not violate the Fourth Amendment.

# TABLE OF CASES

*United States v. Handy,* 788 F.2d 1419; [9th Cir. 1986]

*United States v. Hill,* 939 F.2d 934; [11th Cir. 1991]

*United States v. Hinshaw,* 235 F.3d 565; [10th Cir. 1998]

*United States v. Janis,* 428 U.S. 433 (1976)

*United States v. Knights,* 534 U.S. 112 (2001)

*United States v. Leon,* 468 U.S. 897 (1984)

*United States v. Lopez-Mendoza,* 468 U.S. 1032 (1984)

*United States v. Martinez-Fuerte,* 428 U.S. 543 (1976)

*United States v. Matlock,* 415 U.S. 164 (1974)

*United States v. Mendenhall,* 446 U.S. 544 (1980)

*United States v. Molina-Tarazon,* 279 F.3d 709; [9th Cir. 2002]

*United States v. Montoya de Hernandez,* 473 U.S. 531 (1985)

*United States v. Moreno,* 475 F.2d 44; [5th Cir. 1973]

*United States v. Ogbuehi,* 18 F.3d 807; [9th Cir. 1994]

*United States v. Oyekan,* 786 F.3d 832; [8th Cir. 1986]

*United States v. Pino,* 729 F2d 1357; [11th Cir. 1984]

*United States v. Place,* 462 U.S. 696 (1983)

*United States v. Powell,* 222 F.3d 913; [11th Cir. 2000]

*United States v. Ravinowitz,* 339 U.S. 56 (1950)

*United States v. Robinson,* 414 U.S. 218 (1973)

*United States v. Ross,* 456 U.S. 798 (1982)

*United States v. Santana,* 427 U.S. 38 (1976)

*United States v. Sharpe,* 400 U.S. 675 (1985)

*United States v. Skipwith,* 482 F.2d 1272; [5th Cir. 1973]

*United States v. Sokolow,* 490 U.S. 1 (1990)

*United States v. Torres,* 926 F.2d 321; [3d Cir. 1991]

*United States v. United States District Court for the Eastern District of Michigan,* 407 U.S. 297 (1972)

*United States v. Velez-Saldana,* 252 F. 3d 49; [1st Cir. 2002]

*United States v. Verdugo-Urquidez,* 494 U.S. 259 (1990)

*United States v. Villamonte-Marquez,* 462 U.S. 579 (1983)

*United States v. Welbeck,* 145 F.3d 493; [2nd Cir. 1998

*Vernonia School District v. Acton,* 515 U.S. 646 (1995)

*Warden v. Hayden,* 387 U.S. 204 (1967)

# ANNOTATED
# BIBLIOGRAPHY

Abraham, Henry J. 1998. *Freedom and the Court: Civil Rights and Liberties in the United States.* New York: Oxford University Press. A classic text on civil rights and liberties, including a careful look at the Bill of Rights and its applicability to the states.

———. 1999. *Justices, Presidents, and Senators: A History of the U.S. Supreme Court Appointments from Washington to Clinton.* Lanham, MD: Rowman and Littlefield Publishers. A comprehensive and accessible history of the members of the U.S. Supreme Court, focusing on why individual justices were nominated, how their nominations were received politically, and what legacy their jurisprudence left on the development of American law and society.

Adams, John, and Charles Francis Adams, eds. 1856. *Life and Works of John Adams.* Vol. II. Boston: Little, Brown. Excerpts from Adams's diary and autobiography as well as his notes of debates in the Continental Congress of 1775; part of a ten-volume set.

Adams, John, and L. H. Butterfield, eds. [1755–1804] 1961. *Diary and Autobiography of John Adams.* Vol. III. Cambridge, MA: Belknap Press. An edited version of John Adams's account of his early life.

Adams, John, L. K. Wroth, and H. B. Zobel, eds. 1966. *The Legal Papers of John Adams.* Vol. I. Cambridge, MA: Belknap Press. A collection of the legal papers of John Adams; part of a three-volume set.

Allen, Francis. 1996. *The Habits of Legality: Criminal Justice and the Rule of Law.* New York: Oxford University Press. A broad survey of American criminal justice in a time of troubles, discussing how the habits of legality in American criminal justice can be strengthened, and demonstrating that a closer adherence to the rule of law may contribute to a more rational and effective penal policy.

Amar, Akhil Reed. 1994. "Fourth Amendment First Principles." *Harvard Law Review* 107: 757–819. Questions much of the Supreme Court's modern-day Fourth Amendment jurisprudence, arguing that the justices' preoccupation with warrants and probable cause for all searches and seizures, and the exclusion of illegally seized evidence, is misguided and should be replaced with a "reasonableness" standard.

———. 1997. *The Constitution and Criminal Procedure: First Principles.* New Haven, CT: Yale University Press. An examination of the role of Fourth, Fifth, and Sixth Amendment rights, challenging conventional wisdom on a broad range of topics, most notably the value of excluding reliable evidence in criminal trials.

———. 2000. *The Bill of Rights: Creation and Reconstruction.* New Haven, CT: Yale University Press. A clause-by-clause analysis of the intentions of those who adopted and ratified the Bill of Rights, arguing that the primary purpose of the Bill of Rights was not to protect against tyranny of the majority but rather to protect the rights of the majority from the distant and aristocratic federal government.

Amsterdam, Anthony. 1970. "The Supreme Court and the Rights of Suspects in Criminal Cases." *New York University Law Review* 45: 785–815. Argues that judicial activism in Fourth Amendment jurisprudence is inevitable because of the failure of other political actors and agencies of law to assume responsibility for regulating police practices.

———. 1974. "Perspectives on the Fourth Amendment." *Minnesota Law Review* 58: 349–477. An oft-cited article identifying and discussing a number of basic issues that complicate the development of a single, comprehensive Fourth Amendment theory.

Banks, Christopher P. 2004. "Protecting (or Destroying) Freedom through Law: The USA PATRIOT Act's Constitutional Implications." In *American National Security and Civil Liberties in an Era of Terrorism,* edited by David Cohen and John Wells. New York: Palgrave MacMillan. A selective analysis and critique of major provisions of the USA PATRIOT Act.

Banning, Lance. 1995. *The Sacred Fire of Liberty: James Madison and the Founding of the Federal Republic.* Ithaca, NY: Cornell University Press. A biography following Madison from 1780 until 1792, including his role in the drafting and adoption of the Fourth Amendment.

Barnett, Randy E. 2004. *Restoring the Lost Constitution: The Presumption of Liberty.* Princeton, NJ: Princeton University Press. A forceful and detailed argument stating that courts should adopt a "presumption of liberty," giving the benefit of the doubt to citizens when government restricts their rightful exercise of liberty. Proposes that the government be required to show that laws restricting liberty are both necessary and proper under some enumerated power; discusses the "natural rights" underpinnings of the Bill of Rights and argues for greater reliance on the Ninth Amendment as a source of unenumerated rights.

Basha, Rania M. 2003. "*Kyllo v. United States:* The Fourth Amendment Triumphs over Technology." *Brandeis Law Journal* 41: 939–956. Addresses the more general question of how the heightened sophistication of technology threatens the privacy rights guaranteed by the Fourth Amendment; though in agreement with the holding in *Kyllo,* the author wishes that the justices had gone further by extending the rule beyond the home to other recognized constitutionally protected areas.

Berger, Raoul. 1977. *Government by Judiciary: The Transformation of the Fourteenth Amendment.* Cambridge, MA: Harvard University Press. An influential text arguing that the U.S. Supreme Court's incorporation of the Bill of Rights has dangerously disregarded the intentions of the amendments' framers and has resulted in a judiciary that has become the nation's paramount policymaker, a super-legislature.

Bernardi, Frederick A. 1980. "The Exclusionary Rule: Is a Good Faith Standard Needed to Preserve a Liberal Interpretation of the Fourth Amendment?" *DePaul Law Review* 30: 51–108. Suggests that the exclusionary rule be limited to bad faith violations; asserts that application of the rule outside of the "bad faith" context has a detrimental effect on the citizenry's respect for the law and the courts.

Blackstone, Sir William. 1765–1769. *Commentaries on the Laws of England.* Four volumes. Oxford, England: Clarendon Press. The most influential lawbook and primary legal authority for eighteenth- and nineteenth-century lawyers in the United States.

Bloom, Robert M. 2003. *Searches, Seizures, and Warrants: A Reference Guide to the United States Constitution.* Westport, CT: Greenwood Publishing Group. A reference work on Fourth Amendment issues.

Bloom, Robert M., and Mark S. Brodin. 2004. *Criminal Procedure: Examples and Explanations.* Fourth ed. New York: Aspen Publishers, Inc. A concise guide to understanding the rights of criminal suspects.

Bodenhamer, D. J., and J. W. Ely. 1993. *The Bill of Rights in Modern America.* Bloomington: Indiana University Press. A collection of essays, informed by a historical perspective, focusing on the applicability of the Bill of Rights to contemporary issues.

Bradley, Craig. 2003. "The Middle Class Fourth Amendment." *Buffalo Criminal Law Review* 6: 1123–1161. Examines ten decisions in criminal procedure from two terms of the Supreme Court—five from the October Term 2002 and five from the October Term 2001; suggests that there is a strikingly consistent theme to these decisions: The Court is resistant to new exercises of the power of criminal law enforcement but is reluctant to interfere with police when they are acting with probable cause.

Brant, Irving. 1965. *The Bill of Rights: Its Origin and Meaning.* New York: Mentor Books. A study of the Bill of Rights from its roots in English common law to the mid-1960s, through decisions of the Supreme Court.

Buffaloe, Jennifer Y. 1997. "'Special Needs' and the Fourth Amendment: An Exception Poised to Swallow the Warrant Preference Rule." *Harvard Civil Rights–Civil Liberties Law Review* 32: 529–564. Demonstrates how the Supreme Court has extended the "special needs" exception, making it far too easy for the government to avoid the rigorous requirements of a warrant and probable cause, as required by the very language of the Fourth Amendment.

Bush, President George W. 2001. *Proclamation 7463:* "Declaration of National Emergency by Reason of Certain Terrorist Attacks." Available at http://www.whitehouse.gov/news/releases/2001/09/20010914-4.html. President Bush's invocation of the National Emergencies Act declaring a national state of emergency dating from September 11, 2001.

Cammack, Mark E., and Norman Garland. 2001. *Advanced Criminal Procedure.* St. Paul, MN: West Group. An examination of the procedural aspects of a criminal case once the investigation is complete.

Carr, Robert K. 1942. *The Supreme Court and Judicial Review.* New York: Farrer & Rinehart. A thorough discussion of the establishment, justification, and exercise of judicial review by the Supreme Court.

Chase, Harold W., and Craig R. Ducat. 1974. *Edward S. Corwin's* The Constitution *and What It Means Today.* Princeton, NJ: Princeton University Press. A basic resource in the study of the Constitution, the Bill of Rights, and other amendments.

Clements, Lucinda. 2002. "*Ferguson v. City of Charleston:* Gatekeeper of the Fourth Amendment's 'Special Needs' Exception." *Campbell Law Review* 24: 263–278. Argues, by looking at *Ferguson,* that the justices have closed a gap in the Fourth Amendment "special needs" jurisprudence by clarifying and shrinking the exception; now, whether a search and seizure policy has a primary purpose divorced from law enforcement is a "gateway question" into constitutional "special needs," suspicionless searches.

Cogan, Neil H., ed. 1997. *The Complete Bill of Rights: The Drafts, Debates, Sources, and Origins.* New York: Oxford University Press. Perhaps the most complete and useful historical analysis of the Bill of Rights, including all documentary records and relevant debates in the First Congress and in the state ratifying conventions.

Coke, Sir Edward, and Steve Sheppard, eds. 2003. *The Selected Writings of Sir Edward Coke.* Indianapolis, IN: Liberty Fund. From a leading authority on English common law and a strong defender of individual liberty against the autocratic claims of the Stuart monarchy in the seventeenth century, this three-volume collection of Coke's writings includes annotations of reported cases, selections from his famous *Institutes*, the complete Magna Carta, and Coke's speeches in Parliament addressing such subjects as liberty of speech, freedom from arbitrary arrest, and the English Petition of Right.

Cole, David, and James X. Dempsey. 2005. *Terrorism and the Constitution: Sacrificing Civil Liberties in the Name of National Security.* New York: The New Press. A critique of the U.S. government's response to the terrorist attacks of September 11, 2001; warns that many antiterrorism efforts needlessly sacrifice civil liberties without effectively protecting national security.

Commager, Henry Steele. 1958. *Documents of American History.* Sixth edition. New York: Appleton-Century-Crofts, Inc. A reference work containing virtually every significant document in American history, beginning in the fifteenth century.

Cooke, Jennifer Ison. 2002. "Discretionary Warrantless Searches and Seizures and the Fourth Amendment: A Need for Clearer Guidelines." *South Carolina Law Review* 53: 641–659. Analysis of the contradictions between *City of Indianapolis v. Edmond* and *Atwater v. City of Lago Vista,* emphasizing the need for state legislation to set forth a bright-line rule for police officers to follow when conducting warrantless searches and seizures.

Cook, Joseph G. and Marcus, Paul. *Criminal Procedure.* Matthew Bender Fifth ed. 2001 (with annual supplements through 2005) Lexis Nexis: Virginia, Charlottesville. This law school casebook provides up-to-date coverage of major aspects of American criminal procedure. It features three chapters on the Fourth Amendment, addressing such topics as individual liberty in the context of stops and arrests, Fourth Amendment standards governing the seizure of evidence, and the vindication of Fourth Amendment violations, with emphasis on the exclusionary rule.

Cooley, Thomas McIntyre. 1878. *A Treatise on Constitutional Limitations which Rests upon the Legislative Power of the States.* Fourth edition. Boston: Little, Brown, and Company. A nineteenth-century constitutional law treatise justifying judicial review for legislative acts that infringe upon natural rights.

Corwin, Edward S. [1929] 1955. *The Higher Law Background of American Constitutional Law.* Reprint. Ithaca, NY: Cornell University Press. A classic text rejecting the doctrine of legislative supremacy and advocating the exercise of judicial review to preserve natural rights.

Cray, Ed. 1997. *Chief Justice: A Biography of Earl Warren.* New York: Simon and Schuster. A well-researched and well-written biography of the fourteenth Chief Justice of the United States.

Cuddihy, William J. 1990. *The Fourth Amendment: Origins and Original Meaning, 1602–1791.* University of Michigan Dissertation Services. A lengthy unpublished dissertation from the Claremont Graduate School examining in great detail the original meaning and history of the Fourth Amendment.

Dash, Sam. 2004. *The Intruders: Unreasonable Searches and Seizures from King John to John Ashcroft.* Piscataway, NJ: Rutgers University Press. Covering almost 800 years of history, this book by the chief counsel of the U.S. Senate Watergate Committee examines the factors that led to the Fourth Amendment's protection against unreasonable searches and seizures and laments the considerable erosion of such protections in the last few decades.

Davies, Thomas Y. 1999. "Recovering the Original Fourth Amendment." *Michigan Law Review* 98: 547–750. A lengthy refutation of the commonplace assumption that the framers of the Fourth Amendment meant to create a broad reasonableness standard for warrantless intrusions, concluding that courts today now accord police officers far more discretionary authority than the framers ever intended.

———. 2002. "The Fictional Character of Law-and-Order Originalism: A Case Study of the Distortion and Evasions of Framing-Era Arrest Doctrine in *Atwater v. Lago Vista.*" *Wake Forest Law Review* 37: 239–437. A detailed critique of *Atwater v. City of Lago Vista,* concluding that the Supreme Court's modern-day Fourth Amendment jurisprudence on warrantless searches and seizures is a clear departure from what the framers of the amendment thought about the constitutional arrest authority.

DeGrave, Michael J. 2004. "Airline Passenger Profiling and the Fourth Amendment: Will CAPPS II Be Cleared for Takeoff?" *Boston University Journal of Science and Technology Law* 10: 125–151. Discusses the history of airline passenger profiling in the United States and outlines the proposed operations of the Computer Assisted Passenger Pre-Screening II (CAPPS II) program, concluding that such screening fits squarely within one of the recognized exceptions to the warrant requirement of the Fourth Amendment.

Dickerson, O. M. 1939. "Writs of Assistance as a Cause of the Revolution." In *The Era of the American Revolution.* Richard B. Morris, ed. New York: Columbia University Press. Considered by many to be the seminal essay reestablishing the importance of the Townshend Act as a source of colonial outrage.

Diffie, Whitfield, and Susan Landau. 1998. *Privacy on the Line: The Politics of Wiretapping and Encryption.* Boston: M.I.T. Press. Explores how intelligence and law-enforcement agencies intercept communications and how they use what they intercept.

Dripps, Donald. 2001. "The Case for the Contingent Exclusionary Rule." *American Criminal Law Review* 38: 1-46. Proposes that courts should enter contingent suppression orders that can be avoided if the state pays damages for conducting unreasonable searches and seizures. If the government accepts the offer, it waives its objection to damages set by a judge; if the government declines, the evidence is suppressed. This proposal would allow the judge to punish the police without letting the accused go free.

Dudley, Eric C., Jr. 1998. "*Terry v. Ohio,* the Warren Court and the Fourth Amendment: A Law Clerk's Perspective." *St. John's Law Review* 72: 891–903. A firsthand account of the Supreme Court machinations in the landmark case *Terry v. Ohio,* as told by the law clerk who worked for Chief Justice Warren on the opinion.

Dumbauld, Edward. 1957. *The Bill of Rights and What It Means Today.* Norman: University of Oklahoma Press. A standard reference work on the origins and meaning of the Bill of Rights.

Dworkin, Ronald. 1973. "Fact Style Adjudication and the Fourth Amendment: The Limits of Lawyering." *Indiana Law Journal* 48: 329–368. A critique of the Supreme Court's complex search and seizure law.

Editorial. 2005. "PATRIOT ACT: Court ruling on key section is long overdue," *Detroit Free Press,* February 25, 2005, 10A. Urges judicial review of

Section 215 of the PATRIOT ACT, which, among other things, allows the FBI, with little judicial supervision, to obtain library and Internet records in near secrecy.

Elliot, Jonathan. [1836] 1974. *The Debates in the Several State Conventions on the Adoption of the Federal Constitution.* Four volumes. Reprint. New York: Burt Franklin. A massive compilation of the documentary records of the state ratifying conventions.

Estrada, E. Martin. 2005. "A Toothless Tiger in a Constitutional Jungle: The 'Knock and Announce' Rule and the Sacred Castle Door." *Journal of Law and Public Policy* 16: 77–102. Addresses the enforcement problems surrounding the "knock and announce" rule, arguing that the key purpose of the rule is to avoid unnecessary destruction of property regardless of the legality of an arrest or seizure of evidence following police entry. Suggests that a "knock and announce" violation will rarely serve as a basis for suppression of otherwise legally seized evidence.

Etzoni, Amitai, and Jason H. Marsh. 2003. *Rights vs. Public Safety after 9/11: America in an Age of Terrorism.* Lanham, MD: Rowman and Littlefield. A collection of twenty-one essays that debate the uneasy tension between civil liberties and the "war on terror."

Fairman, Charles. 1949. "Does the Fourteenth Amendment Incorporate the Bill of Rights?" *Stanford Law Review* 2: 5–139. A lengthy examination of the original understanding of the Fourteenth Amendment, concluding that it was not intended to make the Bill of Rights applicable to the states.

Farber, Daniel A., and Suzanna Sherry. 1990. *A History of the American Constitution.* St. Paul, MN: West Publishing Co. A textbook on constitutional history, based largely on James Madison's notes on the debates in the constitutional convention.

Flaherty, David H. 1972. *Privacy in Colonial New England.* Charlottesville: University Press of Virginia. A thorough investigation of personal privacy in colonial New England, including a discussion of the strong resistance among the colonists to general searches and writs of assistance.

Foote, Caleb. 1960. "The Fourth Amendment: Obstacle or Necessity in the Law of Arrest?" *Journal of Criminal Law, Criminology & Police Science* 51: 402–408. A law professor's response to the question, "In the absence of sufficient grounds for an arrest, should the police have a right to stop and question a person as to his identity and reason for being where he is, if the appearance of that person has reasonably aroused police suspicion?"

Franklin, Paula A. 1991. *The Fourth Amendment.* Englewood Cliffs, NJ: Silver Burdett Press. Written for young adults, this volume in the *Amer-*

*ican Heritage History of the Bill of Rights* series traces the origins of the Fourth Amendment.

Friedman, Paul R. 1969. "Scope Limitations for Searches Incident to Arrest." *Yale Law Journal* 78: 433–447. Advocates limits on the warrantless search incident to arrest exception to the Fourth Amendment.

Gilliom, John. 1994. *Surveillance, Privacy, and the Law: Employee Drug Testing and the Politics of Social Control.* Ann Arbor: University of Michigan Press. An exploration of the legal and political battles over employee drug testing.

Glenn, Richard A. 2003. *The Right to Privacy: Rights and Liberties under the Law.* Santa Barbara, CA: ABC-CLIO. Examines the philosophical underpinnings, historical development, and contemporary scope of the right of privacy in the United States.

———. 2004. "Civil Liberties in an Age of Terrorism." *Trial: Journal of the Association of Trial Lawyers of America* 40, No. 4: 18–28. Analyzes the long-standing fault lines between liberty and security, made more relevant by the terrorist acts of September 11, 2001, and the USA PATRIOT Act.

Graham, Fred P. 1970. *The Self-Inflicted Wound.* New York: Macmillan. An easy-to-read overview of landmark Supreme Court cases in the 1960's dealing with rights of persons accused of crimes.

Gray, Horace, Jr. In Quincy, Josiah, Jr. [1865] 1948. *Appendix to Reports of Cases Argued and Adjudged in the Superior Court of Judicature of the Province of Massachusetts Bay, between 1761 and 1772.* Boston: Little, Brown and Company. Reprinted 1948, Buffalo, NY: Dennis & Co. Documents the responses to the issuance of writs of assistance in the American colonies shortly before the American Revolution.

Greenhalgh, William. 2003. *The Fourth Amendment Handbook.* Chicago: American Bar Association. A chronological survey of Supreme Court decisions.

Greenhouse, Linda. 2003. "Knock, Wait 15 Seconds, and then Break In, Justices Rule." *New York Times,* December 2: A1. A brief explanation of the holding in *United States v. Banks,* in which the Supreme Court ruled that a fifteen- to twenty-second wait was under the circumstances of this case, long enough to satisfy the "knock and announce" requirement.

Hale, Sir Matthew. 1736. *History of the Pleas of the Crown.* A treatise on English criminal procedure published posthumously by a leading seventeenth-century jurist; specifically criticizes general warrants and asserts that all warrants must be based on standards of probable cause and particularity.

Hall, John Wesley, Jr. 2000. *Search and Seizure.* Third ed. Two volumes. Charlottesville, VA: Lexis Law Publishing. A two-volume treatise on Fourth Amendment law from its English origins through recent decisions of the U.S. Supreme Court.

Hamilton, Alexander, James Madison, and John Jay. [1787–1788] 1961. *The Federalist Papers.* New York: Mentor. A collection of eighty-five essays written in defense of the Constitution of 1787. To this day, these papers remain the most thorough explication of the constitution of 1787.

Harvard Law Review Editors. 1967. "The Supreme Court 1966 Term." *Harvard Law Review* 81: 69–262. An analysis of leading Supreme Court decisions from the October 1966 term.

———. 2004. "The Supreme Court, 2003 Term: " *Harvard Law Review* 118: 286–296. An explication of *Hiibel v. Sixth Judicial District Court of Nevada,* in which the Court held that prosecution for failing to provide one's name to a police officer during an investigative stop did not violate the Fourth Amendment.

Hawkins, Serjeant William. 1721. *Pleas of the Crown.* A highly influential treatise on English criminal procedure, condemning general warrants long before the controversy over their validity in the 1760s.

Hoffman, Grayson A. 2003. "Litigating Terrorism: The New FISA Regime, the Wall, and the Fourth Amendment." *American Criminal Law Review* 40: 1655–1682. Presents a brief overview of U.S. foreign intelligence law, concluding that the procedures established under the amended Foreign Intelligence Surveillance Act (FISA) are reasonable under the Fourth Amendment.

Holcomb, Jayme Walker. 2002. "Consent Searches: Factors Courts Consider in Determining Voluntariness." *FBI Law Enforcement Bulletin.* A concise summation of the case law on voluntary consent searches.

Holmes, Oliver Wendell. 1897. "The Path of the Law." *Harvard Law Review* 10: 457–478. A landmark speech discussing the development and advantages of the common law and arguing, in effect, that law is ultimately a prediction of what a judge will decide in a future case.

Hudson, David L. 2004. *Rights of Students.* Philadelphia: Chelsea House Publishers. Presented in a point-counterpoint method, this short book examines various topics involving civil liberties in public schools.

Hull, Daniel. 2004. *Memorandum on the Fourth Amendment.* On file in the Law Library, University of Tennessee College of Law. An unpublished research paper explicating the historical background of the drafting of the Fourth Amendment.

Iraolo, Roberto. 2003. "Terrorism, the Border, and the Fourth Amendment.

*Federal Courts Law Review* 2003: 1. Analyzes the rationale and case law pertaining to the exception to the warrant requirement for routine searches and seizures at borders, in a post-9/11 nation where public demand for heightened homeland security inevitably runs headfirst into the Fourth Amendment.

Kamisar, Yale. 1984. "*Gates,* 'Probable Cause,' 'Good Faith,' and Beyond." *Iowa Law Review* 69: 551–615. A detailed analysis of the various opinions in *Illinois v. Gates,* concluding that the Supreme Court, in addition to jettisoning the two-pronged *Aguilar v. Texas* test, essentially modified the exclusionary rule so as not to require the exclusion of evidence obtained in the reasonable belief that the search and seizure was consistent with the Fourth Amendment.

Kamisar, Yale. 1995. "The Warren Court and Criminal Justice: A Quarter-Century Retrospective." *Tulsa Law Journal* 31: 1–55. A sympathetic look at the Warren Court's performance in the field of criminal procedure.

Kamisar, Yale, Wayne R. LaFave, and Jerold H. Israel. 1999. *Basic Criminal Procedure: Cases, Comments, and Questions.* St. Paul, MN: West Group. A standard law school textbook on criminal procedure (in the American Casebook Series).

———. 2002. *Advanced Criminal Procedure: Cases, Comments, and Questions.* St. Paul, MN: West Group. A standard law school textbook on criminal procedure (in the American Casebook Series).

Kaplan, John. 1974. "The Limits of the Exclusionary Rule." *Stanford Law Review* 26: 1027–1055. A law review article defending the view that the exclusionary rule is justified only in terms of its relative utility as a deterrent measure.

Katz, Jason M. 2003. "*Atwater v. City of Lago Vista:* Buckle-Up or Get Locked-Up: Warrantless Arrests for Fine-Only Misdemeanors under the Fourth Amendment." *Akron Law Review* 36: 491–543. A critique of the Supreme Court case authorizing warrantless arrests for automobile drivers who fail to wear a seat belt. Asserts that *Atwater* increases the possibility that individuals will be forced to endure invasive searches, elevates the likelihood that Americans will be forced to deal with various problems associated with arrest and confinement, and increases the opportunities for racial profiling.

Kelley, Angela. 2000. "Excuse Me, but Your House Is Leaking: Thermal Imaging Devices and Fourth Amendment Protection." *American Journal of Criminal Law* 28: 157–177. Criticizes the holding and rationale of the Ninth Circuit's decision in *United States v. Kyllo,* where the judges declared that the use of thermal imaging devices did not constitute a search under the Fourth Amendment. (The Supreme Court later reversed the Ninth Circuit, relying in part on the same reasons articulated in this note.)

Kerr, Orrin S. 2005. "Digital Evidence and the New Criminal Procedure." *Columbia Law Review* 105: 279–318. Suggests how the law of criminal procedure should be modified in response to the increasing number of criminal cases based largely on digital evidence.

Kucharson, M. Casey. 2004. "Please Report to the Principal's Office, Urine Trouble: The Effect of *Board of Education v. Earls* on America's Schoolchildren." *Akron Law Review* 37: 131–170. Critical analysis of the Supreme Court's decision in *Board of Education v. Earls* and its implication for the future of the Fourth Amendment and drug testing. Documents the history and expansion of the "special needs" doctrine and illustrating how the doctrine has whittled away students' Fourth Amendment guarantees.

Kuras, Jeffrey Haningan, Catherine Kreindler Levy, Jennifer L. Burns, and Scott A. Lowry. 2002. "Thirty-First Annual Review of Criminal Procedure: I. Investigation and Police Practices: Warrantless Searches and Seizures." *Georgetown Law Review* 90: 1130–1209. An excellent summary of case law on warrantless searches and seizures, focusing more on the holdings of the Supreme Court and less on the rationales behind the holdings.

LaFave, Wayne R. 1966. "Search and Seizure: 'The Course of the True Law . . . Has Not . . . Run Smooth.'" *University of Illinois Law Forum* 1966: 255–389. A lengthy survey on Fourth Amendment jurisprudence, noting that "no area of the law has more bedeviled the judiciary, from the Justices of the Supreme Court down to the magistrate," than search and seizure.

———. 1984. "'The Seductive Call of Expediency': *United States v. Leon*, Its Rationale and Ramifications." *University of Illinois Law Review* 1984: 895–931. A detailed critique of the good faith exception to the exclusionary rule. Accuses the justices of falling victim to the "seductive call of expediency" and suggests that there is reason to fear that the exception will be both broadly construed and distended, resulting perhaps in the complete abjuration of the exclusionary rule.

———. 1996. *Search and Seizure: A Treatise on the Fourth Amendment.* Third ed. Five volumes. St. Paul, MN: West Publishing Company. A massive and comprehensive examination of the Fourth Amendment, written at an advanced level.

Landynski, Jacob W. 1966. *Search and Seizure and the Supreme Court: A Study in Constitutional Interpretation.* Baltimore, MD: Johns Hopkins Press. A widely recognized and oft-cited historical and analytical treatment of the development of Supreme Court doctrine on search and seizure from the beginning of the republic to the mid-1960s.

Lasson, Nelson B. 1937. *The History and Development of the Fourth Amendment to the United States Constitution.* Baltimore, MD: Johns Hopkins Press. Reprint edition, New York: Da Capo Press. A concise history of the Fourth Amendment in the first 150 years of the republic; part of the Johns Hopkins University Studies in Historical and Political Science.

Lehmann, Nicole J. 1994. "Note: The 'Plain Feel' Exception in *Minnesota v. Dickerson:* A Further Erosion of the Fourth Amendment." *Campbell Law Review* 16: 257–274. Criticizes the Supreme Court's creation of the "plain feel" exception to the warrant requirement of the Fourth Amendment.

Levy, Leonard W. 1974. *Against the Law: The Nixon Court and Criminal Justice.* New York: Harper and Row. An analysis of the criminal justice adjudication of the Supreme Court after the Court's composition had been altered by President Nixon's four appointees: Chief Justice Burger and Associate Justices Blackmun, Powell, and Rehnquist. Following these appointments, the Court was decidedly more sympathetic to concerns of "law-and-order."

———. 1999. *Origins of the Bill of Rights.* New Haven, CT: Yale University Press. From a Pulitizer Prize–winning historian, a panoramic view of the liberties secured in the Bill of Rights, illuminating behind-the-scenes maneuverings, public rhetoric, and political motivations.

Lieber, Francis. 1853. *On Civil Liberty and Self Government.* London: Trubner & Co. A detailed explication of the author's theory of institutional liberty.

Locke, John. [1690] 1960. "An Essay Concerning Civil Government." In *Two Treatises of Government.* Reprint. New York: Mentor. An essay concerning the limits of governmental authority, highly influential on the drafters of the Declaration of Independence and the Constitution.

Love, Brian S. 2004. "Comment: Beyond Police Conduct: Analyzing Voluntary Consent to Warrantless Searches by the Mentally Ill and Disabled." *St. Louis Law Journal* 48: 1469–1500. Proposes a test for courts to employ when faced with the issue of voluntary consent to a warrantless search from a mentally ill or disabled person. Suggests that courts should look beyond the conduct of the police in requesting consent and the officer's perceptions and focus instead on the narrower factual question of whether the person was capable of voluntary consent.

Luna, Eric. 1999. "Sovereignty and Suspicion." *Duke Law Journal* 48:

787–889. Argues that Fourth Amendment jurisprudence should be completely "overhauled." Maintains that vacillating interpretations of the Fourth Amendment have left search and seizure law "randomly strewn across the legal landscape."

Maclin, Tracey. 1997. "The Complexity of the Fourth Amendment: A Historical Review." *Boston University Law Review* 77: 925–974. A critique of Professor Akhil Reed Amar's scholarship on the Fourth Amendment, concluding that Professor Amar ignores "a large segment of history" when he notes that warrantless searches do not always have to be supported by probable cause. This note relies heavily on the scholarship of William J. Cuddihy.

Maltz, Earl M. 2000. *The Chief Justiceship of Warren Burger.* Columbia: University of South Carolina Press. A summary and analysis of the Supreme Court's impact on American law during the chief justiceship of Warren Burger; includes a chapter entitled "The Rights of Criminal Defendants."

Mason, Alpheus Thomas, and Donald Grier Stephenson, Jr. 2005. *American Constitutional Law: Introductory Essays and Selected Cases.* Fourteenth ed. Upper Saddle River, NJ: Prentice Hall. A standard undergraduate constitutional law textbook, including a chapter on Fourth Amendment issues, in which, following an introductory essay on the Fourth Amendment, the authors provide excerpts from leading Supreme Court cases.

*Massachusetts Declaration of Rights,* March 2, 1780. An enumeration of the rights of Massachusetts' citizens; predates the United States Constitution's Bill of Rights and may have influenced its language.

McCullough, David. 2001. *John Adams.* New York: Simon and Schuster. An acclaimed biography of the revolutionary leader and second president of the republic. Discusses the frustration of the colonists in Boston over general warrants and writs of assistance.

McWhirter, Darien A. 1994. *Search, Seizure, and Privacy.* Phoenix, AZ: Oryx Press. A general look at search and seizure law in the United States.

Mericli, Kemal Alexander. 1989. "The Apprehension of Peril Exception to the Knock and Announce Rule." *Search and Seizure Law Report* 16: 129–136. A concise discussion of the history of the "apprehension of peril" exception to the "knock and announce" rule.

Mill, John Stuart. [1859] 1956. *On Liberty.* Reprint. Indianapolis, IN: Bobbs-Merrill. A classic text exploring the limits on governmental authority over the individual.

Mirande, Alfredo. 2003. "Is There a 'Mexican Exception' to the Fourth Amendment?" *Florida Law Review* 55: 365–389. Suggests that warrantless searches and seizures of persons who are "Mexican looking" are commonplace and extend well beyond any recognized exception to the warrant requirement of the Fourth Amendment. Concludes that there is considerable support for the view that with regard to suspected alienage status, there is a *de facto,* unwritten Mexican exception to the Fourth Amendment.

Moenssens, Andre. 2003. "Police Procedures: Some Problems with Warrants." *Forensic Evidence Newsletter, available at* www.forensic-evidence.com (last visited May 15, 2005). An easy-to-read discussion of the basic constitutional requirements for a valid warrant (and many other Fourth Amendment topics); written by a University of Missouri at Kansas City law professor emeritus.

Moran, David A. 2000. "Traffic Stops, Littering Tickets, and Police Warnings: The Case for a Fourth Amendment on Custodial Arrest Doctrine." *American Criminal Law Review* 37: 1143–1164. Suggests that the Supreme Court recognize and develop a fourth category of police-citizen encounters. In addition to the already-recognized consensual encounters, investigative stops, and custodial arrests, the author argues that it would be advantageous to recognize the noncustodial arrest as the fourth type of police-citizen encounter.

Oaks, Dallin. 1970. "Studying the Exclusionary Rule in Search and Seizure." *University of Chicago Law Review* 37: 665–757. Post-*Mapp* examination of import and impact of exclusionary rule.

O'Brien, David M. 2005. *Constitutional Law and Politics: Civil Rights and Civil Liberties.* Sixth ed. New York: W. W. Norton. A casebook of Supreme Court decisions in the area of civil rights and liberties supplemented with commentary and historical information.

Packer, Herbert L. 1965. "Policing the Police." *The New Republic,* September 4, 1965, 17–21. Addresses the role of legislatures and state and federal executives in defining the proper limits of police investigatory power.

Packer, Herbert L. 1968. *The Limits of the Criminal Sanction.* Stanford, CA: Stanford University Press. Analyzes sanctions against offenders in the American criminal justice system, identifying and contrasting two models of criminal justice—the due process model and the crime control model.

*Pennsylvania Declaration of Rights.* The Commonwealth's enumeration of the rights of its citizens; part of Pennsylvania's 1776 constitution.

Persico, Deborah A. 1997. Mapp v. Ohio: *Evidence and Search Warrants.* Springfield, NJ: Enslow Publishers. Analysis of the landmark decision *Mapp v. Ohio* (1961), applying the federal exclusionary rule to the states through the Fourteenth Amendment.

————. 1998. New Jersey v. T.L.O: *Drug Searches in Schools.* Springfield, NJ: Enslow Publishers. Details the Supreme Court case dealing with drug searches by public schools employees and debates the Fourth Amendment rights of students.

Pinard, Michael. 2003. "From the Classroom to the Courtroom: Reassessing Fourth Amendment Standards in Public School Searches Involving Law Enforcement Authorities." *Arizona Law Review* 45: 1076–1125. Meshes the long-standing principles of the Fourth Amendment with the increased law enforcement presence in public schools, the increased interdependency between law enforcement and public school administrators, and the increased use of the criminal justice system to monitor and address behavior previously handled through the school disciplinary process. Suggests a more protective probable cause standard in some circumstances and a more relaxed reasonable suspicion standard in others.

Posner, Richard A. 1981. "Rethinking the Fourth Amendment." *Supreme Court Review,* pp. 49–80. Chicago: University of Chicago. Approaches the Fourth Amendment from the standpoint of an economic interest in privacy rather than from a conventional constitutional law and criminal procedure perspective, arguing that a tort remedy for Fourth Amendment violations is a viable alternative to the exclusionary rule.

Powe, Lucas A., Jr. 2000. *The Warren Court and American Politics.* Cambridge, MA: The Belknap Press of Harvard University Press. Examines the Warren Court in the broad context of the national political environment, emphasizing the consistency between leading decisions of the 1960s and domestic policies of the Kennedy and Johnson administrations.

Raskin, Jamin B. 2003. *We the Students: Supreme Court Cases for and about Students.* Washington, D.C.: Congressional Quarterly Press. Written to help students achieve constitutional literacy on a variety of issues relevant to students, including search and seizure. Contains learning exercises, case excerpts, and discussion prompts.

Scheb, John M. and John M. Scheb, II. 2005. *Criminal Law and Procedure.* Fifth ed. Belmont, CA: West Wadsworth. A college textbook featuring commentary and excerpts from leading criminal justice decisions of the United States Supreme Court, U.S. courts of appeals, and state appellate courts.

Schlesinger, Stephen. 1977. *Exclusionary Injustice: The Problem of Illegally Obtained Evidence.* New York: Dekker. Depicts the Fourth Amendment exclusionary rule as obstructing the introduction of reliable evidence in criminal cases.

Schwartz, Bernard. 1977. *The Great Rights of Mankind: A History of the American Bill of Rights.* New York: Oxford University Press. An informative and readable history of the American Bill of Rights, tracing its development from English antecedents through the late twentieth century; a second edition was published in 1992 by Madison House (Madison, Wisconsin).

Shapiro, B. J. 1991. *"Beyond Reasonable Doubt" and "Probable Cause": Historical Perspectives on the Anglo-American Law of Evidence.* Berkeley: University of California Press. Traces the development of rules of evidence in England prior to the American Revolution with emphasis on the trial and pretrial conduct of attorneys, judges, and law enforcement officers. Illustrates the influence of religious and philosophical precepts on the development of the Anglo-American law of evidence.

Siebert, Fredrick S. 1952. *Freedom of the Press in England 1476–1776: The Rise and Decline of Government Controls.* Urbana: University of Illinois Press. Chronicles early efforts by the English Parliament and Crown to curb publications critical of the government through such devices as seditious libel, and documents the gradual emergence of freedom of the press in England. The English experience significantly influenced early American commitments to freedoms of press and speech.

Slobogin, Christopher. 2002. *Criminal Procedure: Regulation of Police Investigation.* Third ed. New York: Matthew Bender. Includes cases as well as legislative, historical, comparative and empirical materials.

Smith, M. H. 1978. *The Writs of Assistance Case.* London: University of California Press. A historical look at the famous *Paxton's Case* of 1761.

Steiker, Carol. 1994. "Second Thoughts about First Principles." *Harvard Law Review* 107: 820–857. A critique of Akhil Reed Amar's interpretation of the origins of the Fourth Amendment.

Stephens, Otis H. 1973. *The Supreme Court and Confessions of Guilt.* Knoxville: University of Tennessee Press. A historical account of legal developments governing the admissibility of confessions from English origins through U.S. Supreme Court decisions on confessions and police interrogation beginning at the turn of the twentieth century, culminating with *Miranda v. Arizona* (1966). Includes an original empirical study of the impact of this decision on law enforcement agencies and analyzes previously published studies of *Miranda*'s impact.

———. 2004. "Presidential Power, Judicial Deference, and the Status of Detainees in an Age of Terrorism." In *American National Security and Civil Liberties in an Era of Terrorism*, edited by David B. Cohen and John W. Wells. New York: Palgrave MacMillan. Contrasts the traditional law-enforcement model of criminal justice with the military model endorsed by the Bush administration following the attacks of September 11, 2001.

Stephens, Otis H. and John M. Scheb, II. 2003. *American Constitutional Law.* Third ed. St. Paul, MN: Wadsworth. Contains abridged cases and introductory essays covering major aspects of American constitutional law including judicial review, allocation of powers, and individual rights and liberties with a separate chapter on criminal justice.

Story, Joseph. 1851. *Commentaries on the Constitution of the United States.* Second ed. Boston: C. C. Little and J. Brown. An oft-cited treatise on the U.S. Constitution.

Taylor, Telford. 1969. *Two Studies in Constitutional Interpretation.* Columbus: Ohio State University Press. One of two well-researched essays in the volume that address major issues of the 1960's in the areas of search, seizure, and surveillance. The essays are expanded versions of lectures given by Professor Taylor at the College of Law of Ohio State University of April 3 and 4, 1967.

Torr, James D. 2004. *Civil Liberties and the War of Terrorism.* San Diego, CA: Lucent Books. A brief work on civil liberties post-9/11, with a chapter on the USA PATRIOT Act and the Fourth Amendment.

Tucker, St. George. 1999. *View of the Constitution of the United States with Selected Writings.* Indianapolis, IN: Liberty Fund. Written by a professor of law at William and Mary College and an appellate judge in Virginia and originally published in 1803, this book was the first extended, systematic commentary on the U.S. Constitution and an important handbook for law students, lawyers, and judges during the pre–Civil War period.

United States Congress. 2001. "Authorization for Use of Military Force," Pub L. No. 107–40, 115 Stat. 224. General authorization for the use of military force, issued in the immediate aftermath of the attacks of September 11, 2001.

United States Immigration and Naturalization Service. 1979. *The Law of Search and Seizure for Immigration Officers.* Washington, D.C.: Department of Justice. An instructional guidebook on policy and practice for U.S. immigration officers.

*Virginia Declaration of Rights.* June 12, 1776. The Virginia Constitution's enumeration of the rights of its citizens. Like the bills of rights of other early state constitutions, it may have influenced the authors of the federal Bill of Rights.

Wallin, Howard E. 1987. "The Uncertain Scope of the Plain View Doctrine." *University of Baltimore Law Review* 16: 266–286. Focuses on the expansion of the "plain view" exception to the warrant requirement established in *Coolidge v. New Hampshire* (1971).

———. 2002. "Plain View Revisted." *Pace Law Review* 22: 307–345. Focuses on the seminal case of *Coolidge v. New Hampshire* (1971) and its progeny.

Walsh, Brian D. 2002. "*Illinois v. Wardlow:* High-Crime Areas, Flight, and the Fourth Amendment." *Arkansas Law Review* 54: 879–914. Criticizes *Illinois v. Wardlow* (2000), examining how the decision arbitrarily decreases Fourth Amendment protections in certain neighborhoods; suggests that the Arkansas Supreme Court provide greater privacy protection under the Arkansas Constitution than is provided under the U.S. Supreme Court's interpretation of the Fourth Amendment.

Wasserstrom, Silas J. 1989. "The Fourth Amendment's Two Clauses." *American Criminal Law Review* 26: 1389–1396. Law review article discussing the historical relationship between the reasonableness and warrants clauses.

Way, H. Frank, Jr. 1959. "Increasing Scope of Search Incidental to Arrest." *Washington University Law Quarterly* 1959: 261–280. Addresses the problem of expansion of warrantless searches incident to arrest.

Way, H. Frank, Jr. 1980. *Criminal Justice and the American Constitution.* Belmont, CA: Duxbury Press. A casebook on criminal justice including history and commentary.

Westin, Alan F. 1966. "Science, Privacy, and Freedom: Issues and Proposals for the 1970's." *Columbia Law Review* 66: 1003–1050. Discusses the then-emerging right of privacy with emphasis on problems of electronic surveillance.

Wetterer, Charles M. 1998. *The Fourth Amendment: Search and Seizure.* Springfield, NJ: Enslow Publishers. A collection of cases and historical analysis.

White, G. Edward. 1982. *Earl Warren: A Public Life.* New York: Oxford University Press. A biography of the fourteenth Chief Justice, written by a former Warren law clerk and current professor of law at the University of Virginia. Draws heavily on the Chief Justice's public papers.

White, Theodore H. 1969. *The Making of the President, 1968.* New York: Atheneum Publishers. A detailed account of the 1968 presidential campaign, in which the "liberal" criminal rights jurisprudence of the Supreme Court proved to be an important issue.

Wilkey, Malcolm R. 1982. *Enforcing the Fourth Amendment by Alternatives to the Exclusionary Rule.* Washington, DC: National Legal Center for Public Interest. White paper suggesting methods of enforcing the Fourth

Amendment without excluding credible, yet questionably obtained, evidence.

Wilson, Bradford. 1982. "The Origin and Development of the Federal Rule of Exclusion." *Wake Forest Law Review* 18: 1073–1109. Examines the historical development of exclusionary rule, including analysis of *Mapp v. Ohio* (1961).

Zalman, Marvin, and Larry J. Siegel. 1997. *Criminal Procedure*. Second ed. Belmont, CA: West/Wadsworth. An upper-level textbook containing cases and comments on the evolution of criminal procedure.

Zotti, Priscilla Machado. 2005. *Injustice for All:* Mapp v. Ohio *and the Fourth Amendment*. New York: Lang. The story behind the landmark Warren Court decision of *Mapp v. Ohio,* including chapters on oral arguments before the justices, the drafting of the opinion, and the impact of the decision on criminal justice.

# INDEX

# About the Authors

Otis H. Stephens, Jr. (Ph.D. Johns Hopkins University, 1963; J.D. University of Tennessee, 1983) is National Alumni Association Distinguished Service Professor of Political Science and resident scholar of constitutional law in the College of Law at the University of Tennessee. His published books include *The Supreme Court and Confessions of Guilt* and *American Constitutional Law* (co-authored with John M. Scheb II). He has also published numerous articles and book reviews in law and social science journals and has contributed chapters to several scholarly books. He lives with his wife, Mary, in Knoxville, Tennessee.

Richard A. Glenn (Ph.D. Tennessee, 1995) is professor of government and political affairs at Millersville University. He is the author of *The Right to Privacy* and more than forty articles, chapters, essays, and reviews appearing in many journals, books, and other publications, on a variety of U.S. political subjects. He lives with his wife, Lorena, and their sons, Ryan and Andrew, in Lancaster, Pennsylvania.